RECONSTRUCTING

HISTORY

IN MAY 1998, a group of prominent scholars announced the formation of the Historical Society, an organization that sought to be free of the jargon-laden debates and political agendas that have come to distance so many readers from their interest in historical scholarship. Eugene Genovese, president of the Society, explained the commitment to form a new and genuinely diverse organization. "The Society extends from left to right and embraces people of every ideological and political tendency. The Society promotes frank debate in an atmosphere of civility, mutual respect, and common courtesy. All we require is that participants lay down plausible premises, reason logically, appeal to evidence, and prepare to exchange criticism with those holding different points of view. Our goal is to promote an integrated history accessible to the public." From those beginnings, the Society has grown to include thousands of members from Pulitzer-prize winning scholars to general readers, from graduate students to public historians.

In this first book from the Historical Society, several founding members explore central topics in the field, including the sensitive use of historical records, sources, and archives; the debates over teaching history in the public schools; the enduring value of the practice of history; and much more. An engaging and important work, *Reconstructing History* is sure to challenge and inform scholars, students, educators, and the many general readers who have become lost in the culture wars.

ELIZABETH FOX-GENOVESE is the Eléonore Raoul Professor of the Humanities and professor of history at Emory University, and a member of the executive board of the Historical Society.

ELISABETH LASCH-QUINN is associate professor of history at Syracuse University and a recent fellow at the Woodrow Wilson International Center for Scholars.

RECONSTRUCTING HISTORY

THE EMERGENCE OF A NEW HISTORICAL SOCIETY

EDITED BY

Elizabeth Fox-Genovese

&

Elisabeth Lasch-Quinn

Routledge

NEW YORK

LONDON

Published in 1999 by
Routledge
29 West 35th Street
New York, NY 10001

Published in Great Britain by
Routledge
11 New Fetter Lane
London EC4P 4EE

Printed in the United States of America on acid-free paper.

10 9 8 7 6 5 4 3 2 1

Library of Congress Cataloging-in-Publication Data

Reconstructing History: The Emergence of a New Historical Society
[edited by] Elizabeth Fox-Genovese and Elisabeth Lasch-Quinn.

p. cm.

Includes bibliographical references.

ISBN 0-415-92278-X. — ISBN 0-415-92279-8 (pbk.)

1. History—Philosophy. 2. Social sciences and history.
3. Intellectual life—History. I. Fox-Genovese, Elizabeth, 1941–
II. Lasch-Quinn, Elisabeth.

D16.8R343 1999

901—dc21 99-24892

CIP

DEDICATION

TO THE MEMORY OF OUR FATHERS,

Edward Whiting Fox (1911–1996),
Christopher Lasch (1932–1994),
and Henry Steele Commager, grandfather (1902–1998),
beloved historians and teachers

and

To our students,
custodians of the future
of historical studies

CONTENTS

ACKNOWLEDGMENTS

IT WOULD BE IMPOSSIBLE to compile a volume of essays like this one without incurring a multitude of debts, and when draconian time constraints compound the task, the debts increase proportionately. Here, we happily acknowledge ours. First, Deirdre Mullane, who initially proposed the idea of such a book and volunteered her and Routledge's efforts to publish it. Presumably Deirdre did not foresee what she was letting herself in for, but she has gracefully and solicitously seen the project through to completion, sparing us the many reproaches to which she is entitled. Without the generous collaboration of the authors of the essays, there would have been no book, and we are grateful to every one of them, not merely for meeting deadlines (however inconvenient), but especially because working with them has enriched our own understanding of the many dimensions of historical thought. The production staff at Routledge and at Stratford Publishing Services have graciously coped with the challenges and frustrations of keeping everyone on schedule, and we heartily thank T. J. Mancini, Mary Robinson, and their coworkers for speeding the work to its conclusion. Ralph Luker helped to coordinate many essential matters, and Chris Curtis in Atlanta and Heidi Sherman in Washington, D.C., did their best to keep us on track. Our own families have lovingly contributed to the completion of *Reconstructing History* in countless tangible and intangible ways, and we are all the more grateful since in this, as in everything else, without them, nothing would have been possible.

INTRODUCTION

Elizabeth Fox-Genovese and Elisabeth Lasch-Quinn

ALL OF HUMAN EXPERIENCE falls within the purview of historians. Simply by living in time, human beings naturally and inescapably make history. Thus, to paraphrase Aristotle, men and women are history-generating animals. By the same token, women and men depend heavily upon that history—their own and that of others—to live. No matter how radically we believe ourselves to have broken with the past, it never loosens its hold upon us. Amnesia may erase it from our memories, simultaneously erasing our sense of rootedness, but, consciously or not, we remain rooted in the past, and, however indirectly, we are shaped by our society's version of its history.

In many ways, the late twentieth century, reeling under the consequences of a breathtaking rate of change, resembles the amnesiac, although this erasure of memory often is willed rather than imposed. The political and philosophical upheavals of the recent past have called virtually all inherited certainties into question, cultivating the perception that the past is finally dead. For many, the promise of our times lies in the prospect that we may literally make ourselves anew—or better yet, "invent" ourselves. History dampens that dizzying prospect with its sober reminders that if some things change, or appear to change, others assuredly do not. For even as history instructs us in the wondrous accomplishments of which our kind has been capable, it also reminds us of the many ways in which we have fallen short of our ideals. It is sobering to confront a record that features as many, if not more, disasters as triumphs, as much, if not more, villainy as heroism, and to be reminded that we are no better nor worse than those who created it. The "distant mirror" of history, to borrow from Barbara Tuchman's title, rarely offers a flattering reflection. Nor can many of us take unadulterated comfort in the lineage from which we descend. For history, in contrast to myth, offers no evidence of peoples who were uniformly virtuous, and scant, if any, evidence of peoples who were uniformly evil.

The wave of postmodernist relativism and indeterminacy broke later upon the discipline of history than upon literary studies and anthropology, perhaps because so many historians remained attached to the notion that they were building not upon sand but upon the solid ground of fact. The observant nonetheless discerned the signs of the times a-coming in the culture and politics of the 1960s. The emergence of social history, notwithstanding valuable contributions, invited a new personalization of historical scholarship, and the cries for relevance in education heralded a new distaste for the unsettling knowledge that history so often affords. Both tendencies owed much to the political upheavals of the decade, and it soon became widely agreed that a commitment to social justice and true democracy dictated a rejection of "elitist" educational standards, including demands that students learn anything about those of whom they did not approve or who were not personally "relevant" to them. These moves ensured that it would be only a matter of time until history as a field joined the relativist flow.

Historians have not uniformly capitulated to relativism and relevance, doubtless because so many continue to cherish the canons of their craft, to respect the people they study, or to revel in the ways in which history challenges the intellect and the imagination. But history as a field has increasingly been suffering the aftershocks of developments elsewhere. Above all, changes in educational agendas, standards, and curricula have dislodged history from its previously central position. Under these conditions, historians have been implicitly and explicitly reflecting upon the nature of their work, history's place in education, and the place of both in American culture.

Even these incentives, however, cannot readily explain why a group of presumably rational and responsible people, with more than enough to occupy their time, decided to found a new historical society—not a specialized society devoted to one or another subfield, but a comprehensive society that invites the participation of all historians of any rank, specialization, and level of employment (or nonemployment). The answers may be as numerous as the thousand plus historians who have joined The Historical Society in the first few months of its existence. Yet, however diverse, these scholars have converged at key points. *Reconstructing History* explores some of this common ground as a way of responding to at least some of the questions raised by the emergence of The Historical Society. In addition, it sketches some preliminary attempts to rethink the situation of historians and the study of history and to open new directions for both, sometimes by recovering old ones. Many of these essays offer sharp criticism of the current state of the historical profession, historical scholarship, historical education, and even the university and culture at large. Yet their tone and content also betray genuine excitement about the prospect of developing fresh initiatives. In the words of Albert Camus, if a rebel is one who says "no," he or she is also one who says "yes." Thus, even as these essays say "no" to the trivialization and overspecialization of history, they offer a heartfelt and hopeful "yes" to the possibility of a common reconsideration of the purposes and possible results of the study of history.

No one volume, especially at such an early date, nor any two editors, can do justice to the myriad criticisms, worries, and hopes of the society's varied members, much less to those of the countless others who have expressed interest in its plans. The difficulties are compounded by the wide variety of members' and prospective members' views, which range across the political and ideological spectrum and encompass innumerable historical methods and styles, as well as subjects of study. Yet beneath this vast array of diversity, The Historical Society represents a common belief that our ideals and responsibilities as historians require renewal, that contemporary events threaten to compromise those ideals, and that burning questions about the state of the profession must be engaged, even if we differ over the answers. Notwithstanding diversity of tone, purpose, and content, these essays testify to the range of concerns. None should be taken as representative of the views of others or the group as a whole, but the very differences of opinion capture the spirit of the society, which, above all, has emerged in response to the widespread conviction that we need to expand the scope of historical interchange rather than restrict it. Most emphatically, individual critiques of particular scholars by no means constitute group censure, but a respectful wish to give important ideas their proper due by subjecting their implications to scrutiny not always encouraged today. The point is to engage others, not just those with whom we agree, just as their ideas have engaged us. The divergence among the essays represents real political and intellectual differences, while their points of convergence demonstrate, across the lines of ideology, method, and specialization, a deep shared concern for the study, teaching, and intellectual significance of history.

We have divided *Reconstructing History* into five parts. Part I, "The Imperative: The Historical Society as a Critique and a New Ideal," includes what might best be viewed as calls to action. Eugene D. Genovese and Marc Trachtenberg set the tone with their accounts of the circumstances that led to the founding of The Historical Society. Alan Kors and Daniel Littlefield widen the focus in their critiques of current intellectual trends that are undermining historical studies. Acknowledging the discomfort with the prevailing state of the profession, Elisabeth Lasch-Quinn explores the deterioration of conditions within the academy and launches an appeal for historians to collaborate in the development of new structures that may help to restore the dignity and excitement of their work as teachers, scholars, and intellectuals.

In Part II, "History and the Contemporary Intellectual Milieu," Elizabeth Fox-Genovese, Rochelle Gurstein, Gertrude Himmelfarb, and Russell Jacoby reflect upon the ways in which postmodernism, identity politics, and the misreading of historical experience contribute to the distortion and trivialization of history as an intellectual endeavor. Phillip Richards extends the critique to the specific situation of African American intellectuals who are increasingly substituting intellectual fashion for direct engagement with the world around them, especially the plight of their own people.

Part III, "Meditations on the Practice of History," traces variations on these themes as they have figured in the lives of individual historians and in historical studies in general. Leo P. Ribuffo and Deborah A. Symonds reflect upon their understanding of being a historian, while Bruce Kuklick defends the ideal of history as a rule-governed practice in the manner of baseball. Victor Davis Hanson and Paul A. Rahe reflect upon the ways in which contemporary concerns are undermining military history and the history of political theory, while Donald Kagan deplores their role in the erosion of liberal education. One regrettable result of these tendencies, according to Edward Berkowitz, has been the flight from the ideal that Americans of different backgrounds may share common allegiances as citizens of one nation.

All of these issues have resurfaced in recent heated debates about the history that deserves a place in the curricula of our schools and colleges. In Part IV, "An Educational Mission: Standards for the Teaching of History," Diane Ravitch, John Diggins, Sean Wilentz, and Walter McDougall advance four perspectives on the most heated of these debates—the debate over the national history standards. And in Part V, "Historians at Work," Martin J. Sklar, Miriam R. Levin, John Womack, and Louis Ferleger and Richard H. Steckel provide specific examples of the ways in which historians can engage new questions while respecting the standards of their craft.

Many of the authors believe that the study of history is under siege and that its afflictions emanate from a general crisis in education from the lowest to the highest levels. The educational crisis in turn reflects a general cultural crisis, which, in the view of many, threatens an unraveling of the very fabric of American society. The relation between the crumbling of historical studies and of other cherished and vital institutions remains debatable, and we do not assert the one as the cause of the other. But only willful blindness could deny a connection between history's travail and our other cultural problems. What remains indisputable is that, as historians, we must begin by trying to understand the extent and nature of our difficulties and how best to surmount them.

In "The Death of Jane Addams," Edward Berkowitz deplores the cultural temper that is condemning historians to a growing irrelevance to the broader society—to an isolation manifest in their loss of a hold upon the public imagination. Here, as other essays suggest, the problem is not a decline in public interest in history, which remains vigorous, but Hollywood's usurping of the historian's role. Victor Hanson, for instance, deplores the current cinema's proclivity to offer shallow portraits of war, drastically simplifying moral questions and thus distorting the choices made by people in the past and their bearing on our own predicament. Along with Berkowitz, Elisabeth Lasch-Quinn and Alan Kors point to the disengagement of historians from the questions of the day. Both Berkowitz and Lasch-Quinn fault historians for wrapping themselves in a kind of cocoon spun from their personal preoccupations. Kors urges a careful distinction between the drawing of specific policy implications from historical examples and subtler uses of history as a guide to understanding the context of pressing contemporary issues.

Like Berkowitz, many contributors to this volume fault new academic fads for historians' disengagement from—or failure to engage—the public, as well as for the general crisis in the profession. Many agree with Kors that "faddish and ephemeral critical theory, with its simplistic and misleading theories of oppression" has made inroads into the field of history just as it has ravaged other subjects under the guise, particularly repellent to many cultural historians, of cultural studies. Cultural studies and the newly fashionable postmodern history—if they are not one and the same—share a tendency to measure all historical situations by the reductionist standard of a uniform, ubiquitous power. Their notion of method favors a focus on language or texts in complete isolation, even from other works, and a radical relativism that views any conception of external reality or objective knowledge as the suspect product of another's subjective perception. This doctrine undercuts the enterprise of history by asserting that there is "no fixed event"—as Leo Ribuffo puts it in his "Confessions of an Accidental (or Perhaps Overdetermined) Historian"—no chronology, no adequate evidence, and, hence, no way to establish any kind of truth or even accuracy. Not only objectivity, which historians have long questioned, but truth of any kind is dismissed as an impossibility. Indeed, Gertrude Himmelfarb, in "Postmodernist History," systematically delineates what she sees as the basic incompatibility of postmodernism and historical study.

Other essayists fault multiculturalism, as currently conceived, for threatening the quality of historical inquiry and higher education in general. Daniel Littlefield draws on Diane Ravitch's distinction between particularistic and pluralistic multiculturalism to argue that the latter currently pervades academic contexts. The uncritical celebration of formerly oppressed groups, he argues, not only compromises the historical record, which demands greater nuance in order to be understood, but fosters divisiveness in the wider society. A simplistic multiculturalist slant encourages students to take effortless stands rather than learn about the real extent and nature of cultural mixing or interaction, which would demand a far more rigorous examination of the subject matter. John Diggins's analysis of what he views as the wrongheaded multiculturalist slant of the National History Standards also warns against the substitution of celebration—or, in his words, romanticization or therapy—for real learning. The replacement of the historical record of the triumph of power with a feel-good message that all cultures have always been equal sacrifices the possibility of understanding power and how it has been won, lost, and wielded. As just one voice on the uses and potential misuses of history by other fields—in this case, African American literary criticism—Phillip Richards draws subtle but clear distinctions between cultural theory that can bend too far in the service of therapy and substantive literary history, or historically based literary criticism, which he believes actually offers more profound assistance in addressing the predicament of the black intellectual (and black middle class generally) in a newly integrated world.

In "Aristotle and the Study of History: A Manifesto," Paul Rahe maintains that scientific pretensions have actually led scholars to obscure the past under the guise of impartiality. In "A New Intellectual History?" Russell Jacoby explores one case of this process of mystification. He discusses a movement among some late-twentieth-century intellectual historians who have embraced the "linguistic turn" to reject earlier attempts by historians to establish themselves as scientific and instead to turn to modern art and literature as models of the renunciation of "the pretense of realism and objectivity." Jacoby nonetheless finds this redefinition ironic, since these same intellectual historians often resort to incomprehensible "taxonomies and scientistic idioms" and opaque "methodologies and systems." Lasch-Quinn's essay, "Democracy in the Ivory Tower?" focuses on a larger context of overprofessionalization, arguing that the attendant compartmentalization, jargon, and specialization have narrowed scholars' vision and compromised their willingness to draw conclusions that illuminate larger debates. The effects of this intellectual retreat have included the replacement of knowledge with elite expertise, substance with process, and moral inquiry with a mode of "passionlessness or neutrality."

Observers frequently find connections between these trends and disquieting aspects of the contemporary intellectual scene or prevailing social conditions. Elizabeth Fox-Genovese, for instance, sees an intimate connection between the common assumptions that inform cultural studies, postmodernism, and multiculturalism and the general crisis of authority outside of universities. In her view, this radical relativism, which designates all experience subjective and all truth relative, reflects and buttresses the larger social structure of a managerial state, which corrupts and degrades politics into group competition for social benefits.

Donald Kagan writes of a kind of "cultural void" that derives from unbridled skepticism unmediated by a commitment to pass on "shared values and assumptions." Doubt and questioning, he argues, are vital to education, but in the past they rested on some "received moral and civic teachings." It was the acknowledged role of education to prevent those teachings from devolving into "ethnocentric complacency and intolerance" or superpatriotism. In today's universities, where any mention of shared assumptions or teachings is itself suspect as a wrongheaded attempt to defend objective, transcendent universals, the stability afforded by common standards crumbles and nihilism results. In Kagan's words, "Having little or no sense of the human experience through the ages, of what has been tried, of what has succeeded and what has failed, of what is the price of cherishing some values as opposed to others or of how values relate to one another, [the students] leap from acting as though anything is possible, without cost, to despairing that nothing is possible."

Although these authors do not always concur in their diagnoses, most couple their criticism with hints about initiatives they deem promising, inspiring, and necessary. Notably, sometimes hinting at their own role, they deplore the ferocity and polarization of recent public debates about the kinds of issues raised here. It is eminently clear that the level of acrimony, the search for ideological purity by both the right and left, and the oversimplification of central issues impede rather than advance a serious examination of our situation and our possible responses to it. The contributors to this volume vary in the virulence of their style, but most express an unambiguous desire to move beyond the style and content of the divisive and directionless "culture wars." Thus Sean Wilentz worries that the principal casualty of the debate over national history standards has been the amount of history taught in American schools. He warns that the gravest danger derives from the revolution that has replaced history with social studies at the cost of much vital information and interpretation and with the result of a precipitous drop in general levels of knowledge crucial for an educated citizenry. Similarly, Walter McDougall charges that the standards debate has sidestepped the greater questions—now at risk of vanishing entirely—of why we should study history in the first place. Without a full sense of the intellectual, civic, and moral functions of historical instruction, education risks being relegated to only one of those functions, at great cost both to students and to history itself.

Still others temper their criticism of recent developments in historiography with the acknowledgment that some such developments have breathed new life into fields of study and broadened perspectives. Jacoby sees much benefit in the linguistic turn in intellectual history, and Kors acknowledges the contribution of the whole generation that entered universities since the 1960s. Miriam Levin draws on the history of women even as she proposes new directions for the field and argues for its incorporation into a broader investigation of cultural developments that influence the scientific profession. Richards appreciates the vibrancy of African American studies while he worries about the direction some of its currents might lead. None of the contributors to this volume argues for a backward turn but they share a strong commitment to the reintegration of various historical approaches through attention to the larger history of which they are a part.

A number of social critics and political philosophers have issued an urgent call for restoration of a sense of common ideals in politics, community life, and education. Many especially bemoan the loss of shared direction among teachers of the humanities, arguing that fragmentation, whether by "identity," ideology, or narrow specialization, threatens the very future of humanistic study in universities. Several essayists in this volume similarly comment on the need for grounding in a common sense of purpose. The challenge would be daunting in any era, but it is especially formidable in an era in which issues often provoke passionate polarization and the notion of commonality has itself become suspect. The challenge nonetheless merits our most generous response, and it is this challenge, above all, that these essays seek to meet as the surest avenue out of current confusion.

For a start, we must repudiate the radical polarization—the Manicheanism—that assigns all positions to irreconcilable camps and then demonizes one or the other. Referring to the specific case of the debates over modern art, Rochelle Gurstein shows that much more promising alternatives to such simplistic sidetaking and the attendant substitution of reflection or open debate with the exchange of epithets, can be found in the historical study of more nuanced sensibilities. False dichotomies both slight the complexity of issues and demolish hopes for our collective commitments to history, education, and democratic society. Our only prospects for intellectual and educational reconstruction lie in a renewed commitment to civilized and engaged argument with those who differ from us. To avoid the sterile alternative of bitter isolation and retreat requires moving beyond an indifferent, insipid toleration of difference to genuine respect for opponents and a serious grappling with their ideas, even in disagreement.

We can even, as Ribuffo asserts, agree upon the basic assumptions that most historians—by virtue of being historians—share: a belief that "we can more-or-less understand the past" independent of our personal experience; that "we can more-or-less figure out what individuals and groups *intended* by their words and deeds"; and that an understanding of the past demands "atypical seriousness of purpose." On this basis, we can formulate an "ecumenical" standard for the study of history. The essays in the final part of the book offer a modest introduction to the possibilities—from interpretive narrative, to moral inquiry, social criticism, interdisciplinary history, and straight narrative. In a similar spirit, Fox-Genovese posits a kind of historians' compact grounded in a common respect for a fundamental "integrity of evidence and argument." In another strategy for moving us beyond the impasse of postmodern relativism, Kors invokes historians' common capacity for fascination with knowledge for its own sake and our surprise at evidence that challenges our presuppositions. And Kagan finds hope in the possibility of adopting a simultaneously critical and respectful stance toward the past.

Other essays hint at strategies for engaging the issues that trouble all historians: political bias, history's direct and indirect relevance to current issues, the standards of the historian's craft. None is so naïve as to deny that scholars inescapably bring discrete perspectives and values to bear upon their writings and lectures. The real problem of political bias in education concerns the tendency to substitute personal and political loyalties for logic, evidence, and reasoning. To acknowledge the ubiquity of perspective in scholarship means to claim that it inevitably dominates all academic standards. Similarly, the question of the past's relevance to our contemporary situation defies the simple dichotomy between its being merely relevant or irrelevant. The requisite skill lies in the ability—and the integrity required—to distinguish among the ways in which it can be presented as relevant to, or morally instructive for, the present. So, too, standards of excellence, often dismissed as a reactionary defense of elitism, can and must coincide with democratic education. Respect for the integrity of our craft and for the intellectual potential of all our citizens commands us to reject false dilemmas. Above all, the challenges of our times require nuanced distinctions that transcend received categories, but conform to our common sense as historians.

Our best defense against the nihilism and stagnation that plague many students of history, as well as some of the most distinguished historians of our day, lies in a reconsideration of the reasons we study it and believe that it merits a central place in education. In exploring the nature of a liberal education, Kagan evokes its fundamental purposes and argues that we have capitulated to a truncated version more suited to the perpetuation of an elite than to the cultivation of a democratic citizenry. In this perspective, the broad purposes of liberal education include a love of learning as an "end in itself," as a mode of character formation, as preparation for a "useful career in the world," and as a necessary condition for the accountable freedom of citizens.

It is difficult to imagine a more important contribution to a renewed sense of common purpose than the cultivation of our common reverence for a free society. Education serves as the custodian of that reverence, which must be renewed in each generation, as the essential initiation into citizenship. The study of history, in all of its diversity, stands at the center of this project, and, across differences of perspective, ideology, and partisan politics, we aspire to contribute to a history that meets the demands of our times.

PART I

THE IMPERATIVE: THE HISTORICAL SOCIETY AS A CRITIQUE AND A NEW IDEAL

THE HISTORICAL SOCIETY has emerged in response to widespread discouragement about the dominant trends in the historical profession and a commitment to an ideal of a community of historians bound by respect for one another and their craft. The five essays in this section reflect both outlooks, albeit each with a specific balance between the two. During the early months of the society's existence in 1998, Eugene Genovese and Marc Trachtenberg each published an opinion piece (in the *Los Angeles Times* and the *Wall Street Journal,* respectively) that explained the society's origins and goals to the general public. Notwithstanding differences, the two essays converge in emphasizing the imperative to rescue history from the overspecialization, trivialization, faddishness, and political exclusivity into which the main historical organizations and no small number of departments have fallen.

Trachtenberg, a diplomatic historian, has first-hand experience of the "marginalization" that so many groups claim for themselves. Indeed, he recently came across a reference to the "virtual disappearance" of diplomatic history from the curricula of the most prestigious departments. Prevailing fashion in history has denigrated diplomatic history, along with much political, economic, and intellectual history. The fields that were once taken to capture the main developments in the life of any nation are now widely derided as the preserves of elite white men who trod upon the sensibilities and aspirations of those less privileged than they. In their stead, curricula and conventions now feature courses and sessions that focus upon topics such as "feminist studies" and "bodyworks," neither of which acknowledges a historical dimension. Journals now publish articles entitled "A Dual-Gendered Perspective on Eighteenth-Century Advice and Behavior"; "Constructing Menstruation"; "Rationalizing the Body"; and "The Ambiguities of Embodiment in Early America." And as these examples proliferate, it is increasingly difficult to dismiss them as a fad. To the contrary, Trachtenberg argues, they have become the norm—the standard by which candidates for jobs, proposals for sessions, and article and book manuscripts are measured.

In Trachtenberg's view, the heaviest burden of these developments falls upon young scholars "who still believe in the traditional concept of what historical work should be" and "find it much harder to get to first base in their academic careers." Ultimately, however, the cost for our society as a whole is even higher, because the way in which we understand the past directly influences the quality of our culture and our understanding of domestic and foreign relations.

Eugene Genovese deplores the neglect of diplomatic, intellectual, political, and economic history, which, because of their resistance to the ideologically loaded, formulaic claims of race, class, and gender, ". . . are barely tolerated when not treated with open contempt." Genovese attributes the main reasons for this disdain to political intolerance and likens the prevailing atmosphere to the McCarthy period. Chiding those who enjoin dispirited historians to reform the major professional associations "from within," he invokes the imposition of ideological conformity that the associations have tolerated or enforced, "for example by condoning the proscription of those who hold differing views—say, those who oppose abortion on religious principle." History, he reminds us, requires the intellectual freedom that can derive only from the willingness to attend respectfully to the views of others, even—indeed especially—those who hold different political and ideological views. The main rationale for The Historical Society lies precisely in fostering such a climate of intellectual and ideological openness that alone can nurture rich and challenging historical work of every variety—from social history to economic and diplomatic history.

Alan Kors, in an essay that originated as a presentation at an annual meeting of the American Historical Association, takes up similar themes, deploring the politicization that led the AHA in 1982 to pass a "we know as historians" resolution which advised the American public that "Reagan's rearmament and deployment policy would end détente, led to heightened tension between the U.S. and the—erstwhile—USSR, and that a nuclear freeze, not deployment, alone could lead to disarmament." This is not a wisdom, Kors scathingly notes, that the general public needs. Kors shares Trachtenberg and Genovese's dismay with the presumption of those historical associations which take political stands in the name of their purportedly "diverse" members. Above all, however, Kors points to the ignorance of important topics that informs the pronouncements on them. If you disdain the study of diplomatic history, how are you to provide wisdom on the diplomatic questions of today?

All of these essays voice deep concern about historians' apparent flight from the ideals of objectivity and the honest use of evidence. Recognizing history as a demanding and rewarding craft, the essays insist upon the importance of respect for common standards in the practice of that craft. The first requirement is not that historians espouse one or another political position but that they do their work as thoroughly and honestly as possible on the assumption that their colleagues will do the same. Kors further insists that the fashionable preoccupation with theory distracts historians from the intrinsic interest and significance of their work. Long after the world has forgotten prevailing theories of oppression, the nature of slavery and the fate of "nominally or truly freed slaves" will remain historical phenomena of abiding interest. Historians' choice of topics may embody one or another political inclination, but those political inclinations do not preclude a genuine commitment to knowledge for its own sake. In this respect, history invites us to move beyond the limitations of our own situation and biases rather than to wallow in them.

Daniel Littlefield takes up the problems of imposed political conformity in relation to multiculturalism, and, in accord with Diane Ravitch (Part IV), he distinguishes between its pluralistic and particularistic tendencies. Pluralist multicultural, he maintains, offers an ideal to which all historians should aspire: attention to the full range of historical actors necessarily enriches our work. Particularistic multiculturalism, in contrast, narrows our historical focus and undermines the significance of our work. Littlefield thus deplores the tendency of those who protest Eurocentrism simply to replace one centrism with another and thereby to reduce human accomplishment to a matter of gender or race. The struggles over the claims of multiculturalism, he notes, have blurred political lines by confusing its legitimate claims with the political agenda of those who most vociferously defend it. Those who acknowledge "the necessity to respond to a pluralistic society" frequently find themselves at odds with colleagues who share their respect for pluralism but feel obliged "to reject pandering to unreasonable demands of those whose primary purposes may have little to do with education." These divisions frequently lump people of very different views into a single camp, and "because we are so frequently judged by the company we keep, we sometimes avoid honest discussion of educational conundrums."

Elisabeth Lasch-Quinn underscores the importance of attending to the experience of groups that historians have often ignored and analyzes the political intolerance into which worthy initiatives have fallen. Not content to let the matter rest there, she links the particular problems of the historical profession to a general crisis of education and culture. Above all, she mourns the loss of a sense of scholarly community and of the intellectual excitement that drew so many of us to the study of history. Today, she argues, the conditions of our collective intellectual life are inexorably deteriorating under a myriad of external pressures. As the university increasingly comes to resemble one capitalist enterprise among others, historians, like other academics, face mounting pressures. The young especially confront a daunting job crisis and a pressure to "publish or perish" that discourages sustained reflection, independence of judgment, and demanding scholarship. Established scholars live with similar pressures to conform, heavy teaching loads, burdensome committee work, and a collapse of funding for research and travel to conferences. More and more, work within the university is coming to resemble work in other corporations, with the predictable results of declining intellectual courage and the erosion of bonds of collegiality.

We now live in a world in which ideas go at a discount and information is transmitted by sound bite or celluloid image. For historians, Lasch-Quinn writes, the greatest casualty has been our "sense of connection to a pulsating world of ideas, whose purpose transcends individual urges for advancement, supplies a context that adds meaning to such achievement, and provides the mixture of intellectual life and sociability that both compensates for the solitude of writing and research and continually reminds one that grappling with ideas matters here and now." Intellectuals necessarily work alone, but, she suggests, their work ultimately depends upon a sense of membership in a fellowship—a Republic of Letters that simultaneously honors individuality and fosters community. Communities, however, can foster both rigor and egalitarianism only if "dissenting voices and broader questions are not only heard or tolerated, but addressed."

Each of these essays testifies to the hopes that historians' current professional situation has too often deceived. While each member of The Historical Society carries the mark of specific experience and allegiances, including personal experience within the academy and without, some commitments and aspirations bind them all together. Above all, historians are turning to the society to find an intellectual community that simultaneously respects and fosters the vagaries of individual difference and the fellowship of common purpose. At the heart of these aspirations and commitments lies the conviction that history—as education, as scholarship, as of concern to the general culture—is vital to our prospects for a robust and democratic society and cannot be sacrificed on the altar of any person's or group's prejudices or politics.

CHAPTER 1

A NEW DEPARTURE

Eugene D. Genovese

PUBLIC INTEREST IN HISTORY is flourishing: an enthusiastic general audience buys and reads books about history, follows the offerings of the History Channel, and applauds historical films. All the while, much of the history now practiced in the academy is becoming increasingly specialized, careerist, bureaucratized, and politically conformist. The ironies abound and merit savoring. For today's academic history has largely done its work in the name of democracy. History, it claims, must embody the experience and feelings of ordinary people, especially those who have been oppressed, exploited, and barred from the corridors of power. It claims further that a focus on peoples and their victimization should replace nations and their traditions, and that attention to wars, rulers, and political contests should give way to sexualities and personal identities. Great religious and intellectual movements have evaporated under the hot sun of "performance" and the vagaries of "cultural studies."

Few would dispute the rich contributions of much of what was once called the "new" social history. Fewer still would deny the value of the historical sensibility that evokes the variegated legacy of different cultures. The call for a renewal of historical study has little to do with the politics of left, right, or center, much less with the suppression of diversity and multiculturalism. Contemporary academic history is being systematically gutted of the breadth, the drama, and, most dangerously, the tragedy that have accounted

---

Originally published as "Restoring Dignity to the Historical Profession" in the *Los Angeles Times,* May 31, 1998.

for its abiding hold over the public imagination. What remains is a series of vignettes of everyday life that bear an eerie resemblance to the contemporary sensibilities of identity politics.

Since Thucydides, historians of every century and civilization have focused upon the rise and fall of empires, states, and republics, and those subjects continue to fascinate the public. But today's academic historians contemptuously dismiss this legacy as elitist—dead, white, male—history. And indeed, at least in Northern Europe and the United States, the main players in this arena have primarily been white and male—and are now dead. But to condemn them for those attributes amounts to a public confession of intellectual poverty. For better or worse—usually a measure of both—they shaped the world we have inherited. History further demonstrates that, given the opportunity, Asians, Africans, Middle Easterners—and more than an occasional woman—have done the same, sometimes with more admirable results, sometimes with less. Their behavior like ours was one aspect of the human condition. They exercised their power and authority through the wars, diplomacy, and political struggles in which they engaged, as well as through their efforts to write laws, build institutions, establish cultural and intellectual hegemony, and implement their vision of life in a specific society. In most instances, their efforts demonstrably embodied some measure of self-interest. But the alleged selfishness of individuals or ruling classes does not justify our denying their claims upon our attention.

Since diplomatic, intellectual, political, and economic history, among other subjects, prove resistant to race, class, and gender, they are barely tolerated when not treated with open contempt. No matter that, for example, diplomacy may result in a transfer of territory that reshapes the lives of ordinary people, perhaps easing or exacerbating class or ethnic conflict, perhaps inducing a new attitude toward gender roles. It is preposterous to deny the significance of high diplomacy, politics, and intellectual life in the lives of ordinary people, which they influence—and are influenced by—in countless direct and indirect ways. But historians' interest in them does not require that justification. Their real claims upon our attention lie in their intrinsic interest, and our attention to them in turn testifies to our openness to the social life of diverse peoples in its genuine complexity.

The demand that historians privilege race, class, and gender is occurring in an atmosphere that uncomfortably resembles the McCarthyism of the 1950s. It is being imposed by presiding cliques that have made ideological conformity the primary criterion for holding office. Some eminent historians are now lecturing us to "work from within" the establishment organizations rather than form a new historical society. With every respect for their good intentions, let me ask them if the establishment organizations have not imposed the extremism of "political correctness," for example by condoning the proscription of those who hold differing views—say, those who oppose abortion on religious principle. Am I being unreasonable when I ask why eminent colleagues have never uttered a word of protest, much less demanded that those responsible be called to account? For ourselves, we do not deny the right of the prevailing academic establishment to do its thing on its own turf, but we believe that we can build an organization that practices academic freedom in open debate over the large themes that lie at the heart of any history worthy of attention.

We have founded The Historical Society to foster the intellectual and ideological openness that alone nurture rich and challenging historical work of every variety—from social history to economic and diplomatic history. Our charter members include people whose politics range from the Marxist left to the traditionalist right, including every position between them, and we welcome the adherence of all who share our fundamental commitments, independent of their views on other matters. It should say enough that our board of governors includes Paul Gottfried, Gertrude Himmelfarb, Donald Kagan, Franklin W. Knight, Elisabeth Lasch-Quinn, Pauline Maier, Susan Rosa, Joel Silbey, Martin J. Sklar, Sean Wilentz, and John Womack. They have been selected solely on the basis of their professional contributions and represent themselves, not constituencies. It should come as no surprise that that leadership includes blacks and whites, men and women, gays and straights. All we ask of our members is that they lay down plausible premises; reason logically; appeal to evidence; and respect the integrity of all those who do the same.

Historians with diverse views are coming together to establish a dynamic dialogue in which history will once again attract the attention of all those who see it as more than fad or fancy. We intend to create a new community in which civilized exchange will be the pattern of intellectual discourse. For the rest, Professor John H. Roper of Emory and Henry College, a man known for his political moderation and tolerant spirit, said it all: "We simply must restore the dignity of our profession."

CHAPTER 2

THE PAST UNDER SIEGE

A HISTORIAN PONDERS THE STATE OF HIS PROFESSION—AND WHAT TO DO ABOUT IT

Marc Trachtenberg

THIRTY YEARS AGO, when I first became a historian, I thought I knew what historical work should be. I had this notion that the goal was to get at the truth. It seemed obvious that to do that you had to put your political beliefs aside and frame questions in such a way that the answers turned on what the evidence showed.

As everyone knows, this concept of historical work has been under attack in recent years. We have seen the rise of a new brand of history, defined not so much by the kind of subject matter it seeks to "privilege"—above all, issues of gender—but by something more basic.

Increasingly, the old ideal of historical objectivity is dismissed out of hand. The very notion of "historical truth" is now often considered hopelessly naïve. Instead, the tendency is for people to insist that all interpretation is to be understood in essentially political terms. If objectivity is a myth, how can our understanding of the past be anything but an artifact of our political beliefs? Indeed, if all interpretation is political anyway, then why not give free rein to one's own political views? Why not use whatever power one happens to have to "privilege" one's own brand of history?

And in fact a particular brand of history is currently being "privileged." Just look at what goes on at the annual meetings of the main professional organizations, or what gets published in their journals. "A Dual-Gendered

Originally published in the *Wall Street Journal,* July 17, 1998.

Perspective on Eighteenth Century Advice and Behavior"; "Constructing Menstruation"; "Rationalizing the Body"; "The Ambiguities of Embodiment in Early America"—these are the sorts of topics one sees all the time nowadays.

Cyborg Bodies

Or, look at the kinds of courses that now, increasingly, are being taught in major academic departments. One leading university lists a course called "Introduction to Feminist Studies" as part of its history curriculum. Note the title: not women's history, not the history of gender relations, indeed, not history at all, but "feminist studies." You don't have to be an expert in Foucault to deconstruct that.

Another course listed as part of the history curriculum there was called "Bodyworks." The goal of this course, according to the syllabus, was to examine the thesis that "dramatic new ways of imaging, controlling, intervening, remaking, possibly even choosing bodies have participated in a complete reshaping of the notion of the body in the cultural imaginary and a transformation of our experience of actual human bodies." "Using theories of postmodernism," this class would address the questions: "Are there postmodern bodies? And how have they been constructed?" It would explore the thesis that "postmodern bodies are cyborg bodies and that we are all cyborgs."

One sees this sort of thing more and more, and it is not to be dismissed as simply a passing fad. The problem is that the "privileging" of certain types of history necessarily implies the marginalizing of everything else. Those who do trendy work find it relatively easy to get jobs and eventually to get tenure. But younger scholars who still believe in the traditional concept of what historical work should be find it much harder to get to first base in their academic careers. Many drop out of graduate school when they see which way the wind is blowing. And many talented undergraduates see what is going on and decide not to go to graduate school in the first place.

The result is that the profession as a whole is gradually being transformed. Last year [in 1997], for example, I came across a reference to the "virtual disappearance" of diplomatic history, my own field, from the curriculum of "major departments." Can it be that people really think that courses in "feminist studies" are more important, and more worthy of being taught in history departments, than courses concerned with the problem of war and peace? It's hard to believe, but increasingly that seems to be the case.

This is a serious problem, not just for the academic community but for the country as a whole, because the way the past is understood—and, even more than that, the quality of historical culture—is a matter of profound importance to society at large.

So what's the solution? If there is an answer, it has to come from within the profession, and in fact something important has been going on. Two months ago [in April 1998], a new organization for professional historians, The Historical Society, officially came into being. The scholars who joined this new body—there were more than two hundred charter members—were no monolithic bloc. Some of them resented the politicization of the major professional organizations (a charge that the leaders of these organizations do not even bother to deny). Some especially disliked what they saw as the parochial and exclusionary attitude of the newly dominant groups, reflected most notably in what went on at annual meetings of the established organizations. Some simply found the status quo boring and wanted above all to put some intellectual excitement back into their professional lives.

Discontent and Action

But these people all had one thing in common: a deep dissatisfaction with the status quo, a discontent strong enough to lead them to break with the established organizations and to say through their action that something new was needed.

Who are the scholars who have joined the new Historical Society? Just tired old conservative white male professors, who had been left behind by the transformation of the profession and who wanted nothing more than to turn back the clock to the good ole days when they were in the saddle? As it turns out, the new society includes some of the most distinguished scholars in the profession. Its membership covers the whole political spectrum. Its president, Eugene Genovese, one of the nation's most eminent historians, is an ex-Marxist and still certainly a man of the left. It includes black scholars who, given the rawness of the black historical experience, bridle at the idea that there is no such thing as historical reality and that everything is just a construct. It includes women who resent being told that they should be doing "feminist history." And it includes many of our best younger scholars who feel, with some justification, that they are not getting a fair shake from the system.

Will the new organization transform the profession? A few months ago, I thought the establishment of this new group would be little more than a symbolic gesture. I was astonished by the response, and now I am more optimistic.

The real battles, of course, will be fought in the universities, and an organization like this can scarcely change things overnight. But the new society can show through its example what historical work should be and what a professional historical organization should be. If it succeeds at that, it might well have a major impact on the future of historical culture in America.

CHAPTER 3

THE FUTURE OF HISTORY IN AN INCREASINGLY UNIFIED WORLD

Alan Charles Kors

DECEMBER 1992

MY SUBJECT, as suggested by the president of the American Historical Association (AHA) is "the state of history in a world that is increasingly unified by technology, a global economy, and such common problems as ecological exploitation, ethnic tension, and political disillusionment." It is, from my sense of the present and of the profession (and I am not a historian of the contemporary), an ironic list. Indeed, the world is, in some sense, increasingly unified by the technology of the developed nations and by dependency upon the productive powers of free markets in what is probably "early," not, as historians are wont to say, "late capitalism." These are not (nor, necessarily, should they be) the most favored historical subjects.

The parameters of ecological exploitation ought to be defined, at least in significant part, by precise science, but few historians seem more than marginally interested in precise science these days. Political disillusionment is a curious addition. I take it that the end of the communist calvary and the evidence of its catastrophic legacy, coupled with academic anguish over twelve years of Republican administration in the United States, indicates that now, everyone is disillusioned. In fact, the ex-dissidents, the aspiring democrats in

Originally presented in a slightly different form at the Presidential Plenary Session of the American Historical Association, December 1992.

cultures that seemed fated to permanent, unaccountable tyranny, and the classical liberals I know are filled with wary, alert optimism—not disillusionment. As for ethnic tension, it has been with us, everywhere, through all of recorded history, and for all we know as historians, aversion to difference might well reflect, alas, one of those ancestrally functional and now dysfunctional evolutionary legacies from which culture only partially saves us. Evolutionary, let alone sociobiological or ethological discourse among historians, however, is distinctly out of favor, despite the increasing wish to comment on the boundary between biology and culture without knowing any biology.

In terms of the disparate quality of the fundamental lives of peoples, however, there is not now and never has been any "unified world," increasingly or otherwise. Most of the world's people still live lives that are, if not solitary, then poor, nasty, brutish, and short—hungry, ill-housed, and truly helpless before natural and human power, variations on a theme by Somalia and Serbia, or indeed by seventeenth-century (and later) Germany. Further, a factor of great moral interest to scholars and teachers, freedom of thought, criticism, and expression does not typify the human world. In most societies, including some that live materially quite well, honest critics and scholars risk their freedom or lives to state even obvious truths, and certainly are not rewarded by deanships, tenure, fellowships, and the power to educate the next generation and determine the curriculum. When Salman Rushdie was asked what he read in the first year of his hiding from holy assassins, he answered that he read the French Enlightenment, for insight and strength. Say what one will about Eurocentric, Enlightenment value judgments and relativism, but I fondly hope that the cultural norms of peer review adopted by Rushdie's critics do not become a part of our own "multiculturalism." Count me as a moral absolutist on that.

Historians in general, it seems safe to say, have not chosen to nurture the sort of knowledge that the world so desperately needs now: how to effect transformations from centrally planned to market economies; or how to create and sustain democratic cultures capable of supporting the flawed but real practice of accountable institutions. Given the nature of historical study, however, both in practice and in the abstract, this is not necessarily a loss to the world. It was the AHA, after all, that in 1982 passed its prescient "we know as historians" resolution advising the public that President Reagan's rearmament and deployment policy would end detente, lead to heightened tension between the United States and the erstwhile Soviet Socialist Republics, and that a nuclear freeze, not deployment, alone could lead to disarmament. The world certainly does not need either wisdom such as that, or the help of an intellectual community that submits questions of complex historical analysis to a majority referendum.

More significantly, it is dubious that historians possess a kind of knowledge that ought to give them, as AHA President Wakeman phrased it, "intellectual leadership." To me what we do above all, or, at least, what we do at our best, is to recreate, patiently, the historical contexts and trends of people's social, cultural, political, intellectual, and institutional lives; or, indeed, of their sexual lives and gender relations above all, with categories particular to if not derived from the periods, places, and groups under study. All of our immersion, empiricism, digging, and familiarity with time and place often make us quite good at that. We are at our worst, I fear, when we overreach as metatheorists of the human condition, flying from a few particulars and a smattering of this or that faddish and ephemeral critical theory to pronouncements on matters where contextual historical knowledge ought to inform diplomacy, psychology, domestic policy, ethology, economics, and social theory, for example, but where it scarcely can do more than that. In two generations, almost no one except intellectual historians will remember Foucault, Lacan, Fanon, Derrida, Althusser, Gramsci, or Lukacs, but people still will want to know about the forms and varieties of human political, social, cultural, and intellectual behavior as it existed, evolved, and was experienced in the diversity of human times and places. Theories of oppression, for example, will come and go, but slavery and the fate of nominally or truly freed slaves will remain as historical phenomena. Indeed, such theories only can be assayed if there is an historically informed contextual knowledge against which they may be tested. Theories of linkage between thought and social context will come and go, but the emergence and evolution of Islam, the formation and transmission of Confucian or Hindu structures of thought, the European transformation of natural knowledge in the seventeenth and eighteenth centuries, the myriad folk cultures of ordinary lives at different times and places, and, indeed, the culture wars of the late twentieth century will remain as objects of our fascination with the history of human understanding, and the human structuring of phenomena and value. What historians respond to best is that fascination, that curiosity about the past and variety of the forms of human life. It is a current commonplace to define all things as political, but the higher primates, ourselves included, are marked by curiosity. Historical study, at some level, responds to the desire to hold up the evidence of a human past and regard it from a variety of angles, some of them personal, some political, and some simply or complexly part of the chain of human *curiositas* and *scientia*.

It is in some sense undoubtedly true that the very choice of historical topics itself is political, but it is possible for the human spirit to want to inquire honestly, for the sake of knowledge, into a chosen topic. As historians, we are so often surprised and forced by evidence to modify our deepest views, contrary to initial working hypotheses and, indeed, contrary to desire, even when personally invested in such views. The enemy of honest inquiry is tendentiousness, and it is generally the bane of historical writing. As Francis Bacon noted in his cautions against "the Idols of the Mind," we are prone to error—from the limits of human powers, from individual bias, from the equivocation of our words, from the inveterate flaws of those inherited human theories that we take as nature's own. To overcome such propensities for self-deception and illusion, Bacon urged, we need to guard, above all, against those things we wish to believe; we need to devise tests of precisely the hypotheses to which we are drawn; we need to learn from the behavior of the world; and we need to be skeptical of both our own powers and of the force of received tradition.

The kaleidoscope of history may be somewhat less confusing than the full kaleidoscope of nature, but the political and psychological gratification of certain beliefs makes history at least as prone to self-deception as was seventeenth-century natural philosophy. Some claim for history today a conceptual revolution as fundamental as that embodied in Copernicus or Galileo, but we should recall that for every one Galileo among subverters of the canon, there were hundreds of ill-fated systematizers, alchemists, and astrologers whose work led simply to bizarre, if historically interesting, dead ends. The more we deem our histories to be guides to current human behavior, the greater the danger of our anachronisms, our self-indulgence, and our natural tendentiousness.

What I suspect the agenda here to be is less the "increasing unification" of the "world" than the changing demographics of American and academic life, a process that in a variety of ways and for a variety of reasons has altered, for many, the nature of historical theory and practice. The movement into history of generations radicalized or reradicalized by the sixties and its legacies; of ethnic groups, my own included, previously absent from academic life; of gays and lesbians who need not or courageously will not hide their identities from bigotry; and of women with often essential feminist commitments, has introduced new agendas, questions, and perspectives into our discipline. For many, the task of history now is, above all, the recovery of ignored voices, the demystification of power, the restructuring of our conceptions from new perspectives, and the empowerment of groups deemed historically victimized. As general phenomena, none of these developments is new in the history of history, but in much less than one generation, the content of journals, the topics of meetings, the voices of historians and the first-year colloquia of graduate students have changed dramatically. These processes have broadened the scope and perspectives of history and have altered certain fundamental understandings, but, given the ferment they have occasioned, not without exacerbating disquieting tendencies that traditionally have plagued the profession: theorizing without appropriate criticism or testing; overreaching beyond competence and knowledge; intolerant political intimidation; and, to say the least, tensions in the air that we well might seek to mitigate.

I suggest some means toward a more irenic *modus vivendi:*

1. Fields should be defined by subjects and questions, not by theoretical commitments, and certainly not by politics or answers. The histories of Jews, Christians, or Muslims, for example, may not legitimately be the preserve of particular sectarian perspectives. Similarly, the history of gender should be open to study from a wholly pluralistic array of perspectives: gender-feminism, sociobiology, class and status analysis, functionalist social theory, and a comprehensive "etcetera." The analysis of power is not a radical preserve. Both conservatives and radicals often forget that Mosca, Pareto, and Michels, before Gramsci, and from the Right, sought to demystify and decode the myths by which power justified itself. Historians need intense debates and intellectual competition among a diversity of methodological and interpretive schools and theories.
2. Work should be evaluated for its descriptive, analytic, or explanatory power, not for its provenance and certainly not for its political good faith. Indeed, across the spectrum, we should in some sense be harshest in our evaluation of sloppy work done by people whose intellectual (or other) goals and commitments we share. One's liking for companions on a path does not entail that it is leading one anywhere valuable. The profession is tolerating often egregiously partial and prepossessed work, across the spectrum, for ideological reasons.
3. We all should avoid the temptation to clone ourselves. In particular, hiring, tenure, promotion, and peer review should be moments when all of us bend over backward to be intellectually pluralistic, judging work by its intellectual force, its provocation of vital debate, and its shedding of light on historical phenomena, even if we should shed that light from other directions. We have a right to demand probative research, rigorous inquiry, and logical relationship of explanation or theory to data, but not to demand that someone share our particular ideological, theoretical, or political commitments. If the latter is what people mean by boasting that their professional life is an extension of their politics, the future of a pluralistic historical community is dim indeed.

The best educators always have preferred open, critical minds to spellbound disciples. It was my Marxist professors, devoted to scientific inquiry and honest debate, who introduced me to Hayek, von Mises, and Pareto; it was my religious professors who sent me to Marx, Holbach, Diderot, and the atheistic tradition. If history as a discipline can offer anything to the world, it can offer that sense of the value of open-mindedness, competing interpretations, and intense debate in the pursuit of knowledge about the human past. The great antidote to parochialism is indeed knowledge of human diversity, but the truly mysterious "other," awesome in its diversity, and always awaiting historical attention, is our human selves in other times, other places, and other forms of being. Such a gift will seem small in light of the presentistic agendas and metapretensions increasingly prevalent, but it is, I suspect, the deepest gift our vocation has to offer.

CHAPTER 4

POLITICS AND MULTICULTURALISM

Daniel C. Littlefield

A MAJOR ISSUE facing us today as teachers and interpreters of our nation's history is the conflict commonly associated with the term "multiculturalism." Recent controversies, moreover, have raised the issue to a level of public visibility, if not concern. The term is a loaded one and we may begin by assessing its content. In recent pronouncements,[1] Diane Ravitch made a useful distinction between what she called "pluralistic multiculturalism" and "particularistic multiculturalism," or, as she clarified her terminology, pluralism or multiculturalism on the one hand, and particularism on the other. We have reached a stage, she said, where "cultural pluralism is now generally recognized as an organizing principle of this society." The idea of the "melting pot" has been rejected and "children now learn . . . that differences among groups are a national resource rather than a problem to be solved. Indeed, the unique feature of the United States is that its common culture has been formed by the interaction of its subsidiary cultures." This may be called the multicultural consensus. But while the "pluralists seek a richer common culture . . . the particularists insist that no common culture is possible or desirable." Thus one needs blacks to motivate blacks, Latinos to motivate Latinos, women to motivate women, and so forth. Human accomplishment is reduced to a matter of race and gender.

Those who have called for a rejection of what they style "Eurocentrism" have a sound case for the broadening of American education to reflect the

Originally published in slightly different form in the *OAH Council of Chairs Newsletter,* October/December 1991.

country's diverse cultural heritage. The achievements of women and people of color need to be represented, nay, to be recognized as commonplace, in the story of America's development. Such people need also to be among those doing the teaching. But it is not wise to replace one "centrism" with another. Some proponents of change come dangerously close to a willingness to celebrate the achievements of women, blacks, and other people of color not to illustrate that people regardless of gender and color are capable, but rather simply because they are blacks or women. They argue for courses or programs not as a means to illustrate or celebrate a common humanity but as a vehicle to magnify the accomplishments of a particular group. And where these accomplishments are lacking they are willing to fudge the issue because what they seek is an image, not the courage, triumphs, and failure of human beings engaged in common and uncommon endeavors. They use symbols to foster group identities and political agendas rather than education. Such image-building hinders the solution of real pedagogical problems by providing administrators and others in power an easy way out. Responding to political pressures, they may establish ill-conceived programs in ethnic or other studies rather than ponder alternative ways to answer legitimate concerns (as, for example, integrating those studies into existing courses or units). Once such programs are established, the problem remains to plague a new group of students, teachers, and administrators, or the same group at a later time, among other reasons because these programs often are deliberately isolated from the regular curriculum.

The demands of a just multicultural society are complex, and we may find no easy answers; worse, the problems often promote demagoguery. It is, for example, a lot easier today to be a black conservative than it might once have been. Most black people are more socially conservative than most white people think, but black opportunists can now find acceptance and support (economic and otherwise) among white conservatives who desire to prove that they are not racist, but who oblige their black proponents to mouth platitudes or back platforms that do not benefit the majority of the black community. A lot of money can be made nowadays by people who say the right thing. At the very least, they can get a lot of publicity. Moreover, the lines between liberal and conservative positions are being blurred; that is to say, positions once associated primarily with wealthy, conservative, white people are now finding resonance among people who are neither white nor wealthy, as is the case with public funding for private schools in situations where the public schools are inadequate. More often than one would have thought possible, blacks from working-class backgrounds now find themselves speaking before the conservative Heritage Foundation. Whether or not people there can develop any serious appreciation for the concerns of minorities and the poor, whether or not they have any real interest in what blacks or others have to say beyond the limits of their own preconceptions, nevertheless, the situation is new. It has the potential of encouraging greater discourse among those who do not normally attempt to communicate. Perhaps there is even a chance for greater understanding. There is at least a chance to change some stereotypes. In any case, traditional lines are no longer clear.

This blurring of traditional lines is nowhere more apparent than in the debate provoked by Dinesh D'Souza. "Distort D'Newza," as he was apparently known in his student days as editor of the *Dartmouth Review,* evidently continues to be guilty of inaccuracies and oversimplifications. Nevertheless, as Eugene Genovese suggests, he has adduced an opportunity to discuss important educational issues.[2] Members of our profession who have been (and one hopes and supposes will continue to be) friends and allies find themselves on opposite sides of the argument over *Illiberal Education* because of their different emphases: the necessity to respond to a pluralistic society versus the obligation to reject pandering to the unreasonable demands of those whose primary purposes may have little to do with education. Feelings become strained because one side of the argument is supported by those who would deny the current multicultural reality altogether, grouped, in this case, with those who take the same position from a sense of social balance and intellectual integrity rather than from cultural blindness or moral obtuseness. Because we are so often judged by the company we keep, we sometimes avoid honest discussion of educational conundrums. For example, some might avoid criticizing a conceptually flawed ethnic studies program for fear of being viewed as against the idea of ethnic studies. No one wants to be seen as giving aid and comfort to the enemy. Scholars can be notoriously contentious and one may expect disagreements but we ought at least to be clear about the areas of disagreement and not push each other to extremes.

Special studies programs should be a means to an end not an end in themselves. I find it ironic, for example, that some of the people who talk so glibly about Afrocentrism have little knowledge about, or interest in, Africa. Students in my African American history classes are increasingly impatient with the section on the African background—not that they are always enthralled with the rest of the material. They are often more willing to take positions than they are to study. In fact, a real multicultural education requires the absorption of *more* material, not less. Ideally, it suggests interrelationships between Western and other cultures and particularly the extent to which American culture is the result of the blending of European and other cultures. Any program that is based on a rejection of that basic concept of American society is one that will further not education and understanding but rather dissention and miscomprehension. Any program that fosters isolation and particularism should be resisted.

At one southern university where I taught in a conservative department, the chairman regularly taught a graduate history seminar in which he occasionally asked members of the department to address the class concerning their specialty. I was asked only once, during a semester when he had one or two black students in the class and I was asked to talk about my secondary field of African history. There are two ways one can view that situation: On the one hand, the chairman had black students and thought perhaps that they should be addressed at least once by a black professor (they did not work with me) on a topic that had some black content. This would indicate a degree of sensitivity and concern. On the other hand, if what I said had value, it should have been valuable to all, regardless of race. I once discussed this with the only woman in the department, whose response was "Well, Dan, if you're unhappy here, I don't see why you stay."

But if ignoring or segregating the expertise of black scholars is objectionable, so too is tolerating unreasonable conduct or demands, even those rationalized on the basis of race or gender. And candor requires me to say that some do act that way. A person where I now work has evidently made a career of using issues of race and gender to further her personal goals, and the department has made a practice of giving in to the strategy. Indeed, if it works, why not? Pride and integrity might dictate otherwise, but unprincipled behavior is not confined to white males even if one assumed that they have held much of the ground. On their part, white males sometimes evince unprincipled behavior these days by making gutless concessions to people who take advantage of the real need for diversity; and having made the concessions, usually to someone of dubious qualifications, use the concession to argue the injustice of worthwhile concepts. The dearth of qualified women and minorities should not be used as an excuse to retain or coddle charlatans or incompetents simply because they are black or female. That benefits no one—except those opposed to their hiring.

There is a difference, however, between encouraging a more inclusive approach to education and insisting that everyone toe the same line; in adopting and enforcing outlooks deemed to be "politically correct." The evidence suggests that I once was denied a job at a prominent West Coast university for failure to meet such a test. When asked how I "treated" women in my courses, rather than asking for clarification, I interpreted the question to mean how I dealt with them in the subject matter. I ought to have responded simply that I made an honest effort to integrate the history of women (and others) into my coursework and that, insofar as I knew, I made a greater effort to do so than anyone else in the department, including one woman, where I currently taught. Misjudging my audience by thinking that that might sound too self-serving, assuming that we already shared a common perspective, and recalling that a woman in my class had once asked why I didn't do more on women, I replied that I didn't do enough, pleading constraints of time. It never occurred to me that my response might be taken as evidence of insensitivity. I intended to suggest that there might be honest differences over whether my "treatment" of women was adequate, and it was something we might have discussed. I certainly did not mean to indicate an unwillingness to consider ways to reorganize the course, which I periodically do anyway. Instead, the discussion moved on to a consideration of particular books. But I had already failed a political test and so apparently I was reported. Support I thought I had rapidly evaporated in face of the opposition. That may be as it should be. Perhaps departments should strive for unanimity in hiring as much as possible for the sake of harmony. But I was disappointed that I could be so easily dismissed because of a perception that I was "politically incorrect" and have otherwise reasonable people cave in at the mere suspicion. Ironically, one who rapidly abandoned my support was himself recently the target of a charge of racism in connection with a textbook series he had a hand in developing, despite his obeisance in all the right directions, and heartfelt determination to be responsible as well as fair. The exigencies of political correctness are not always easy to meet.

Justice and political correctness are not always, one might even suggest that they are seldom, coterminous. I would argue for multiculturalism because it is just, not because it is politically correct. Moreover, it is wise and beneficial and accords with reality. But multiculturalism does not benefit us and it does not accord with reality when we confuse our political and educational needs.

Notes

1. "Multiculturalism: E Pluribus Plures," and "Multiculturalism: An Exchange," *American Scholar,* 59, no. 3 (summer 1990): 337–54 and vol. 60, no. 2 (spring 1991): 267–76.
2. *The New Republic,* April 15, 1991.

CHAPTER 5

DEMOCRACY IN THE IVORY TOWER?

TOWARD THE RESTORATION OF AN INTELLECTUAL COMMUNITY

Elisabeth Lasch-Quinn

AT THE RISK of charges of nostalgia or idealism, it is time to contemplate the nature of the collective intellectual life that most historians share on a daily basis. Certain recent historical works inspire awe; occasional forums hint at the riches that only historical inquiry can offer; pockets of community sprout up that support independence of thought by permitting open debate and exploration of ideas in a context of tremendous encouragement. Yet in the larger picture, overwhelming trends in recent years have sapped the life-force of the public dimension of the profession, distancing the study of history from what it can be at its most compelling. Time pressures, a degree of resignation or complacency, an overly individualistic notion of career—these and other factors may well have allowed trends in academia and in Western culture more broadly to compromise the vision of those who decided to devote their lives to the practice of history in the first place. That vision involved pursuing such work in the company of an engaged, even enthralled, community of scholars and thinkers whose existence raises not only the level of engagement but its quality and significance.

Such a community, even (or especially) if one finds oneself at odds with the views of other members, can provide support for rigorous intellectual achievement unavailable elsewhere. A sense of connection to a pulsating world of ideas, whose purpose transcends the urge for individual advancement, supplies a context that adds meaning to such achievement, and provides the mixture of intellectual life and sociability that both compensates for the solitude of writing and research and continually reminds one that grappling with ideas matters here and now. Pockets of community surely do exist, but not generally along such lines; the likemindedness of members generally rules out the kind of exchange possible in a context of open, but supportive, disagreement. Of course just the right mix of support and confrontation—that which allows for lively debate, prevents participants from taking personal affront, and ends with mutual edification—is difficult to achieve. But if this ideal recedes too far it risks disappearing altogether. This ideal, after all, is the goal not only of education but of democratic deliberation, the two of which are inextricable.

Several forces have eaten away at the ideal of an intellectual, continually self-educating community. Recent years have witnessed a heightening of trends, including overspecialization, the drive for intellectual or political conformity, careerism, obsessive gatekeeping, rising concerns for process over substance, the triumph of relativism and subjectivism in scholarship, the bureaucratization of academic life, the cult of professional expertise, the imperialism of schools of education, the shrinkage of job prospects in the classical areas of knowledge, and the commercialization of the university. These and other factors have created a situation in which scholars often shy away from genuine engagement with others in open dialogue, from unpopular conclusions, and from large questions that take them beyond the safe ground of narrowly delimited fields of expertise. The effects have been devastating not only for practicing historians but also for the level of historical understanding and inquiry in public life.

The retreat of an ideal of a genuine, open community among historians functions to the detriment and demoralization of many in the profession, helping to keep or drive out valuable potential contributors, discouraging many within, and setting an uninspiring example for younger scholars. Either by choice or in response to various pressures—foremost among them the sour job market of the last three decades—many individuals committed to serious history make their livings in ways other than permanent academic jobs. That reality has had a tremendous impact on those individuals and on the formal profession itself, which is seriously impoverished by its own isolation.

Any observer must acknowledge the randomness, injustice, and error that has consigned some members of this generation of scholars to the periphery of the historical profession and compelled others to practice their craft from another discipline or in nonacademic venues altogether. In order for a certain ideal of intellectual life to flourish, meaningless distinctions must be set aside. It is time that those making serious contributions to historical understanding be acknowledged as such *by historians,* just as they are, in many cases, acknowledged by other disciplines and by the public.

The creation of new structures of intellectual life is a matter of dire importance. The constricted academic job market, and the perennial question of how intellectual work (especially work that fails to fit neatly into current economic imperatives) will find material support, is only one side of the problem. The other is that many of the realities of academic life increasingly keep it from being a desirable intellectual life at the individual and collective level. Such bureaucratic constraints as tight budgets and shrinking departments, the attendant rise in committee work, an increase in teaching loads, pressure for participation in top-down academic reforms, and inflated quantitative expectations for hiring, tenure, and promotion, all take the focus off the study, contemplation, and exchange needed for fruitful intellectual production, whether aimed at teaching or publication.

This crisis of purpose is a loss not only to the particular historian or to historical scholarship but to the larger project of democratic deliberation, which relies on education, particularly of the sort history can provide, in order to function at all. Mere toleration of different perspectives is too thin an educative philosophy to support democratic aspirations. The best traditions of Western democracies include a sustained attack on social inequality and self-perpetuating social hierarchies and ingrained patterns of deference. In the twentieth century, however, this attack on hierarchy took a misguided turn into the arenas of taste, standards and ideals.[1] Many believe that an extreme version of relativism as a philosophy of life is the only ethos that rightfully fits our shared desire for universal citizenship rights and equality. But the consequences of this relativism—precisely for *democratic* education—have been disastrous.

According to radical relativism, the imperative that each individual and group perspective be granted a hearing often translates into an assumption that each perspective is equally valid. Enlightened citizens in the relativist world are bound to tolerate different perspectives without actually challenging them, since each speaker, by virtue either of culture or experience, has a kind of unassailable authority. Since each perspective theoretically possesses equal validity, ideas—imbued with their subjective origins—become viewpoints and each viewpoint demands a hearing (but little more). The resulting vague sense that acceptance of diversity has been achieved stands in for democratic engagement. Such expressions pass themselves off as democracy in action, as the logical consequence of movements for social equality. Full visibility—or audibility—supposedly comprises full participation. And full participation must mean democracy is at work.

The problem with this arrangement is that tolerance pure and simple not only shows a severe shrinkage of the faculties of hope and imagination, which might demand more of our collective life, but also is precisely *undemocratic.* A flourishing democracy does, of course, presume civic participation, but the unchallenged self-expression of self-righteously subjective perspectives—so well exemplified by the talk-show mode, a therapeutic style of expression that confirms prejudices and thus further balkanizes audiences—is an impoverished, if not insidious, notion of participation. Democracy demands not the mere airing of feelings but diverse ideas as well, as it must find a way to allow citizens to understand, evaluate, and make decisions based on knowledge. Without a public sphere created by the kind of dialogue made possible, as Jürgen Habermas put it, when individuals put their personal stake in an idea on hold for the purpose of reasoned discussion, democracy devolves into interest group politics, and the notion of the general good—essential to democratic life—vanishes. What is more, previously disfranchised groups may win temporary victories in this setting, but in the long run equality itself loses out to an unstable cycle of vengeance. In addition, individual dissent within such groups often draws dismissal or attack. The point of the democratic process, as political philosopher Jean Bethke Elshtain establishes in *Democracy on Trial,* is not that each group should get its day in the sun but that full participation, rights, and equality are merely aspects of a social life bound by mutual obligations and devoted to self-government and shared prosperity, that is, merely aspects of a collective life worthy of our inclusion.[2]

In an open, egalitarian society that strives for freedom from coercion and for self-government, the quality of education takes on supreme importance. Education should involve schooling, to be sure, but should go well beyond institutions to include intellectual activity more broadly; the learning that aims at mastery and understanding and not just at career making. This ideal is familiar to those whose very posture toward life revolves around education as the primary project of the self. This notion of education's role in character building is mandatory for the high level of individual responsibility and competence that is necessary for true self-government (rather than a species of paternalistic self-deception) at the community and national level. This stance is also one of the most fundamental sources of hope in the face of past individual and group mistakes and shortcomings. Those who have conceived of history as moral inquiry are among the few who have kept this aspect of education alive.

Beyond the character-building role of education is its ability to foster the climate of open inquiry, civil debate, and collective discussion that is indispensable for democracy. An entire school of political philosophy currently defends the vital role of associational activity described by Tocqueville in his *Democracy in America.*[3] In certain prepolitical forms, citizens learn the arts of debate, persuasion, respect of other points of view, and other fruits of genuine engagement for a higher purpose—precisely the prerequisites for democratic politics. Of course, associational life (even certain expressions of family life) also introduces people to the richness of collective life, which in turn raises concrete images of the good society that is worth constructing, joining, and defending.

All signs suggest that the modern university—one of the most promising places for such an introduction to collective life—largely fails today to provide the flourishing intellectual environment best suited to fulfill democracy's unique requirement for both excellence and egalitarianism. The university is clearly in deep trouble. A shocking indication of its affliction can be found in the pressures for conformity that beset campuses in the 1990s despite all too recent memories of such pressures in the 1950s and 1960s. Renowned scholars such as Yale English professor David Bromwich and University of Massachusetts feminist Daphne Patai have written of the stifling conformity of today's universities and colleges. Based on endless accounts from students and professors, as well as materials from specific cases, Bromwich's *Politics by Other Means* and Patai's *Professing Feminism* (written with Noretta Koertge) carefully document a situation in which careers have been ruined, students have been cornered into studying particular subjects or reaching desired conclusions, and teachers have been barred from teaching in certain areas, all in the service of a prevailing orthodoxy.[4]

These and other authors have cited numerous cases in which individuals whose ideas were deemed too controversial were denied jobs, tenure and promotion, publication, or, if they managed to surmount these hurdles, were ostracized in all relevant communities to which such independent thinkers might otherwise turn for support (if not agreement), from department to university or college to profession. While an outcry eventually arose in response to the most extreme and obvious torts, some of the most vocal objections to conformity came from those on the right, rather than from left independents like Bromwich and Patai, and it was clear that such objections came only because much of the current pressure seemed to be for a kind of left-liberal orthodoxy. One wondered whether, with the changing of the political tide, objections from the right would still be raised. As Bromwich makes clear, similar pressures for conformity currently originate on the right in the form of overly rigid attempts to enforce notions of the canon, as though education had more to do with imbibing "culture" than engaging it critically and independently. The voice of those who address the educational crisis as a question of principle—often the independent element of any shade of the spectrum whose thought cannot be reduced to simplistic political categories—

cannot be ignored. In any climate, it is not just democracy that rests on free expression and rightly applied standards; so does education.

Russell Jacoby's brilliant analysis of the changes in the structures of intellectual life over the course of the twentieth century, *The Last Intellectuals,* requires the sustained attention of anyone interested in the current state of the university. Jacoby argues that the pressures for conformity have not resulted solely from a short-term drive for ideological purity. Rather, American intellectuals made a fateful compromise when they moved from a state of often precarious financial and intellectual independence to more secure positions in colleges and universities.

Early twentieth-century intellectuals were often fiercely independent in their thinking and relied on either the "small magazines of opinion and literature" or larger venues, from the *New Republic* and *Partisan Review* to the *New York Times* or *Fortune.* They "wrote for the educated reader," "viewed themselves as men and women of letters," and "sought and prized a spare prose." Those who strived toward this ideal with little institutional support of any kind absolutely relied on informal communities of writers and others wrestled with the issues of the day. Their often painful battles to make ends meet and still have time for their most creative work made the option of university life incredibly attractive. According to Jacoby, when the famous intellectual Daniel Bell left *Fortune* magazine in 1958 to work in a university, he cited "four good reasons": "June, July, August, and September." Academic life, Jacoby points out, offered "salaries, security, summers."[5]

Unfortunately, in Jacoby's eloquent phrasing, "In recasting the lives of intellectuals, intellectual life was recast." It might seem that steady institutional support should have paved the way for a new independence of mind, particularly since tenure (once attained) specifically protected freedom of speech. Certainly, it accomplished just that for some key figures. However, the move to the university also brought new "rules," changing the criteria for advancement. "A successful career depended on impressing deans and colleagues, who were interested more in how one fit in than in how one stood out," Jacoby argues. Different intellectual products resulted from the change of setting: "To vary an old proposition, cafe society gives rise to the aphorism and essay; the college campus yields the monograph and lecture—and the grant application." The long-term costs include the supplanting of "leathery independence" with "political timidity," plain style with "unreadable communiqués sweetened by thanks to colleagues and superiors," and the recasting of intellectuals as specialized academics. To Jacoby, this shift explains the dearth of broad-minded intellectuals of the likes of Dwight MacDonald or Irving Howe in the generation born after 1940, a tragedy of incalculable proportions.[6]

While Jacoby's "missing intellectuals" do seem to comprise "a vacancy in culture, the absence of younger voices, perhaps the absence of a generation,"[7] there are still clearly some voices worth listening to—his own is just one example. Jacoby's rhetorically dramatic portrait also leaves out the crowning glory of universities and colleges: their students. Granted, the growing emphasis on professional accreditation at the expense of the value of a liberal arts education in itself, together with the insidious recasting of students as consumers, attacks the almost inviolable teacher-student relation upon which true education rests. Yet, wherever there are students, there are opportunities (however rare) for serious intellectual work. And intellectual community still survives in some places, and is even fostered by exceptional administrators. Academia, for all its faults, has occasioned the production of important works that many outside it agree demand a full reckoning. However, those works often stand alone; many experience them as isolated achievements rather than as contributions to an ongoing discussion that involves us all. Often it seems that only a limited segment of the nonacademic press and the atypical periodicals *Salmagundi,* the *New Republic, Commentary, Dissent,* and the like continue to believe in this ongoing discussion and its urgency. Notable exceptions aside, the academic press seems unconcerned with the urgency of that discussion. Academic scholars often seem oblivious to what goes on in this domain, which refrains from specialized terminology or the conventions of academic style out of responsibility to a varied readership and the standards of the world of letters.

The overprofessionalization[8] of scholarship, as it has played itself out in the twentieth century, has a great deal to do with the disengagement of many scholars from their own times and from one another. The universities have accepted the model of compartmentalization of knowledge and competence from the world of commerce, along with its notion of specialized expertise. Overspecialization has become so common that it is now valid for historians to devote their whole careers to the study of only one brief time period, a particular confined locale, or a single aspect of the past, which prevents most of them from considering the implications of history for understanding humanity, its context, and its predicaments. Give and take among academic historians all too often takes the form of exchange of minutiae rather than exploration of central, debatable arguments or implications. An academic's defense of his or her work often consists of appeals to special authority rooted in familiarity with obscure archival materials rather than in readings of published materials to which many have access. This is not to say that archival materials do not have their place—often they are the only way to get at answers about the past—but that scholars have the responsibility to translate their gist keeping in mind an audience. There is no reason that the special skills they require to analyze their documents (such as languages or prior knowledge) should lead them to write inaccessibly. Unfortunately, scholarly specializations have developed their own jargon and rituals that serve more often than not to exclude the uninitiated.

There is a dominant creed in American schools of education which, casting itself as "progressive," argues that the process of learning is more important than the content. Proponents reiterate a cynical belief that students cannot retain much actual knowledge at all, but can only learn how to learn. This ethos has led to a current situation in which high school teachers take very few courses in the actual content of what they intend to teach but many courses in teaching methods and the psychology of students. Looking for new markets for their ideas, adherents of this view have recently seized on the fresh terrain of the university, and if unimpeded, will gladly extend their techniques to a new habitat. Together with technology that encourages mental passivity (like television), they have helped bring public education to its knees.

While many academics, particularly historians, frown upon this emphasis on process over substance, they help perpetuate its equivalent in the realm of scholarship. The emphasis on technique in education, after all, paralleled a greater emphasis on technique in all of life, a major contribution of the move toward professionalization. Taking the emphasis off soundness of ideas or workmanship, the new professions often sought to establish themselves and their credibility by spelling out their own codes of proper technique. An obsession with technical procedures often replaced open exploration or dialogue. Frenetic publication of works of questionable quality in the drive to "publish or perish" has created a glut of works for historians to master and overspecialization has helped individuals feel justified in concentrating only on the scholarship of one narrow subject. Any sense of what makes one study more compelling than another is dispensable, so long as technique has been mastered, only to be replaced by a lack of consensus about which works have achieved true importance. This shift rules out the possibility that all historians can be expected to have read some works in common, eroding a necessary precondition for any kind of intellectual community.

While a certain degree of specialization is necessary to delve deeply into an area of inquiry, the current degree of overspecialization serves as much as a damper on bold work as the more explicit pressures for political conformity. To obtain or hold jobs, or gain an audience, scholars have to prove, after all, that their work fits somewhere in the contemporary academic scene and must gain support within the ranks of some existing specialization. Work that crosses or breaks boundaries, or harks back to categories now deemed passé, threatens the existing arrangements and thus usually fails to gain acceptance. The result is that often mediocre work, because it ruffles the least feathers, survives instead.

The great irony of our own time, of course, is that the transgression of boundaries, especially since the 1960s put its stamp of approval on modernism, has become a way to enforce specialization and professionalization so that works that genuinely provide new syntheses, deploy archaic styles, or fail to meet narrow requirements are dismissed, often with the aid of political name calling. (The term "neoconservative" springs to the lips to describe anyone interested in reviving older forms or reconsidering past conclusions as possibly more valid than current ones.) "Academic pseudo-radicalism," as described by historian and social critic Christopher Lasch in his *Revolt of the Elites,* poses as a revolutionary force but lives off the very complacency and elitism that threaten democracy outside of universities. Self-professed academic revolutionaries defend their "professional privileges" with claims of specialized expertise and champion their "incomprehensible jargon as the language of 'subversion.'"[9]

Many on the right have seized on the antics of academic subversives as evidence that the universities have become politicized. As Jacoby points out, their complaint is merely thinly disguised outrage that the politics involved are left-wing. Demands to depoliticize education terrify the left, which (often correctly) suspects cries for a more neutral, scientific, or objective history as merely an attempt to impose a different political orientation on the classroom and on scholarship. An example of the common terms of debate appears in Arthur Marwick's recent work *The Sixties.* In his introduction, Marwick castigates the simplistic theorizing of postmodernist history which "supports predetermined theories about language, ideology, narratives, and discourse, as agents of bourgeois hegemony." But he goes on to suggest that there are just two kinds of history:

> It is an inescapable fact of the intellectual world in which we live today that there is, on the one side, the non-metaphysical, source-based scientific history of the historians and, on the other, the metaphysical history of those committed to left-wing causes (or, alternatively, to the nihilistic philosophy that humanity is helpless in face of the impersonal structures of bourgeois thought and language).

Over the ensuing nine hundred pages it becomes increasingly clear through statements such as "life became more varied and enjoyable" and the sixties were "phenomenally innovative, phenomenally liberating," that Marwick, not surprisingly, does reveal a position on his material despite his voluminous use of sources.[10]

The question is not how to remove perspective from history, which is impossible, or banish even illuminating theory, which is counterproductive, but how to struggle against preconceived notions, take into account perspectives other than one's own, and present a compelling analysis or narrative that rings as true as possible. Passionlessness or neutrality, professionalization's favorite mode, is only another kind of subjectivism in disguise; like radical relativism, and *unlike* engaged moral inquiry, it fails to make crucial distinctions based on the quality, coherence, support, and truth of particular ideas because it disengages itself from argument. We need to recover a concept of argument as something other than group or individual self-expression without turning down the dead end of cold rationalism, a path political philosopher Michael Oakeshott eloquently warns us not to take.[11]

For some, a successful attack on the current politicization of the academy by the left is a frightening notion, for it is difficult to imagine anything but counterreaction. But in fact, bias need not be stamped out in individual works of scholarship (which includes teaching), but restrained from reigning in a crude fashion, particularly in places where it has no business at all. It is impossible to consider where the profession of history would be, after all, without the interpretations offered by everyone from the Columbia historians Henry Steele Commager, Richard Hofstadter, and William Leuchtenberg to the historically-minded scholars in a range of fields such as sociologists David Riesman and Norbert Elias. The distinction we need to make is not between scientific and "metaphysical" history, but between that which self-righteously stays within strict confines of its own bias and that which constantly challenges itself to confront and take into account opposing views. Whether more narrative or more analytical, this kind of engaged history enters the debate self-consciously and open to challenge rather than remaining closed and aloof.

In this regard we need to consider the implications of Jacoby's notion that the nature of intellectual achievement corresponds to some degree to the structures within which it was produced. If the nature of today's universities compromises originality, excellence, and genuine intellectual diversity, then clearly new structures—whether formal or informal, whether independent or part of existing institutions—must come into being. Through accident or frustration, many intellectuals already turn away from today's universities in their quest for structures conducive to the most lively forms of intellectual life and the communities needed to sustain them. More will undoubtedly follow if the real spirit and ideal of university life is not recovered. Currently, small groups of specialists are the closest thing to an intellectual community to be found and the constricted job market necessitates that these individuals be far-flung. Members of small specialized fields are unembarrassed in their assumption that attendance at conferences—supposedly an opportunity to participate in the apotheosis of intellectual life—provides them primarily with a chance to see their friends and exchange gossip. It is not considered odd that a multitude of concurrent sessions divides the potential audience into tiny cadres of specialists, ruling out interaction across subfields that could develop a sense of the larger community and encourage participants to think beyond the confines of their own area of expertise.

Sadly, the experience of genuine intellectual community is more the exception than the rule, although many choose university life with just that ideal in mind. The balkanization of intellectual life results in work that is too internally self-referential to be of interest to others and which is ignorant of burning issues in other areas of inquiry or cultural life generally—issues inevitably connected to the study of history. The revitalization of intellectual life demands that we work hard to make crucial distinctions of all kinds: between mere tolerance and genuine engagement; between radical relativism and valid judgements; between group self-expression and democracy; between process and content; between unmitigated bias and reasoned argument; between scientific objectivity and moral inquiry; between publications as lines on a curriculum vita and as contributions to the world of letters; between education as a business and education as a life of learning; between professional hierarchies and the leveling tendency of great ideas. The recovery of a sense of what it means to be consumed by the life of the mind—the driving force of the university at its best—demands the retrieval of a larger, living context for intellectual production for those involved in it. Communities that serve the imperatives both of rigor and of egalitarianism are ones in which dissenting voices and broader questions are not only heard or tolerated, but addressed.

Notes

1. Forthcoming work by historian Rochelle Gurstein addresses the long-term roots of this change; see, for instance, "Taste and the 'Conversible World': The Invention of Aesthetic Sensibility in the Eighteenth Century." Unpublished paper, courtesy of the author.
2. Jean Bethke Elshtain, *Democracy on Trial* (New York: Basic Books, 1996).
3. Jean Bethke Elshtain and Theda Skocpol are just two of the best-known scholars who have brought renewed attention to such institutions. Other scholars, from Ray Oldenberg to Robert Putnam, have emphasized the informal qualities of forms or activities that provide the shared experiences that bind communities together.
4. David Bromwich, *Politics by Other Means: Higher Education and Group Thinking* (New Haven, Conn.: Yale University Press, 1992); Daphne Patai and Noretta Koertge, *Professing Feminism: Cautionary Tales from the Strange World of Women's Studies* (New York: Basic Books, 1994).

5. Russell Jacoby, *The Last Intellectuals: American Culture in the Age of Academe* (New York: Farrar, Straus and Giroux, 1987), 7, 14.
6. Russell Jacoby, *The Last Intellectuals,* 15–16, 31.
7. Russell Jacoby, *The Last Intellectuals,* 3.
8. By professionalization, I mean the process by which so many professions, like the profession of history, took form in the late nineteenth and early twentieth centuries, as described in Robert Weibe's *Search for Order, 1877–1920* (New York: Hill and Wang, 1980) and Burton Bledstein's *Culture of Professionalism: The Middle Class and the Development of Higher Education in America* (New York: Norton, 1976), for example. The emphasis was on professional identity, internal codes of legitimizing practitioners (and delegitimizing others), and expert knowledge. Professionalism can also refer to a more benign (in my view) set of standards and ideals related to mastery and craftsmanship.
9. Christopher Lasch, *The Revolt of the Elites and the Betrayal of Democracy* (New York: Norton, 1994), 178.
10. Arthur Marwick, *The Sixties: Cultural Revolution in Britain, France, Italy, and the United States, c.1958–c.1974* (Oxford: Oxford University Press, 1998), 20, 347, 803.
11. Michael Oakeschott, *Rationalism in Politics and Other Essays* (Indianapolis: Liberty Press, 1991).

PART II

HISTORY AND THE CONTEMPORARY INTELLECTUAL MILIEU

Superb essays of social criticism in their own right, the essays in this section, taken together, fill in many pieces of the complicated puzzle which is our strange inheritance: a contemporary cultural milieu characterized by, among other things, extremes of relativistic subjectivity and tremendous divisiveness. It is a truism that the cultural milieu has a bearing on the quality and character of the intellectual life of a given social world, but the details of this relation are always far less evident. Here we encounter authors who examine the relation between larger cultural or intellectual developments of recent times and the resulting openings and constraints—both in form and content—in the arena of scholarship and thought generally.

Elizabeth Fox-Genovese sees the main problem of contemporary intellectual and civic life to be a general crisis of authority, or the diminishing of any shared or articulated understanding of possible legitimate bases for jurisdiction of any kind. She views today's intellectual battles, often disturbing in their acrimony, as aligned along two camps: the "liberal modernists" and the "postmodern culturalists." While the two sides are often pitted against one another, they share more than they let on, particularly a propensity to see the world as centered on the individual's subjective experience and an unquestioning acceptance of relativism. Their differences are primarily matters of degree, except when it comes to the issue of authority, where the postmodernists verge off into skepticism about any form of authority as inherently oppressive while the modernists maintain a belief in the individual as the repository of authority.

Postmodernist skepticism of morality as a mask for power grubbing contrasts with the liberal individualism of those like Lionel Trilling, who maintained a belief in the need for self-discipline and morality as prerequisites for individual freedom. Contemporary liberals, however, fail to engage in open confrontation with the question of authority because they themselves, in their failure to see legitimate authority beyond the individual, helped set the stage for the further erosion of authority. This erosion, exemplified in postmodernism, underpins an abdication of the sources of self-governance by the populace in the face of the incursions of the managerial state, with dire consequences for both intellectual integrity and democratic citizenship.

Along similar lines, Rochelle Gurstein points out that the main sides in today's "culture wars," taken over issues like obscenity in modern art and music, have much in common. While liberals see themselves as advocates of "freedom and progress," "sophistication and urbanity," pitted against prudish, moralizing "puritans," both liberal reformers and those who advocate some restraint on obscenity (usually nothing stronger than limits on public funding) share a common disregard for the nineteenth-century "reticent sensibility," which modernism has largely obscured both from contemporary culture and from the historical record. Turn-of-the-century battles between reformers such as birth control advocates and proponents of censorship set the pattern for later debates by conflating intrusive moralizing with reticence, which entails such qualities as "keen sensitivity toward the feelings of others," "sympathy," "reserve, tact, discretion, propriety, delicacy, and tenderness," as well as "courtesy, politeness, civility, decency, honor, refinement, cultivation, grace, and elegance." Adhering to a distinction between the public and private spheres, a notion of shame dismissed by moderns as emotionally damaging to individuals, and a stress on moral standards and taste, advocates of reticence have easily been targeted as suspect for acting contrary to the imperatives of individual liberation and progressive openness. In fact, as Gurstein makes clear, the notion of reticence is vital for *protecting* public life from the predations of commercialism, unbounded individualism, and the loss of any sense of the sacred. The use of "puritanism" as an epithet, according to Gurstein, has foreclosed public discussion of the all-important matter of the quality of our shared world. The dismissal of reticence as a form of puritanism prevents us from cultivating the "virtues necessary for a common world and flourishing public life."

Gertrude Himmelfarb's essay also treats the issue of liberationism gone awry, examining its effects particularly on the study of history in the form of postmodernism. Like Fox-Genovese, she sees the debate between modernists and postmodernists as central for understanding contemporary intellectual life and expresses grave worries about the radical relativism and other features of postmodernist scholarship, which she spells out at the start of her piece. Modernists (who fare better in Himmelfarb's rendering than in Gurstein's), and historians generally, openly acknowledged the challenges of recreating a record of what transpired in the past and freely admitted to the partiality and contingency of reality and truth. Where they differ with postmodernists is that they choose to rise to the challenge and attempt to transcend the cultural blinders of their own time in their quest to understand the past on its own terms. Postmodernists, guided by "absolutistic relativism," however, follow their rejection of absolute truth so far as to reject the search for truth altogether as a valid inquiry. In fact, truth becomes, in their eyes, a coercive mask for the assertions of power. Rather than revising the findings of their predecessors, they repudiate in a wholesale fashion the inheritance of traditions of all kinds: historical study as it has been practiced; conventions such as evidence and reasoning; in fact, "all pretense of rational, 'enlightened' discourse." While promulgated in the extreme by only a small number, such an outlook wields disproportionate influence, with its allure of the avant-garde, its invitation to create any version of history one likes, and its seeming acceptance of diversity in the form of its embrace of "aphoria." But, as Himmelfarb illustrates in an eloquent discussion of conflicting notions of the meaning and limits of historical imagination, the cult of particularism and suspicion of truth deny our common humanity and the reality of existence as well as undermine the whole enterprise of contemplating and discovering meaning, encouraging a radical cynicism that might well constitute "intellectual and moral suicide."

Russell Jacoby examines some of the authors discussed by Himmelfarb, and agrees that their radical relativism and self-conscious conflation of fiction and reality (he quotes intellectual historian Hayden White's statement that history is primarily a "fiction-making operation") are disturbing and "explosive" matters. However, looking at postmodernist scholars, he criticizes the recent "linguistic turn" in intellectual history for its formalistic tendencies as well. Under the guise of rebels throwing off the cloak of oppressive tradition, these historians have questioned the assumptions underlying all language and historical study and in so doing have, according to Jacoby, brought "welcome ferment" to the field. Their primary thrust came from a rejection of scientistic pretense on the part of historical study, including claims to universal objectivity it could not bear, and they urged instead an embrace of the literary and artistic which would tie history, in White's view, to a larger intellectual world and thus enliven it. Despite this promising start, the linguistic turn ended up as an embrace of method "as an end in itself," with a mode of analysis that attempted to examine historical writing by quantifying and classifying stylistic devices while losing sight of content. Advocates of a radical new departure thus ended up mired in a "new cautiousness," complete with its multiple qualifications and "technical prose" (one scholar condemned a particular work of history as "too readable"), seemingly furthering the breach between literary stylists and historians, whose language they considered appropriate when characterized by "rigor, structure, and technique." Claiming to question the authority of language and historians who aspired to legitimate their discipline through scientific claims, they ended up promulgating the insular "language of the professional scholar" through their formalism.

The final essay in this section examines what it means when contemporary scholars position themselves this way simultaneously as antiauthoritarian and as experts, specifically in the arena of African American studies. Like the other essayists in Part II, Phillip Richards sees recent trends in literary criticism beginning to have a palpable impact on the study of history, but he focuses on the ways history is being used in other fields. Like Jacoby, he acknowledges the major contribution literary critics have made in enlivening debate and drawing attention to important works of literature. Also like Jacoby, however, he points to what he sees as a kind of disjuncture between the ostensible drive of some leading scholars to liberate readers and students from old pieties and hierarchies, on the one hand, and the actual effects of the framework they purvey. In this case, Richards sees the concept of "signifying," brought to such wide attention by Harvard theorist Henry Louis Gates, Jr., as deflecting attention from the content of a given piece of writing—whose discussion would raise questions of validity, among others—to its form, or from meaning to "social function." Richards places Gates's critical theory in the larger context of its emergence, linking it to the problem of the encounter of the black intellectual with the integrated world of the academy. He argues that the notion of signifying and the framework it represents tends to provide a kind of therapeutic adjustment to the unresolved tensions raised by the contemporary predicament of middle-class blacks. This notion of literature and history as handmaidens to a therapeutic goal rather than as avenues to a self-conscious quest for realistic understanding represents, Richards writes, a radical departure from earlier literary historical study. This earlier tradition, as exemplified by the work of Sterling Brown, provided a genuine form of resistance to racial discrimination even while it paved the way for blacks' entry into the world of letters.

Each of these authors examines a cultural and intellectual milieu in which individual liberation has become celebrated as a supreme value, buttressed by intellectual trends that help erode confidence in older customs or concepts now seen by many as impossibly backward: authority, truth, reticence, morality, knowledge. They point to a central contradiction in the embrace of individual freedom and extreme relativism so common among the thinkers they analyze: that new limitations arise when liberation from all inherited constraints is actually taken seriously as an intellectual and social project in the absence of a vision of freedom made possible only by a sense of desirable and legitimate restraints. This is the project in the midst of whose unfolding we find ourselves, and which we are obligated to understand and confront.

CHAPTER 6

HISTORY IN A POSTMODERN WORLD

Elizabeth Fox-Genovese

THE CATACLYSMIC EVENTS of the twentieth century have literally remade the world and have redrawn its maps. With the conclusion of the Cold War, dawn has apparently broken upon a new era of peace and unimaginable prosperity. The appearance has troublesome and deceptive aspects, but even the illusion that commerce and consumption have displaced warfare as the main purpose of peoples and societies has led some to ask whether we have finally arrived at the end of history. Those, like Francis Fukuyama, who pose the question in this fashion understand history in Hegel's sense as the unfolding conflict between antagonisms—thesis and antithesis—that are eventually subsumed in a synthesis in which "normal" life dominates everything, leaving no great story to tell.[1] The end of history in this sense thus signals the demise of politics and warfare as the hallmarks of human attempts to coexist in a world of finite and unequally distributed resources. It remains debatable whether our time is, indeed, inaugurating history's demise, but if history is dying, it is dying a lingering death. For those most intent upon discrediting "traditional" history are no less intent upon claiming its mantle for themselves. However unintentionally, they are confirming history's role as the chronicle of conflicts over the varied resources that people tend to covet—honor and preeminence as well as material goods and natural resources.

As the chronicle of conflicts, history has always been contested, and, as the teller of the tale, the historian wields a unique power to allocate blame and praise, rewarding some historical actors and condemning others. In this respect, as most historians have understood, the writing of history is—and always has been—a political act. Since Herodotus and Thucydides, historians have grasped the political significance of their craft and have shaped their interpretations to ground a people's sense of itself in the present and its plans for the future. Political leaders have heeded the call, often turning historian themselves, sometimes to justify their own actions, sometimes to weigh their own times against previous times. Viewing history as a wellspring of political illumination, figures as different as the Earl of Clarendon, Thomas Babbington Macaulay, Woodrow Wilson, Charles de Gaulle, and Winston Churchill have drawn upon the power of historical precedents to promote or justify the wisdom of their own strategies even as they have politicized historical interpretations to serve immediate political ends. Nor have political leaders and professional historians monopolized that understanding. The shrewd in all walks of life—think of grandmothers' cautionary tales to grandchildren—have always recognized that to shape a society's understanding of its own history constitutes a political asset of the highest order.

Given the richness of this tradition, late-twentieth-century historians' wide-eyed discovery that all history is inherently political carries disconcerting echoes of the wonderment of Molière's *bourgeois gentilhomme,* who marveled that he was speaking prose. This disingenuousness would slyly suggest that politics plays no role in the attack upon the political purposes of "traditional" history. Yet contemporary, postmodernist history aims not to drain politics from history but to replace one politics with another. In this respect, it implicitly confirms what it explicitly contests, namely that the use of history for political purposes has never been confined to a specific social or political group. History, as transmitted through epic, saga, cautionary tale, and oral tradition, has been deployed to reinforce the authority of older generations over younger, as well as of kings over subjects or of shamans over believers. Above all, it has served as a reminder that the past in some measure shapes the present and the future, that the struggles and accomplishments of one generation derive from—and are, to a greater or lesser degree, limited by—those of its predecessors. Doubly contested as a continuing struggle to shape the account of human conflicts, history can never be expected to effect an exact recreation of the past, nor to be neutral with respect to the past, present, or future. History constitutes an intervention in human affairs.

What distinguishes the postmodernists' assault upon the traditional practice of history from its predecessors is its transparent effort to discredit history as a distinct intellectual practice. In this respect, postmodernist history aligns itself with the move to cultural studies throughout the humanities, positioning itself as the champion of populism against the pretensions of elitist modernism. On the postmodernists' telling, modernists cling to discredited standards and values, which they use to exclude others from the corridors of intellectual prestige. Yet their charges of complacency, elitism, logocentrism, and assorted other sins fall wide of the mark, and it is difficult to tell if they continue to launch them out of bad faith or genuine misunderstanding. Most of the modernists they are attacking adhere to one or another variant of the post–World War II liberalism that is captured in the work of Lionel Trilling, notably *The Liberal Imagination,* and they normally adhere to a demanding conception of high culture, which they tend to distinguish from popular culture.[2] But the more sophisticated among them fully understand that their inherited modernism is visibly decomposing in front of their eyes. Little in Trilling's work justifies charges of a reactionary commitment to an unchanging and unrevisable elitist vision of culture, not least because his liberalism was grounded in a discriminating sense of the significance of (changing) historical context.

The many American intellectuals of Trilling's generation who came from lower-class or ethnic families were preeminently conscious of their own standing as outsiders, and none knew better than they that their astonishing rise to positions of intellectual and cultural authority would have been difficult, if not impossible, in an earlier period or in almost any country other than the United States. Never deluded about the pretensions and elitism of the WASP establishment, the postwar liberals nonetheless remained committed to the individualism in which previous liberal thought had been grounded. Like their predecessors, they tended to assume that the authoritative individual would be male and probably white, although not necessarily Anglo-Saxon or Teutonic. These assumptions have come under sharp attack from the postmodern culturalists, who dismiss them as narrow, exclusionary, and bigoted. The postwar liberals, however, never intended their individualist assumptions to justify the exclusion of any specific individual, no matter what his or her origins. For them, individualist criteria were intended only to distinguish accomplished and authoritative intellectuals from the uneducated masses, who were primarily defined by their membership in specific groups. In this respect, they remained loyal to the venerable modernist conception of the Republic of Letters (what the distinguished critic Lewis Simpson calls the Third Realm), the fellowship of those who primarily defined themselves by their practice of and commitment to the unencumbered life of the mind.[3] They remained, in other words, committed to an ideal that combined the search for truth with the cultivation of excellence in conception and execution. In their view, members of this republic necessarily relinquished parochial loyalties and prejudices in return for entry into the charmed circle. No aspect of an individual's background—or identity—disqualified him or her for membership, but membership did require that specifics of class, race, sex, religion, and national origin be transcended or left at the door.

In this respect and others, liberal individualism embodied a direct challenge to traditional notions of authority, notably authority extrinsic to the individual. What it did not embody was a rejection of authority *per se*. Liberals of this stripe expected the individual to internalize the authority once attributed to God, tradition, or rulers. The weakness of their conception—the tragedy, if you will—lay in their failure to take full account of the transformation of the political and material conditions of their world. The individualism they championed had historically depended upon a measure of political autonomy grounded in an absolute private property that endowed the individual with a direct stake in responsible governance and the health of civil society. The emergence of the managerial state in the United States as well as in Europe consolidated the abdication—or destruction—of the last vestiges of the individual's political independence and, in so doing, decisively and dangerously transformed the understanding of liberalism itself. In a world in which democratic governments primarily manage and mediate competing claims upon public entitlements, the notion of a common good—literally, a *res publica*—for which individuals are responsible and to which they subordinate their private, antisocial interests has collapsed. In the grim, if disturbingly plausible, view of Mary Ann Glendon, distinguished professor of law, the intertwining oligarchies of "big business and government" have "authorized a modern form of bread and circuses, an array of new sexual freedoms to compensate for the loss of the most basic right of all, the right of self-government."[4]

Glendon demonstrates that the escalating emphasis upon rights has disastrously eroded our national political life. Robert George and John Gray, among others, concur with her judgment that rights have superseded politics, assuming a primary and essentially prepolitical status. Thus Gray observes that "the end result . . . is not the simple transposition of political life into legal contexts but rather the corrosion of political life itself. The treatment of all important issues of restraint of liberty as questions of constitutional rights has the consequence that they cease to be issues that are politically negotiable."[5] The implications of this development for the relations between the liberal humanities and cultural studies can hardly be exaggerated. Briefly, the liberal humanities, including history, emerged within and articulated the cultural aspirations of the citizens of a politically vigorous republic, while cultural studies have emerged within and articulate the cultural aspirations of the subjects of the postmodern managerial state.

With respect to intellectual and cultural questions, the liberal modernists and the postmodern culturalists have considerably more in common than we are wont to acknowledge. Or, to put it differently, the lines between the two camps are not nearly as sharp as polemicists on both sides would lead us to believe. The more thoughtful contemporary modernists do not reject the claims of relativism nor do they oppose the move toward a more "inclusive" social history. They do not deify great historical figures or deny the significance of their social and cultural location. Postmodernists, for their part, have not broken as decisively with modernist individualism as they seem to think or would have others believe. Both camps combine elements of modernist and postmodernist thought in a fragile and still exploratory tension. Significantly—some would say ironically—the unbridgeable divide between them concerns their respective attitudes toward the location and legitimacy of authority and the forces and events that decisively shape the consciousness of and relations among individuals.

What assuredly does not distinguish either group is allegiance to one or another of the conventional political camps. Today, the designation "liberal" encompasses a broad political spectrum, ranging from the unreconstructed celebrants of the free market who represent the most direct descendents of nineteenth-century classical liberals—thus Milton Friedman properly scorns the label "conservative" and calls himself a "radical liberal"—to the radical left wing of the Democratic Party, a portion of which openly calls itself "democratic socialist." Even within the rarefied world of academic politics, the defenders of liberal modernism include people from the far left to the far right. And, strange as it may seem, a comparable, if lesser, political diversity characterizes the postmodernist camp, which may include right-wing libertarians as well as self-proclaimed leftists. In this respect, neither camp represents a distinct political position, despite those on both sides who would claim otherwise, especially when defaming their opponents. But then, American politics has ever tended to cluster at the center, with few serious challenges from either extreme. This perspective should help us to recognize that just as modernists and postmodernists do not espouse radically opposed intellectual and theoretical positions, so they do not espouse radically opposed political positions, although in any given instance political passions on either side may run high. If so, you may well counter, how does one explain the ferocity with which the two camps frequently assail one another? Is the apparent opposition between them merely the result of a misunderstanding?

The opposition is—with apologies to those who acknowledge no "reality"—real enough, but it eludes conventional taxonomies, and, for self-serving reasons, neither camp has been eager to reflect upon its nature. The great and possibly nonnegotiable divide concerns the nature and claims of authority especially as they relate to the individual. Postmodernist history draws much of its appeal from the contemporary obsession with identity politics. The more sophisticated proponents of identity politics disguise their purposes under the broad pieties of "gender, race, and class," which they take to circumscribe any worthy history. On their telling, to meet the standards of gender, race, and class, history must focus upon those who qualify as "marginalized," "disempowered," or "victimized." Their agenda includes the demolition of previous historical styles or topics, which they condemn as manifestations of intellectual and political conservatism. Above all, they charge their liberal predecessors with an elitism that stonewalls the overdue claims of innumerable groups whose sensibilities find no echo or reflection in the great texts or events of the liberal tradition. And they increasingly promote a postmodernist view of historical theory and practice, especially by challenging their predecessors' allegiance to standards of historical objectivity.

Identity politics is riding the crest of the cultural currents of our times, which fuel the struggle to secure maximum prestige for oneself or for the group with which one identifies. It especially encourages the widespread conviction that, to be relevant, history must directly engage the experience or traditions of the individual. More, an acceptable history must promote the self-esteem of the individual both by celebrating the virtue of the individual's forbears and by denouncing the iniquities of others, especially if they happened to be white and male. While these qualifications have resulted in an array of absurdities, their main accomplishment has been to discredit historical work that focuses upon those who wielded social, political, economic, intellectual, or religious authority. For adherents of these views, the logic is simple: Those who exercised power must, by definition, have been oppressors of others (presumably more virtuous and worthy than they) and, therefore, undeserving of historical respect or even attention. Why confuse our minds with the possibility that those whom we self-righteously condemn might have had some intrinsic interest or, heaven forfend, some redeeming qualities?

This cultivated blindness to the complexity of human affairs provides an easy target for ridicule, which it is receiving in abundance. It is also easy to understand. Confronting a daunting array of pressures, today's students are understandably inclined to embrace anything that simplifies the requirements imposed upon them. Manicheanism comes naturally to the young, who welcome neat demarcations between good guys and bad. So does self-exploration. Students are not to blame if they instinctively gravitate toward a quasi-autobiographical history that casts their people, and hence themselves, as simultaneously meritorious and victimized and, above all, as the main characters in the story. We may fairly assume that, in greater or lesser degree, such proclivities are ubiquitous, and we may, by the same token, assume that they alone do not account for the current struggles over history.

Identity politics is a peculiarly American phenomenon, although, with waves of global migration, other countries are succumbing. To complicate matters, the collapse of the colonial empires and, more recently, the Soviet Union has unleashed an explosive preoccupation with ethnic and national identity throughout the world. As a nation of immigrants, the United States has a long record of attempting to bind peoples of different ethnic and national origin into a unified citizenry. The accelerating growth of the global economy has, however, sorely strained the sense of identification with the United States as a nation, especially since related cultural developments have, however paradoxically, encouraged both more narrowly personal and more diffusely cosmopolitan forms of allegiance. The main casualty of this development, especially among American academics, has been loyalty to the nation and openness to received versions of its history.[6]

Postmodernism, in contrast, is a European import that has reached history via philosophy and literature. By the time American historians discovered postmodernism, identity politics had already prepared a fertile ground for its reception, and the two have become increasingly intertwined. For analytic purposes, however, the distinction merits attention. Postmodernism embodies an attack upon Enlightenment and modernist assumptions about the nature of knowledge and the relation between knowledge and "reality." Above all, it concerns epistemology and ontology—that is, the nature of our ability to know and the nature of being—and it takes as its special mission the destabilization of both. Composed of disparate strands, postmodernism resists tidy definitions, especially since different postmodernists mobilize aspects of it for different purposes. Among American academics, postmodernism is probably best known for its emphasis upon relativism, for its rejection of binary categories, and for its emphasis upon the role of language or discourse in the "construction" of reality. All of these strands conjoin in a general attack upon authority or "power" and in the preeminence accorded to the individual—especially the individual's biases or perspective—in the construction of knowledge.

The modernists against whom the postmodernists rebel themselves rejected previous assumptions about the reliability of knowledge and the stability of a world under the direct authority of God. But they retained confidence in the human mind's ability to know—to form clear and distinct ideas—and in the ability of that knowledge to capture the complex reality external to it. If anything, they effectively transferred the ability to grasp reality from the mind of God to the mind of man, thereby virtually deifying the individual, whom they viewed as the locus of political and cognitive sovereignty. This intellectual revolution carried within it the seeds of instability, but the proponents of individualism, notably intellectuals and the European bourgeoisie, sought to foreclose their development by encouraging the individual to internalize a healthy measure of authority or self-discipline. Modernists, in other words, refrained from a full-scale revolt against authority, insisting only that authority must derive from individuals rather than be imposed upon them. They assumed that the possible differences among individuals' interests would be negotiated within the contours of an implicit social compact. In practice, this assumption led to acceptance of the principle of majority rule and respect for minority views. No party to the compact would have the right to obliterate any other: dissidents would respect the rule of the majority, secure in the confidence that the majority would protect their freedom to express their views.

In comparison to the earlier theocentric world view, enlightened and modernist thought contained a heavy dose of relativism—an inescapable consequence of the emphasis upon the cognitive sovereignty of the individual mind. But these liberals believed that shared standards of morality and honesty would protect society against the extreme logical consequences of that relativism. Thus even as they recognized the importance of historical and social context in shaping beliefs and customs, they counted upon a common acceptance of fundamental concepts to ground moral norms. Notwithstanding significant theoretical inconsistencies, these views coalesced in a broad liberalism the practical coherence of which depended upon the sense of responsibility that limited the independence of purportedly autonomous individuals. Academic postmodernism, in contrast, aims to liberate individuals from such constraints, even when self-imposed. In this view, all limitations upon the freedom of the individual necessarily represent forms of domination, frequently ideological domination. Consequently, despite frequent denials, academic postmodernists promote a radical relativism, according to which any theory, narrative, or judgment reflects the standpoint of the person who expounds it. And this postmodern relativism feeds directly into identity politics, for which it is often taken to provide a high theoretical justification.

Today, this wave of radical relativism, which is engulfing the academy and debunking all claims of scholarly objectivity, is winning a growing constituency among historians, who had initially resisted its appeal. The new cohort of postmodernist historians is campaigning against efforts to identify clear historical facts of any kind, arguing that our knowledge of the past depends entirely upon the records in which the knowledge has been preserved. They point out that such records inevitably suffer from the same ideological biases that corrupt all written texts and, accordingly, should not be trusted. In their view, it necessarily follows that any claim of historical objectivity adheres to the principles of logocentrism that have distorted all previous forms and theories of knowledge. Their position thus combines the reasonable claim that no historical source should uncritically be taken at face value with the unreasonable claim that no historians are capable of surmounting their own—and possibly their sources'—biases in order to present an honest, disinterested interpretation that adheres to the highest standards of their craft. These attitudes permit one to wonder why postmodernists bother with history at all. Bizarre as it may seem, many postmodernists pride themselves on being historicists, but what they call history consists primarily in exposing the class, race, and gender biases that pervades historical texts. Heavily influenced by the work of Michel Foucault, they are more concerned with deconstructing history (understood as what has been written in or about the past) than in attempting to reconstruct history (understood as what happened in the past).

This skepticism about our ability to provide an objective or faithful account of the past has intertwined with a growing cynicism about public action, which postmodernists dismiss as the exercise of domination. Feeding into popular mistrust of politicians, this cynicism has eroded notions of leadership, service, and heroism, even as it has discredited the significance of political and military action. I do not wish to belabor the intellectual impoverishment frequently attacked as "political correctness," but rather to underscore the challenges that confront contemporary historians. Has the general crisis of confidence that pervades culture, intellectual life, and politics effectively invalidated history as a discipline and, especially, as a valuable perspective upon the vicissitudes of the human condition?

It is worth noting that the claims of intellectual relativism also figure prominently in the natural sciences, where they indeed originated, but with notably different results. Above all, scientists have not allowed the acknowledgment of relativism and indeterminacy to undermine the credibility of their enterprise as a whole or of their specific findings. To paraphrase a leading nuclear physicist, scientists sustain the integrity of their work on the basis of a working agreement: that we agree on what we are talking about and that we are honest. Although historians have not formulated the premise as succinctly, those who remain loyal to the possibilities and value of historical scholarship have effectively done the same. The philosophical status of the "fact" as the faithful mirror of "reality" may be problematic, but a responsible and self-respecting historian proceeds on the assumption that appropriate standards of evidence and verifiability establish a base line for the phenomena and events we may reasonably accept as factual. Such tacit agreements necessarily constitute the foundation of any intellectual discipline as a discipline. The only requirement lies in the foundational agreement about the objects of investigation and the willingness to respect prevailing canons of intellectual honesty. Conversely, the failure to meet that requirement results in a radical personalization of appropriate criteria that effectively explodes the discipline as a common, professional undertaking—a craft that may be taught, learned, and used instructively to illuminate aspects of our contemporary situation.

Adherence to what we might call an intellectual compact with respect to the integrity of evidence and argument does not, however, imply or necessitate agreement about questions of theory or method or even about subject matter. Academic postmodernism, especially as informed by identity politics, does not begin to exhaust the implications of postmodernist theory, which is opening some fresh and promising perspectives in theology and science.[7] I cannot do justice to those developments here, but two main currents merit at least a brief mention. Catholic theologians, notably Karol Wojtyla, now Pope John Paul II, have drawn upon postmodern theory, which they combine with Scholasticism and other currents of Christian thought, to criticize the liberal model of the autonomous and atomized individual and to substitute a conception of the individual—or human person—as integrally connected to and dependent upon others.[8] Meanwhile, scientists have been criticizing the foundationalism according to which scientific reasoning must always move from the smallest unit to the larger, from the nature and behavior of discrete atoms or molecules to general systems or laws. Increasingly, scientific research is finding that the behavior of particles in a system—say, molecules in a gas—may vary considerably and even randomly without affecting the essential structure of the system. Both of these developments potentially point in different directions than does prevailing academic postmodernism, and both open exciting possibilities for historians, who may find them a rewarding departure from liberal modernism. But the validity and interest of historical work does not depend upon the adoption of any single theory or method.

Above all, history requires that we acknowledge the tragedy that shadows human experience. The attempt to divide the world tidily into the good guys and the bad invariably results in a mechanical, unidimensional account. For if history teaches anything, it teaches that any group of people will contain both good and bad. The proportions may vary from one population to another, but to deny the presence of both in any group is to deny that group its humanity and to transform it into an abstraction. History challenges us to consider human experience from the varied—and frequently antagonistic—points of view of the different participants in any situation or event.

Proverbially, history has been understood as the collective memory of a people or society, and, in our own time, that understanding has led to the conviction we are all entitled to our own memories, which themselves are entitled to as much respect as any others. But the emphasis upon the personalization of memory virtually erases the proper understanding of history, which implicitly requires the recognition of multiple—and frequently conflicting—individual memories. The recovery of a personal past results in autobiography or genealogy, each of which has its intrinsic value. History, in contrast, focuses upon the interaction of individuals and groups, and this multiple focus generates its abiding political significance.[9] Individual lives have always been shaped by the imperative that diverse social groups coexist within finite boundaries on the basis of finite resources. It is enough to recall what Karl Marx said on this matter: Man makes his own history, but not under conditions of his own choosing. The challenge for people to make their history has provoked greed and generosity, heroism and villainy, wisdom and stupidity, and infinite combinations of these qualities. Only in the aggregate and over the broad sweep of time do we begin to envision the good and the evil of which our kind is capable. History helps us to reflect upon the record and envision new possibilities.

Postmodernist history is implicitly or explicitly challenging these assumptions, preferring a Manichean view that casts the powerful, however defined, as villains. At the heart of their vision lies the rejection of authority, including the authority of circumstance—often known as reality or necessity. The liberal modernists, for their part, have proved reluctant openly to engage the problem of authority perhaps because their entire tradition was built upon a repudiation of illegitimate, external authority. In defense of the freedom of the individual, pioneering liberals beheaded monarchs, disestablished churches, broke free of imperial dominance, abolished slavery, and secured the suffrage for women. With such a pedigree to ground their identity, they have found it increasingly difficult to mount a considered defense of authority, especially as they have retreated from their early Christian moorings. The culturalists, for their part, have been equally reluctant to undertake a candid discussion of authority because they have built their position and assembled their eclectic constituency on a simple extension of the initial liberal premise. They claim to be defending the freedom of the individual against the escalating usurpation of cultural and social tyranny. In their case, the issue is not a reluctance to come to a belated defense of authority, but rather a reluctance to admit publicly that, in essence, they deny the legitimacy of all authority—human, natural, or divine.

Since the dawn of liberal individualism, authority has hovered, like the ghost of Banquo, over the continuing discussion of the claims and necessary limits of individual freedom. Authority figures as the ubiquitous silence or erasure in texts that explore freedom. Thomas Hobbes has never enjoyed a warm welcome from the theorists of freedom, who would prefer to forget that it is virtually impossible to understand the more palatable John Locke without him. Hobbes, Locke, and their legion of successors participated in one central conversation: How may we acknowledge the individual as the locus of sovereignty and cognition—as self-governing and self-knowing—while simultaneously protecting the equal freedom of all other individuals who, perforce, compete with him for material goods, offices, honor, and prestige? Locke answered the question with a fiction: The individual's freedom is grounded in his property, which, however extensive, represents the fruits of his labor, and individuals will collaborate in governance because of their respect for one another's property. Locke's fiction, accordingly, emphasized the harmony of interests among propertied individuals and the dependence of the nonpropertied upon them. Hobbes had answered the question with another fiction: Since all individuals—women as much as men—are equal by virtue of their ability to kill one another, by cunning if not by brute force, they can never trust one another to negotiate fairly. Moved by mistrust of other individuals, they accordingly relinquish their sovereignty to an absolute sovereign, who will govern in what he deems the best interests of all.

For three centuries and some, Hobbes's conception of the government that befitted a society of individuals languished in moral and intellectual exile. Only an arrant reactionary could claim that the freedom of the individual depends upon the power of an absolute sovereign. During these centuries, liberal individualism unfolded under the long shadow of Locke, and its defenders took comfort in the knowledge that upstanding individuals internalized authority and exercised that becoming self-discipline that Sigmund Freud subsequently called repression. By the twentieth century the premium on self-discipline began to fray, and, from the 1960s on, it has unraveled at an escalating rate, until the more radical postmodernists pronounced it not merely dead, but damned.[10] What they failed to grasp was that almost in direct proportion to their success in liberating the individual from the shackles of social, cultural, and sexual restraint—normally described as bigotry or discrimination—the state was assuming the authority once ascribed to individuals. The ghost of Hobbes returned in the form of the managerial state, which maintained order by distributing entitlements, while countless groups squabbled over their respective "rights" to one or another piece of the state's pie.

Sadly, cultural prestige—a place in the curriculum, public validation of one's identity, a cut of cultural resources—emerged as an increasingly important aspect of that pie. The postmodern culturalists, often unwittingly, have developed the theoretical justification for the jockeying over the distribution of cultural spoils. The core arguments are all too familiar: Political and intellectual reputations owe nothing to the putative quality of the work and everything to the politics of reception; the idea of an integrated or essential self is a self-serving elitist fiction; dominant ideologies, like texts, are constructed to work upon the unwitting by binding them to hegemonic premises; notions of good and evil serve merely to mask the interests of the dominant group; contemporary readers, especially historians and critics, constitute the true repositories of a work's meaning. The list could be extended indefinitely, and, in truth, each of these claims has a measure of validity. We do bring greater skepticism, if not greater sophistication, to reading than previous generations. Enlightenment and modernist certainties have not withstood the hurly-burly of our postmodern world. But the postmodernist attack does not ultimately concern the ways in which we read or even the choice of what we study, both of which could be negotiated with the modernists. The attack concerns the legitimacy of privileging any text, actor, political regime, or any method of interpretation. It targets, in short, the legitimacy of authority in any form. (Permit me to note what I will not pursue here, namely that the attack on authority does not preclude and often encourages the mobilization of totalitarian tactics in launching it.) And its ultimate tragedy lies in the postmodernists' failure to recognize that, in repudiating authority, they have only facilitated the imperial reach of the managerial state to which they turn to satisfy their demands.

The tragedy of the liberal modernists also lies in the failure to acknowledge the sway of the managerial state and its pervasive influence upon cultural and intellectual life. Trilling was right to insist upon the inescapable political dimension of literature and uncommonly brave to lament the absence of a vigorous conservative opposition, which might force us "to become more intelligent" and "require us to keep our ideas from becoming stale, habitual, and inert."[11] He could hardly have been expected to foresee that the last vestiges of a left political opposition would also fall away with the collapse of communism, leaving nothing but a cultural, sexual, and identity politics. The postmodernist challenge did not encourage liberal modernists to rethink the relation between their rhetoric and the political realities that engulfed them. If anything, it led them to foreclose the development of their thought as a coherent and comprehensive project. Thus, the acceleration of the cultural struggles on the campuses led to a rigidification rather than a reinvigoration of liberal humanities. Above all, the liberal modernists suffered from their inability to mount a robust and capacious vision of legitimate authority that simultaneously respected the (measured) freedom of the individual and the (legitimate) claims of the community.

Trilling ascribed special virtues to the novel as a genre and worried that its decline augured a decline in political and individual freedom. It is hard to believe that even Trilling fully grasped the prescience of his passing remarks, but it is no less hard to deny him an impressive understanding of the real stakes in a rapidly changing game. Trilling celebrated the novel for its special effectiveness as an agent of the moral imagination. For the novel, he insists, draws the reader into the moral life, challenging him to examine his own motives and to see the world afresh. In this way, the novel invites the reader to respect and appreciate the human diversity of a world that may not conform to conventional expectations and, beyond that, enjoins the virtues of forgiveness and understanding. Perhaps the most striking aspect of Trilling's passage lies in his unapologetic linking of morality and freedom. Here, I quote him at some length:

> For our time, the most effective moral agent has been the novel of the last two hundred years. . . . [I]ts greatness and its practical usefulness lay in its unremitting work of involving the reader himself in the moral life, inviting him to put his own motives under examination, suggesting that reality is not as his conventional education has led him to see it. It taught . . . the extent of human variety and the value of this variety. It was the literary form to which the emotions of understanding and forgiveness were indigenous. . . . At the moment its impulse does not seem strong, for there never was a time when the virtues of its greatness were so likely to be thought of as weaknesses. Yet there was never a time when its particular activity was so much needed, was of so much practical, political, and social use—so much that if its impulse does not respond to the need, we shall have reason to be sad not only over a waning form of art but also over our waning freedom.[12]

Trilling's reflections apply as readily to history as to the novel, since, notwithstanding the distinction between "fact" and "fiction," history also engages its readers in moral reflection upon the extent and value of human variety. History, if anything more than the novel, invites us to reflect upon the balance between change and continuity in human experience: In what ways do people and societies change—perhaps even progress—and in what ways do they remain, if not the same, at least recognizable? And our time, even more than Trilling's, is prone to dismiss the virtues of historical study and moral reflection as weaknesses rather than strengths.

It would be preposterous to expect history to remain immune to the rapidly changing currents of our times, including the temptations of postmodernism and identity politics. For reasons that defy facile explanation, the iconoclasm and nihilism that inform much postmodernist thought are proving powerfully seductive, especially to academics. Nor may we reasonably expect history to remain a vital force in our culture if historians retreat into a modernist bunker. Indeed, as Trilling's sad warnings confirm, many of the worst tendencies in contemporary culture and society derive directly from the tensions within liberal modernism itself. Liberal modernism never made its peace with authority, and today its own antiauthoritarian proclivities are flowering, notably in the postmodernist repudiation of all forms of authority—including the authority of the moral or intellectual compact without which history as a craft or an intellectual undertaking collapses.

Postmodernists regularly reduce morality to a ploy of the powerful to control the weak. And our world is showing a disconcerting tendency to concur, viewing morality as primarily concerned with the defense or infringement of individual rights. Morality thus becomes nothing but a weapon in a Hobbesian struggle over resources. Trilling, however, viewed morality as a common or social concern, a habit of virtue, generosity, understanding, and respect for others that, however paradoxically, guaranteed the freedom of the individual. He effectively linked freedom and authority, implicitly claiming that without authority freedom is impossible. Notwithstanding the maddening imprecision of this vision, it affirms both freedom and authority as necessarily both individual and social. More, it rejects the understanding of freedom as the repudiation of authority, just as it rejects the understanding of freedom as narrowly a matter of individual right. Neither a right nor a commodity, freedom emerges as a form of stewardship for a shared respect for moral authority.

For historians, that stewardship primarily entails the willingness to respect the standards of our craft, which include the honest use of evidence and the continuing attempt to reach fair and nonpartisan judgments. If we lose the ability or the will to acknowledge that those whom we regard as political villains might also have been honorable men and women, we lose our ability to write a history that rises above the level of a party platform or position paper. If we lose the ability or the will to acknowledge that circumstances have always constrained human action—and arguably human beliefs and values as well—we lose the ability to write a history that captures the heroism and tragedy of human attempts to shape the social, political, and material world. If we fail to respect the constraints of circumstance or the humanity of our ideological opponents, we will effectively confess our inability to respect people who differ from us in background, conviction, or situation. The fabled "diversity" of our postmodern world should preeminently have encouraged us to cultivate these virtues and move beyond the more complacent tendencies in liberal modernism. Instead, it is drawing us into a relativism that, by denying the authority of any external reality, repudiates the idea of history as an intellectual practice or a collegial profession.

Notes

1. Francis Fukuyama, *The End of History and the Last Man* (New York: Free Press, 1992).
2. Lionel Trilling, *The Liberal Imagination* (Garden City, N.Y.: Doubleday Anchor, 1950).
3. Lewis P. Simpson, *The Dispossessed Garden: Pastoral and History in Southern Literature* (Athens: University of Georgia Press, 1975).
4. Mary Ann Glendon, "The End of Democracy? A Discussion Continued," *First Things* 69 (1997): 23. See also Mary Ann Glendon, *Rights Talk: The Impoverishment of Political Discourse* (New York: Free Press, 1991) and Paul Edward Gottfried's *After Liberalism: Mass Democracy and the Administrative State* (Princeton: Princeton University Press, 1998).
5. John Gray, *Enlightenment's Wake* (New York and London: Routledge, 1995), 74, cited by Gottfried. See also, Robert George, *Making Men Moral: Civil Liberties and Public Morality* (Oxford: Clarendon Press, 1993).
6. For further exploration of these topics, see the essays by Berkowitz, Diggins, McDougall, Ravitch, and Wilentz in this volume.
7. For a good introduction, see Nancey Murphy, *Anglo-American Postmodernity: Philosophical Perspectives on Science, Religion, and Ethics* (Boulder, Colo.: Westview Press, 1997).
8. Karol Wojtyla, *Person and Community: Selected Essays,* trans. by Theresa Sandok (New York: Peter Lang, 1993). See also, Rocco Buttiglione, *Karol Wojtyla: The Thought of the Man Who Became Pope* (Grand Rapids, Mich.: Erdmans, 1997).
9. For an exploration of aspects of this problem, see Elizabeth Fox-Genovese and Eugene D. Genovese, "The Political Crisis of Social History," *Journal of Social History* 10 (1976), 205–20.
10. For an exploration of aspects of this theme, see Gurstein in this volume.
11. Trilling, *Liberal Imagination,* viii.
12. Trilling, *Liberal Imagination,* 215.

CHAPTER 7

ON THE OBSOLESCENCE OF "PURITANISM" AS AN EPITHET

Rochelle Gurstein

For almost a hundred years now, the charge of puritanism has guaranteed the accuser the prestige of being on the side of progress, free speech, and sexual emancipation. To utter this epithet has been to announce and celebrate one's own receptivity to advanced art and unorthodox "lifestyles"; it has been the preeminent sign of one's capacity for regarding all aspects of the human condition without flinching or passing judgment. To label one's opponent a puritan has been, above all, to theatrically display one's own sophistication. Puritanism has become the unanswerable indictment, the ultimate smear, occupying much the same territory in contemporary cultural disputes as the final, damning charge "Crritic!" in the ever escalating exchange of insults between Vladimir and Estragon in *Waiting for Godot*.

With so many automatic advantages to be gained, it is no surprise that in many of the most contentious battles of the culture wars during the 1990s, those on the side of progress have detected the recrudescence of puritanism everywhere. The most obvious example, of course, are the Jesse Helmses of the world who are all too happy to play the old, familiar role of moralizing, bible-thumping hick against the depraved elite. Both sides were quick to don their threadbare costumes in the clamor over whether the National Endowment for the Arts should fund museums that exhibit slick, sexually graphic work like Robert Mapplethorpe's photographs, just as they tried to breathe

Originally published in a slightly different version in *Salmagundi,* 101–102, (1994), 95–116.

new life into their hackneyed lines when it came to the obscenity trial of 2 Live Crew and movies like *The People vs. Larry Flynt.* But what distinguishes the most recent culture skirmishes from earlier ones is that, increasingly, old-time freedom fighters have found themselves in the most unbohemian company—mainstream news pundits, Hollywood, the Time-Warner entertainment corporation, academics, and the art establishment of museums and foundations. What is more, they have found themselves at war not only with puritanical senators from the South and the religious right, but with those who were once their comrades—avant-garde artists, radical feminists, and cutting-edge legal theorists.

The crime of the latest artistic vanguard and its champions is to devote their energies to extra-aesthetic considerations of identity politics, making and judging art according to utilitarian, political, or moral standards rather than aesthetic ones, which was previously the defining mark of the philistine. The crime of the new feminism associated with Catharine MacKinnon and Andrea Dworkin is to attack pornography as an instrument of male domination of women, thereby putting into question its alleged emancipatory promise and in the bargain, its protection by the First Amendment. For old-school liberals, these artists and feminists, who should have known better, are even worse than the religious right, and thus they take special pleasure in yoking them together under that most durable term of derision, "puritan."

It appears that puritan-baiting, which first developed at the turn of this century as a concerted attack on Victorian manners and morals, has become such a venerable tradition that it continues on even in the absence of any real Victorians. Let us remember that what is at issue here is not the legendary prudery of the Victorians, who allegedly covered the "limbs" of furniture with skirts, invented the term "white meat" for the indelicate phrase "chicken breast," or blushed at hearing married people speak of retiring for the night. Nor is it a battle over the artistic value of modern novels like *Ulysses* or *Women in Love*—and such battles, it must be stressed, have been few in the history of obscenity law. Rather, our contemporary cultural disputes that incite the epithet puritanism center on the obligation of the NEA to support museums displaying Mapplethorpe's photographs, whose only claim to distinction is that they chronicle the most extreme reaches of sexual violence, and on the right of pornographers to their trade in women's flesh.

Even the most eager heir to the title of puritan, Jesse Helms, is worlds apart from the real thing. "I'm not talking about banning [Mapplethorpe's] works," Helms insisted. "I'm talking about subsidizing them."[1] The capacity to make this distinction places Helms in a different realm from the late-nineteenth-century purity crusader who symbolized for an entire generation the puritan as censor, prurient prude, neurotic, and fool: Anthony Comstock.

Comstock, like most of his contemporaries, treated all representations, images, and discussions of sex as obscene; sex-education pamphlets and notorious French picture postcards belonged to the same category. Helms's distinction between censorship and sponsorship would have been lost on Comstock. Moreover, contemporary feminist accounts of sexual violence within the home, Antioch College's explicit "Sexual Offense Policy," and the televised Anita Hill–Clarence Thomas sexual harassment hearings—not to mention the Starr Report and almost all of the public discussion of the Lewinsky affair—would have provided the grounds not for another round of puritan-baiting, but rather for obscenity prosecution. In 1873, with the help of the YMCA, Comstock pushed legislation through Congress that banned all materials relating to sex, including birth control information and devices, from the public mails. Not only was his name inscribed in the legal annals—the law was known as the Comstock Act—it also became an epithet in its own right in 1905 when George Bernard Shaw, responding to the threat that Comstock would ban his play *Mrs. Warren's Profession,* invented the sneer "comstockery": "Comstockery is the world's standing joke at the expense of the United States. Europe likes to hear of such things. It confirms the deep-seated conviction of the Old World that America is a provincial place, a second-rate country-town civilization after all."[2]

With all the commotion about modern-day puritanism, one would think that such people wielded real power, like Comstock, who, in his role as special prosecutor, had the authority of federal and local government to bring distributors of obscenity to justice. One would never know that Helms's attempt to prevent the NEA from funding works considered obscene was roundly defeated seventy-three to twenty-four in the Senate, or that both Mapplethorpe's photographs and 2 Live Crew's rap music were found *not* obscene by juries in Cincinnati and Florida respectively and that they can be purchased at neighborhood stores everywhere, or that MacKinnon and Dworkin's antipornography ordinance in Indianapolis was almost immediately repealed, or that there have been almost no successful obscenity prosecutions since the mid-1960s—all this in a country with a most unpuritanical appetite for pornography valued in the billions.

Since the new puritans command no real power, why do they continue to provoke the ire of liberals today? The time has come to ask why our contemporary disputes about art, pornography, and mass culture are invariably formulated in these thoroughly exhausted terms. Why, in all of these arguments about the quality and character of our common world—since nothing less is at stake here behind all the bluster—is there a singleminded focus on ridiculing and rooting out impotent puritans, the code word for an anemic version of reactionary politics, censorship, philistinism, and sexual repressiveness? Our best hope for moving beyond our current stalemate is to return to the origins of this style of argument—to the turn of this century—to understand how and why the attack on puritanism emerged. This is especially important because this mode of debunking not only bade a final and definitive farewell to all that was Victorian but also introduced many of the key words of modernity which still define our interminable present-day controversies. And if the terms of those controversies are as depleted as I have been suggesting, then the obsolescence of "puritanism" as an epithet also points to the exhaustion of many of its associated values.

"Puritanism" as an epithet made a sudden, explosive appearance in the opening decades of the twentieth century, when an angry generation of feminists, birth-control champions, anarchists, free-speech lawyers, cultural critics, realist novelists, and Greenwich Village bohemians attacked their forebears for willfully evading what they considered to be the most pressing issue of life—sex. Randolph Bourne spoke for his entire generation when he charged, "Certainly the older generation is rarely interested in the profounder issues of life. . . . It shies in panic at hints of sex-issues."[3] This habit of evasion, or what was commonly called "the conspiracy of silence," the younger generation blamed for deforming intimate life and giving rise to a hypocritical double standard of sexual conduct; at the same time, they denounced it for stunting the imagination, for making artistic achievements negligible and culture provincial.

The distinguishing feature of this assault was the young radicals' equation of nineteenth-century manners and morals with puritanism, and puritanism with a pathological dread of sensual pleasures. In his devastating satire, "The Puritan's Will to Power" (1917), Bourne defined puritans as those people who "give up the primitive satisfactions of sex and food and drink and gregariousness and act the ascetic and the glumly censorious." They were not, however, content to rest there. Bourne noted that "the true Puritan is at once the most unselfish and the most self-righteous of men" in that he feels superior in his acts of renunciation, he is proud of his humility, and attains power by forcing everyone to act in the same supposedly selfless way. "In the compelling of others to abstain, you have the final glut of puritanical power." With this emphasis, Bourne divested the puritan of his historical and theological contexts and successfully redefined him as a nasty, manipulative character type thinly disguised as social reformer. He then disposed of this figure with one cutting remark: "The Puritan is a case of arrested development."[4]

Puritanism was also another name for the general state of ignorance about reproduction. Appalled by the miserable conditions of huge families and by the desperation and ruined health of women forced into a life of perpetual childbearing, outspoken reformers like Margaret Sanger and Emma Goldman tirelessly assailed the Comstock Act. Sanger denounced "the hundreds of thousands of abortions being performed in America each year . . . [as] a disgrace to civilization." With the lives of countless women at stake, Sanger marshalled all of her rhetorical energy to slay her enemy. Setting dramatic terms that would have remarkable staying power, she formulated the controversy over birth control as a battle between evasion and knowledge, reaction and progress, in short, between puritanism and emancipation: "I lay the blame for [abortions] and the illness, suffering, and death resulting from them at the door of a government which in its puritanical blindness insists upon suffering and death from ignorance rather than life and happiness through knowledge and prevention."[5]

Repeatedly, radicals complained that their elders' recoil from the life of the senses had warped their intimate life. In "The Hypocrisy of Puritanism" (1910), Emma Goldman censured puritanism for "repudiat[ing], as something vile and sinful, our deepest feelings; but being absolutely ignorant as to the real functions of human emotions, Puritanism is itself the creator of the most unspeakable vices." Critics held puritanism responsible for devising an impossibly strict moral code which required absolute abstinence before marriage, lifelong abstinence for all who did not marry, and sexual relations exclusively in the service of procreation within marriage. And it was precisely the impossibility of adhering to this stringent code that had led to "the double standard" with its attendant vice of prostitution, which Goldman characterized as puritanism's "most cherished child, all hypocritical sanctimoniousness notwithstanding." "Out of the unchallenged policies of continence, abstinence, 'chastity,' and 'purity,'" Sanger angrily observed, "we have reaped the harvests of prostitution, venereal scourges, and innumerable other evils." Puritanical taboos about sex, seen in the light of Freud's writings, were also the cause, in Sanger's words, of "neurosis and hysteria on the one hand; or concealed gratification of suppressed desires on the other, with a resultant hypocrisy and cant." She criticized the way earlier generations had attempted "to control, civilize, and sublimate the great primordial natural force of sex, mainly by futile efforts at prohibition, suppression, restraint, extirpation. Its revenge, as the psychoanalysts are showing us every day, has been great. Insanity, hysteria, neuroses, morbid fears and compulsions."[6]

Birth control champions sought to rectify this intolerable state of affairs by making information about sexual hygiene widely available through public lectures, by distributing pamphlets, and by creating institutions like Sanger's widely publicized but short-lived Brownsville birth control clinic in 1917. Their efforts, however, were repeatedly impeded by the Comstock Act; they often landed in jail for short stints, and the newspapers covered their exploits.

In their defense of open speech about reproduction, these reformers initiated a line of argument that would be repeated with tedious regularity by later advocates of exposure both in social reform and the arts. They envisioned history as a long march of progress led by courageous individuals who were always before their time. Just as free speech had guaranteed victories against the absolutism of the church and the state, so it was necessary in the battle against puritanical laws banning birth control material—which they envisioned as the latest event in this grand saga.

Because every rebel knew this story, every rebel also knew in advance the role he or she might play in this pre-scripted cultural drama. Shocking the bourgeoisie and challenging the law were the twin aspirations of the earliest birth control leaders: "Let us insist upon Birth Control now—even in the face of statutes, magistrates, courts, and jails," exclaimed Jessie Ashley. "The rebel spirit is of great social value; it keeps the race from becoming craven." With the same obvious pleasure in provocation, Sanger described the stance of her short-lived journal, *The Woman Rebel,* as "To look the world in the face with a go-to-hell look in the eyes; to have an idea; to speak and act in defiance of convention." Confident that their cause was just, birth control champions chided their contemporaries for being on the wrong side of history. When Sanger's sister, Ethel Byrne, staged a hunger strike to protest her imprisonment for distributing birth control material at the Brownsville clinic, the *New York Tribune* predicted, "It will be hard to make the youth of 1967 believe that in 1917 a woman was imprisoned for doing what Mrs. Byrne did." The unanswerable claim that "history is on our side" was also advanced by an early chronicler of the birth control movement, Victor Robinson: "In the unending annals that recount the struggle for freedom and progress, history will reserve a bright page for the Pioneers of Birth Control." In this way, birth control advocates were able to seize the high ground, insinuating that to question the legitimacy of their endeavors was to place oneself in opposition to the hallowed liberal values of freedom and progress.[7]

And when H. L. Mencken entered the fray, the mere mention of puritanism would be enough to vanquish one's opponent instantly. While Mencken had little sympathy with the birth control movement, its enemies—puritanism, Comstock, comstockery, and censorship—were his enemies, and he launched a merciless attack on all of them in his "Puritanism as a Literary Force" (1917).[8] That Mencken was able to compile a number of definitive catalogues of the puritan's alleged crimes testifies to the abundance of material that was already in wide circulation at the time. I will quote at length from two of his indictments. In the first, we witness the roasting of the puritan as censor; in the second, the skewering of the puritan as philistine:

> The Puritan's utter lack of aesthetic sense, his distrust of all romantic emotion, his unmatchable intolerance of opposition, his unbreakable belief in his own bleak and narrow views, his savage cruelty of attack, his lust for relentless and barbarous persecution—these things have put an almost unbearable burden upon the exchange of ideas in the United States.

And:

> [Puritanism] is, indeed, but a single manifestation of one of the deepest prejudices of a religious and half-cultured people—the prejudice against beauty as a form of debauchery and corruption—the distrust of all ideas that do not fit readily into certain accepted axioms—the belief in the eternal validity of moral concepts—in brief, the whole mental sluggishness of the lower orders of men.

With these dazzling verbal displays, Mencken impressed his audience that he and they belonged to a superior sort of society—"the civilized minority." In the same way that birth control champions succeeded in joining their cause with the cherished liberal values of progress and freedom, Mencken joined his with the winning modern values of sophistication and urbanity. He took special pleasure in using the puritan of old to make comstockery—which, for Mencken, was puritanism in its modern guise—appear even more laughable by comparison. Distinguishing between the old puritanism and the new, Mencken emphasized the "difference between *re*nunciation and *de*nunciation, asceticism and Mohammedanism, the hair shirt and the flaming sword."

> The new Puritanism is not ascetic, but militant. Its aim is not to lift up saints but to knock down sinners. Its supreme manifestation is the vice crusade, an armed pursuit of helpless outcasts by the whole military and naval forces of the Republic. Its supreme hero is Comstock Himself . . .

The "essential fact of the new Puritanism," scoffed Mencken, was "its recognition of the moral expert, the professional sinhound, the virtuoso of virtue."

It was this smug devotion to the policing of private morals that Mencken despised most about the new puritanism and he detected its pernicious influence not only on reform projects from Prohibition to purity leagues, but also on the realm of culture where "literature was conceived, not as a thing in itself, but merely as a hand-maid to politics or religion." Puritanism as a literary force had led to the "wholesale and ecstatic sacrifice of aesthetic ideas, of all the fine gusto of passion and beauty, to notions of what is meet, proper, and nice." Proudly displaying his own hard-won capacity to separate moral from aesthetic judgment—a capacity that distinguishes the sophisticated modern from the old-fashioned provincial—Mencken repeatedly tore into American critics for their inability to "estimate a piece of writing as a piece of writing, a work of art as a work of art." And American novelists whom he suspected of moralism—"the virtuous, kittenish [William Dean] Howells" was his favorite target—he ridiculed for "timorousness and reticence which are the distinguishing marks of the Puritan." From this time on, anyone employing the epithet "puritanism" would have the satisfaction of knowing that he or she belonged to the fortunate minority of modern, sophisticated, urbane people who were open to new ideas and unconventional art.

While Mencken is the undisputed master of puritan-baiting, this showy brand of debunking also was performed by many of his accomplished followers. Heywood Broun and Margaret Leech's *Anthony Comstock, Roundsman of the Lord* (1927) combined the smart-set style with a smattering of psychology, producing the definitive portrait of the puritan as censor, and the censor as "neurotic" and "fool." With an air of amusement, they noted that by the turn of the century Comstock was already a popular target of ridicule. By the time of his death in 1915, "to his youthful countrymen, he had become a great tradition, a joke, a scapegoat." They also had a great deal of fun with his private life, mocking his "puritanism," sneering at his close relationship with his "beloved," "pious" mother, and drawing simpleminded Freudian conclusions about his marriage to a woman ten years his senior. In an afterword on censorship, Broun repeated what by the 1920s had become the stock indictment of those who were shocked by obscenity: "It is not lustful thoughts which mar human personality, but only the sense of shame." Taking obvious pleasure in inverting Comstock's arguments about the relation of obscenity and shameful conduct, Broun asserted that "Comstock spread shame about very widely and it was a force much more debilitating than any exotic notions which might have come from the books he seized."[9]

Drawing on work from the emerging fields of ethnography and anthropology, many moderns came to believe that obscenity and other moral questions were shaped by time and place, and therefore, always evolving. In consequence, forward-looking people like Broun had only contempt for those who would ban what later, more progressive generations might find perfectly acceptable. With the rise of moral relativism, disputants often pictured themselves as occupying separate moral universes, and found it increasingly difficult to persuade an opponent of the rational superiority of a given argument. Sharp-witted debunking swiftly sank into nasty name-calling: "As things are constituted," Broun concluded, "it is pretty safe to assume that any given censor is a fool. The very fact that he is a censor indicates that."

While the fury of the original attack against puritanism suggests that the young radicals had much to despise about their elders, it is important to note that even this first generation was accused by their contemporaries of having exaggerated the threat of puritanism. As early as 1915, Randolph Bourne—no friend of puritanism—criticized "crusaders" like Mencken and Theodore Dreiser for "beat[ing] at a straw man of Puritanism which, for the younger generation, has not even the vitality to be interesting." Responding to Mencken's "Puritanism as a Literary Force" a few years later, Bourne observed that younger writers seemed wholly oblivious to the "cultural terrorism" that Mencken attributed to puritanism. Not only had Mencken overestimated its power, he had also misjudged the strength of comstockery. Pointing to the large number of publishers and magazines willing to bring out "vigorous and candid work," Bourne concluded that "comstockery in art must be seen as an annoying but not dominating force."[10] By 1918, the debunking style itself had become a cliché. In a review of a history of puritanism that appeared in *The New Republic,* well known puritan-baiters such as Mencken, Theodore Dreiser, Walter Lippmann, Van Wyck Brooks, Floyd Dell, and *Seven Arts Magazine* were singled out for censure:

> In fact, the whole younger set, including Mr. Dreiser, never see the word "Puritan," without getting out their axes, refreshing their memories of Freud and Forel, remembering bitterly the small towns they were brought up in, thanking god they can find the way to Greenwich Village, even if they do not live there—and then taking another whirl at the long-suffering men whose manners and customs, distorted and unillumined by that unearthly light in which they lived, have yet been the mold in which our country's laws, literature, education, religions, economics, morals, and points of view have become purified.[11]

That these criticisms were voiced at the very beginning of this argument suggests that puritanism as a force in American private and cultural life was never as powerful as its detractors would have us believe. How, then, can we account for its remarkable durability as epithet? In their urgency to defeat comstockery and puritanism, the young rebels who came of age in the final decades of the nineteenth century discredited the manners and morals of their century wholesale, thereby giving an entire century a bad name based solely on their opposition to its most obnoxious representatives. Yet by the close of the nineteenth century, a competing and, I would argue, more representative sensibility—what I will call the reticent sensibility—had reached its apex. This sensibility, however, has largely become alien or conflated with puritanism, so thoroughgoing and effective has the attack on puritanism been over the past hundred years.

Courtesy, politeness, civility, decency, honor, refinement, cultivation, grace, and elegance were essential components of the reticent sensibility, and keen sensitivity to the feelings of others was the distinguishing mark of the reticent person. Sympathy was the keynote here, and reserve, tact, discretion, propriety, delicacy, and tenderness provided an array of finely modulated approaches toward the privacy of others. A crystalline expression of this sensibility can be found in a letter Charles Eliot Norton wrote to John Ruskin in 1873, in which he apologized for not being able to return a copy of a letter his close friend had sent him. In his pained description of his "old custom" of burning not only "trivial notes" but also extremely personal letters—"those that are like intimate talks, when confidences are given to which no third person would be privy"—Norton invoked the sanctity of privacy and with it, the respectful distance owed to intimate matters: "I hold these last letters sacred, and often make a holocaust of what it pains me to sacrifice, and of what I would keep among my treasures if I could be sure they would be buried with me." Norton's confession to Ruskin that he has burned "those [letters] in which you told me of sorrowful experience in love, for they were secrets between you and me" reveals a crucial component of the reticent sensibility: personal affairs, because they can only be made intelligible by the sensitive rendering of a trusted intimate, must be protected from the unsympathetic gaze of strangers lest they become slight or ridiculous.[12]

This defining characteristic of the reticent sensibility—which obviously has nothing to do with prudery—depended on a shared sense of which things were large and sturdy enough to withstand the glare of publicity, and which things were so personal, fragile, or vulnerable that they required the cover of privacy if they were to retain their significance and emotional vibrancy. Matters that were too small—like published gossip or everyday life represented in the new realist fiction—were liable to appear trivial; matters that were too personal—like sexual intimacy, no matter whether it was couched in clinical or literary language—were liable to become obscene. Far from being enthusiasts of censorship, the most articulate spokesmen of the reticent sensibility were dedicated to protecting the quality of the public sphere: they feared that invasions of privacy and obscenity—which, for them, were the same thing—would "pollute" the public domain, blunt public standards of taste and sensibility, and coarsen the tone of public discussion. While they were concerned with controlling private sexual conduct, their sense of obscenity was shaped, above all, by a sense of proportion. Judges typically defined obscenity as the "indecent," by which they meant "the wanton and unnecessary expression or exposure, in words or pictures, of that which the common sense of decency requires should be kept private or concealed," that which is "unbecoming, immodest, unfit to be seen or heard."[13]

Not only was a finely wrought sense of proportion required to insure a high tone to common life and public discussion; decisions about which things should appear in public also required a highly modulated sense of the sacred and the shameful. In W. S. Lilly's "The New Naturalism" (1885), it becomes clear that the understanding that moderns have uncritically derided as puritan is actually at one with the perspective of all societies that recognize limits to human knowledge and, consequently, approach the unknowable with awe and wonder:

> The great ethical principles of reserve, shame, reverence, which have their endless applications in civilized life, prescribe limits to imagination as to action. There are moods of thought which do not yield in heinousness to the worst deeds—moods of madness, suicidal and polluting. To leave them in the dark is to help towards suppressing them. And this is a sacred duty. "We are bound to reticence," says George Eliot, "most of all by that reverence for the highest efforts of our common nature, which commands us to bury its lowest fatalities, its invincible remnants of the brute, its most agonizing struggles with temptation, in unbroken silence."[14]

For the rebels at the turn of the century, the crimes that could be laid at the feet of Comstock and his followers dictated a merciless policy of take no prisoners. But, in fact, the only point at which Comstock's prejudices intersected with the reticent sensibility was in their shared concern that private matters not see the light of day. Comstock's impolite and evangelical unmasking of his opponents' misdeeds, the better to reveal his own superior morality, shares much with Mencken's theatrical style of debunking, which served to display and reinforce his sophistication; it has nothing to do with Norton's solicitude for the feelings of others and his concern about which things should appropriately appear in public. This first generation of rebels, exasperated by the antics of comstockery and impatient for change, can be forgiven for conflating reticence with puritanism; caught in the heat of the battle, they had no time to reflect upon the cost of a strategy that would end by making the concept of reticence incomprehensible as anything other than evasion, repression, or prudery. It is not so easy today to forgive the reigning attitude that nothing is sacred and, consequently, everything speakable.

Seen in this light, the squabble over the NEA leaves no doubt that the long-running drama of the avant-garde against the puritan has given way to farce. Any self-respecting provocateur should be courting rejection from "establishment" institutions; the NEA's approval of a museum retrospective signals that the rebel has either failed to shock the bourgeoisie or that he or she is naïve at best and at worst a hypocrite. Rather than grumbling about their right to funding, avant-gardists should have set up a *salon des refusés,* except that museums of contemporary art, frantic to keep up with the times, have robbed artists of this prerogative. Playing the puritan card in this controversy is an irresponsible diversionary tactic. Instead of questioning whether something has gone wrong with the practice of art when those who become celebrities document sexual torture or make glossy cibachromes of a crucifix submerged in the photographer's own urine, the puritan-baiter acts as if all is well, or as if there is nothing wrong that a little more artistic freedom or a little more NEA funding cannot fix. Old-school libertarians are so invested in the myth of the martyred genius that they have somehow missed the extraordinary success of today's "bad boys." Soho, Fifty-Seventh Street, Chelsea, the Whitney Biennial, not to mention the auction houses and the international art extravaganzas, are not threatened by Senator Helms and others. Those throwbacks invigorate them by providing an old-fashioned enemy, which, for a blissful moment, lets them imagine they still have a cause around which to rally. Instead of circulating petitions, staging conferences, and sending letters to editors about the threat of puritanism, the art world needs to come to terms with its amazing successes. If art is to continue as anything other than tried-and-true scandals, sophomoric mischief, simpleminded political sloganeering, mind-numbing collage, or trite academic abstraction, thinking people will need to grapple with the surprising turn of events that has put an end to the avant-garde as an adversary culture and instead made it into a tradition, as Harold Rosenberg pointed out thirty years ago.

Critics who complain of puritanism of the left are more searching. Drawing attention to the way the arts in recent times have become increasingly politicized, they rightly point out that great art always has a dimension beyond its political, moral, or social use. They fail, however, to take account of why that essential quality seems to matter little today. Today's artists find themselves disinherited by the modernist tradition that culminated in abstract expressionism on the one hand, or beating the dead horse of avant-gardism on the other; in addition, they find themselves living in a society beset by hard, even brutal times. Under such conditions, some artists have begun to worry whether art is not a luxury product, and whether its historical claim of disinterestedness has not made it and them literally useless. Instead of simply dismissing their often desperate efforts as puritanism of the left, it is important to recognize them as the fruits not only of a corrupted practice, but also of a mean, grasping national culture. Politically correct art and the politics of identity, with their cult of victimhood and tirades against power, are the most recent revelations of the failure of our liberal, commercial society to cultivate the virtues necessary for a vital common world and flourishing public life, an unfulfilled task that has shadowed our republic since its founding. They represent our incapacity to imagine shared projects that endure over time and transcend the individual; they point up our failure to regard legacies bequeathed us by past generations as anything other than old-fashioned relics to be thrown over for the latest inventions or repressive codes to be undermined in the name of emancipation.

Just as controversies over obscene and politically correct art testify to the disappearance of shared standards of judgment and taste and the receding of a durable common world, recent feminist criticism of pornography and sexual harassment speaks to the disintegration of common standards of decency and the destruction of intimacy. It is precisely here that denunciations of puritanism do us no good at all. First, the graphic quality of these descriptions places people who speak this way in the unpuritanical company of late-nineteenth-century sex radicals whose frank accounts of domestic sexual violence landed them in jail for distributing obscenity. Their unblinking chronicles of sexual coercion and intimidation cannot simply be waved away as evidence of prudery, moralism, or humorlessness; any sympathetic reader has to be alarmed by the frightful vulnerability that some women feel in their intimate relations with men. More than anything else, such writings are confessions of the desperation and alienation that has now penetrated even the sphere of intimacy, which was supposed to be a refuge from and antidote to such things. They reveal that intimate life has suffered the same lamentable consequences as public life in a society animated by the debunker's mantra that nothing is sacred: both have become increasingly brutal, threatening, coarse, indecent, and ugly. And it is this recognition that has pushed some feminists to demand pornographers be prosecuted under existing obscenity laws, some colleges and universities to institute codes regulating speech and sexual behavior, and some legal scholars to call for an expansion of the concept of sexual harassment.

When feminists whose rallying cry is "pornography is the theory, rape the practice"[15] are told even by thoughtful champions of free speech that "the speech we hate is as much entitled to protection as any other,"[16] they respond, why does the right of the pornographer or the artist to "offend" take priority over the actual harm suffered by the victims of such "speech"? That they invoke the victim's suffering points to the extreme limitation of our contemporary legal framework: the law, because of its adversarial role as defender of individuals' rights, is forced to hunt for victims whose rights have been violated and therefore deserve state intervention. While feminists have made a powerful case against pornography in exactly these terms when they argue that it not only degrades women and incites violence against them, but also reflects and furthers the structural inequality of women in our society, the legal fixation on victims has made it difficult to imagine let alone address the public dimension of the harm. This is because the legal paradigm lacks the conceptual range to take account of the harm suffered by society at large, especially the way the tone of public conversation is cheapened and sensibilities coarsened when our common world is deluged with images and discussions that formerly evoked shame. When private matters are indiscriminately flooded with light, they are liable to become either obscene like pornography, or laughable like the countless jokes in circulation about President Clinton and Monica Lewinsky.

At this late date, to speak of shame and decency is to invite the epithet "puritanism," which effectively puts an end to any further discussion, since no right-thinking person wants to be on the side of prudery and censorship. Yet if my argument has any merit, the power of this epithet is based on a series of historical mistakes: first, the reigning sensibility of the late nineteenth century was not prudish and censorious, but reticent; second, Anthony Comstock—the model for the caricature of the puritan—represents a deformed offshoot of the reticent sensibility; third, while the rebels at the turn of the century had much to complain of, they exaggerated the repressiveness of their times; and finally, our own times are neither repressive nor puritanical. For these reasons, puritanism as an epithet should at last be retired.

This is not to suggest an uncritical embrace of the nineteenth-century reticent sensibility, but rather to reconsider—now that the battles for birth control and free expression have long been won—what was valuable in it. One of its most penetrating insights was that overfamiliarity with unseemly things led to inurement or, in nineteenth-century language, to the corruption of taste, judgment, and sensibility. Whereas a delicate sensibility was the very sign of cultivation for the party of reticence, a loss of sensitivity was precisely what enthusiasts of exposure had been hoping for all alone. In 1911, the free speech advocate Theodore Schroeder boasted that his "sex sensibilities" had become "considerably blunted . . . partly as a result of my study of sexual psychology." Even more to the point, he questioned whether "'blunted sensibilities' are not a good kind to be encouraged in the matter of sex—as we now discuss matters of liver or digestion—with an absolute freedom from lascivious feelings?"[17] Almost ninety years later, in a world where art experts brag of their capacity to detect the persistence of classical forms in a Mapplethorpe photograph of a man violating another with his fist; where academics praise teenagers for their appreciation of the "allegorical" and "parodic" codes of vernacular African American traditions in the sexually brutal, hate-filled songs of 2 Live Crew; where bored souls daily display their willingness to endure lurid confessions of sexual deviation and perversity on TV talk shows; and where the editors of the *New York Times* turn the front page of their newspaper into a gallery of the most invasive photographs of the vulnerable, dead bodies of victims of murder, war, natural catastrophes, and accidents, we have the answer.

Notes

1. "Senate Passes Compromise on Arts Endowment," *New York Times,* October 25, 1990.
2. Shaw quoted in Morris L. Ernst and Alexander Lindey, *The Censor Marches On* (New York: Doubleday, 1940), 60.
3. Randolph Bourne, "This Older Generation," *Atlantic Monthly* (September 1915), *The Radical Will: Randolph Bourne, Selected Writings, 1911–1918,* edited by Olaf Hansen (New York: Urizen Books, 1977), 159–68.
4. Randolph Bourne, "The Puritan's Will to Power," *The New Republic* (April 1917), in Hansen, *Radical Will,* 301–6.
5. Sanger quoted in Victor Robinson, *Pioneers of Birth Control* (New York: Voluntary Parenthood League, 1919), 101–2.
6. Emma Goldman, "The Hypocrisy of Puritanism" (1910) in her *Anarchism and Other Essays* (1917 rpt; New York: Dover Publications, Inc., 1969), 170. Margaret Sanger, *The Pivot of Civilization* (New York: Brentano's, 1922), 246, 200, 229.
7. Ashley quoted in Robinson, *Pioneers,* 90. Margaret Sanger, *An Autobiography* (1938 rpt; New York: Dover, 1971), 110. The *New York Tribune,* quoted in David M. Kennedy, *Birth Control in America: The Career of Margaret Sanger* (New Haven: Yale University Press, 1970), 86.
8. H. L. Mencken, "Puritanism as a Literary Force" in his *A Book of Prefaces* (New York: Alfred A. Knopf, 1917), 197–284.
9. Heywood Broun and Margaret Leech, *Anthony Comstock, Roundsman of the Lord* (New York: Literary Guild of America, 1927).
10. Randolph Bourne, "Traps for the Unwary," *The New Republic* (May 1915), in Hansen, *Radical Will,* 480. Bourne, "H. L. Mencken" (March 1918), in Hansen, *Radical Will,* 472, 473.
11. R.E.R., "The Young Modern and the Puritan," *The New Republic* 16 (August 17, 1918), 84.
12. Norton to John Ruskin (April 2, 1873) in *The Correspondence of John Ruskin and Charles Eliot Norton,* edited by John Lewis Bradley and Ian Ousby (Cambridge, Mass.: Cambridge University Press, 1987), 285, 286.
13. *United States v. Bennett,* 16 Blatchford 339 (1873).
14. W. S. Lilly, "The New Naturalism" *Fortnightly Review* 38 (August 1, 1885), 240–56.
15. Laura Lederer (Ed.), *Take Back the Night: Women on Pornography* (New York: William Morrow, 1980).
16. Ronald Dworkin, "Liberty and Pornography," *New York Review of Books,* August 15, 1991.
17. Theodore Schroeder, "Obscenity, Prudery, and Morals" and "Psychologic Study of Modesty and Obscenity" in his *"Obscene" Literature and Constitutional Law: A Forensic Defense of Freedom of the Press* (New York: Privately Printed, 1911), 102, 276.

CHAPTER 8

POSTMODERNIST HISTORY

Gertrude Himmelfarb

FOR THE HISTORIAN, as for the philosopher, the quarrel between the Ancients and the Moderns is being superseded by a quarrel between the Moderns and the Postmoderns. If the great subversive principle of modernity is historicism—a form of relativism that locates the meaning of ideas and events so firmly in their historical context that history, rather than philosophy and nature, becomes the arbiter of truth—postmodernism is now confronting us with a far more subversive form of relativism, a relativism so radical, so absolute, as to be antithetical to both history and truth. ("History," in this context, refers to writings about the past rather than the past itself.) For postmodernism denies not only suprahistorical truths but historical truths, truths relative to particular times and places. And that denial involves a repudiation of the historical enterprise as it has been understood and practiced until very recently.

Postmodernism (or poststructuralism—the terms are by now used interchangeably—or "pomo," as it is familiarly called in academic circles and computer networks) is best known as a school of literary theory. But it has become increasingly prominent in such other disciplines as history, philosophy, anthropology, law, and theology (and in architecture, where it has a more specialized meaning). Its forefathers are Nietzsche and Heidegger, its fathers Derrida and Foucault; that the latter have vigorously disputed each other does not diminish the enthusiasm of disciples who find them equally congenial and compatible. From Jacques Derrida postmodernism

Originally published in *On Looking into the Abyss* (Knopf, 1994).

has borrowed the vocabulary and basic concepts of "deconstruction": the "aporia" of discourse, the indeterminacy and contrariness of language, the "fictive" and "duplicitous" nature of signs and symbols, the dissociation of words from any presumed reality. From Michel Foucault it has adopted the idea of power: the "power structure" immanent not only in language—the words and ideas that "privilege" the "hegemonic" groups in society—but in the very nature of knowledge, which is itself an instrument and product of power. The combined effect of these doctrines is to impugn traditional rational discourse as "logocentric," "phallocentric," "totalizing," "authoritarian."[1]

In literature, postmodernism amounts to a denial of the fixity of any "text," of the authority of the author over the interpreter, of any "canon" that privileges great books over lesser ones. In philosophy, it is a denial of the fixity of language, of any correspondence between language and reality—indeed, of any "essential" reality and thus of any proximate truth about reality. In law (in the United States, at any rate), it is a denial of the fixity of the Constitution, of the authority of the founders of the Constitution, and of the legitimacy of law itself, which is regarded as nothing more than an instrument of power. In history, it is a denial of the fixity of the past, of the reality of the past apart from what the historian chooses to make of it, and thus of any objective truth about the past.

Postmodernist history, one might say, recognizes no reality principle, only the pleasure principle—history at the pleasure of the historian. To appreciate its full import, one should see it in the perspective of what might be called "modernist" history, now generally known as "traditional" history.

Modernist history is not positivist, in the sense of aspiring to a fixed, total, or absolute truth about the past. Like postmodernist history, it is relativistic, but with a difference, for its relativism is firmly rooted in reality. It is skeptical of absolute truth but not of partial, contingent, incremental truths. More important, it does not deny the reality of the past itself. Like the political philosopher who makes it a principle to read the works of the Ancients in the spirit of the Ancients, so the modernist historian reads and writes history in that spirit, with a scrupulous regard for the historicity, the integrity, the actuality of the past. He makes a strenuous effort to enter into the minds and experiences of people in the past, to try to understand them as they understood themselves, to rely upon contemporary evidence as much as possible, to intrude his own views and assumptions as little as possible, to reconstruct to the best of his ability the past as it "actually was," in Leopold von Ranke's celebrated and now much derided phrase.

Like modernist literature and art, modernist history is an exacting discipline, requiring a great exercise of self-restraint, even self-sacrifice. The greatest of modernist poets, T. S. Eliot, once said, "The progress of an artist is a continual self-sacrifice, a continual extinction of personality."[2] And so it is with the historian, who strives constantly to transcend his own present in order to recapture the past, to suppress his own personality in order to give life to generations long dead. This self-sacrifice is all the greater because the historian is well aware that his effort will never entirely succeed, that the past will always, to some degree, elude him.

Historians, ancient and modern, have always known what postmodernism professes to have just discovered—that any work of history is vulnerable on three counts: the fallibility and deficiency of the historical record on which it is based; the fallibility and selectivity inherent in the writing of history; and the fallibility and subjectivity of the historian. As long as historians have reflected upon their craft, they have known that the past cannot be recaptured in its entirety, if only because the remains of the past are incomplete and are themselves part of the present, so that the past itself is, in this sense, irredeemably present. They have also known that the writing of history necessarily entails selection and interpretation, that there is inevitable distortion in the very attempt to present a coherent account of an often inchoate past, that, therefore, every historical work is necessarily imperfect, tentative, and partial (in both senses of the word).

Historians have also known—they would have to be extraordinarily obtuse not to—that they themselves live and act and think in their own present, that some of the assumptions they bring to history derive from, and are peculiar to, their own culture, that others may reflect the particular race, gender, and class to which they belong, and that still others emanate from ideas and beliefs that are unique to themselves as individuals. It did not take Carl Becker, in 1931, to discover that "Everyman [is] his own historian";[3] or Charles Beard, in 1934, to reveal that "each historian who writes history is the product of his age."[4] Beard pointed out that these propositions had been familiar "for a century or more"—thus antedating even Marx. Forty years before Beard delivered his famous presidential address to the American Historical Association, William Sloane, professor of history at Columbia University, inaugurated the first issue of the *American Historical Review* with a lead article announcing: "History will not stay written. Every age demands a history written from its own standpoint—with reference to its own social conditions, its thought, its beliefs and its acquisitions—and thus comprehensible to the men who live in it."[5]

It is useful for historians to be reminded of what they have always known—the frailty, fallibility, and relativity of the historical enterprise—if only to realize that these ideas are not the great discoveries of postmodernism. Yet in their familiar form, they are very different from the tidings brought by postmodernism. For the presumption of postmodernism is that all of history is fatally flawed, and that because there is no absolute, total truth, there can be no partial, contingent truths. More important still is the presumption that because it is impossible to attain such truths, it is not only futile but positively baneful to aspire to them.

In a sense, modernism anticipated and tried to forestall the absolutistic relativism of postmodernism by creating a "discipline" of history. Conscious of the deficiencies both of the historian and of the historical record, acutely aware of the ambiguous relationship between past and present, the profession created a discipline of checks and controls designed to compensate for these deficiencies. This is the meaning of the historical revolution that drew upon such diverse sources as Enlightenment rationalism, Germanic scholarship, and academic professionalism to produce what was once called "critical history."[6]

Critical history puts a premium on archival research and primary sources, the authenticity of documents and the reliability of witnesses, the need to obtain substantiating and countervailing evidence; and, at a more mundane level, the accuracy of quotations and citations, prescribed forms of documentation in footnotes and bibliography, and all the rest of the methodology that goes into the "canon of evidence." The purpose of this methodology is twofold: to bring to the surface the infrastructure, as it were, of the historical work, thus making it accessible to the reader and exposing it to criticism; and to encourage the historian to a maximum exertion of objectivity in spite of all the temptations to the contrary. Postmodernists scoff at this aim as the antiquated remnant of nineteenth-century positivism. But it has been the norm of the profession until recently. "No one," the American historian John Higham wrote, "including the 'literary' historians, rejected the ideal of objectivity in the ordinary sense of unbiased truth; no one gave up the effort to attain it; and no one thought it wholly unapproachable."[7] This was in 1965, well after Becker and Beard had "relativized" history but before Foucault and Derrida had "postmodernized" it.

Here lies the crucial distinction between modernism and postmodernism, between the old relativistic relativism, one might say, and the new absolutistic version. Where modernism tolerates relativism, postmodernism celebrates it. Where modernism regards the obstacles in the way of objectivity as a challenge and makes a strenuous effort to attain as much objectivity and unbiased truth as possible, postmodernism takes the rejection of absolute truth as a deliverance from all truth and from the obligation to maintain any degree of objectivity.

From the postmodernist perspective, modernist history is as uncritical as the history it professes to transcend—as mythical and honorific as Nietzsche's "monumental" history. And it is all the more spurious because it conceals its ideological structure behind a scholarly façade of footnotes and "facts" (in quotation marks, in the postmodernist lexicon). To "demythicize" or "demystify" this history, postmodernism has to expose not only its ideology—the hegemonic, privileged, patriarchal interests served by this history—but also its methodology, the scholarly apparatus that gives it a specious credibility. This is the twofold agenda of postmodernism: to free history from the shackles of an authoritarian ideology, and to release it from the constraints of a delusive methodology. The ultimate aim is even more ambitious: to liberate us all from the coercive ideas of truth and reality.

This is not the familiar kind of historical revisionism that revises or reinterprets a particular account of a particular event or period. It goes well beyond that, for it is profoundly skeptical, even cynical, about all of traditional history—its assumptions and intentions, methods and conclusions. It is not so much a revision of modernist history as a repudiation of it.

Theodore Zeldin was one of the first historians (as distinct from philosophers of history) to launch a serious, sustained assault upon modernist history. That history, he claimed—traditional narrative history—is dependent upon such "tyrannical" concepts as causality, chronology, and collectivity (the latter including class as well as nationality). To liberate history from these constraints, he proposed a new history on the model of a *pointilliste* painting, composed entirely of unconnected dots. This would have the double advantage of emancipating the historian from the tyranny of the discipline, and emancipating the reader from the tyranny of the historian, since the reader would be free to make "what lines he thinks fit for himself."[8] More recently, Zeldin has gone so far by way of liberation as to liberate himself from history itself, this time by invoking a literary model. "Free history," he now finds, can take the form only of fiction[9]—in testimony to which he has written a novel entitled *Happiness.*

Not all postmodernists go as far as Zeldin in seeking that ultimate liberation from history, but all share his aversion to the conventions and categories of traditional history. Following Derrida's strictures against "chronophonism," Dominick LaCapra has deconstructed historical chronology, explaining that even so simple a fact as the date of an event depends on "what is for some historians a belief and for others a convenient fiction: the decisive significance of the birth of Christ in establishing a chronology in terms of a 'before' and 'after.'"[10] The modernist historian might say that the issue is not what some historians happen to believe but what contemporaries at the time believed—an argument unpersuasive to the postmodernist who is as skeptical of the authority of contemporaries as of all other authorities.

Narrative history—"narrativity," as the postmodernist says—is the primary culprit, not only because it depends upon such arbitrary conventions as chronology, causality, and collectivity, but also because it takes the form of a logical, orderly structure of discourse that is presumed to correspond, at least in some measure, to the reality of the past, and thus communicates, again in some measure, a truth about the past. This is the illusion that the postmodernist seeks to expose: that the narratives of history are anything more than the rhetorical, literary, aesthetic creations of the historian.

The aestheticization of history is most evident in the work of the leading postmodernist philosopher of history, Hayden White. To the traditional historian, this kind of philosophy of history appears to be more philosophical than historical and more literary than philosophical. Thus, one of White's essays is titled "The Historical Text as Literary Artifact,"[11] and one of the chapters in his most influential work, *Metahistory,* is called "The Poetics of History." The preface to *Metahistory* explains that each of the subjects, from Hegel to Benedetto Croce, represents a particular aspect of the "historical imagination": metaphor, metonymy, synecdoche, and irony.[12]

For White, as for postmodernists generally, there is no distinction between history and philosophy or between history and literature—or between history and "antihistory," which is why he can describe the psychoanalytic study *Life against Death* as a brilliant work of "antihistory," and then insist that its author, Norman O. Brown, is surely worthy of consideration as a "serious historian."[13] All of history, in this view, is aesthetic and philosophical, its only meaning or "reality" (again, in quotation marks) being that which the historian chooses to give it in accord with his own sensibility and disposition. What the traditional historian sees as an event that actually occurred in the past, the postmodernist sees as a "text" that exists only in the present—a text to be parsed, glossed, construed, and interpreted by the historian, much as a poem or novel is by the critic. And, like any literary text, the historical text is indeterminate and contradictory, paradoxical and ironic, rhetorical, and metaphoric.

In postmodernist history, as in postmodernist literary criticism, theory has become a calling in itself. Just as there are professors of literature who never engage in the actual interpretation of literary works—and even disdain interpretation as an inferior vocation—so there are professors of history who have never (at least to judge by their published work) done research in or written about an actual historical event or period. Their professional careers are devoted to speculation about the theory or philosophy of history—metahistory—and to the active promotion of some particular methodology or ideology of history.

But it is not only metahistorians who reject such naïve notions as reality and truth. More and more practicing historians are beginning to share that attitude, almost unwittingly, reflexively. An essay in the *American Historical Review* casually observes that while "contemporary historians seldom believe anymore that they can or should try to capture 'the truth,'" this does not absolve them from passing judgment on their subjects. In support of this proposition, the author cites an earlier president of the American Historical Association, Gordon Wright, who had given it as his credo that "our search for truth ought to be quite consciously suffused by a commitment to some deeply held humane values."[14] The quotation actually speaks against the thesis of this article, for Wright made that commitment to humane values as part of "our search for truth." But that was in 1975, when it was still possible to speak respectfully of the search for truth—and, indeed, to speak of truth without the ironic use of quotation marks.

Hard cases, it is said, make bad law. History, however, all too often consists of hard cases, and historical methods are designed to accommodate them. For all historians, traditional and "new" alike, the hardest case in modern history is surely the Holocaust. It is especially hard for postmodernists, who face the prospect of doing to the Holocaust what they do to all of history—relativizing, problematizing, ultimately aestheticizing or fictionalizing it. One postmodernist historian, Jane Caplan, raises the problem, only to confess that she cannot resolve it.

> To put it bluntly, what can one usefully say about National Socialism as an ideology or a political movement and regime via theories that appear to discount rationality as a mode of explanation, that resist the claims of truth, relativize and disseminate power, cannot assign responsibility clearly, and do not privilege (one) truth or morality over (multiple) interpretation? . . . It is one thing to embrace poststructuralism and postmodernism, to disseminate power, to decenter subjects, and all in all let a hundred kinds of meaning contend, when *Bleak House* or philology or even the archaeology of knowledge are the issue. But should the rules of contention be different when it is a question, not simply of History, but of a recent history of lives, deaths, and suffering, and the concept of a justice that seeks to draw some meaningful relation between these?[15]

The difficulty is compounded by the existence of a school of thought that relativizes, deprivileges, decenters, indeed, deconstructs the Holocaust so thoroughly as to deny its reality. It is this "revisionist" thesis that postmodernists would like to avoid. But they can do so only by the kind of verbal legerdemain that is their stock-in-trade—and that has created the problem in the first place.

Hayden White poses the dilemma and attempts to solve it. If all historical narratives ("modes of emplotment," in the postmodernist vocabulary) are rhetorical devices, if no one mode can be judged to be more "true" to the "facts" than any other because there are no "facts" from which one may elicit "truths," is there any basis on which to choose among the alternative modes? Can one say, for example, that the comic or pastoral modes are unacceptable as "representations" of the Holocaust? Are there any limits on the kinds of stories that can responsibly be told about the Holocaust? There could be such limits, White reasons, only if one believes that the events themselves possess some inherent "meaning," so that there is some correspondence between the "facts" and the mode of emplotment. But since that is not the case, since the comic and pastoral modes, like any others, are "figurative" rather than "literal," White concludes that there are no limits to the kinds of stories the historian might choose to tell and no grounds on which to reject one or another mode.[16]

Indeed, the comic mode, White points out, has been effectively used in a comic-book version of the Holocaust, in which the Germans are portrayed as cats, the Jews as mice, and the Poles as pigs. Art Spiegelman's *Maus* is a story within a story: the author is trying to extract from his father the story of his parents' experiences as well as that of the Holocaust itself. And both stories are ironic, White says, with all the characters—not only the perpetrators, victims, and bystanders, but the father and son as well—resembling beasts rather than human beings. White himself finds this comic-book version of the Holocaust "one of the most moving narrative accounts" he knows, "not least because it makes the difficulty of discovering and telling the whole truth about even a small part of it as much a part of the story as the events whose meaning it is seeking to discover."[17]

It is typical of the postmodernist to find this account of the Holocaust so moving, "not least" because it makes of the Holocaust as much a metahistorical problem as a historical event—and to be moved, as well, by this ironic (and evenhanded) treatment of the subject, in which everyone looks like a beast. The comic-ironic mode is congenial to the postmodernist because it has the double effect of converting history into metahistory, thus distancing the historian from anything that might resemble truth or reality, and of dehumanizing the subjects of history, thus transforming history from a humanistic discipline into a critique of humanism.

Yet White is eager to differentiate himself from the revisionist historian who, in a more simpleminded and less ironic fashion, denies the truth and reality of the Holocaust. He finds the solution to his dilemma in Derrida's concept of the "middle voice." It is this middle voice, neither passive nor active, that can express "something like the relationship to that event," something like the "reality" of the Holocaust, without falling into the fallacy of "realism." And that voice can express not only the reality of the Holocaust but the entire "new form of historical reality," including "total war, nuclear contamination, mass starvation, and ecological suicide."[18]

This attempt to deconstruct (White never uses that term) the Holocaust without denying it, to affirm something like a "reality" that is not a reality, to make the Holocaust "unique" and at the same time part of a larger phenomenon—all of this, obviously, raises many problems. The historian Martin Jay (himself more a Marxist or historicist than a deconstructionist) takes White to task for compromising his principles: "In his anxiety to avoid inclusion in the ranks of those who argue for a kind of relativistic 'anything goes,' which might provide ammunition for revisionist skeptics about the existence of the Holocaust, he undercuts what is most powerful in his celebrated critique of naive historical realism."[19] Carlo Ginzburg (whose work superficially resembles that of the postmodernist), is distressed not by White's abandoning his principles but by his remaining true to them. He quotes a moving passage from a letter by Pierre Vidal-Naquet, whose mother died at Auschwitz and who had earlier written an essay refuting the arch-revisionist Robert Faurisson. The *affaire Faurisson,* Vidal-Naquet says, convinced him that the old Rankean notion of reality cannot be dismissed and that there is "something irreducible" that, for better or worse, can only be called "reality." "Without this reality," he asks, "how could we make a difference between fiction and history?"[20]

If in the hard case of the Holocaust some postmodernists find it uncomfortable to aestheticize or fictionalize history, they have no such qualms about less sensitive subjects. Committed to the fictive nature of history, liberated from "fact fetishism," uninhibited and unapologetic in the exercise of the "imaginative creation" that is presumed to be of the essence of the historical imagination, postmodernist history may well take the form of fictional history.

This new kind of fictional history is very different from the familiar genre of historical fiction. The historical novel, as it has evolved from Walter Scott to the flourishing industry that it is today, has never been a challenge to traditional history because it has been understood as a distinctive form of fiction, not of history—as historical fiction, not fictional history. Only when history itself is problematized and deconstructed, when events and persons are transformed into texts, when the past is deprived of any reality and history of any truth, does the distinction between history and fiction become blurred or elided. It is then that fictional history becomes a form of history rather than fiction, and that history itself may be seen as "historiographic metafiction."[21] By the same token, biography is said to have embraced a new methodology, a "'freedom' from fact," that makes it "ultimately fiction."[22]

Many historians who shy away from any suggestion of fictional or even "metafictional" history welcome the invitation to be "imaginative," "inventive," "creative"—words bandied about so frequently in the profession today that one almost does not notice them or consider their implication. Yet they have contributed to the widespread tendency, as the late Arnaldo Momigliano observed, to treat history as "another genre of fiction."[23] Where once historians were exhorted to be accurate and factual, they are now urged to be imaginative and inventive. Instead of re-creating the past, they are told to create it; instead of reconstructing history, to construct or deconstruct it. A recent French study of Richelieu asks, only partly tongue-in-cheek, "Did Richelieu—Armand Jean du Plessis—exist? Didn't the narratives invent him?"[24]

Formerly, when historians invoked the idea of imagination, they meant the exercise of imagination required to transcend the present and immerse oneself in the past. This is the genius attributed to the great nineteenth-century historians: "empathy, imagination, the attempt to place oneself in an historic situation and into an historic character without prejudgment."[25] For the postmodernist it means exactly the opposite: the imagination to create a past in the image of the present and in accord with the prejudgment of the present-minded historian.

History, Macaulay said, is a "debatable land" governed by two hostile powers, Reason and Imagination, falling "alternately under the sole and absolute dominion of each." But he then went on to place significant limits on the dominion of the imagination.

> A perfect historian must possess an imagination sufficiently powerful to make his narrative affecting and picturesque. Yet he must control it so absolutely as to content himself with the materials which he finds, and to refrain from supplying deficiencies by additions of his own. He must be a profound and ingenious reasoner. Yet he must possess sufficient self-command to abstain from casting his facts in the mould of his hypothesis.[26]

Later in the essay Macaulay described the "art of historical narration" as the ability to affect the reader's imagination "without indulging in the licence of invention." And he compared the historian to the dramatist, "with one obvious distinction": "The dramatist creates: the historian only disposes."[27] Even Macaulay's great-nephew G. M. Trevelyan, the most "literary" of historians, put the imagination under strict constraints:

> The appeal of history to us all is in the last analysis poetic. But the poetry of history does not consist of imagination roaming at large, but of imagination pursuing the fact and fastening upon it. That which compels the historian to "scorn delights and live laborious days" is the ardour of his own curiosity to know what really happened long ago in that land of mystery which we call the past.[28]

If postmodernism appeals to the creative imagination of the historian, it also appeals to the political imagination. Yet its political implications, like much else about it, are ambiguous. Some radicals criticize it for being so unremitting and negative in its rejection of modernity that it provides no grounds for resistance. "Since it commits you to affirming nothing," says Terry Eagleton (a Marxist and "new historicist"), "it is as injurious as blank ammunition."[29] Jürgen Habermas goes so far as to call Foucault and Derrida "Young Conservatives" because of their "de-centered subjectivity" and "irreconcilable antimodernism."[30] The social critic Michael Walzer criticizes Foucault for not being a "good revolutionary," because Foucault does not believe in the reality of the state or ruling class and therefore cannot believe in the overthrow of the state and of the ruling class; neither is he a good reformer, because he has no "regulative principles with which we might set things right."[31]

Other commentators emphasize the radical and subversive effect of postmodernism in general and of the ideas of Foucault and Derrida in particular. One of Foucault's admirers sees him as "continuing the work of the Western Marxists by other means";[32] another describes his "radical reformism" not as a form of passivity but as a "tactical hyper-activism."[33] Peter Stearns finds in postmodernism the support for non-Marxist forms of radicalism, such as the "currently-fashionable protest ideologies of the academic world"—antiracism, antisexism, environmentalism. "Postmodernists," he observes, "are clearly spurred by a desire to find new intellectual bases for radicalism, given the troubles of liberalism and socialism."[34] Eagleton, having criticized postmodernism for being negative and passive, makes a point of exempting Derrida from these strictures. "Derrida is clearly out to do more than develop new techniques of reading: deconstruction is for him an ultimately *political* practice, an attempt to dismantle the logic by which a particular system of thought, and behind that a whole system of political structures and social institutions, maintains its force."[35]

Postmodernism, as Eagleton suggests, is far more radical than either Marxism or the new modish radical causes, if only because it denies the Enlightenment principles to which they are committed: reason, truth, justice, morality, reality.[36] And in denying the rhetoric and the values of the Enlightenment, it subverts the society and polity that invoke that rhetoric and those values. Thus, in rejecting the "discipline" of knowledge and rationality, postmodernism also rejects the "discipline" of social and political authority. This is the clear implication of Foucault's "Power/Knowledge" thesis, in which knowledge, the "regime of truth," is identified with the political regime of domination and oppression.[37] And it is as clearly implied in Derrida's critique of the modernist tradition—in his description, for example, of "organized narration" as "a matter for the police," a "force of order or law."[38]

The political implications of Hayden White's "metahistory" are no less obvious, although it displays a confusing (but not untypical) combination of deconstruction and Marxism. The Marxism is most conspicuous in his interpretation of traditional history as a reflection of the class interests of the bourgeoisie. White's essay on the German historian Johann Droysen, subtitled "Historical Writing as a Bourgeois Science," describes history (and not only Droysen's history) "as part and parcel of the cultural superstructure of an age, as an activity that is more determined by than determinative of social praxis."[39] Another essay, "The Politics of Historical Interpretation," explains the function of the "discipline" of history: "We do not have to impute dark ideological motives to those who endowed history with the authority of a discipline in order to recognize the ideological benefits to new social classes and political constituencies that professional, academic historiography served and, *mutatis mutandis,* continues to serve down to our own time."[40]

Provoked by the charge that his own form of relativism promotes "the kind of nihilism that invites revolutionary activism of a particularly irresponsible sort," White protests that he is against revolutions, "whether launched from 'above' or 'below' in the social hierarchy." His relativism, he says, is a counsel of tolerance rather than license. Besides, in advanced countries revolution is likely to result in the consolidation of oppressive powers, since those who control the "military-industrial-economic complex hold all the cards." Instead of a political revolution of the traditional kind, he proposes, in effect, a metarevolution, which would replace the "bourgeois ideology of realism," typified by the conventional "discipline" of history, by a view of the past as a spectacle of "confusion," "uncertainty," and "moral anarchy." Only such a "utopian," "eschatological" idea of history, he argues, is consistent with "the kind of politics that is based on a vision of a perfected society."[41]

In the familiar vocabulary of postmodernism, this anarchic, utopian view of history is translated as "indeterminacy." And indeterminacy is inherently radical insofar as it is a standing invitation to *creatio ex nihilo.* Having discredited the bourgeois discipline of history, having deconstructed both the texts of the past and the texts of all previous histories, the historian finds himself with a tabula rasa on which he may inscribe whatever past he likes. Thus the principle of indeterminacy lends itself, paradoxically, to any determinacy at all—to any part or the whole of the race/class/gender trinity, for example. By the same token, it lends itself to any kind of radical ideology the historian may choose to impose on history. (But not to any kind of conservative ideology, which implies a respect for tradition and the givens of the past, and rejects the very idea of a tabula rasa.)

The radical potential of postmodernism has been seized most enthusiastically by feminist historians, who find the old Marxism and even some forms of the new radicalism unresponsive to their concerns. It is no accident (as a Marxist would say) that so many postmodernist historians are feminists, and that postmodernism figures so prominently in feminist history. Joan Wallach Scott explains the political affinity between the two:

> A more radical feminist politics (and a more radical feminist history) seems to me to require a more radical epistemology. Precisely because it addresses questions of epistemology, relativizes the status of all knowledge, links knowledge and power, and theorizes these in terms of the operations of difference, I think poststructuralism (or at least some of the approaches generally associated with Michel Foucault and Jacques Derrida) can offer feminism a powerful analytic perspective.[42]

Feminist history is consciously and implacably opposed not only to traditional history but to earlier varieties of women's history. It belittles the kind of women's history that focuses on the experiences of women in particular events and periods. It even rejects the idea of "mainstreaming" women's history into general history—the "add-women-and-stir recipe," as it is now called.[43] The new feminist history, unlike the old women's history, calls for the rewriting and "reconceptualizing" of all of history from a "consciously feminist stance" or "feminist perspective," so that it may be "seen through the eyes of women and ordered by values they define"[44]—the eyes and values of the feminist historian rather than of the women who are the ostensible subjects of history. And these values, many feminists believe, are inimical not only to the substance of traditional (and traditional women's) history, but also to its methodology and mode of discourse: the logic, reason, and coherence that are themselves expressive of a patriarchal ideology.

It is this repudiation of traditional history that makes postmodernism so congenial to the feminist, and that makes its "radical epistemology," as Scott says, conducive to a radical feminist politics.[45] Just as traditional history is an instrument for patriarchal power, so feminist history is an instrument for feminist power. Some feminists are more candid than others in discussing their political agenda. "We are all engaged," the authors of one essay explain, "in writing a kind of propaganda. Our stories are inspired by what could be called a world view, but what we would call politics." Since there is no objective basis for one story rather than another, the only grounds for judging one better than another are "its persuasiveness, its political utility, and its political sincerity." But the political rationale of feminist history is itself a problem, these feminists point out, for political utility might be best served by concealing or denying the theory upon which this history is based. To "problematize the past, reality, and the truth," as a properly feminist history should, is to write a history that is difficult to read and, therefore, politically inexpedient. It would surely be more persuasive if such a history assumed the "mantle of objectivity" and "mythologized" its own interpretation by presenting it as true. The authors of this essay sympathize with those feminists who resort to this stratagem, but they themselves resist it. A truly radical history, they believe, requires nothing less than a totally demythicized history.[46]

Thus it is that the "poetics" of history becomes the "politics" of history. Postmodernism, even more overtly than Marxism, makes of history—the writing of history as much as the "praxis" of history—an instrument in the struggle for power. The new historian, like the proletariat of old, is the bearer of the class/race/gender war—or, rather, wars. And here lies another quandary.

What is sauce for the goose . . . If the feminist historian can and should write history from her perspective and for her political purposes, why should the black historian not do the same—even if such a history might "marginalize" women? And why not the working-class historian, who might marginalize both women and blacks? (Feminists have criticized E. P. Thompson and other radical historians on just this ground.) And why not the homosexual historian, who might marginalize heterosexuals? For that matter, why not the traditional dead-white-male (or even live-white-male) historian, who might marginalize (who has, in fact, been accused of marginalizing) everyone else?

If "Everyman his own historian" must now be rendered "Everyman/woman his/her own historian"—or, as some feminists would have it, "Everywomyn her own herstorian"—why not "Every black/white/Hispanic/Asian/Native American . . ."? Or "Every Christian/Jew/Catholic/Protestant/Muslim/Hindu/agnostic/atheist . . ."? Or "Every heterosexual/homosexual/bisexual/androgynous/polymorphous/misogynous . . ."? And so on, through all the ethnic, racial, religious, sexual, national, ideological, and other characteristics that distinguish people. This sounds like a *reductio ad absurdum,* but it is little more than is already being affirmed in the name of multiculturalism.

Multiculturalism has the obvious effect of politicizing history. But its more pernicious effect is to demean and dehumanize the people who are the subjects of history. To pluralize and particularize history to the point where people have no history in common is to deny the common humanity of all people, whatever their sex, race, class, religion. It is also to trivialize history by so fragmenting it that it lacks coherence, focus, sense of continuity—and finally meaning.[47]

From a postmodernist perspective, this is all to the good, for it destroys the "totalizing," "universalizing," "logocentric," "phallocentric" history that is said to be the great evil of modernity. Postmodernist history, like postmodernist literary theory, celebrates "aporia"—difference, discontinuity, disparity, contradiction, discord, ambiguity, irony, paradox, perversity, opacity, obscurity, anarchy, chaos. "We require a history," Hayden White explains, "that will educate us to discontinuity more than ever before; for discontinuity, disruption, and chaos is our lot."[48] The modernist accuses the postmodernist of bringing mankind to the abyss of nihilism. The postmodernist proudly, happily accepts that charge.

It may be said that postmodernist history is of little importance in the profession at large, that it is confined to a self-described "vanguard" that has few disciples in theory and fewer still in practice. In sheer numbers, this may be the case, although it is difficult to make such a quantitative calculation. But the question of influence is not determined by numbers, as anyone who has followed the fortunes of Marxism in the academy and in the culture at large is aware; Marxism in the 1930s was far more influential than the number of avowed Marxists would suggest. And so it is with any intellectual or cultural movement. The word "vanguard" itself is deceptive. In its original military meaning, it referred to the advance troops of the army, and the efficacy of the vanguard was assumed to depend on the size and strength of the troops behind it. In its present cultural sense, a vanguard may exist and thrive, and profoundly affect social and cultural values, without any army—with "fellow travelers" in place of troops. It is a long time since anyone has been foolish enough to ask, "How many divisions has the Pope?"

Postmodernism is less prevalent among historians than among literary critics, although there are some who regard it, even in history, as "the orthodoxy of today."[49] But if it is not the dominant orthodoxy, it does exercise a disproportionate influence in the profession, because it tends to attract so many of the best and the brightest, especially among the young. How can clever, ambitious young historians resist the new, especially when it has the sanction of some of their most distinguished elders? How can they resist the appeal to be on the "cutting edge" of their profession, when it carries with it not only the promise of advancement but the allure of creativity, imagination, inventiveness? And not only creativity but liberation from the tedium and rigor of the old discipline of history?

This last is a matter of more than passing importance, in explaining both the attraction of postmodernist history and its influence. Postmodernism, even more than the older varieties of the new history, makes obsolete any course on methodology, because any prescribed methodology is regarded as arbitrary and privileged. The absence of such a course, the lack of any training in what used to be confidently called the "canon of evidence"—even more, the disrespect for any such canon—is itself a fact of considerable importance in the training (or non-training) of young historians. This methodological liberation has done more to transform the profession, making it less of a discipline and more of an impressionistic art, than any conscious conversion to postmodernism. It may, indeed, prove to be the lasting influence of postmodernism.

But what of postmodernism itself? Will it last? Is it just another of those intellectual fashions that periodically seize the imagination of a bored and fickle academia? Whatever happened to existentialism? In France, the source of most of these fashions, deconstruction is already passé. Can it survive much longer here? Given the volatility of intellectual and academic life, it is easy to imagine a not-so-distant future when postmodernism will be succeeded by something proudly calling itself "postpostmodernism."

In history, as in literature and philosophy, there almost certainly will be—the signs are already here—a disaffection with postmodernism, if only because the appeal of novelty will wear off.[50] The "herd of independent minds," in Harold Rosenberg's memorable phrase, will find some other brave new cause to rally around. Out of boredom, careerism (the search for new ways to make a mark in the profession), and sheer bloody-mindedness (the desire to *épater* one's elders), the young will rebel, and the vanguard of today will find itself an aging rear guard—much as the "new history" (social history) of an earlier generation has been displaced by this newer (postmodernist) history. What is not at all clear, however, is the nature and degree of the rebellion—whether it will be a counterrevolution leading to a restoration (or partial restoration) of an older mode of history, or whether it will usher in a still newer mode, the configuration of which we cannot begin to imagine.

One might think that a counterrevolution is already under way in the form of the "new historicism," a linguistic version of Marxism which interprets "cultural productions" as the symbolic forms of material productions. But while some of the members of this school (Frederic Jameson and Terry Eagleton, most notably) criticize postmodernism for being excessively aesthetic and insufficiently revolutionary, they are also attracted to those aspects of it that they recognize as truly subversive. Thus Eagleton praises feminist postmodernism not only for insisting that women have equal power and status with men, but for questioning the legitimacy of all power and status. "It is not that the world will be better off with more female participation in it; it is that without the 'feminization' of human history, the world is unlikely to survive."[51] In the common cause of radicalism, structuralists and poststructuralists, new historicists and deconstructionists, have been able to overlook whatever logical incompatibilities there may be among their theories. (This presents no great problem for deconstructionists, who have an infinite tolerance for contradiction and no regard for "linear" logic.) Like the communists and socialists of an earlier generation, they have formed a popular front, marching separately to a common goal. Thus the new historicism, so far from presenting a real alternative to postmodernism, has become an ally of it, if a somewhat uneasy one. One critic complains of the merger of Marxism and deconstruction, producing the latest oxymoron, "materialist deconstruction."[52]

It is a cliché—and a true one—that no counterrevolution is ever quite that, that the status quo ante is never fully restored. In the case of history, what will stand in the way of a restoration of traditional history is not, as one might think, ideology; one can foresee a desire to return to a more objective and integrated, less divisive and particularistic history. What will be more difficult to restore is the methodology that is at the heart of that history. A generation of historians (or several generations as these are reckoned in academia) lacks any training in that methodology and may even lack the discipline, moral as well as professional, required for it. When Eagleton speaks of the "laid-back" style of postmodernism, he does not mean that it is casual, colloquial, or commonsensical—on the contrary, by normal standards of discourse, it is contrived, abstruse, and recondite—but rather that it renounces all pretense of rational, "enlightened," "linear" discourse.[53] In the case of history, this has meant abandoning not only the conventions regarding the presentation and documentation of evidence, but the very idea of objective evidence, reasoning, coherence, consistency, factuality. The postmodernist argument is that these are the "totalizing," "terroristic" practices of an "authoritarian" discipline.[54] But they are also the hard practices of a difficult discipline. Gresham's law applies in history as surely as in economics: bad habits drive out good; easy methods drive out hard ones. And there is no doubt that the old history, traditional history, *is* hard.

Hard—but exciting precisely because it is hard. And that excitement may prove a challenge and inspiration for a new generation of historians. It is more exciting to write true history (or as true as we can make it) than fictional history, else historians would choose to be novelists rather than historians; more exciting to try to rise above our interests and prejudices than to indulge them; more exciting to try to enter the imagination of those remote from us in time and place than to impose our imagination upon them; more exciting to write a coherent narrative while respecting the complexity of historical events than to fragmentize history into disconnected units; more exciting to try to get the facts as right as we can than to deny the very idea of facts; even more exciting to get the footnotes right, if only to show others the visible proof of our labors.

The American political theorist William Dunning said that one of the happiest days of his life was when he discovered, by a comparison of handwriting, that Andrew Johnson's first message to Congress was actually drafted by George Bancroft. "I don't believe," he wrote to his wife, "you can form any idea of the pleasure it gives me to have discovered this little historical fact."[55] Every serious historian has had this experience—the pleasure of discovering a fact that may appear in the published work in a subordinate clause or footnote, but that, however trivial in itself, validates the entire enterprise, because it is not only new but also true.

Postmodernism entices us with the siren call of liberation and creativity, but it may be an invitation to intellectual and moral suicide. Postmodernists boast that in rejecting metaphysics, they are also delivering themselves from humanism. In his essay "The Ends of Man" (playing upon the two meanings of "ends"), Derrida quotes Heidegger approvingly, "Every humanism is metaphysical," and goes on to explain that metaphysics is "the other name of ontotheology."[56] Similarly, Foucault, in his celebrated account of "the end of man," mocks those who cling to the old humanism.

> To all those who still wish to talk about man, about his reign or his liberation, to all those who still ask themselves questions about what man is in his essence, to all those who wish to take him as their starting-point in their attempts to reach the truth . . . to all these warped and twisted forms of reflection we can answer only with a philosophical laugh—which means, to a certain extent, a silent one.[57]

A corollary of the end of man is the end of history. If the liberation from metaphysics means a liberation from humanism, it also means a liberation from history. Hayden White commends those historians of the nineteenth century who "interpreted the burden of the historian as a moral charge to free men from the burden of history."[58] One may think it bizarre to attribute that intention to Ranke, Macaulay, or Parkman, but one cannot doubt that it is indeed the aim of postmodernism. To free men from the "burden" of history is to free them from the burden of humanity. Liberationist history is not a new and higher form of the discipline; it is the negation of the discipline.

If we have survived the "death of God" and the "death of man," we will surely survive the "death of history"—and of truth, reason, morality, society, reality, and all the other verities we used to take for granted and that have now been problematized and deconstructed. We will even survive the death of postmodernism.

Notes

1. This description of postmodernism by a postmodernist may read like a parody, but it is all too typical of the genre:

   > . . . indeterminacy and immanence; ubiquitous simulacra, pseudo-events; a conscious lack of mastery, lightness and evanescence everywhere; a new temporality, or rather intemporality; a polychronic sense of history: a patchwork or ludic, transgressive or deconstructive approach to knowledge and authority; an ironic, parodic, reflexive, fantastic awareness of the moment; a linguistic turn, semiotic imperative in culture; and in society generally the violence of local desires diffused into a terminology of seduction and force.

   From Ihab Hassan, *The Postmodern Turn: Essays in Postmodern Theory and Culture,* quoted, not ironically, by Gabrielle M. Spiegel, "History and Post-Modernism," *Past and Present,* May 1992, 194 n. 3.
2. T. S. Eliot, "Tradition and the Individual Talent" (1917), in *Selected Essays 1917–1932* (New York: Faber and Faber, 1932), 7.
3. This is the title of Becker's book published that year. Twenty years earlier, Becker had made much the same point in an article in *The Atlantic Monthly.*
4. J. H. Hexter, *On Historians* (Cambridge, Mass.: Harvard University Press, 1979), 16–17.
5. Hexter, *On Historians,* 18–19.
6. This is very different from Nietzsche's sense of "critical" history—a history in the "service of life," in contrast to "monumental" history, which celebrates a mythical past, and "antiquarian" history, which is pure pedantry. It is also different from the recent usage of "critical," as in "critical legal theory," which is a cross between deconstruction and Marxism. The original sense of "critical history" is exactly the opposite—an attempt to be as rigorous, accurate, objective, and scholarly as possible.
7. John Higham, *History* (Englewood, N.J.: Prentice Hall, 1965), 90.
8. Theodore Zeldin, "Social History and Total History," *Journal of Social History,* 1976, 10: 242–44. An art historian finds the same "democratizing purpose" in the original *pointilliste,* Georges Seurat, who is said to have tried to create an art that would be "a sort of democratically oriented, hightype painting-by-dots which would totally wipe out the role of genius, the exceptional creative figure, in the making of art, even 'great art'" (Linda

Nochlin, *The Politics of Vision: Essays on Nineteenth-Century Art and Society* [New York: Harper and Row, 1989] 182.

9. Theodore Zeldin, *London Review of Books,* September 1, 1988.
10. Dominick LaCapra, "Rethinking Intellectual History and Reading Texts," in *Modern European Intellectual History: Reappraisals and New Perspectives,* edited by LaCapra and Steven L. Kaplan (Ithaca, N.Y.: Cornell University Press, 1982), 78. By this reasoning, a Jewish historian would be justified in giving the date of the fall of the Bastille as the 20th of Tammuz 5549—which is accurate but, the traditional historian would say, irrelevant and profoundly unhistorical.
11. Hayden White, *Tropics of Discourse: Essays in Cultural Criticism* (Baltimore: Johns Hopkins University Press, 1978), 81 ff.
12. Hayden White, *Metahistory: The Historical Imagination in Nineteenth-Century Europe* (Baltimore: Johns Hopkins University Press, 1973), 9–10. White did not coin the term *metahistory,* but he gave it its present connotation and is responsible for its widespread usage. It had earlier been used in the sense of mythical history rather than the philosophy or theory of history.
13. Hayden White, "The Burden of History," *History and Theory,* 1966, 5:129; reprinted in *Tropics of Discourse,* 45.
14. Michael Kazin, "The Grass-Roots Right: New Histories of U.S. Conservatism in the Twentieth Century," *American Historical Review,* 1992, 97:155. (The quotation about "humane values" is from Gordon Wright's presidential address, *American Historical Review,* 1976, 81.)
15. Jane Caplan, "Postmodernism, Poststructuralism, and Deconstruction: Notes for Historians," *Central European History,* September/December 1989, 274, 278.
16. Hayden White, "Historical Emplotment and the Problem of Truth," in *Probing the Limits of Representation: Nazism and the "Final Solution,"* edited by Saul Friedlander (Cambridge, Mass.: Harvard University Press, 1992), 37 ff.
17. White, *Historical Emplotment,* 41.
18. White, *Historical Emplotment,* 51–52.
19. Martin Jay, "Of Plots, Witnesses, and Judgments," in *Probing the Limits,* 97.
20. Carlo Ginzburg, "Just One Witness," in *Probing the Limits,* 86. On postmodernism and the Holocaust, see also James E. Young, *Writing and Rewriting the Holocaust: Narrative and the Consequences of Interpretation* (Bloomington, Ind.: Indiana University Press, 1988); David H. Hirsch, *The Deconstruction of Literature: Criticism after Auschwitz* (Hanover, N.H.: Brown University Press, 1991).
21. Linda Hutcheon, "The Postmodern Problematizing of History," *English Studies in Canada,* December 1988, 371 and *passim* (reprinted in *A Poetics of Postmodernism: History, Theory, Fiction* [New York: Routledge, 1988]).
22. Ira Bruce Nadel, *Biography: Fiction, Fact and Form* (New York: Saint Martin's Press, 1984), 77–78. See also David Lodge, review of a biography of D. H. Lawrence, *New York Review of Books,* February 13, 1992, and Lodge's letter, *New York Review of Books,* April 9, 1992, 56, for his own rather tortuous endorsement of this view.
23. Arnaldo Momigliano, "Biblical Studies and Classical Studies: Simple Reflections upon Historical Method" (1981), in *On Pagans, Jews, and Christians* (Middletown, Conn.: Wesleyan University Press, 1987), 5.
24. Quoted by David Bell, "Fallen Idols," *London Review of Books,* July 23, 1992, 13.
25. J. H. Plumb, *The Death of the Past* (Boston: Houghton Mifflin, 1970), 135.
26. Thomas Babington Macaulay, "History" (1828), *Works,* edited by Lady Trevelyan (London, 1875), 5: 122–23.
27. Macaulay, "History," 131, 144.

28. Quoted by J. H. Plumb, *The Making of an Historian, Collected Essays* (Athens: University of Georgia Press, 1988), 1: 183.
29. Terry Eagleton, *Literary Theory: An Introduction* (Minneapolis: University of Minnesota Press, 1983), 145. Another Marxist, Frederic Jameson, complains that Foucault paralyzes "the impulses of negation and revolt" (quoted by David Couzens Hoy, ed., *Foucault: A Critical Reader* [Oxford: Blackwell, 1986], 11).
30. Jürgen Habermas, "Modernity Versus Postmodernity," *New German Critique,* winter 1981, 13. Some sources have Habermas identifying these postmodernists as "Neoconservatives" (e.g., David Couzens Hoy, "Jacques Derrida," in *The Return of Grand Theory in the Human Sciences,* edited by Quentin Skinner [Cambridge: Cambridgeshire, 1985], 61; Lawrence D. Kritzman, ed., Michel Foucault, *Politics, Philosophy, Culture: Interviews and Other Writings 1977–1984* [New York: Routledge, 1988], xi). But he explicitly (and in italics) calls them "Young Conservatives" in contrast to the "Neoconservatives" who accept some of the agenda of modernity—most notably, science and capitalist growth. See also Habermas, "Taking Aim at the Heart of the Present," in *Foucault: A Critical Reader,* 103–8; and the comments on this essay by Hubert L. Dreyfus and Paul Rabinow, "What Is Maturity? Habermas and Foucault on 'What Is Enlightenment?,'" in *Foucault: A Critical Reader,* 109–21.
31. Michael Walzer, "The Politics of Michel Foucault," in *Foucault: A Critical Reader,* 55, 67.
32. Mark Poster, *Foucault, Marxism and History: Mode of Production Versus Mode of Information* (Cambridge: Polity Press, 1984), 40.
33. A. Keith Gandal, "Michel Foucault: Intellectual Work and Politics," *Telos,* spring 1986, 122. See also Rebecca Comay, "Excavating the Repressive Hypothesis," in the same issue of *Telos;* Derek D. Nikolinakos, "Foucault's Ethical Quandary," *Telos,* spring 1990; Russell A. Berman, "Troping to Pretoria: The Rise and Fall of Deconstruction," *Telos,* fall 1990.
34. Peter N. Stearns, "Social History Update: Encountering Postmodernism," *Journal of Social History,* 1990, 449. For a more extended discussion of the politics of postmodernism, see Peter Shaw, "The Politics of Deconstruction," in *The War Against the Intellect: Episodes in the Decline of Discourse* (Iowa City: University of Iowa Press, 1989); Catherine Zuckert, "The Politics of Derridean Deconstruction," *Polity,* spring 1991; Jonathan Arar, ed., *Postmodernism and Politics* (Minneapolis: University of Minnesota Press, 1986).
35. Terry Eagleton, *Literary Theory,* 148. (Italics in the original.)
36. Foucault's last essay, published posthumously, is a labored attempt to reinterpret Kant's "What Is Enlightenment?" so that his own philosophy might appear to be less irreconcilably opposed to the Enlightenment. But the essay does justice neither to Kant nor to himself (*The Foucault Reader,* edited by Paul Rabinow [New York: Pantheon Books, 1984], 32–50).
37. Michel Foucault, *Power/Knowledge,* edited by C. Gordon (New York: Pantheon Books, 1981), 131.
38. Jacques Derrida, "Living On," *Deconstruction and Criticism,* edited by Harold Bloom, et al. (New York: Continuum, 1990, [1st ed., 1979]), 104–5.
39. Hayden White, *The Content of the Form* (Baltimore: Johns Hopkins University Press, 1987), 101.
40. White, *Content,* 60–61.
41. White, *Content,* 63, 72, 81, 227 n. 12.
42. Joan Wallach Scott, *Gender and the Politics of History* (Ithaca, N.Y.: Cornell University Press, 1988), 4.
43. Peter Novick, *That Noble Dream The "Objectivity Question" and the American Historical Profession* (New York: Cambridge University Press, 1988), 496.

44. Joan B. Landes, *Women and the Public Sphere in the Age of the French Revolution* (Ithaca, N.Y.: Cornell University Press, 1988), 1–2; Scott, *Gender,* 3, 6; Bonnie S. Anderson and Judith P. Zinsser, *A History of Their Own: Women in Europe from Prehistory to the Present* (New York: Harper and Row, 1988), xviii. See also Philippa Levine, "When Method Matters: Women Historians, Feminist Historians," *Journal of British Studies,* October 1991. Peter Novick claims that by the late 1970s the idea that history could legitimately be written from a feminist perspective "was no longer being argued; it was a settled question, beyond argument" (496).
45. Yet even this radical epistemology is not always radical enough. It is an embarrassment to feminists, for example, that Foucault, having exposed the fallacy of "sexual essentialism," persists in using traditional masculine language and rarely cites works by women. (Irene Diamond and Lee Quinby, *Feminism and Foucault: Reflections on Resistance* [Boston: Northeastern University Press, 1988] xv–xvi). One commentator (a man, as it happens) apologizes for retaining in his translations Foucault's "relentlessly masculine forms" of pronouns, and his use of "homme" to mean "humanity" (James Miller, *The Passion of Michel Foucault* [New York: Simon and Schuster, 1993], 389).
46. Ellen Somekawa and Elizabeth A. Smith, "Theorizing the Writing of History or, 'I Can't Think Why It Should Be So Dull, for a Great Deal of It Must Be Invention,'" *Journal of Social History,* 1988, 22: 154–60. (The title of this essay is taken from a remark by a character in Jane Austen's *Northanger Abbey.* Edward Carr used it as the epigraph of *What Is History?* [New York: Vintage Books, 1961].)
47. For recent statements by "new" as well as traditional historians deploring the "Balkanization" of history, see Gertrude Himmelfarb, "Some Reflections on the New History," *American Historical Review,* 1989, 94: 663–64. Official recent proposals for a multicultural curriculum in the schools have stimulated the same fears. See, for example, Arthur M. Schlesinger, Jr., *The Disuniting of America* (New York: Norton, 1992).
48. Hayden White, *Tropics of Discourse,* 50.
49. Lionel Gossman, *Between History and Literature* (Cambridge, Mass.: Harvard University Press, 1990), 289.
50. Lionel Gossman, for example, says that he once welcomed postmodernist history as a "salutary release from the smug certainties of historical positivism," but has come to believe that it promotes a "facile and irresponsible relativism" (*Between History and Literature,* 303). See also Joyce Appleby, "One Good Turn Deserves Another: Moving Beyond the Linguistic: A Response to David Harlan," *American Historical Review,* 1989, 94: 1326–32.

    Lawrence Stone exaggerates the movement away from postmodernism when he asserts, first, that "it seems as if at least some of the leaders of the 'linguistic turn' are backing away from this radical elimination of the reality principle," and then concludes that "nearly everyone, except perhaps Schama, seems to be retreating from this position." ("History and Post-Modernism," *Past and Present,* May 1992, 192–93). There is a large gap between "at least some" to "nearly everyone." One recalls Stone's earlier prediction of a "revival of narrative," based on such works as Le Roy Ladurie's *Montaillou,* Eric Hobsbawm's *Primitive Rebels,* and E. P. Thompson's *Whigs and Hunters*—none of which is anything like traditional narrative history. That prediction was shortly belied by the postmodernist "linguistic turn," which is even more antithetical to narrative history than the earlier mode of social history.
51. Terry Eagleton, *Literary Theory,* 150. For different views of the relationship of postmodernism to the new historicism, see "Patrolling the Borders: Feminist Historiography and the New Historicism," *Radical History Review,* January 1989; H. Aram Veeser, ed., *The New Historicism* (New York: Routledge, 1989); Brook Thomas, *The New Historicism*

and Other Old-fashioned Topics (Princeton: Princeton University Press, 1991); Frederic Jameson, *Postmodernism: Or, the Cultural Logic of Late Capitalism* (Durham, N.C.: Duke University Press, 1991).

52. Howard Felperin, *Beyond Deconstruction: The Uses and Abuses of Literary Theory* (Oxford: Oxfordshire, 1985), 72.
53. Terry Eagleton, "Awakening from Modernity," *Times Literary Supplement,* February 20, 1987, 194.
54. It is curious to find Foucault and Derrida trading these charges against each other. Derrida accuses Foucault of a "logocentrism" and "structuralist totalitarianism . . . similar to the violences of the classical age." (Jacques Derrida, "Cogito and the History of Madness," in *Writing and Difference* [Chicago: University of Chicago Press, 1978], 57). Foucault, in turn, charges Derrida with exercising a "limitless sovereignty" over the text, permitting him to "restate" it "indefinitely." (Miller, *Passion of Foucault,* 121 quoting Foucault, *Histoire de la folie à l'âge classique* [Paris: Librairie Gallimard, 1972], 603). On another occasion Foucault describes Derrida's rhetoric as "obscurantisme terroriste." He writes so obscurely, Foucault complains, that one cannot figure out exactly what he is saying, and then, when one criticizes it, he replies, "You don't understand, you are an idiot." (John R. Searle, "The Word Turned Upside Down," *New York Review of Books,* October 27, 1983, 77.
55. John Higham, *History,* 103.
56. Jacques Derrida, "The Ends of Man," in *Margins of Philosophy* (Chicago: Harvester Press, 1982), 116.
57. Michel Foucault, *The Order of Things: An Archaeology of the Human Sciences* (New York: Pantheon Books, 1973 [1st French ed., 1966]), 342–43. White's chapter on Foucault is entitled "Foucault's Discourse: The Historiography of Anti-Humanism" (*Content of the Form,* 104 ff).
58. Hayden White, "The Burden of History," 133 (*Tropics of Discourse,* 49). For critiques of this essay, see Arnaldo Momigliano, "The Rhetoric of History and the History of Rhetoric: On Hayden White's Tropes," *Comparative Criticism: A Yearbook,* 1981, 259–68; G. R. Elton, *Return to Essentials: Some Reflections on the Present State of Historical Study* (Cambridge: Cambridge University Press, 1991), 27–49.

CHAPTER 9

A NEW INTELLECTUAL HISTORY?

Russell Jacoby

GENERALIZATIONS ABOUT SCHOLARLY disciplines require audacity. Abundant materials and findings of even small fields undermine, if not refute, generalizations. Who can keep up? In 1987 alone, scholars published 215 articles on John Milton, 132 on Henry James, and 554 on William Shakespeare.[1] "The sheer bulk of material being published," remarked Robert Markley, editor of the journal *The Eighteenth Century,* "means that it is almost physically impossible to read as fast as new readings are mass-produced."[2] Statements about "the" direction of Burke or Shakespeare studies inevitably seem misleading or wrong; several, perhaps scores, of specialists contradict a summary of the field.

Intellectual history is no different. Generalizations about its direction or contours seem arbitrary. Although small, the field seems too large to permit valid statements about its direction. Is there a turn toward rhetorical studies? A revival of contextual approaches to great figures? A shift to popular ideas of social groups? These questions seem to sabotage clear answers. The matter always seems to depend on who is looking where.

For teachers, especially in graduate programs, at least one honorable reason justifies the very slippery effort to reflect on a field: the need to educate others (and self).[3] In addition, a unique reason spurs reflections on intellectual history: a nagging sense of decline.[4] To prove convincingly a decay of intellectual history is probably impossible—and unnecessary. It suffices to note that for some years social history attracted younger scholars and more

Originally published in the *American Historical Review,* April 1992.

attention. Intellectual historians were, or felt, neglected and excluded. Dominick LaCapra complained that intellectual history has been "relatively marginal to the discipline of history."[5] Referring to the "monumental bromide" that history has "many mansions," he declared in the mid-1980s that "today social history tends to occupy many of the mansions and intellectual history a number of the shacks."[6] This perception—true or false—has inspired many articles about the "crisis" of intellectual history.[7]

Inasmuch as it forced intellectual historians to reconsider their identities—are they social historians *manqués* or something else?—the decline harbored an advance. "With a mixture of trepidation and excitement," Martin Jay observes, intellectual historians have joined "the maelstrom of theoretical disputation that now characterizes the humanities as a whole."[8] John E. Toews remarks on a "a new self-confidence" and a new common orientation among intellectual historians; they accept "semiological theory in which language is conceived of as a self-contained system of 'signs.'"[9] Michael Ermarth concurs. "There are now compelling reasons to speak definitely of 'old' and 'new' styles of European intellectual history." We are "in the midst of a shift in 'episteme.'"[10]

Among the historians who have spearheaded the rethinking of intellectual history, perhaps the most committed is Hayden White. "No one writing in this country at the present time," Dominick LaCapra has stated, "has done more to wake historians from their dogmatic slumber than has Hayden White . . . One might, without undue hyperbole, say that White's writings have helped to reopen the possibility of thought in intellectual history."[11] Allan Megill has judged White's *Metahistory* as "clearly the most important work" in its field "published in the last generation."[12]

A continuity marks Hayden White's work. He has always grappled with the venerable issue of the specificity of history.[13] His earlier contributions explored the relationship of history and science. He translated (and co-translated) two books on this topic, *From History to Sociology* (1959) by the Italian Crocean, Carlo Antoni; and *Human Sciences and Philosophy* (1969) by the French Marxist, Lucien Goldmann. Against the claims of the positive sciences, both books defended the uniqueness (and superiority) of history.

With chapters on Wilhelm Dilthey, Ernst Troeltsch, Friedrich Meinecke, and Max Weber, Antoni argued that German thought "declined" from historicism to sociologism; invariant categories surrendered the flux and change of history.[14] Antoni faulted Dilthey for substituting a vacant typology in which "the types are always the same" for a "concept of becoming." Weber's sociology expressed "an epoch which has ceased to believe in history and has banished ideas of development, unfolding and progress to a place among the myths of optimism." Antoni concluded his discussion of Dilthey this way:

> Once the real movement and novelty of history were denied, it was inevitable that history be transformed into typology and sociology . . . Dilthey in his uncertainty, oscillation and desperation foreshadowed a crisis . . . In the throes of that crisis, the German intellectual world turned to the interpretation of history and life in a skeptical and relativistic mood.[15]

In a translator's introduction, White echoed these fairly desperate words as he outlined three forms of historicism. One dissolves history into the natural sciences; another unifies history and science by timeless metaphysical principles. In negating human responsibility and freedom, these historicisms were determinist and "vicious." However, a third form, what he called "aesthetic historicism," won White's sympathies. Affirming "man's freedom and individual creativity," this historicism assumed that "a true vision of history must begin . . . with the subject, the historian living in the present." It "went too far," White added, "abandoning reason completely."[16] But White's discussion remained vague, since individual historians went virtually unnamed. Dramatically (and elusively), he charged that all these historicisms expressed "partial views and thus unhealthy views, and this unhealthiness was manifested in the violence and anarchy that they spawned or justified."[17]

White's subsequent writings remain loyal to the fundamental ideas of Antoni or Goldmann.[18] He defends historical knowledge as exceptional, and he resists subordinating history to science. Within this continuity, however, White's idiom and position have shifted. This can be put in two different ways; either he classifies history as a literary endeavor or he considers all the humanities essentially literary. He chips away at the uniqueness of history in order to accent its links to literature and literary criticism. This means that the stuff of literature—subjectivity, language, and rhetoric—is the stuff of history.

Two essays from the later 1960s, "The Burden of History" (1966) and "The Tasks of Intellectual History" (1969), might be regarded as White's prolegomenon to a new intellectual history; his tentative and earlier formulations became confident, even militant. In the first, he set forth the problem: for over a century, historians have defended themselves from scientists who derided their discipline as vague and subjective. The historians replied that history was not an exact science like physics, but "a kind of art." Yet when reproached by literary artists for failure to appropriate literary modes, the historians backtrack, claiming their field is a science, and "historical data do not lend themselves to 'free' artistic manipulation."[19]

For White, this position no longer satisfies. It irritates both scientists and artists, and it insulates historians from the latest artistic and scientific developments. In short, history's mediating position between science and art is obsolete. The conclusion? Historians must embrace modern art and literature, and to some extent modern science. When historians defend the "art" of history, however, they usually envision nineteenth-century realism. They remain fixated on "antiquated notions" and "outmoded conceptions of objectivity." Modern art has long surrendered the pretense of realism and objectivity. Historians must do the same. [20]

This entails realizing that historical "explanation" is not exhausted by the "category of literally truthful," but can be judged by the "richness of the metaphors." "Methodological and stylistic cosmopolitanism" necessitates understanding that "there is no such thing as a *single* correct view of any object under study, but that there are *many* correct views, each requiring its own style of representation." Recognizing facts is "the problem that the historian, like the artist, has tried to solve in the choice of the metaphor." While White alludes to the problem of "radical relativism," he believes this program will allow historians to rejoin the artistic and intellectual dialogue of our time.[21]

"The Tasks of Intellectual History" signalled a more politically radical White, dissatisfied with "the pessimistic and accommodationist tone of intellectual historiography." Nietzschean and Marxist tones permeate this essay. "Intellectual history is rather like vicarious sex: neither satisfying nor, ultimately, very helpful as a guide to action . . . intellectual history substitutes for the color of the market place, the battlefield, and the parliament, the odor of the study, the library, and the academic hall." He bemoaned that the historical profession saddled intellectual history with conventional methods; when intellectual historians advance new perspectives they must buck *"the essentially antitheoretical bias that prevails in the profession at large."*[22]

White's *Metahistory* (1973) presented the ideas he developed over the previous six years.[23] All history contains a "deep" verbal structure; this structure or metahistorical element shapes the histories. Exactly how White proceeds to analyze this structure is complicated and at times byzantine. For instance, he finds sixty-four varieties of historical writing, but the main argument is sufficiently clear.[24] All history is inextricably poetic and linguistic; it interprets and molds facts more than discovering or finding them. For this reason, histories can be approached as literature and analyzed using tropes of poetic language (metaphor, metonymy, snynecdoche, and irony). This means, among other things, that no single history is more "realistic" than another. "The best grounds for choosing one perspective on history rather than another are ultimately aesthetic or moral."[25]

In his essays from the mid-1970s, White elaborated on these ideas, championing a method underlining language, style, metaphor, and rhetorical strategies. "There has been a reluctance," White wrote in "Historical Text as

Literary Artifact" (1974) "to consider historical narratives as what they most manifestly are: verbal fictions, the contents of which are as much *invented* as *found* and the forms of which have more in common with their counterparts in literature than they have with those in the sciences."[26]

While White does not dismiss the "found" or factual dimension of history, he directs our attention to that formed or imagined by the historian. In a brief analysis White argues that E. P. Thompson's *The Making of the English Working Class* is a contrived work; Thompson "makes" the English working class by consciously or unconsciously utilizing a basic tropic model in which "groups actually pass in a finite movement from a naïve to an ironic condition in their evolution." White has "lingered" on the "tropological unpacking of the structure of Thompson's discourse" because Thompson "claims" to be studying "concrete historical reality." [27]

White's contribution harbors many virtues. He forces historians to rethink their relationship to literature and style. "History as a discipline is in bad shape today," he writes, "because it has lost sight of its origins in the literary imagination. In the interest of *appearing* scientific and objective, it has repressed and denied to itself its own greatest source of strength and renewal."[28] White insists that rhetorical choices saturate the historical project; all facts and accounts are already interpretations and decisions. His works compel historians to attend to their initial and fundamental preconceptions. This is all to the good.

His contribution, however, also tilts toward relativism and, perhaps more seriously, toward formalism. White almost bites the relativistic bullet. Historical material does not dictate anything; the historian selects and interprets.

> Historical situations do not have built into them intrinsic meanings . . . Historical situations are not *inherently* tragic, comic or romantic. All the historian needs to do to transform a tragic into a comic situation is to shift his point of view . . . *How* a given historical situation is to be configured depends on the historian's subtlety in matching up a specific plot structure with the set of historical events that he wishes to endow with a meaning of a particular kind. . . . This is essentially a literary, that is to say fiction-making, operation.[29]

The problem is evident. Inasmuch as intrinsic meaning is depreciated, the historian's discourse is elevated: the key is how he or she "emplots" material. The stuff of history can be plotted in numerous ways, dependent on skill. Does this mean that all histories are equally true and false? These objections are familiar to White. "I have never denied that knowledge of history, culture, and society was possible; I have only denied that a scientific knowledge, of the sort actually attained in the study of physical nature, was possible."[30] Or he writes that he acknowledges "historical events" differ from "fictional events." Yet what interests him are "the fictions of factual representation"—the way history and fiction "overlap, resemble or correspond with each other."[31]

Even as he seeks to avoid slipping into complete relativism, White comes exceedingly close. His essay "The Politics of Historical Interpretation" (1982) addresses the professionalization of history, which for White entails the "repression" of history's utopian, imaginary, and sublime moments. "Imagination is disciplined by its subordination to the rules of evidence." Conservatives, radicals, and Marxists rejected a "visionary politics" developed by romantic and marginal thinkers—Jules Michelet, Friedrich Schiller, Friedrich Nietzsche—and by fascists.

> We must guard against a sentimentalism that would lead us to write off such a conception of history simply because it has been associated with fascist ideologies. One must face the fact that when it comes to apprehending the historical record, there are no grounds to be found in the historical record itself for preferring one way of construing its meaning over another.[32]

White digs a hole for himself and strains to climb out—unsuccessfully to Carlo Ginzburg, who almost indicts White for succumbing to a Gentilean subjectivism and fascism.[33] Though politically the most explosive issue, relativism hardly exhausts the problems with White's *oeuvre;* moreover, it might divert attention from weaknesses more germane to intellectual history—White's formalism.

His formalism is explicit. White occasionally refers to himself as a "formalist": "My method, in short, is formalist."[34] The implications are not spelled out, however. "The tropological theory of discourse," states White, "could provide us with a way of classifying different kinds of discourses by reference to the linguistic modes that predominate in them rather than by reference to supposed 'contents' which are always identified differently by different interpreters."[35] The promise here is clear: abandon the "contents" (in quotes since they cannot really be established) for the linguistic structure. The problem is also clear: critical scrutiny and evaluation turn into categorizing. In looking at historical work, the questions become how do we classify it? What are its principal tropes? [36]

The relationship of categorizing to wider knowledge cannot be discussed in a brief compass, and probably no extended discussion suffices inasmuch as this relationship varies by the field of knowledge. For the humanities, categorizing tends to be insufficient, if not inadequate and superficial; it remains external, appraising structure and types. It smacks of a static nonhistorical approach. It becomes formalistic.[37] White once knew this, having criticized Arthur O. Lovejoy and Ernst Cassirer for this failing: "Their organizational principles are uniformly typological . . . on the whole they avoided the problem of intellectual historical dynamics. They tended to view the history of consciousness as an intra-mural or domestic affair within consciousness itself."[38] Now White himself seems to do this. He writes:

> A semiological approach to the study of texts permits us to moot the question of the text's reliability as witness to events or phenomena extrinsic to it, to pass over the question of the text's "honesty," its objectivity. . . . This is to shift hermeneutic interest from the content of the texts being investigated to their formal properties.[39]

A fundamental irony colors White's formalism; his *oeuvre* develops out of a tradition underscoring the uniqueness of the humanities (and history). He consistently rejects as misguided efforts to imitate scientific neutrality and objectivity. Yet he bills his formalism as more objective, almost more scientific, than approaches that evaluate contents and contexts. Indeed, he seems to dismiss these as impressionistic and subjective. The literary intellectual historian revels in the superiority of a hardnosed formal and structural method. "The utility" of the semiological analysis, White proclaims, "is to be assessed solely in terms of quantitative criterion, namely, its capacity to account for more of the elements of any given text, of whatever length, than any contending 'content'-orientated method could match."[40] He offers an inspection of *The Education of Henry Adams* as an example of his method.

In this space it is possible to comment only on one aspect of White's analysis: his own rhetoric. He assumes the idiom of the cool scientist scoffing at the emotionalism of the artist. He first dissects a 1961 preface to the book by D. W. Brogan, which seems to White completely "impressionistic and unsystematic. . . . It provides absolutely no criterion for assessing the validity of the various generalizations." Brogan's approach is completely unsuitable "as a model of analysis." It seems totally "arbitrary," based on "personal taste, inclination or ideological commitment." Against this intuitive and subjective commentary, White offers a "semiological perspective" that "can provide a theoretically grounded reading of this text, which would give an account for every element of it."[41]

Here, as elsewhere, White sounds like the analytic logician who can finally dispense with cloudy speculations of poet philosophers. The aim of a complete study of *The Education of Henry Adams* would be "to characterize the types of messages emitted in terms of the several codes in which they are cast and to map the relationships among the codes thus identified both as a hierarchy of codes and a sequence of their elaboration."[42] White's introduction to *Metahistory* is titled "The Poetics of History." But this is the language—and cadence—of aggressive science.[43] White's rebellion against positivism ends in a scientific formalism.

White has not been alone in his effort to reorient intellectual history; by his energy and productivity Dominick LaCapra has joined, and perhaps surpassed him. In broadest terms, their contributions run parallel: they both have sought to rescue history (and intellectual historians) from a certain unconsciousness; they have forcefully drawn attention to the problems of language and text; and they both want to push intellectual history in a literary direction.[44] Again, it is difficult to fault the project. Few can object to rethinking assumptions about intellectual history.

If kindred in approach, much separates LaCapra from White. Unlike White, he emphatically identifies with the field of intellectual history and worries about its health. Beginning with his second book, LaCapra's work directly or indirectly broaches questions of the methods and parameters of intellectual history. His book on Jean-Paul Sartre (1978) opens with a discussion of intellectual history.[45] A collection ten years later (1989) closes with an essay, "Intellectual History and Critical Theory."[46]

LaCapra is more pugnacious than White. "I have long felt that the annual convention of the American Historical Association (AHA) is second only to that of morticians in the liveliness of its addresses and interchanges. A little controversy might . . . be welcomed."[47] LaCapra enjoys intellectual strife. In an essay, he defends "the provocative role of hyperbole."[48] In addition, he tackles subjects that seem especially unsuited for his method: LaCapra admits that Jean-Paul Sartre has "explicitly rejected a theory of the text" that he employs.[49]

LaCapra also is less systematic than White, and for that reason is sometimes difficult to follow. This is not a statement about personal style, but theoretical orientation. Despite their many similarities, White and LaCapra appeal to different traditions. Both reject a naïve, common sense approach to history; both underscore the linguistic strategies of historical texts. Yet in conceptualizing these strategies, White looks to the formalism of Northrop Frye, LaCapra to the deconstructionism of Jacques Derrida.[50] Like Frye, who always had an "obsession with form,"[51] White prizes the patterns he believes structure texts. And like Derrida, LaCapra challenges systems that he judges float above a text. Derrida's "oft-quoted maxim *'il n'y a pas de hors-texte'* [there is no outside-the-text] is not a charter for formalism," LaCapra writes. "It is a critique of the attempt to ground the work and play of textuality in some extratextual foundation."[52]

On this issue, LaCapra criticizes White. While unstinting in his praise, he protests that White remains committed to the passive "historical record" and an "idealistic mythology." He fails to appreciate Derrida. For LaCapra, texts and language in White seem too traditional; White avoids the "problem of interplay between structure and play in the text and one's relation to it"; he misses "the tense interplay among elements in the language of the text."[53]

This is a persistent note in LaCapra, almost an antidogmatic dogma. Time and again he insists on the complexities, ambiguities, and tensions of "the text." For instance, in *A Preface to Sartre,* he complains that "ambiguity is domesticated and controlled [in Sartre] by its insertion into the totalizing human project." LaCapra objects that "what is almost invariably left in the dark or repressed by Sartre is the intercourse between structure and play in his own use of language." His criticism of Sartre appeals to what LaCapra calls Derrida's "'minimal' program" that posits "the contest and contestation between structure and play." For this approach, Sartre's life can be ignored, since it offers few clues to his thought. "Sartre remains too much the same and does not change enough—at least as far as his writing is concerned."[54]

LaCapra's next major effort examined the 1857 trial of Gustave Flaubert, a terrain in which "intellectual history and literary history converge." He explained that a trial "is a locus of social reading that brings out conventions of interpretation in a key institution." Indeed, he offers his book as a "test case" of his methodological program.[55] Is he successful? LaCapra's energy and devotion are admirable; his commitment to a close textual reading can hardly be faulted. For instance, he inspects the novel's dedication to Flaubert's lawyer, who defended the author when the government charged that *Madame Bovary* offended public morality; and LaCapra finds some extra punctuation in the translation. "Paul de Man, in his 'substantially new translation' of the novel, has introduced into the dedication six commas more than Flaubert himself used, thereby accentuating one's doubts about its intention."[56]

Some of LaCapra's main points seem unexceptional. The trial "reduced the radical negativity of the novel to manageable proportions either to condemn or to praise its author."[57] For LaCapra, these juridical "readings" avoid the novel's seditiousness. Yet it is hardly surprising that neither the prosecutor nor defense went beyond a simple interpretation of *Madame Bovary;* neither were, or wanted to be, literary critics. They argued whether the book offended public morality by celebrating adultery. For LaCapra, this showed a superficial understanding of the novel.

LaCapra believes that *Madame Bovary* is marked by shifting narrative voices creating an "indeterminacy" that "unsettles the moral security of the reader." LaCapra has much to say about Flaubert's "dual style" and a variant of it, his "free indirect style," which also undermines a simple reading of the book. In fact, LaCapra has so much to say about Flaubert's style that, except in passing, he never returns to Flaubert's trial. Occasionally, he mentions that "the trial of course did not investigate the problem of the so-called free indirect style." In the conclusion, he reiterates that in understanding *Madame Bovary* neither the prosecutor nor defense "went beyond viewing the issue of standard conformity or deviance."[58]

To be just a little unfair, the trial of Flaubert was for LaCapra a foil for a literary analysis of *Madame Bovary.* His learned and engaged discussion draws on numerous critics as well as Flaubert's letters and a few events of 1848. However, LaCapra is not very interested in the trial or even in historically situating Flaubert's style. He analyzes Flaubert's style as found in *Madame Bovary.* "My own argument," he concludes, "has been that the problem of narration or modes of 'representation' in *Madame Bovary* is indeed complex. . . . One minimal point I have tried to establish is that one cannot simply take the most lapidary statements concerning pure art . . . from the letters [of Flaubert] and interpret the novel as their unproblematic realization."[59] In his essays and books, LaCapra continuously repeats this "minimal point": texts cannot be reduced to other texts or contexts; texts are complex. As a method, this appears to be beyond dispute; no one wants to promote reductionism. Yet LaCapra's position becomes a dogma, a methodological pronouncement that sabotages interpretations.

LaCapra shares with other new intellectual historians several characteristics. They see themselves as beleaguered, a few rebels facing a powerful and unsympathetic profession. They generally stay clear of direct encounters with other historians; that is, they develop methodological critiques of historians, but at arm's distance. The method becomes an end itself. In his major programmatic essay "Rethinking Intellectual History and Reading Texts," LaCapra reiterates that intellectual historians have succumbed to various reductionisms: a documentary approach, contextualism, presentism. "The predominance of a documentary approach," LaCapra writes, "is one crucial reason why complex texts—especially 'literary' ones—are either excluded from the relevant historical record or read in an extremely reduced way."[60] Yet he rarely tells us which historians or what histories are guilty of these sins.

This needs some qualification. The few efforts of the new intellectual historians to criticize deficient history do not seem illuminating. The examples usually are secondary or marginal.[61] Apart from briefly discussing E. P. Thompson, in one of his rare bids to demonstrate how "the figurative level of the discourse" guides a modern historian, White selects a passage from "a no-nonsense purveyor of facts." The passage he chooses comes from A. J. P. Taylor's *The Course of German History.*[62] This is an odd choice. Taylor's book is generally considered extremely tendentious and polemical. Few books are less neutral—all the details are marshaled to show that Luther led to Hitler. It takes no great acumen to show that Taylor's language abets his project.

To his credit, LaCapra has sought several direct encounters with writings of other historians. Yet the results are decidedly mixed. Against provocative interpretations, LaCapra argues that texts are complex and indeterminate. He evaluates *Wittgenstein's Vienna,* by Allan Janik and Stephen Toulmin, which he states belongs to "the standard repertory of the intellectual historian." The book puts forth "a striking argument" based on a "contextualist approach" that interprets a text by way of other writings and individuals.[63]

LaCapra finds "extremely reductive" their argument that the *Tractatus* is fundamentally ethical. "The text becomes a vehicle for ideas, discursive arguments, and essential positions." He objects to their appeal to Karl Kraus, Robert Musil, Ludwig Wittgenstein's letters, and *fin-de-siècle* Vienna to bolster their case. Yet LaCapra does not go much beyond arguing that Wittgenstein and the *Tractatus* preclude any interpretation. It is fair enough to question Wittgenstein's emphatic statement about the ethical core of the *Tractatus,* but LaCapra seems to prefer ambivalence and indeterminacy.

Does the relation between what Wittgenstein directly and indirectly states, LaCapra asks, "authorize one to say that the text is essentially ethical—or essentially anything else for that matter?" In effect, LaCapra answers negatively: the text is essentially about nothing (or is essentially nothing). Wittgenstein's *Tractatus,* like any text, is "the scene of an interplay between different forces—forces of unification and dissemination—whose relation must be taken as a matter of inquiry."[64] To LaCapra, a convention of historians resembled an assembly of morticians, but here one sniffs the stale air of the endless seminars. Nothing is ever figured out or resolved; everything is judged a complex matter demanding more study.

His criticism of Carlo Ginzburg's *The Cheese and the Worms* raises valid objections, yet returns insistently to the proposition of textual complexity. "My emphasis would be on the complex, often distorted interaction of levels or aspects of culture and the attendant relations between orthodoxy and heterodoxy in social and intellectual life."[65] Ironically, the critique of Ginzburg by this militantly unconventional or anti-traditional historian could have been made by an ordinary empiricist who prizes facts. LaCapra charges that Ginzburg fails to sift carefully through his texts, generalizes too widely and boldly, is too anecdotal and informal, and does not offer enough evidence. He complains that "the diffuse narrative and anecdotal style [of Ginzburg] facilitates the treatment of it [oral culture] in vague, piecemeal, and allusive terms."[66]

The point is not that LaCapra is wrong, but that in one of the few detailed criticisms of other historians, his own position is little more than a call for textual prudence.[67] Unhappy with Ginzburg's interpretation of an inquisition report, he asks, "At the very least, the reader deserves a transcription of the inquisition register itself to be in a better position to test the use and the interpretation made of it."[68] LaCapra sounds very much like a traditionalist upset that a researcher has been insufficiently cautious.

As with White, what begins as a call for a radical departure in historical thought ends up sounding very familiar: the importance, complexity, and ambiguities of the text are continuously reiterated—a proposition advanced for decades by literary critics. To be sure, what is familiar is neither bad nor wrong. Yet as with White, in two respects, the circle has been closed. The new intellectual historians undercut emphatic arguments with the truism of textual complexity. The world of interpretations turns grey; everything is complicated, indeterminate, feasible. Moreover, the method becomes the object. LaCapra criticizes the fetish of archives and documents, as if facts themselves advance knowledge and truth; however, he glorifies a textual technique, as if method exists apart from its object.

Might White and LaCapra, despite themselves, harbor affinities toward a positivist science? The point is not to fling about vague charges over some alleged scientism, as if science were evil. Rather it is this: White, LaCapra, and other new intellectual historians emerge out of a tradition that sought to rescue, if not cultivate, the uniqueness of history; this project does not entail denigrating science, but distinguishing history from its formal, quantifying, and objective elements. Yet the very language of the new intellectual historians (and often the program) smacks of a formalism and objectivity associated with the sciences.

The theorists of a literary intellectual history disdain the "impressionist and unsystematic," White's objection to D. W. Brogan's preface. They want the language of rigor, structure, and technique. LaCapra often criticizes the language of historians; he never states that he finds it too literary, but his objections amount to the same. For LaCapra, the idiom seems too pictorial, accessible, or subjective. These are defects, which LaCapra implicitly contrasts to language that is abstract, technical, structured—the vocabulary of the professional scholar.

LaCapra criticizes the "premium" bestowed on "straightforward prose (the no-jargon rule)."[69] He faults "the diffuse narrative and anecdotal style" of Ginzburg's *The Cheese and the Worms*.[70] He protests that Robert Darnton is "too accommodatingly readable" and that this style lends itself "to gloss over problems and smooth over knotty points that may call for critical thought."[71] He objects to the conformity of the traditional "men and ideas" intellectual history with its "highly readable but diverting mode of introducing readers to the text."[72] He finds that Carl E. Schorske's polished style mirrors his simplified vision of Viennese culture. With Schorske, "an almost Viennese flair for the elaborate elegance of the nicely turned phrase and a butterflylike delicacy in moving from *topos* to *topos* . . . engender an enchanting world of words."[73] The palpable disdain for the less than technical prose suggests the new intellectual history secretly admires the science it openly rejects. [74]

Other historians have followed or accompanied White and LaCapra in advancing a new intellectual history. Unfortunately, their contributions—for instance, Sande Cohen's *Historical Culture,*[75] Allan Megill's, "Recounting the Past: 'Description,' Explanation, and Narrative in Historiography,"[76] and David Harlan's "Intellectual History and the Return of Literature"[77]—reveal the same ills. These pieces share an extravagant appeal to new theories and approaches, a dramatic portrayal of the depth and power of the opposition to these theories coupled with no clear reference to the nature of that opposition, and a sketch of a new intellectual history outlining a new formalism or textual prudence.

Cohen's *Historical Culture,* however, may be *sui generis.* By reason of its dense jargon, *Historical Culture* resists not simply a comparison with other new intellectual histories, but any evaluation. Yet it features an enthusiastic blurb by White. "The most original contribution to historiographical theory since Paul Ricoeur's *Time and Narrative*. . . . A brilliant achievement!" LaCapra reviewed it generously. "Cohen is on the mark in mounting a sustained critique of the recent overvaluation of narrative, and his plea for theory and criticism is timely and forceful."[78] Cohen's main argument parallels that of the other new intellectual historians.

Liberally citing Roland Barthes, Jean Baudrillard, Jean-François Lyotard, and postmodern French critics, Cohen identifies his work as a "modified version of deconstruction theory." Like other new intellectual historians, he challenges an oppressive order, "academic historiography" that is "part of the overall requirement for cultural stability."[79] His method—if it can be called that—is formalistic inasmuch as it dissects the language of historians.

Cohen's own language requires more than a passing comment. His prose is so opaque that the book comes with a glossary, but the glossary needs a translator or an editor. *Actantial/actant,* reads an entry, "refers to the complex exchange between what a 'historical' narration allows to be the subject of doing (for example, capitalism treated as the actant of innovation or capitalism presented as the subject of dialectical transformations) and the reader's ability (generally) to acknowledge primary roles of action as necessary to a culture."[80] This is Cohen when succinct.

Cohen admits that his terms are "radically unfamiliar," but it "must be so." The usual academic discourse evades and absorbs. His "decoding" requires "a discourse that slows reading, that refuses to convince a reader by its cadence or even rightness." He succeeds in this. "If transcendence is a permanent possibility of semiotic-intellectual destruction," runs a typical sentence, "because its minimal function is to make unthinkable the negation of that 'which ties one to reality' and holds one in place, this superfunction today is perfected in contexts where language is hypervalorized as the 'indispensable,' 'needed,' 'necessary,' 'required,' and so on, basis of enculturation."[81]

The issue is not Cohen, but whether the concentration on language by the new intellectual historians ignores their own language. Does their critique of narrative foster the illusion that conceptual subversion requires an unreadable prose? This seems to be the case. Again, the paradox is striking. These historians seek to restore or rethink history's links to the humanities and literature. They want to free history of scientific pretensions; they ponder metaphors, rhetoric, and imagination. Yet they author, even champion, insular and cramped writings distant from literature.

A rare devotion to an argument distinguishes *Historical Culture.* Cohen claws his way through historical texts by Peter Gay, E. P. Thompson, and Ferdinand Braudel sentence by sentence for hundreds of pages. This is no mean achievement; such intensity is typically brought to bear on poetry, short fiction, or the densest philosophy, not the prose of historians. Cohen cannot be charged with avoiding specifics. By virtue of its singlemindedness, *Historical Culture* makes a point.

One example must suffice for Cohen's method. He spends well over a page on the first sentence of Peter Gay's appendix to *Weimar Culture,* which reads "The Weimar Republic was proclaimed on November 9, 1918, by the Social Democrat Philipp Scheidemann."[82] Cohen objects to the pretense of neutrality and matter-of-factness: Gay writes neither, "'As I hope to prove, the Weimar Republic was proclaimed in order to. . . .'" nor, "'What was *called* the Weimar Republic by x.'" Rather, Gay's sentence encourages "passive cognition." "The reader is blocked from considering the status of such namings." The opening sentence, Cohen concludes elegantly, is "both a performative (see Barthes) and what Derrida has called a detour for the reappropriation of presence."[83]

The argument complements that of other new intellectual historians, and its truth remains salutary. Narratives suppress issues by carrying along the reader. Even the plainest sentences betray cultural assumptions, and inasmuch as historians write—or study—texts, they must weigh language. This radical insight, however, slides into its opposite: a new cautiousness. Nothing can be stated without multiple qualifications and clauses. Sprinkles of "as I hope to show" and "what is called," or scare quotes around every other word supposedly subvert a passive narrative. LaCapra also backed away from decisive arguments of Ginzburg, Toulmin, and Janik. "As I see it," Cohen writes in his conclusion citing Baudrillard, the historical narratives exclude the "reciprocity and antagonism of interlocutors, in the ambivalence of their exchange." They leave out the questions "'What do you mean by . . . ?'"[84] These questions are essential, but an obsession with ambivalence and interchanges hardly betters an obsession with clear facts.

David Harlan also wants to restore and rethink the link between history and literature. He writes that "now, after a hundred-year absence, literature has returned to history . . . The return of literature has plunged historical studies into an extended epistemological crisis." Apart from stating that the "return of literature" was "prepared" by Ferdinand de Saussure, Harlan makes no effort to indicate when literature deserted history. What is this "one-hundred year absence"?[85] Does it include, for instance, Vernon Parrington's *Main Currents in American Thought*?

In his *American Intellectual Histories and Historians* (1927), Robert Allen Skotheim calls this "no doubt the most famous American history of ideas ever published," noting that it was frequently criticized for excessively discussing literature.[86] Or, if this is too far afield, what of Carl E. Schorske's *Fin-de-siècle Vienna* (1980)? Its first chapter is titled "Politics and Psyche: Schnitzler and Hofmannsthal."[87] Or James H. Billington's *The Icon and the Axe* (1966)?[88] Or Raymond William's *Culture and Society 1780–1950* (1958)?[89] Do these belong to the period when intellectual historians expelled literature? To Harlan, probably none of these count, since they may be too flat-footed in their employment of literature. Harlan is not really bothered by absence of literature from history; however, he is irked by the absence of a different beast: literary theory.

This sleight-of-hand or confusion facilitates the stance that Harlan shares with other new intellectual historians. He sees himself as besieged, combatting a serious and well-armed enemy. He calls the opposition (the contextualists), a powerful force, "the dominant and now conventional orthodoxy . . . well placed, well organized and increasingly intolerant of alternative approaches." He offers as evidence John P. Diggins's book on Thorstein Veblen, *The Bard of Savagery*. Diggins's effort to recontextualize and rewrite Veblen received a critical review and comment in several historical journals, meaning "the American historical establishment would have none of it."[90]

Harlan also alludes to one of the odder pieces by LaCapra, "On Grubbing in My Personal Archives." Although LaCapra also challenges contextual reductionism, he made an exception. LaCapra found highly significant that his own book *'Madame Bovary' on Trial,* which he characterizes as a book by "a full professor at a 'major research institution,'" was sharply criticized in the "official publication of the American Historical Review" by an assistant professor from the bush leagues. Moreover, after a reply from LaCapra, Professor James Smith Allen of Phillips University in Enid, Oklahoma, did not back down.[91] LaCapra took umbrage.

> I would suggest that the very fact that a relatively unknown assistant professor from a relatively unknown university is willing not only to write a critical review but to follow it up with a rather imperious letter [a reply to LaCapra's response] indicates that he must be fairly certain he is indeed invoking conventional wisdom and will have the large majority of the profession in his corner . . . the hegemonic voice of historiography . . . speaks through him [the reviewer].[92]

Allan Megill exhibits less posturing in his essay, yet he, too, vaguely refers to an army of historians stamping out new theories. Opponents are everywhere, but he hardly finds any. His examples of historical writings also seem askew; only one comes from a historian, another he invents, still others derive from textbooks. He shares with Harlan an ostentatious appeal to sophisticated paradigms, hinting that common historians will be unable to follow his subtlety. "The force and implications of this essay's distinction between recounting and explanation," Megill notes toward his conclusion, "are likely to be misunderstood by many readers." Or he states, "Yet, even among historians of some sophistication, there remains a tendency to underrate the force and scope of the hermeneutical insight that all perception is perspectival."[93]

What are the issues? The idioms of Harlan and Megill diverge from one another, but their general efforts run parallel. Like LaCapra and White, they resist what they consider scientistic approaches to history and texts, and they appeal to new literary theories. Harlan argues against both the "radical contextualists" and those who seek "to recover authorial intention." Postmodern literary theory subverts these reductionist methods. "Texts do not point backward, to the historical context or putative intentions of their now-dead authors; they point forward, to the hidden possibilities of the present."[94]

Harlan becomes a bit misty-eyed and mystifying; he writes about the need to recognize that "every text, at the very moment of its inception, has already been cast onto the waters, that no text can ever hope to rejoin its father, that it is the fate of every text to take up the wanderings of a prodigal son that does not return."[95] Megill is more sober. He challenges "professional orthodoxy" that elevates causal explanation over more subjective interpretations or descriptions.[96] For two reasons, historians still denigrate descriptions and esteem scientific approaches and explanations: their "prejudice for universality" and their "hermeneutic naïveté, or the belief in immaculate perception." Both are derived from the continuing prestige of "science," especially the belief that science requires a neutral observer seeking general laws. "It is widely held in philosophy and in social science that only knowledge of the general or universal (as distinguished from the local or particular) is truly scientific."[97]

Turning first to *The Mediterranean and the Mediterranean World,* Megill challenges conventional opinion by avowing that Fernand Braudel's masterpiece is "narrative history." This truth has been missed because of a traditionalism that identifies narrative as a chronicle or sequence of actions. Yet narrative is much more, combining four elements: action, happening, character, and setting. The first two are "events," which means they "occur"; the latter two are "existents," which means they "simply are." "Emphasis on one of the four elements perforce limits the attention given to the others." To clarify, Megill offers a formula:

$$(AH) \times (CS) = k$$

The formula means "action times happening [that is, 'events'] times character times setting [that is, 'existents'] equals a constant." Unfortunately, what these elements are, and why they must stand in an inverse relation remains obscure. We are assured, however, that only traditionalists or the "uninformed" will deny the truth of this formula.[98] With this formula we see that Braudel's book is narrative history.

The same irony that marks the work of White and LaCapra is evident here. The new intellectual historians resolutely seek to escape a baneful positivism that erases the specificity of history; they reject a search for general, causal, and objective laws; they want to attend fully to the ambiguities of the text and the subjectivity of the historians who interpret the texts. But these laudable aims vaporize in the course of their contributions. Instead of reviving historical thinking and nurturing subjectivity, they promote empty taxonomies and scientistic idioms. They celebrate bold theories and revel in cautious truisms. They cherish a more literary history, and offer pale methodologies and systems.

New history, new social history, new intellectual history: especially in history, "new" is suspect. Yet that does not mean nothing changes or should change. By their energy and thoughtfulness, the new intellectual historians have brought a welcome ferment to a quiet field, and the story is far from over. An initial report suggests, however, that they succumb to bloodless scholasticism and cold formalism.

Notes

1. Edward B. Fiske, "Lessons," *The New York Times,* August 2, 1989, B8.
2. Robert Markley, "Stop the Presses: A Modest Proposal for Sa(l)vaging Literary Scholarship," *The Eighteenth Century,* 29, no. 1 (1988):72. "It becomes increasingly difficult to decide what to read; confronted by the twenty-five entries in the 1984 *MLA Bibliography* under *Macbeth,* how can one decide which books and articles are worth reading?" (72).
3. Another motivation surfaces: the desire to preserve or expand a professional field. Education passes into fief building: define a field so it (and its students) can survive and perhaps prosper. "I dislike to yield territory to sociologists, political scientists, etc.," wrote Frederick Jackson Turner, "on which the historian may raise good crops." (Turner in a letter, September 5, 1914; cited by Michael Kammen, *Selvages and Biases: The Fabric of History in American Culture* [Ithaca, N.Y.: Cornell University Press, 1987], 78.) Dominick LaCapra admits that his own concerns about intellectual history partly bear witness to "an obvious 'territorial imperative.'"(Dominick LaCapra, *Rethinking Intellectual History* [Ithaca, N.Y.: Cornell University Press, 1983], 24.)
4. "Decline from what?" or "From when?" it might be asked. Some date modern intellectual history from James Harvey Robinson's course at Columbia before World War I. See Franklin L. Baumer, "Intellectual History and its Problems," *Journal of Modern History,* 21 (1949): 191. Others look to Vernon L. Parrington's two volumes, *Main Currents in American Thought,* published in 1927. Still others look to Arthur O. Lovejoy, his teachings, writings, and organizations. See Dorothy Stimson, "The History of Ideas Club," in George Boas et al., *Studies in Intellectual History* (Baltimore, Md.: Johns Hopkins University Press, 1953), 174–96. In any event, John Higham, who has been monitoring its health for forty odd years, reported that "as late as 1934," an official bibliography of the American Historical Association ignored intellectual history. (John Higham, "The Rise of American Intellectual History," *American Historical Review,* 56 (April 1951): 462.) Over the next decades, however, the cumulative impact of Charles Beard, James Robinson, Vernon Parrington, Perry Miller, Merle Curti, Arthur Schlesinger, and others took effect. By the later 1940s, the quantity and quality increased to the point that some commentators believed intellectual history was "the profession's outstanding achievement of the last decade." Higham quoting Thomas Cochran in John Higham, "The Rise of American Intellectual History," 467. In the 1950s, one historian referred to "the rapid rise of intellectual history to prominence in the world of American scholarship." John C. Greene, "Objectives and Methods in Intellectual History," *Mississippi Valley Historical Review,* 44 (1957–58):58. Another noted it "has never been more popular. It attracts increasing numbers of students who regularly produce a sizeable body of very creditable work." R. Richard Wohl, "Intellectual History: An Historian's View," *The Historian,* 16 (1953): 62.
5. Dominick LaCapra, *Soundings in Critical Theory* (Ithaca, N.Y.: Cornell University Press, 1989), 199.

6. Dominick LaCapra, "On Grubbing in My Personal Archives: An Historiographical Exposé of Sorts," *Boundary 2,* 13 (1985): 59.
7. Announcements of a "crisis" in the field start appearing in the late 1960s, and intensify over the next fifteen years. By the early 1970s, Higham wrote of the field as having "passed the zenith of its influence." "American Historiography in the 1960's" in John Higham, *Writing American History: Essays on Modern Scholarship* (Bloomington: Indiana University Press, 1970), 169. A report from 1975 observed a "crisis" and malaise in that young scholars no longer specialize in intellectual history. "The field was no longer rising, but rapidly declining." Gene Wise, "The Contemporary Crisis in Intellectual History Studies," *Clio,* 5 (1975): 55. Intellectual history, offered another historian, "now seems as dated as narrow ties." Paul K. Conkin, "Intellectual History: Past, Present, and Future," in *The Future of History,* edited by Charles F. Delzell (Nashville, Tenn.: Vanderbilt University Press, 1977), 111. Laurence Veysey's survey of American historical scholarship in 1979 celebrated the productivity and diversity of American historians—and used the declining field of intellectual history to prove his point. "In 1976, some thirty-five to forty [book] titles alone were published in the rather arcane and unfashionable subfield of American intellectual history, an area that some scholars pronounce to be dying." Laurence Veysey, "The United States" in *International Handbook of Historical Studies,* edited by Georg G. Iggers and Harold T. Parker (Westport, Conn.: Greenwood Press, 1979), 157. A year after Veysey, Robert Darnton confirmed that disease has struck the field. "The trend toward self-doubt and beleaguered self-assertion can be found wherever intellectual historians discuss the state of their craft." Once intellectual historians, he observed, "saw their discipline as the queen of the historical sciences." Now they have been dethroned and humbled. The next year, William J. Bouwsma confirmed the diagnosis. "The decline of intellectual history appears obvious, and probably irreversible." William J. Bouwsma, "From History of Ideas to History of Meaning," (1981) in his *A Usable Past: Essays in European Cultural History* (Berkeley: University of California Press, 1990), 337.
8. Martin Jay, "The Textual Approach to Intellectual History," in *Fact and Fiction: German History and Literature 1848–1924,* edited by Gisela Brude-Firnau and Karin J. MacHardy (Tübingen: Francke Verlag, 1990), 77.
9. John E. Toews, "Intellectual History after the Linguistic Turn," *American Historical Review,* 92 (October, 1987): 881–2.
10. Michael Ermarth, "Mindful Matters: The Empire's New Codes and the Plight of Modern European Intellectual History," *Journal of Modern History,* 57 (1985): 507. For a very different perspective, see the spirited exchange between F. R. Ankersmit and Perez Zagorin. Ankersmit, "Historiography and Postmodernism," *History and Theory,* 28 (1989):137–53; Zagorin, "Historiography and Postmodernism: Reconsiderations" and Ankersmit, "Reply to Professor Zagorin," both in *History and Theory,* 29 (1990): 263–96. See also the discussion in *Theory and Society,* in which Fritz Ringer argues for a more sociological intellectual history. Fritz Ringer, "The Intellectual Field, Intellectual History, and the Sociology of Knowledge"; Charles Lemert, "The Habits of Intellectuals"; Martin Jay, "Fieldwork and Theorizing in Intellectual History"; and a "Rejoinder" by Ringer, all in *Theory and Society,* 19 (1990): 269–334. For a judicious overview, see Donald R. Kelley, "Horizons of Intellectual History: Retrospect, Circumspect, Prospect," *Journal of the History of Ideas,* 48 (1987): 143–69.
11. Dominick LaCapra, *Rethinking Intellectual History: Texts, Contexts, Language* (Ithaca, N.Y.: Cornell University Press, 1983), 72.
12. Allan Megill, Review Essay on Theodore Hamerow, *Reflections on History and Historians,* in *History and Theory,* 27 (1987): 98.

13. For a different view of White's development, see Hans Kellner, "A Bedrock of Order: Hayden White's Linguistic Humanism," in Kellner, *Language and Historical Representation: Getting the Story Crooked* (Madison, Wis.: University of Wisconsin Press, 1989), esp. 193–202.
14. For a good overview of Antoni, see Antonino Pagliaro, "Ricordo di Carlo Antoni" in Antoni, *Storicismo e antistoricismo* (Naples: Morano, 1964), 3–32. See also, Gennaro Sasso, *L'illusione della dialettica: Profilo di Carlo Antoni* (Rome: Edizioni dell'Ateneo, 1982), esp. 39–72; and Michele Biscione, *Interpreti di Croce* (Naples: Giannini, 1968), 95–187, which stresses Antoni's links to Croce.
15. Carlo Antoni, *From History to Sociology: The Transition in German Historical Thinking,* translated by Hayden V. White (Detroit, Mich.: Wayne State University Press, 1959), vii, 32, 167, 38.
16. Hayden V. White, "Translator's Introduction," Antoni, *From History to Sociology,* xix–xx, xxi–xxii.
17. Hayden V. White, xxiv. Of course, White may be referring to the knotty issue of historical thought and Naziism. To follow Georg Iggers, with Heidegger and others, "historicism . . . reached the end of its road: the last eternal values and meanings had dissolved. All that was left was historical, temporal, and relative." Georg G. Iggers, *The German Conception of History* (Middletown, Conn.: Wesleyan University Press, 1968), 244–45.
18. White wrote no introduction to the Goldmann text (Lucien Goldmann, *The Human Sciences and Philosophy,* translated by Hayden V. White and Robert Anchor [London: Jonathan Cape, 1969]), but he discussed Goldmann in an essay published the same year as his translation: Hayden White, "The Tasks of Intellectual History," *The Monist,* 53 (1969), especially 623–25. In general, Goldmann, influenced by Georg Lukács and other Western Marxists, argued for the specificity of history. "We are here concerned with a fundamental difference between history, which studies human behavior and the physico-chemical sciences, which study inanimate matter. The physico-chemical sciences study facts solely in their external or sensible aspect; the historian deals with consciously realized actions . . . of which he must, above all, discover the *meaning* . . . and an *objective* meaning which often differs from the conscious meaning in an important way." (Goldmann, *The Human Sciences and Philosophy,* 32–33.) For a good overview of Goldmann, see his *Cultural Creation in Modern Society* (Oxford: Basil Blackwell, 1977), esp. the introduction by William Mayrl, 3–29; and Mary Evans, *Lucien Goldmann: An Introduction* (Sussex: Harvester Press, 1981).
19. Hayden V. White, "The Burden of History" (1966) in his *Tropics of Discourse: Essays in Cultural Criticism* (Baltimore: Johns Hopkins University Press, 1978), 27.
20. Hayden V. White, *The Burden of History,* 29; 42–43. White discussed *Life Against Death* by Norman O. Brown (then his colleague at the University of Rochester) as exemplifying a new artistic history. "By a series of brilliant and shocking juxtapositions, involutions, reductions, and distortions" he "forces the reader to see with new clarity" (45).
21. Hayden V. White, *The Burden of History,* 47–48.
22. Hayden V. White, "The Tasks of Intellectual History" *The Monist,* 53 (1969): 608, 609–10, 616.
23. Richard T. Vann argues that the work of Louis Mink, for instance, his essay "History and Fiction as Modes of Comprehension" (1970), played a key role in White's ideas; see his "Louis Mink's Linguistic Turn," *History and Theory,* 26 (1987), esp. 5–8. One element from White's earlier program no longer appears in his later writings: the almost "new age" hope expressed in "The Burden of History" that history will embrace contemporary science as well as art.

24. White distinguished five levels in all historical work: chronicle, story, emplotment, argument, ideology. The first two involve how events are organized. The "plot" (or emplotment), however, is more decisive, since it is the manner in which the historian gives meaning to the chronicle/story. Following Northrop Frye, White suggests at least four different emplotments: romance, tragedy, comedy, and satire. "A given historian is forced to emplot the whole set of stories making up his narrative in one comprehensive or *archetypal* story form" (8). Beyond the emplotment lies the explicit argument or explanation, which is founded on "different notions of the nature of historical reality" (13). White distinguished four types of historical explanation: formist, organicist, mechanistic, and contextualist. On the last level, the ideological, White also posits four types: anarchist, conservativism, radicalism, and liberalism. While there appear to be sixty-four possibilities—four different emplotments, explanations, and ideologies—White suggests elective and homological affinities exist among these levels. In any event, White goes on to state that a "particular *combination* of modes of emplotment, argument and ideological implication" makes up a "historiographical style" (29–38). All in Hayden V. White, *Metahistory: The Historical Imagination in Nineteenth-Century Europe* (Baltimore, Md.: Johns Hopkins University Press, 1973). This style is fundamentally linguistic and poetic, and is White's real concern. It also can be classified in four ways, using the four basic literary tropes: metaphor, metonymy, synecodoche, and irony. In his essential book *In Defense of Rhetoric,* Brian Vickers judges severely White's fetish of "four," and especially his reduction of rhetoric to four tropes. This he regards as a piece with the "reduction, fragmentation, and misapplication of rhetoric in modern literary discourse." Vickers, *In Defense of Rhetoric* (Oxford: Oxford University Press, 1989), 441–42, 453. Another historian of rhetoric, Nancy S. Struever, makes a similar and equally tough assessment of White; see her "Topics in History," in *Metahistory: Six Critiques, History and Theory,* Beiheft 19 (1980): 66–79.
25. White, *Metahistory,* xii.
26. White, *Tropics,* 82.
27. White, *Tropics,* 15–19.
28. White, *Tropics,* 99.
29. White, *Tropics,* 85.
30. White, *Tropics,* 23.
31. White, *Tropics,* 121.
32. White, "The Politics of Historical Interpretation," in his *The Content of the Form: Narrative Discourse and Historical Representation* (Baltimore, Md.: Johns Hopkins University Press, 1987), 67, 72, 74–75. It is always tempting to turn the rhetoric of the rhetoricians against themselves. The critic of "facts" says here, "One must face the fact . . . there are no grounds." What fact?
33. See Carlo Ginzburg's critique of White, "Just One Witness" and commentary by Martin Jay, "Of Plots, Witnesses and Judgements" both in *Probing the Limits of Representation, Nazism and the "Final Solution,"* edited by Saul Friedlander (Cambridge, Mass.: Harvard University Press, 1992), 82–107. At least part of White's argument is neither wrong nor new; it has been discussed that fascism and Nazism successfully exploited a mythic dimension that liberals, conventional conservatives, and Marxists abandoned. For instance, this argument has long marked the writings of George L. Mosse; see his *Nationalization of the Masses* (New York: New American Library, 1977). See also Jeffrey Herf, *Reactionary Modernism: Technology, Culture and Politics in Weimar and the Third Reich* (Cambridge, Mass.: Cambridge University Press, 1986), esp. ch. 1. Yet White seems to be stating something more than this—or perhaps less.
34. White, *Metahistory,* 3.
35. White, *Tropics,* 21.

36. For a critique of White's tropes for sidestepping the issue of historical truth, see Arnaldo Momigliano, "The Rhetoric of History and the History of Rhetoric: On Hayden White's Tropes," in *Comparative Criticism: A Yearbook*, 3, edited by E.S. Shaffer (Cambridge, Mass.: Cambridge University Press, 1981), 259–68.
37. This is a huge topic. Innumerable versions of formalism exist: the formalism of Northrop Frye; New Criticism and Russian Formalism, and many others. In politics and program, for instance, New Criticism and Russian Formalism seem very different. Nevertheless, they do share certain elements. See Ewa M. Thompson, *Russian Formalism and Anglo-American New Criticism: A Comparative Study* (The Hague: Mouton, 1971).
38. White, "The Tasks of Intellectual History," *The Monist,* 53 (1969): 613.
39. White, *The Content of the Form,* 192–3.
40. White, *The Content of the Form,* 194.
41. White, *The Content of the Form,* 196.
42. White, *The Content of the Form,* 196–7, 208.
43. In a sympathetic discussion, Reinhart Koselleck calls White's work a "scientifically grounded linguistic metahistory." Koselleck, "Einführung" to White, *Auch Klio Dichtet oder Die Fiktion des Faktischen* (Stuttgart: Ernst Klett Verlage, 1986), 6.
44. See generally, Lloyd S. Kramer, "Literature, Criticism, and Historical Imagination: The Literary Challenge of Hayden White and Dominick LaCapra," in *The New Cultural History,* edited by Lynn Hunt (Berkeley: University of California Press, 1989), 97–128.
45. The first words (of the main text) of his Sartre book run "Intellectual history has often followed. . . ." Dominick LaCapra, *A Preface to Sartre* (Ithaca, N.Y.: Cornell University Press, 1978), 19.
46. LaCapra, "Intellectual History and Critical Theory" in *Soundings in Critical Theory,* 182–209.
47. LaCapra, "On Grubbing in My Personal Archives," 46.
48. LaCapra, *Soundings in Critical Theory,* 2.
49. LaCapra, *A Preface to Sartre,* 23.
50. One element of their divergence: In keeping with his more rigorous formalism White refuses to distinguish between high and popular culture. "The linguistic model provides us with a basis for dissolving the distinction, hierarchical and essentialist in nature, between high culture on the one side and low, folk or popular culture on the other. This distinction . . . precludes the possibility of a genuine science of culture." White, "Structuralism and Popular Culture," *Journal of Popular Culture,* 7 (1974): 775. LaCapra resists losing all these differences; see for instance his "Culture and Ideology," in LaCapra, *Soundings,* 133–54.
51. Albert C. Hamilton, *Northrop Frye: Anatomy of his Criticism* (Toronto: University of Toronto Press, 1990), 40.
52. LaCapra, "Criticism Today," *Soundings,* 19.
53. LaCapra, "A Poetics of Historiography: Hayden White's *Tropics of Discourse,*" in *Rethinking Intellectual History,* 80–81.
54. LaCapra, *A Preface to Sartre,* 90, 26, 223, 39.
55. Dominick LaCapra, *"Madame Bovary" on Trial* (Ithaca, N.Y.: Cornell University Press, 1982), 7, 10.
56. La Capra, *"Madame Bovary" on Trial,* 53.
57. La Capra, *"Madame Bovary" on Trial,* 53, 54.
58. La Capra, *"Madame Bovary" on Trial,* 60, 127, 210.
59. La Capra, *"Madame Bovary" on Trial,* 211.
60. LaCapra, *Rethinking Intellectual History,* 33.
61. See Anthony Pagden's comments in "Rethinking the Linguistic Turn: Current Anxieties in Intellectual History," *Journal of the History of Ideas,* 49 (1988): 527.

62. White, *Tropics,* 107–8.
63. All citations from "Reading Exemplars: *Wittgenstein's Vienna* and Wittgenstein's *Tractatus,*" in LaCapra, *Rethinking Intellectual History,* 84–117.
64. LaCapra, "Reading Exemplars," 102, 116.
65. LaCapra, "The Cheese and the Worms: The Cosmos of a Twentieth-Century Historian," in *History and Criticism* (Ithaca, N.Y.: Cornell University Press, 1985): 63.
66. Dominick LaCapra, *"The Cheese and the Worms,"* 55.
67. LaCapra also has discussed the work of Carl Schorske, Robert Darnton, and Roger Chartier. See his "Is Everybody a *Mentalité* Case? Transference and the Culture Concept" in his *History and Criticism,* and "Chartier, Darnton and the Great Symbol Massacre," in his *Soundings.* Again LaCapra makes some good points, but he repeatedly objects to the reductionist "reading" of texts. "One question that nonetheless arises as Schorske carries out his program," he asks, is whether he "tends to collapse in a reductive direction whereby the artifact or text is explained as a very restricted . . . response to a 'larger context.'" *History and Criticism,* 82. "On a methodological level, an overly reductive process is operative in Darnton's own understanding of reading and symbolic meaning." *Soundings,* 79. LaCapra is responding to Darnton's book, *The Great Cat Massacre and Other Episodes in French Cultural History* (New York: Basic Books, 1984), as well as a discussion of it by Darnton and Chartier; the latter's "Text, Symbols and Frenchness," is now in his collection, Roger Chartier, *Cultural History: Between Practices and Representations,* translated by Lydia G. Cochrane (Cambridge: Polity Press, 1988), 95–111.
68. LaCapra, *"The Cheese and the Worms,"* 63.
69. LaCapra, "Intellectual History and Critical Theory," 196.
70. LaCapra, *"The Cheese and the Worms,"* 54–55.
71. LaCapra, "Chartier, Darnton and the Great Symbol Massacre," 82.
72. LaCapra, *A Preface to Sartre,* 20.
73. LaCapra, "Is Everyone a *Mentalité* Case?" 84.
74. To be fair, LaCapra has raised the problem of "expertise . . . becoming enclosed in its own dialect or jargon." See "Rethinking Intellectual History and Reading Texts" in his *Rethinking Intellectual History,* 65.
75. Sande Cohen, *Historical Culture: On the Recoding of an Academic Discipline* (Berkeley: University of California Press, 1986).
76. Allan Megill, "Recounting the Past: 'Description,' Explanation, and Narrative in Historiography," *American Historical Review,* 94 (1989): 627–53.
77. David Harlan, "Intellectual History and the Return of Literature," *American Historical Review,* 94 (1989): 581–609.
78. Dominick LaCapra, in a review of Sande Cohen, *Historical Culture,* in *American Historical Review,* 92 (1987): 376. LaCapra also made some serious criticisms. Mark Poster offered an ambiguous blurb: "No historian who reads and comprehends this book will ever write in the same way again." Was this praise or warning?
79. Cohen, *Historical Culture,* 10, 17.
80. Cohen, *Historical Culture,* 327.
81. Cohen, *Historical Culture,* 2, 46.
82. Peter Gay, *Weimar Culture: The Outsider as Insider* (New York: Harper and Row, 1968), 147. To be sure, Cohen's choice of writings seems somewhat eccentric, if not misleading. For instance, he takes up Peter Gay, but he does not select Gay's *Freud* or *Voltaire's Politics* or *Bourgeois Experience,* but what he calls a text "representative of historical works read by an audience as a confirmation of the act of synthesis" (p. 110). An inattentive reader might think he is analyzing the conclusion to Gay's *Weimar Culture,* but it is an appendix to that book. Gay directs those "unfamiliar with modern German history" to this appen-

dix, but observes it "obviously makes no claim to originality" (Gay, xv). Cohen employs sixty pages to reflect on this seventeen page appendix, but he never manages to state the obvious: this text was a minor addition to the main book.

83. Cohen, *Historical Culture,* 113.
84. Cohen, *Historical Culture,* 325.
85. "For a provocative discussion of literature's return specifically to history," Harlan refers the reader to Linda Orr, "The Revenge of Literature: A History of History," *New Literary History,* 18 (1986–87): 1–22. Yet this piece contains only the most marginal and fleeting references to historians.
86. Robert Allen Skotheim, *American Intellectual Histories and Historians* (Princeton: Princeton University Press, 1966), 145–148.
87. Carl E. Schorske, *Fin-de-siècle Vienna* (New York: Vintage Books, 1981), 3–23.
88. James H. Billington's *The Icon and the Axe: An Interpretive History of Russian Culture* (New York: Vintage Books, 1970).
89. Raymond William, *Culture and Society, 1780–1950* (Garden City, New York: Doubleday, 1960).
90. Harlan, "Intellectual History and the Return of Literature," 594, 607.
91. Allen is author of numerous essays on the nineteenth century French reading and publishing, and two books: *Popular French Romanticism: Authors, Readers and Books in the 19th Century* (Syracuse, N.Y.: Syracuse University Press, 1981); and *In the Public Eye: A History of Reading in Modern France, 1800–1940* (Princeton, N.J.: Princeton University Press, 1991).
92. LaCapra, "On Grubbing in My Personal Archives," 49.
93. Megill, "Recounting the Past," 646, 636. Megill likes these formulations. It would be difficult to satirize the following: "Even historians aware of the hermeneutic tradition often resist the self-reflexive implications. Note, for example, Quentin Skinner's apparently unwitting reduction of post- to pre-Heideggerian hermeneutics . . ." (637). Since text is the name of the game, it is tempting to begin at the beginning of his text. Megill thanks four research assistants and thirty colleagues for their comments. For an essay, this is an act of intimidation.
94. Harlan, "Intellectual History and the Return of Literature," 604. See the criticism of Harlan following his article: David A. Hollinger, "The Return of the Prodigal," *AHR,* 94 (1989): 610–21.
95. Harlan, "Intellectual History and the Return of Literature," 600.
96. Megill, "Recounting the Past," 631.
97. Megill, "Recounting the Past," 632, 634. Megill's essay may be bidding, not simply for a shift toward a hermeneutical history, but for itself as a notable effort on that behalf; rhetorically, it almost offers itself as a rejoinder to Hempel's 1942 "Function of General Laws in History" (which Megill cites), that was required reading for a positivist philosophy of history. Hempel sought to push history toward the exact sciences by promoting a search for general laws. His essay began: "It is a rather widely held opinion that history . . . is concerned with the description of particular events of the past rather than with the search for general laws." Hempel considered this "unacceptable" and tried to show why. Carl G. Hempel, "The Function of General Laws in History," edited by Patrick Gardiner, *Theories of History* (Glencoe, Il.: Free Press, 1959), 344–45. Forty-five years later, Megill begins almost identically, but argues the reverse proposition: "It is a rather widely held opinion among professional historians that the truly serious task of historiography . . . is the task of explanation," that is, causal and general laws. It is difficult to figure out why Megill imagines that in decades since Hempel's essay the positivist currents have become stronger; Hempel and others who advanced similar arguments

never made much impact, and surely their influence has diminished, not increased, since the 1940s. "When Carl Hempel applied Karl Popper's concept of a 'covering law' to history," James T. Kloppenberg has written, "and when Mandelbaum elaborated his own objectivist theory, few historians were persuaded." James T. Kloppenberg, "Objectivity and Historicism: A Century of American Historican Writing," *American Historical Review,* 94 (1989): 1022.

98. Megill, "Recounting the Past," 645.

CHAPTER 10

HENRY LOUIS GATES, STERLING BROWN, AND THE PROFESSIONAL LANGUAGES OF AFRICAN AMERICAN LITERARY CRITICISM

Phillip M. Richards

HENRY LOUIS GATES has achieved broad renown as a literary critic who writes widely on political, social, and cultural issues. His work shows an awareness of the network of understandings—traditional and topical, rational and charismatic—on which such a literary critical role must be grounded.[1] Early in his career, he conceptualized an African American literary canon based on the concept of "signifying," setting forth certain historical narratives, critical sites, and professional gestures that have since become influential among critics of African American literature and some historians. Although this critical discourse dramatized the black literary experience as a counterculture to the Anglo-American literary tradition, the language of signifying often remains unable to address the deepest concerns of the black middle class, concerns to which Gates's criticism often alludes. If literary criticism and historical commentary are ways in which educated people discuss their condition, one rightly worries about the sterility of vernacular criticism as a discourse for confronting such intraracial crises as the black bourgeoisie's competitive disadvantage in upper-class American society, the meaning of increased social mobility, and its relationship with the *lumpen* poor.

At its heart, signifying is an indirect means of argument, whereby an assertion is made through a figure of speech.[2] The signifying statement forces the reader or receiver to understand a statement by means of an act of interpretation that takes him far beyond the literal meaning of the statement. An excellent example of signifying—an example showing the issues involved in this essay—is given in the footnotes of Gates's *The Signifying Monkey*. Here, Gates asks a black colleague Dwight Andrews whether he has ever heard of signifying. Andrews's ironic response asserts Gates's naïveté by an indirection typical of signifying.

> While writing this essay, I asked a colleague, Dwight Andrews, if he had heard of the signifying monkey as a child. "Why, no," he replied intently. "I never heard of the signifying monkey until I came to Yale and read about him in a book." I had been signified upon.[3]

Gates's anecdote shows the way in which signifying can be a figurative judo whereby the weight of a superior party's intention is turned against itself. More broadly stated, signifying calls attention to the social function of communication as well as its meaning. Andrews's response is not only an ironic play upon his literal statement but also a commentary upon the social meaning of Gates's question. Drawing upon these aspects of signifying, Gates's theory elevated a street ritual of lower-class black life to a discourse of literary influence, a metaphor for the ethos of African American culture, and a gesture of black self-consciousness *vis à vis* Anglo-American culture.

As a transplanted ritual of lower-class life, signifying not only dramatizes the dynamics of literary tradition but also acts out the black speaker's thwarted appropriation of Anglo-American culture. In Gates's literary theory, signifying therefore constitutes the way in which black authors revise the rhetoric of their literary predecessors and also project ironic attitudes toward a European American world, which African Americans appropriate but do not fully inhabit in white American society. Although literary critics primarily have made use of the paradigm of signifying, some social historians of the early American republic have been drawn to signifying as a means to describe the beginnings of autonomous black public expression. Through this adaptation of the signifying paradigm these social historians have shown literate blacks exercising their freedom from the restraints of acculturation to American life.

Significantly, the performative and expressive style of signifying diverges from the tradition of middle-class African American literary criticism. The African American literary criticism of earlier figures, such as the distinguished Howard critic Sterling Brown (1901–1989), Saunders P. Redding (1906–1988), and Arthur P. Davis (1904–1996), was a conversation between different voices defined by distinctive cultural and social perspectives.[4] The distinguishing feature of this genre of literary criticism was its tendency to question the class's various ideological constructs, moral *dicta,* and social conventions. At its best, this criticism sustained those literate social understandings that must be renewed to adapt a middle class to historical change.[5] However, the expressive rhetorical style of signifying cannot sustain the inquiry or analysis that this process of intellectual renewal requires. Vernacular deconstructive literary criticism has tended toward self-justifying ideological ends that obstruct rather than further a fresh self-consciousness in black intellectual discourse. An examination of Gates's influential literary discourse—influential for historians as well as for literary critics—reveals that the earlier critical writing of Sterling Brown exemplified a more rigorous intellectual conversation than present-day canonical interpretation now permits. This earlier black criticism allowed critics to call their bourgeoisie's own presuppositions and cultural inclinations into question far more effectively than vernacular critics do at present.

To be sure, Gates, like earlier critics, speaks to a middle class alienated from American culture by ideologies of racism. However, Sterling Brown, Arthur P. Davis, and Saunders Redding sought to instill an intellectual self-consciousness that eroded ideological certainty through the resistance of literary argument and historical fact. Gates, on the other hand, appropriated currently fashionable intellectual methods in the service of a therapeutic adjustment of black marginality to the "integrated world" of elite institutions.

By the term therapeutic, I refer to a specific psychological and social ethos that has been an object of discussion since Philip Rieff's influential book, *The Triumph of the Therapeutic: Uses of Faith After Freud.* In this ethos, modern man has found overarching social and cultural meanings not in external institutions but rather in himself. Society is seen not as the ground of human experience and meaning, but rather as a restriction on the self's realization of true meanings. The ethos of the therapeutic inculcates honesty as a norm, advocating not only sincere expression of feeling but the cultivation and expression of all feeling. Signifying in this sense allows middle-class black critics to express alienation as an assertion of self that transcends the racist restrictions of white society. As a cathartic expression of the self, however, signifying can mark a therapeutic adjustment to a white society that challenges a black writer's sense of worth at a level deeper than that of expression.[6]

The broad appeal of Gates's discourse and methods not only in literary studies but across disciplines points to their function as a therapeutic response to the alienation of the black middle class within integrated society. The figurative and expressive gestures of signifying implicitly signal the black speaker's freedom from the restraints of white society. Arguments about an entrapment in a pernicious white culture or discourse, however, may mask the more immediate cause of personal devaluation in an alien professional or intellectual world. And the masking of a personalized response to dislocation may account for the deeply consensual acceptance that the ethos of signifying has won within the profession of letters.

An example of the influence of this appropriation of signifying for middle-class therapy appears in a recent professional address repeated in the *Publications of the Modern Language Association.* There, black literary critic Nellie McKay echoes a commonplace of Gates's "signifying" canon. Gates suggested that Phillis Wheatley had been examined by a group of white male guarantors who wrote the note of attestation that preceded her 1773 collection of verse. Although Gates himself cites no explicit evidence of such a group oral examination, his account of Wheatley's "examination" persists as a central theme in his literary criticism and personal essays.[7] For Gates this "examination" was an exemplary episode in Enlightenment thought about race.

> This curious anecdote, surely one of the oddest oral examinations on record, is only a tiny part of a larger, and even more curious, episode in the Enlightenment. Since the beginning of the seventeenth century Europeans had wondered aloud whether or not the African "Species of men," as they most commonly put it, could ever create formal literature, could ever master "the arts and sciences." If they could, the argument ran, then the African variety of humanity and the European variety were fundamentally related. If not, then it seemed clear that the African was destined by nature to be a slave.[8]

Within the context of the atmosphere of the "test," Wheatley's literary composition becomes an assertion of her humanity, her capacity to "master 'the arts and sciences.'" And implicitly, this exhibition of cultural mastery in the face of white disbelief became an important motif in the subsequent canon of African American literature.

In a recent address, Nellie McKay refers to Phillis Wheatley's oral examination by her white male guarantors, taking her account from Gates's speculative reconstruction of the event.[9] However, in McKay's version, Gates's speculation is hardened into an actuality that dramatizes the ideology underlying Gates's canonical project.[10] By ideology, I do not refer to Clifford Geertz's spacious conception of those cultural symbols that generally organize human life, but instead to a narrowly political, social, or economic view of the world founded on a tightly knit, highly limited set of principles.[11] Gates's canonical ideology draws upon the metaphor of Wheatley's "examination" to dramatize the black middle class's sense of vulnerability in the integrated white world. The picture of the young black female facing examination by a body of all-white male examiners was immediately recognizable to academic audiences as a typical interracial confrontation in the recently integrated elite academy of the seventies and eighties. In McKay's essay, the Wheatley scenario becomes a signifying assertion about an academic playingground in which the intellectual capacities of blacks have not yet been proved. McKay is referring to an enduring historical scene, put bluntly, where blacks may have entered prestigious institutions, but still experience interrogations akin to those of Wheatley. Implicitly, McKay asserts that Wheatley and the black middle-class academic are the victims of a white racism, masking itself as inquiry.

This scenario defined Wheatley's adversarial performance as a therapeutic black victory over white expression. As an ideological narrative, the Wheatley scenario distributes a superior moral authority to the black poet who successfully confronts her white opponents in a conversation between black writers and white audiences that will, one assumes, repeat itself. Slyly, the tale refers not only to Wheatley's historical confrontation between poet and white guarantors but to the confrontation between the story's black author, skeptical white readers, and amused black onlookers perusing the text. In this enduring contest, McKay's Wheatley rewards a bourgeois black audience with the defeat of its white enemy. Similarly, Gates's historical scenario of black literacy as a parodic response to white judgment has become for some historians and literary critics a shorthand for asserting an adversarial and oppositional role of black expression toward the white Euro-American culture.

To be sure, Gates is not the first canonical critic to invent a literary strategy that gives intellectual and moral authority to a certain kind of academic reader and historical scenario. This ideologically directed pattern of identifications will—in some important ways—put readers in mind of F. O. Mathiessen's *American Renaissance.* Mathiessen created a mid-nineteenth-century canon of American fiction and poetry, stressing notions of aesthetic and moral complexity grounded in Coleridgean ideas of organic form. Assembling texts by Poe, Emerson, Thoreau, Hawthorne, and Melville, Mathiessen established canonical criteria of complex imaginative vision as well as fierce moral inquiry.[12] His early critical texts also addressed a middle class entering the elite university and the profession of literature in unprecedented numbers during the fifties.[13] The canonical motifs of ethical and political inquiry invited this audience's adversarial, moral inquiry into America's growing technological, political, and military role in the mid-twentieth-century world. Mathiessen's program of inclusive reading, formal understanding, and thematic inquiry was a means of identifying with the contrarian stance assumed by Melville and Thoreau against the liberal-capitalist order of their day. Mathiessen's tradition initiated a period of American studies as serious social inquiry of a liberal, anticommunist bent in the mid-1950s—and a conception of the literary critic as a social judge. In doing so, Mathiessen's inquiry spawned other work including R. W. B. Lewis's *The American Adam,*[14] which considered the ethical and cultural problems of New World innocence; Leo Marx's *The Machine and the Garden,*[15] which engaged the issues of nineteenth-century representation of technological transformation; and Richard Poirier's *World Elsewhere,*[16] which examined the problems raised by nineteenth-century canonical authors.

Mathiessen's moral-political ethos and persistent influence were shared by Lionel Trilling, whose appropriated notions of Hegelian spirit, among other ideas, played an important role in shaping a perspective for moral and aesthetic inquiry.[17] It is, I think, no accident that the two most significant black voices of this period, those of Ralph Ellison in *Shadow and Act*[18] and Nathan Scott in a number of his early essays (particularly *The Wild Prayer of Longing* and *The Broken Center*)[19] clearly echoed the interpretive and ideological strategies of Mathiessen and Trilling, as well as of figures such as Philip Rahv and Irving Howe.

Gates's early criticism attempted to wield the ideological authority that had been manipulated before by Mathiessen and Trilling.[20] However, Gates's canonical motifs place far more attention upon the rhetoric of professional politics and therapeutic responses to racism than upon moral and aesthetic inquiry. Interpretations such as Gates's addressed themselves directly to those tensions revealed by Jacqueline Fleming[21] and Thomas Sowell,[22] who not only addressed black middle-class disorientation in the university but linked it to differentials in academic ability, ethnic culture, and achievement—differences that were to become a central issue in the debates about affirmative action in the newly integrated elite institutions of the American academy.

Not surprisingly, Gates's ideological thrust emerges from myths about primal black selfhood and society. There the parodic play of "signifying" had an important ritual function. From his beginnings, Gates emphasized a highly nostalgic view of black parodic play, grounded both in family and in a timeless origin in an ahistorical past:

> Let me expand this idea a bit. For as long as I can remember, I have been fascinated with the inner workings of black culture, its linguistic and musical resources. My fascination with black language stems from my father's enjoyment of absolute control over its manipulation. My father has mastered black language rituals, certainly; he also has the ability to analyze them, to tell you what he is doing, why, and how. He is a very self-conscious language user. He is not atypical. It is amazing how much black people, in ritual settings such as barbershops and pool halls, street corners and family reunions, talk about talking. Why do they do this? I think they do it to pass these rituals along from one generation to the next. They do it to preserve the traditions of the "race." Very few black people are not conscious at some level of peculiarly black texts of being. These are *our* texts, to be delighted in, enjoyed, contemplated, explicated and willed through repetition to our daughters and to our sons. I acknowledge my father's capacities not only to pay him homage but because I learned to read the tradition by thinking intensely about one of its most salient aspects. This is my father's book, even if cast in a language he does not use.[23]

This gesture of filiopiety lies at the heart of *The Signifying Monkey* and its historical myth. Gates's literary history of the folk is one in which successive generations of increasingly mobile blacks improvise jazz-like upon the creations of the past. The tradition is one not only of Wheatley-like authority, but successful variations from generation to generation. And the standards of judgment are those of aesthetic delight and individual mastery.

Gates is primarily concerned with the aesthetic and therapeutic benefit made possible by spontaneous improvisation of story upon story in the African American literary tradition.[24] But these improvisations are judged from the standpoint of an adversarial chauvinism, a patronage rebellion via a return to one's roots. This folk myth evokes the timeless premodern community of signifying black storytellers. By contrast, the black folk community for Sterling Brown was deeply historical, marked by those continuities and changes experienced by blacks as they moved from the rural South to the North.[25] As a result of its appeals to the standards of a primal folk world and the cosmopolitan academy, Gates's language resonates with a confusion of norms that perhaps reflected the cultural dislocations of the black bourgeoisie to whom they were addressed. What Robert Redfield might call big and little traditions consort strangely here. Gates's father is a master theorist, a scholar of a chattering ethnic group of lesser scholar-talkers who talk about talking. The lower- and middle-class community itself—its rituals and gathering sites—is an eternal literary seminar of black culture. Black people are scholars of signifying before the fact of any academic or systematic intellectual initiation. Somehow this deep mythic identity expresses a wished-for ease in academic life.

An odd dislocation in black intellectual life therefore emerged as Gates applied signifying to the didactic, exemplary, and leadership roles of African American intellectual life. And this dislocation has only deepened the contradiction in his criticism between its cathartic, mythic aspect and his didactic intentions as a middle-class cultural leader. Henry Louis Gates has made himself into a professionalized black man of letters, a kind of literary intellectual that emerged in the twentieth-century segregated black colleges between the wars. This phenomenon, evident in the persons of critics such as Sterling Brown at Howard University, Saunders Redding at Hampton Institute, and Arthur P. Davis, Jr., also at Howard University, emerged amidst a rising black middle class about to assume a major role in African American bourgeois communities in the South and North. These critics brought to the task of humanist middle-class conversation the new methods and ideas of elite American English departments. In particular, figures such as Brown and Davis fused the profession's often divergent intellectual strands of professionalized critical practice, broad humanism, and to a lesser extent, traditional literary historical concerns. In the university, they confronted an older generation of "race men" who lacked the young critic's newly minted professional training.

Gates's distinctiveness lies in his particular response to the crisis faced by the black middle class entering elite integrated colleges. Gates became acutely aware of a professional "lag" in African American literary studies—just as Davis and Brown had been aware in the first third of the century. Early in his professional career Gates played an important role in an influential National Endowment for the Humanities seminar at Yale, where he and other young black critics from newly integrated elite departments directly addressed the need of African Americans to assimilate the advanced contemporary skills of the profession to black literary studies. And the responses drawn by the product of this seminar, *The Reconstruction of Instruction,* pointedly spoke to its implication of black professional backwardness and displacement within the academy.[26]

Like his predecessors, Davis and Brown, Gates has sought to carry the profession's newest methodologies to the black middle class. Early in his career, he was an apostle for the emerging French modes of interpretation in the seventies—and his early essays in *Figures in Black* as well as parts of *The Signifying Monkey* are clearly pedagogical in their attempt to describe, elucidate, and exemplify structuralist and poststructuralist methods for a black audience. Like Brown and Davis, Gates engaged in this task as a moral and cultural pedagogue seeking to initiate his audience into the task of making aesthetic discriminations linked to the formation of social and political values.

Significantly, Gates self-consciously compared himself and his methods with those of his predecessors, especially Brown and Redding. Gates's prefaces to important works by Charles A. Davis, his mentor at Yale, and by Saunders P. Redding often reveal Gates's attempts to make his predecessors appear to anticipate his own theories. His varied literary production, which included a literary critical monograph, *The Signifying Monkey,* the fugitive literary essays in *Loose Canons,* the cultural commentary of *Thirteen Ways of Looking at a Black Man,* and the autobiography *Colored People,* resembled that of Brown, Arthur P. Davis, and Redding, who all followed the broad careers of the man of letters. They too composed anthologies such as *The Negro Caravan* and *Calvacade,* wrote significant literary histories and book reviews, and engaged in informal journalism and personal essay writing.

At the same time, a paradoxical problem emerged as Gates, the postmodernist critic, found primal unchanging structures in black life where others found significant differences of class and cultural orientation. Where Gates saw racial solidarity, Brown could speak of "the disorganization" of lower-class ghetto life.[27] Gates's identification of a therapeutic self with the black lower class was of course an important part of the black American student culture of the sixties and seventies, yet in the late nineties it poses a serious threat. In identifying—or playing—with the pleasurable, self-admittedly antisocial, sometimes nihilistic cultural styles of the masses, black intellectuals engaged in symbolic rebellions. These interpretative strategies may have given black critics release, but they still celebrate social and cultural attitudes at odds with the meritocratic society in which blacks increasingly compete. At one point, Gates seriously speaks of signifying as a form of countersocialization, a cultural style adopted from birth. Gates's signifying ritual implicitly invites the middle class to identify with those lower-class values which they must reject for their own mobility. Celebrating middle-class taboos was a black bourgeois way of rejecting a racist white audience, yet that celebration implied serious middle-class ambivalence toward the meritocratic society and itself.[28]

As Roger Abrahams and Charles Keil, important scholars of signifying and tricksterism make clear, the signifying ritual was an important part of lower-class black culture. And the middle-class appropriation of tricksterism implicitly raises the question of the relative power of the protesting middle class as opposed to the true despair of the powerless poor. Is this lack of power a true basis for shared interest between the middle class and the poor and what would the consequence of such an allegiance be? What did the gestures of black lower-class men without jobs have to do with the cathartic gestures of upwardly mobile upper-middle-class blacks confronting competition in an integrated work world shaped by a technocratic elite? This confusion is deepened by the identification of these lower-class figures with primordial icons. If the lower class is the basis of the bourgeoisie's therapeutic values, then how can the *lumpen* be led or even properly criticized by the black middle class?[29] Where in the literary discourse of signifying is there a procedure for a self-consciousness that would identify those virtues of the *bourgeoisie* worthy of cultivation? Gates's language implies the bourgeoisie's willingness to equate its folk wisdom with professional expertise, without the kind of discrimination between types of knowledge that a historically aware critic such as Brown would make. This easy conflation has devastating consequences for Gates's theory as a middle-class professional ideology.

We encounter consequences of this ideological reading—and a shrewd correction of its confusions—when we consider Ralph Ellison's *Invisible Man.* For Gates, Ellison's revision of the central narrative tropes and images of Richard Wright's *Native Son* evokes the therapeutic pride in the primal, signifying black folk group. The literary transformations of *Invisible Man* were not merely a matter of "influence" between writers, but a kind of "signifying" Oedipal battle in which Ellison staked out a new stylistic territory for himself in his struggle with a black precursor.[30]

> By explicitly repeating and reversing key figures of Wright's fictions, and by defining implicitly in the process of narration a sophistication more akin to Zora Neale Hurston's *Their Eyes Were Watching God,* Ellison exposed naturalism as merely a hardened convention of representation of "the Negro Problem" and perhaps in part of "the Negro Problem" itself. I cannot emphasize enough the huge import of this narrative gesture to the subsequent development of black narrative forms. Ellison recorded a new "way of seeing" and defended both a new manner of representation and its relation to the concept of presence.[31]

And the product of Ellison's bold transformation was aesthetic accomplishment and creation which are celebrated for their own sake. Here Ellison's bold transformation—somewhat like a romance figure's magical transformation of nature—becomes more important than those moral, social, and political issues that Gates explicitly identifies as "the negro problem." Ellison, like the father master-artist of Gates's mythical anecdote, establishes himself as a griot-like African American artist who magically transforms past tales into myth. And at the core of this remaking is a new creation that is a good in and of itself. It is no accident that paternal and filiopietistic language are invoked, for both a new artist and a new creation are coming into being here. An aesthetic discrimination is established: we admire Ellison's artistry for the skill with which it reworks Wright's fiction into a newly made world.[32] Indeed we are less concerned with the aesthetic product of the imagination here than with the imaginative power of transformation by which social reality has been transcended.

Gates's reading of *Invisible Man* as a critique of Wright's realism is, I believe, one of the most powerful and affecting interpretations in *The Signifying Monkey.* It is now difficult to read the fiction of Richard Wright, Ralph Ellison, and Ishmael Reed without reference to the patterns of parody and artistic autonomy that *The Signifying Monkey* discerns within and between these authors' texts. However, it is just as true to say that Ellison—if he shares the technique of Gates's trickster—is deeply aware of the moral limitations of tricksterism as a vision of life. And Ellison can not only affirm the trickster figure through his own parodies—which Gates discovers—but also criticize the notion of signifying as a way of life through the characterization of the novel's Harlem hustler, Rinehart. Rinehart—as the Joycean pun in his name suggests—is morally empty. This is to say that the manipulative creativity of signifying can exist in a social vacuum without the human depth or connection necessary to become a historical force. For all of its claims to autonomy, signifying ultimately can be an expression of impotence.

Historians also have been drawn to the discourse of signifying, and they have had to confront the cultural and moral incompleteness of signifying as a cultural vision. The signifying paradigm has inevitably influenced some excellent recent social historians of early African American history, such as Graham Hodges and Shane White.[33] In drawing upon Gates's notion of "the Talking Book" and "signifying," the historians of early African American literacy have shown the way in which blacks were able to put their own impress upon the processes of the acquisition of oral culture in the New World. Graham Hodges's account of the transformation of oral into written culture in John Jea's slave narrative and preaching is an astute and erudite example of the new social history applied to the study of African American literature. And to Gates's credit, his notion of signifying as a form of cultural identity formation and resistance has clearly alerted Hodges to Africanizing aspects of Jea's passage into literacy.

At the same time, Hodges has necessarily understood that Jea's transformation also is a process of Americanization. To take on the constraints of the literary and cultural conventions of the Anglo-American tradition is to bind oneself within the imperatives of the larger white culture. Jea's literacy, as Hodges's astute introduction shows, is a process of professionalization that preoccupies him during much of his adult life. To become literate for Jea is not only to assert a modified "oral" identity but to move within the strictures of churchly institutions that defined their power by the manipulation of the written word.[34] In this respect the vantage of "signifying" oversimplifies a complicated process of Americanization.

My point is not that Gates's method does not produce coherent and at times illuminating interpretation. However, interpretations that aim at therapeutic and ideological ends are often one-dimensional in their interpretation of art and history. These interpretations are in and of themselves inadequate to the richness of significant art and criticism that frequently correct one-dimensional views of life. Another way of saying this is considered as cures for estrangement and dehumanization, Gates's criticism often reproduces, in its objects of study, the alienation that it seeks to address. Merely to parody a cultural form or mock an opponent is not to engage in a meaningful confrontation—whether politically or culturally—with him.

In this context, one way of understanding Sterling Brown is to see him as an opponent of the self-justifying, ideological brand of criticism exemplified by *The Signifying Monkey.* Brown's literary criticism pursues the self-consciousness that can both value the rhetoric of signifying and—Ellison-like—see its moral and cultural limitations. To be sure, Brown rarely reflected—as few New Critics did—on the individual, social, and political ends of his criticism. But he did meditate on a problem that was similar to that which Gates addresses in fashioning a response to middle-class dislocation. Brown too wrote perceptively about his middle-class alienation from American literary culture, linking the middle class's slackness in cultivating literary interests with the demeaning characterizations of blacks in early-twentieth-century American literature and popular culture.[35]

Brown went on to make another important point. He observed a black middle-class ideology of cultural accommodation that led black lower-class figures to denigrate black folk culture in the name of maintaining black bourgeois cultural standards. These perceptions allowed Brown to make a telling description of the black middle-class public that he wished to convert to literature. Uncritically accepting middle-class white ideology, the black middle class rejected and feared lower-class representations of blacks. It was not surprising that the black bourgeois, as Brown hinted, preferred playing cards to reading books.

In response, Brown sought to create a black middle-class self-consciousness critical of assumed racial ideologies that defined not only American life but the African American point of view as well. The astuteness of Brown's criticism lay in the ways that he sought to train his audience to see literature as a means of questioning and criticizing its own appropriations of inherited American ideologies of race in American society. Brown's criticism therefore rejected both the easy identifications and rejections that a socially insecure black audience might make through ideological strategies such as Gates's. In order to do so, Brown drew upon a sociologically, economically, and politically detailed realism.[36]

Brown described realism with less theoretical elaboration than many present-day critics might require—there were limitations to living in an age that was less interested in theory than ours is today. And we must often follow his criticism, as we follow many great critics, by its rhetorical strategies as well as by its explicit doctrines. But let me assert that the ethos of Brown's criticism aimed at positing the work as a complex imitation of social reality—an objective world outside the reader. This world of art was the site of myriad narratives, scenarios, and visions with which the reader might compare himself and his vision of the world. Such portraits forced the reader's discrimination between his own moral or social viewpoint and that of the fictional world before him. Such comparisons and contrasts only sharpened the reader's awareness of his own values and their consequences. And from the vantage of this reading, the audience was prepared to engage in self-criticism.

This was a literary strategy that enforced a kind of moral and social discrimination between the political and social situations of the *bourgeois* and *lumpen* that Gates's method of signifying pointedly ignores. The reader's sympathetic attachments, in Brown's view of reading, were necessarily made on the basis of sustained moral and social reflection. And not surprisingly, Brown, like present-day African American thinkers, found himself deeply concerned with the relation between the black middle and lower classes, an issue growing throughout the Great Migration, which Brown himself observed as a young man.[37] Brown wished for his threatened black middle class to be able to see the heroic and tragic elements of black folk life hidden by earlier ideological representations that served the interests of post-Reconstruction white supremacy. Moreover, his realism was—as the growing complexity of his literary criticism makes clear—an increasingly sophisticated way of speaking of the function of literature in creating self-understanding and a viable historical consciousness. Brown's exemplary textbooks *The Negro in American Fiction* (1937) and *The Negro in American Poetry and Drama* (1937) portrayed both African American and American literature in narratives that showed an increasing tendency toward realistic portrayal.

The objective point of view in much new critical formalism was ultimately crucial to Brown's demystifying ends and to his own role as an ironic interpreter, undoing his society's deepest racist myths, myths that impeded the African American's self-consciousness even as they advertised therapeutic benefit. The encounter with a world of fiction, poetry, or drama apart from the reader therefore provided the African American literary audience an opportunity to discover itself and its political, social, and economic interests in a new and (it was hoped) illuminating context. The techniques of formalist interpretation allowed Brown to parse literary, moral, and ultimately political problems. Part of the benefit of realistic portrayal was that it encouraged an imitation and reconstruction of social reality that challenged racist mythology in the name of a deeper, more credible "real world," a "universal" realm of human experience. Although the reader might discover established literary forms and philosophical meanings in a text, the work of art was a construct—a fiction in the sense of a made thing outside of the reader. And as she or he discovered characters, points of view, and plots, the reader encountered representations, perspectives, and a history against which she or he might differentiate and therefore come to define her- or himself. This method suited the examination of questions of racial autonomy, identity, literature as protest and art, characterization as self-examination, and the role of blacks in a new Southern regionalist consciousness.

Brown's conception of critical awareness played a similar role in describing black folk culture as a disciplined, historically grounded view of the world. This is to say that the folk were—in Brown's vision—engaged in their own versions of realism and formalism that might generate self-conscious ways of looking at the world. However, for Brown, the folk culture of the slaves represented not religious escape, imaginative reworking of the world, or mere fantasy, but rather a reflective representation of the world of bondage. Slave tradition did not passively accept new elements but rather weighed them against the inherited values of earlier bondsmen's art and sayings—carefully choosing and rejecting the offerings of the present to reproduce for the future.[38] Writing in Washington in the twenties and thirties amidst the Great Migration, Brown, furthermore, understood both the powerful transformations of this reflective dimension of folk life, which, like any other dimension of life, had a historical being. He therefore did not make folk reflection into an eternal truth: it could be lost and recovered throughout the course of human experience. To appropriate folk culture—as Brown argued that the best Southern regionalists, white and black, of his time were doing—was to enter into this sphere. But black "folk interpreters" in the city juke bars were perfectly capable of "losing" the "best" part of "their" tradition.

Brown's appreciation of the techniques of realism allowed the black middle-class reader not only to abandon his culture's racial stereotypes but also to acquire a positive sense of kinship with a sometimes threatening white world. Brown's essays invite his middle-class reader to taste the fiction of Thomas Hardy, Émile Zola, Gustave Flaubert, and James Joyce, as well as a developing realistic regionalism represented by writers such as Howard Odum, Julia Peterkin, Paul Green, and others.[39] The African American and American traditions that dismantled racist stereotypes also connected black writers and readers with broader European and American traditions that preached a self-conscious conception of man and his relation to society. In discriminating between the insights of realism and the false consciousness of narrowly ideological art, African American critics allied themselves unexpectedly with a world of white twentieth-century peers with whom they shared a critical view of experience. At the heart of Brown's conception of regionalism and formalist interpretation was a discourse by which the black middle class not only viewed itself with more discrimination, but also shed its parochialism and alienation to embrace a cosmopolitan world with a place for blacks of intellect and disciplined intellectual consciousness.

Not surprisingly, Brown's realism and formalism allowed him to criticize black writers who fell into the ideological trap of racist representation held out by American culture. His method encouraged black audiences to make critical discriminations about the work of black writers such as Zora Neale Hurston, many of whom wrote important novels during the Harlem Renaissance.[40] Brown urged that blacks might be the worst victims of the false consciousness of those racial ideologies permeating American literature. And he was deeply aware of the ways in which the ideologies of American white supremacy—which Brown found pervasive in a poem such as Vachel Lindsay's "The Congo"—might shape not only black art but its cultural as well as social sensibility.

In a number of his remarkable book reviews, Brown demonstrated a sensibility that was marked by self-awareness of its own historical moment, careful stylistic discrimination, respect for formal complexity, distrust of racial ideologies well established in American culture since the antebellum era, and a dialectical suspicion of the reader's own tendency to seduction by fantasy or propaganda. Such a sensibility ran through Brown's earlier favorable review of Langston Hughes's 1929 autobiographical novel, *Not without Laughter.* Brown affirmed this short fiction as a well-wrought account of an interesting family, an account that gave universal interest to the particular struggles of lower-class black life.

It is easy to see why Sterling Brown wanted his audience to read this book. To be sure, Brown as well as Hughes, Alain Locke, and many of the other intellectuals of the period, read the high modernist writers like Joyce and Eliot. But it is worth noting that little of the great high modernist work finds sustained attention in the essays addressed to the black bourgeoisie. Already—and in the spirit of Hughes—Brown is deeply concerned with works about blacks by both white and black authors that will immediately illuminate the political, social, and economic condition of the black middle class. And thus, we find careful attention given to Hughes's autobiographical novel (which might on another level in Brown's scheme be considered "minor literature") and the same fidelity to literary detail as in an Edmund Wilson review of a book by André Malraux.

Hughes's early novel finds complexity in the world of a young black boy growing up in turn-of-the-century Kansas, and that complexity is treated with sympathy and tact. The novel's folk world—the main characters father, Jim Boy, his mother, Angie, and his sister, Harriet—is depicted in its full vitality, tragic resistance to modernity, and sentimental virtues. *Not without Laughter* engages in a realistic examination of the black world, subjecting it to scrutiny as a site of issues of class, region, and economics. At the same time, the book's narrator, like the book's hero himself, is able to find a mixed view of life—sometimes vital, sometimes expressive, and sometimes tragic—in the life of the folk.

The narrator transcends the bigoted values of a middle-class aunt and uncle who embody an uncritical rejection of the folk as undesirable. At the same time, however, the book subjects the hero's family to the pressures of migration, resettlement, and urban life so that bourgeois values are not only affirmed as vital for survival but ultimately form the basis of the sensibility that the book cultivates. All of these issues touch upon the sort of social and self-consciousness that Brown aimed to give his middle-class audience. At the core of this self-consciousness, of course, was the dialectical capacity to criticize one's own middle-class limitations, but also to see one's strengths *vis à vis* those blacks who needed them most. And it is such an act of sensitive self-criticism that yields the novel's most impressive critical insight.

Brown, like many of his age cohort of black intellectuals, was deeply critical of middle-class limitations, bourgeois snobbery toward the folk, and, more broadly speaking, a tendency toward an intellectual narrowness that cuts the individual off from the fullness of experience. However, he criticizes Hughes for stereotyping the book's most conspicuous black bourgeois figure, and in doing so, Brown shows the way in which his own critiques can lapse into a sterile and limited view of the world.

> Of all of his characters, Mr. Hughes obviously has least sympathy with Tempy. She is the arriviste, the worshipper of white folks' ways, the striver. "They don't 'sociate no mo' with none but de high toned colored folks." The type deserves contempt looked at in one way, certainly looked at in another it might deserve pity. But the point of the reviewer is this: that Mr. Hughes does not make Tempy quite convincing. It is hard to believe that Tempy

> would be as blatantly crass as she is to her mother on Christmas Day, when she says of her church "Father Hill is so dignified, and the services are absolutely refined! *There's never anything niggerish about them—so you know, mother, they suit me.*"[41]

In many ways, this is a critique of the black intellectuals, who, given the ideological therapeutic ways of some intellectuals, can often forget their own intellectual depth and complexity. It is right to say that Tempy would be more sympathetic to her mother on this tragic Christmas morning. The deepest danger of intellectual life was its own subordination to the ideological convenience of the intellectual. Brown never forgot this.

It is worth imagining the response that Brown and Arthur P. Davis would give to Gates's and McKay's presentation of Wheatley at her orals examination. I imagine that they would be sensitive to research that shows that Phillis Wheatley's guarantors included Mather Byles, a highly visible eighteenth-century critic of neoclassical literature. They might point out that Wheatley's patrons also included Samuel Hopkins, a Newport, Rhode Island, antislavery activist. Wheatley wrote, too, in the era of the American Revolution when republican ideologies were mobilized against slavery. That is, she wrote during a time in which her resistance to racism and slavery concerned not only her opponent but like-minded critical patrons, political figures who also had a deep investment in resisting their nation's sins. These facts may not have diminished the distance that race put between her and her white supporters. But black writers such as Wheatley have always had their adversaries and allies as well as their sly enemies. Those ententes and worlds of patronage have often been difficult to negotiate. Certainly, though, in closing our eyes to these areas now discussed by scholars of Wheatley, we close our eyes to these facets of present-day black existence. The ideological narrowness we impose upon Wheatley is ultimately a narrowness that we impose upon ourselves.

In actual critical practice, Gates's literary discourse works—perhaps toward a reduction of the tensions of professional assimilation, but certainly not toward the intellectual and moral self-consciousness that could be achieved by a deeper rejection of those stereotypes and ideological forms to which his canonical strategies have sometimes tended. To put the matter differently, what is most valuable—in an aesthetic sense—about Gates, the critic of African American life, is his sensibility: a voluble quick assimilation of literary critical discourse, high culture, and African American literary culture. However, beneath the surface of that odd folk-professional skill, celebrated in his essays, is an emptiness. I find this emptiness in the sensibility of assimilation to middle-class African American moral life itself. It does not give us the framework of moral and social discriminations necessary in order to understand the black middle class's entrance into a world of increasing cultural and social complexity.

Notes

1. For the sociological understanding of intellectual life that informs this paper, see Edward Shils, *Center and Periphery: Essays in Macrosociology* (Chicago: University of Chicago Press, 1975) and *The Intellectuals and the Powers, and other Essays* (Chicago: University of Chicago Press, 1972).
2. Quoted from Roger Abrahams in Henry Louis Gates, Jr., *The Signifying Monkey: A Theory of African American Literature* (1989 rpt; New York: Oxford University Press, 1988), 53–54.
3. Henry Louis Gates, Jr., *The Signifying Monkey:* 265.
4. On these writers see Joanne V. Gabbin, Sterling Brown, *Building the Black Aesthetic Tradition.* (Westport, Conn.: Greenwood Press, 1985) and Sterling A. Brown, *A Son's Return: Selected Essays of Sterling A. Brown,* ed. Mark A. Sanders (Boston, Mass.: Northeastern University Press, 1996). For bibliographies that bear on the careers of Saunders Redding and Arthur P. Davis, see *From the Dark Tower: Afro-American Writers 1900–1960* (Washington, D.C.: Howard University Press, 1981).
5. On the concept of social knowledge that underlies these formulations, see Peter Berger, *The Sacred Canopy: Elements of a Sociological Theory of Religion* (Garden City, N.Y.: Doubleday, 1967); Peter Berger and Thomas Luckmann, *The Social Construction of Reality: A Treatise in the Sociology of Knowledge* (Garden City, N.Y.: Doubleday, 1966).
6. Philip Rieff, *The Triumph of the Therapeutic: Faith After Freud* (New York: Harper & Row, 1966). For a useful synopsis of recent writers on the therapeutic ethos, see James L. Nolan, Jr. *The Therapeutic State: Justifying Government at Century's End* (New York: New York University Press, 1998), 1–21.
7. Henry Louis Gates, Jr. "Writing, 'Race' and the Difference It Makes" in *"Race," Writing and Difference,* ed. Henry Louis Gates (Chicago: University of Chicago Press, 1989). This essay was reprinted in *Loose Canons: Notes on the Culture Wars* (New York: Oxford University Press, 1992), ch. 3.
8. Gates, "Writing, 'Race' and the Difference It Makes," 7.
9. Nellie Y. McKay, "Naming the Problem That Led to the Question 'Who Shall Teach African American Literature?'; or Are We Ready to Disband the Wheatley Court?" in *PMLA* 113 (1998), 359–69. Ross Posnock also repeats this fable of Wheatley's examination to represent her as "a freak to be carefully monitored" in Ross Posnock, *Color & Culture: Black Writers and the Making of the Modern Intellectual* (Cambridge, Mass.: Harvard University Press, 1998), 5.
10. "In search of authentication she [Wheatley] appeared with them [her poems] before eighteen white men of high social and political esteem, 'the Best Judges' for such a case in colonial Boston. Wheatley's owners and supporters arranged this special audience to promote her as a writer. According to popular wisdom of the time, Africans were intellectually incapable of producing literature. None of the Anglo Americans beyond her immediate circle could imagine her reading and writing well enough to create poetry. But when the examination was over and the men were satisfied among themselves that Wheatley was the author of the poems, they put into writing an 'attestation' that declared the works hers and, by extension, eligible for publication under her name." McKay, 360.
11. On Geertz's conception of ideology, see Clifford Geertz, "Ideology as a Cultural System" in *The Interpretation of Cultures: Selected Essays by Clifford Geertz* (New York: HarperCollins, 1973). For Shils, see "On Ideology" in *The Intellectuals and the Powers,* 23–41.

12. F. O. Mathiessen, *American Renaissance: Art and Expression in the Age of Emerson and Whitman* (1970; reprint, New York: Oxford University Press, 1941), see esp. ch. 1 and ch. 4.
13. Discussions such as these often underestimate the broad influence of the democratization of the American university as well as the concurrent intellectualization of American elites in the fifties and sixties. On these very important phenomena, begin with Edward Shils, "Intellectuals and the Center of Society in the United States" in *The Intellectuals and the Powers*, 224–72.
14. R. W. B. Lewis, *The American Adam: Innocence, Tragedy, and Tradition in the Nineteenth Century* (Chicago: University of Chicago Press, 1964).
15. Leo Marx, *The Machine and the Garden: The Pastoral Ideal in America* (New York: Oxford University Press, 1964).
16. Richard Poirier, *A World Elsewhere: The Place of Style in American Literature* (New York: Oxford University Press, 1966).
17. See, for instance, the essays in Lionel Trilling, *The Liberal Imagination: Essays on Literature and Society* (1974; reprint, New York: Scribner's, 1949), especially "Reality in America" and "Huckleberry Finn."
18. Ralph Ellison, *Shadow and Act* (1964; reprint, New York: Random House, 1964).
19. Nathan A. Scott, Jr., may be the most distinguished example of the way in which the humanism of the 1950s provided the basis for a black critic's entry into the broadest arenas of literary criticism, which had hitherto been highly segregated, and nearly closed to all but a few blacks. See for instance, *The Broken Center: Studies in the Theological Horizon of Modern Literature* (New Haven: Yale University Press, 1966); *Negative Capability: Studies in the New Literature and the Religious Situation* (New Haven: Yale University Press, 1969); *Three American Moralists: Mailer, Bellow, Trilling* (Notre Dame, Ind.: University of Notre Dame Press, 1973); *The Wild Prayer of Longing: Poetry and the Sacred* (New Haven: Yale University Press, 1971).
20. Gates speaks with an alarming directness about the cynical manipulation of canonical authority in literary criticism throughout *Loose Canons* (Chicago: University of Chicago Press, 1992).
21. For the work of Jacqueline Fleming and allied recent studies that report or interpret findings on black college students in white colleges, see Jacqueline Fleming, *Blacks in College* (San Francisco: Jossey-Bass Publishers, 1976); Joe R. Feagin, Hernan Vera, Nikitah Imam, *The Agony of Education: Black Students at White Colleges and Universities* (London: Routledge, 1996).
22. Thomas Sowell, *Education: Assumptions versus History: Collected Papers* (Stanford: California Hoover Institution Press, Stanford University, 1986); *Education: Myths and Tragedies* (New York: McKay, 1971).
23. Gates, *The Signifying Monkey*, xi–xii.
24. See qualifications on this point in Gates, *The Signifying Monkey*, xx–xv.
25. Compare Gates's timeless conception of the folk-world with that of Sterling Brown, which stresses the historical elements of continuity and change in the lives of the transplanted Southern black folk.

    The migration of the folk Negro to the cities, started by the hope for better living and schooling, and greater self-respect, quickened by the industrial demands of two world wars, is sure to be increased by the new cotton picker and other man-displacing machines. In the city the folk become a submerged proletariat. Leisurely yarn-spinning, slow-paced aphoristic conversation become lost arts; jazzed-up gospel hymns provide a different sort of release from the old spirituals; the blues reflect the distortions of the new way of life. Folk arts are no longer by the folk for the folk; smart businessmen now put them up for sale. Gospel songs often become show-pieces for radio slumbers, and the blues become the double-talk of the dives. And yet, in spite of the commercializing, the folk roots often show a stubborn vitality. Just as the transplanted folk may show the old credulity, though the sophisticated impulse sends them to an American Indian for nostrums, or for fortune-telling to an East Indian "Madame" with a turban around her head rather than to a mammy with a bandanna around hers; so the folk for all their disorganization may keep something of the fine quality of their old tales and songs. Assuredly even in the new gospel songs and blues much is retained of the phrasing and the distinctive musical manner. Finally, it should be pointed out that even in the transplanting, a certain kind of isolation—class and racial—remains. What may come of it, if anything, is unpredictable, but so far the vigor of the creative impulse has not been snapped, even in the slums.

"Spirituals, Seculars, Ballads," in *A Son's Return*, 263.

26. Dexter Fisher and Robert Stepto, eds., *Afro-American Literature: The Reconstruction of Instruction* (New York: Modern Language Association of America, 1979).
27. For Henry Louis Gates's recent dismay over the failure of literary criticism and literary intellectuals to address the plight of the black lower class, see "Harlem on Our Minds" *Critical Inquiry* 24 (autumn 1997), esp. 6, 11–12.
28. On the theme of the ambivalence of the new black middle class, see Adolph Reed in *W.E.B. Du Bois and American Political Thought: Fabianism and the Color Line* (New York: Oxford University Press, 1997), 169–76.
29. Roger Abrahams, *Deep Down in the Jungle . . . : Folk Narratives from the Streets of Philadelphia* (Chicago: Alpine, 1970); Charles Keil, *Urban Blues* (Chicago: University of Chicago Press, 1966).
30. Elsewhere in *The Signifying Monkey,* Gates has, in what he would call a signifying passage, shown his own straightforward borrowing of Harold Bloom's *The Anxiety of Influence* (86–88). Much of this academic playfulness directed toward Bloom, Lanham, Wimsatt, Frye, de Man, and others is a parodic borrowing from the most fashionable styles in the Yale English department of the late sixties and early seventies.
31. Gates, *The Signifying Monkey,* 106–107.
32. Gates, *The Signifying Monkey,* 72–74.
33. Shane White, "'It Was a Proud Day'; African Americans, Festivals, and Parades in the North, 1741–1834," *Journal of American History,* 81 (June 1994):35–37; Graham Hodges, *Black Itinerants of the Gospel: The Narratives of John Jea and George White* (Madison: Madison House, 1993); David Waldstreicher, *In the Perpetual Midst of Fetes: The Making of American Nationalism, 1776–1820* (Chapel Hill: University of North Carolina Press, 1997).
34. Graham Hodges, *Black Itinerants,* 23.
35. Sterling A. Brown, "Our Literary Audience" in *A Son's Return,* 139–48. For the American and in particular the antebellum heritage of racial stereotypes of racialist ideologies see Brown's central essay, "Negro Character as Seen by White Authors" in Brown, *A Son's Return,* 149–83.
36. Brown, "Our Literary Audience," passim.
37. For an excellent account of the impact of the Great Migration in Washington, D.C., see Sterling Brown, "The Negro in Washington," in *A Son's Return,* 25–46.
38. See Brown, *A Son's Return,* 209.
39. For examples of Brown's reviews of these critics, see Brown, "Fabulist and Felossofer—A Review," *Opportunity* 6 (July 1928): 211–12; Brown, "An American Epoch," *Opportunity* 9 (June 1931): 187; Brown, "Poor Whites," *Opportunity* 9 (October 1931): 317–20.
40. See Brown's shrewd review of Hurston's *Their Eyes Were Watching God,* "Luck is a Fortune," in *A Son's Return,* 291–92.
41. Sterling Brown, "Not without Laughter," *Opportunity* 8 (September 1930), 279–80.

PART III

MEDITATIONS ON THE PRACTICE OF HISTORY

In offering their meditations on the practice of history, the authors in this section explore many of the themes raised in this volume's introduction and earlier essays, from the role of subjectivity in history to the state of the social sciences and education generally. But they do so here in the context of their broader ruminations about how and why we study history. Through engrossing autobiographical forays, illustrative stories and examples, or excavations of past alternatives for considering contemporary questions, these essays shed light on historians' larger sense of purpose, the intrinsic rewards of studying the past, the craft of history, and some elements of what might be called a historical sensibility. This sensibility helps explain the disjunction many historically-minded observers experience between their own attitudes and those of others who fall prey to some of the current cultural tendencies elaborated in earlier sections of the book.

Leo Ribuffo's entertaining sketch of his own career opens with observations that will ring familiar to many readers. He discusses his encounter with a kind of self-righteous amnesia among those who simultaneously fail to see the relevance of learning about a time through which they did not live and assert authoritative knowledge of their own times based on personal encounter. Ribuffo grants that there should be "no unbridgeable gap" between an untutored observer and a historian, but reflects on the ways in which the contemporary frame of mind—with its personal, subjective assumptions taken to the extreme—can run contrary to the sensibility historians largely share. Despite their many differences, those who study the past tend to be driven by a belief that parts of the past can be known, even without firsthand experience, that the will of past actors can be discerned, and that attempting to unravel these matters requires the utmost seriousness. In a discussion of his own intellectual trajectory, Ribuffo hardly denies all connection between personal outlook and intellectual products, but illustrates that the exact nature of such connections should never be assumed. His comments urge openmindedness not only to the past on its own terms, but to the enormously diverse, or "ecumenical" ways in which we can and do approach the study of the past.

Based on her experiences at the Scottish Record Office, Deborah Symonds also articulates a historical sensibility that counters the contemporary assertion that there can be "no knowable past," a claim she finds "sad," "perverse," and a sign of "desolation." The initial encounter with original sources—smelling a dusty old volume, for instance—immediately eats away at such assertions; even further she reflects on how her immersion in documents concerning a woman tried for the murder of her own daughter illustrate the ways in which maintaining a healthy skepticism, searching for corroboration and reasonable proof, and other difficult tasks of the historian can help establish that the woman and her predicament did, at least, exist. The task of research is "humbling, refining, and tempering," and necessitates a kind of "sympathy with the dead" (words she borrows from Adam Smith) which prevents the dismissal of the record of their lives as merely some kind of "contested cultural narrative." Perhaps most revealing, Symonds admits that ultimately the woman's story itself took on a fascination for her that transcended any simplistic theoretical formula according to which it could be categorized.

Like Symonds, Bruce Kuklick explores the rewards of studying the past—in this case by drawing an intriguing analogy between the sport of baseball and the study of the humanities to show that both constitute practices, sharing aspects of a craft, with "traditions, norms, standards of workmanship." This accumulated wisdom rules out crude claims of relativism, revealing that not all work is of equal value. While frequent debates take place within practices, shared standards and particular virtues result from actual performance of the work. The intrinsic rewards, moreover, are less easily found outside the practice than external rewards like money and prestige. In order to discover the nature of particular practices, the virtues they produce, and their relation to the institutions on which they rely, he urges a kind of "historical moral philosophy," both as a suggestion for historiographical directions and as a way to keep in sight the satisfactions and ethical moorings of a particular practice.

Victor Hanson's essay moves from this wider arena of historical practice to the specific predicament of the contemporary military historian. He makes a case against the dismissive nature of current ideology-driven views that can cast suspicion on historians of warfare, as if all study of war must translate into a wholesale endorsement of it. Instead, Hanson sees the challenge of studying war as inextricably tied to a weighty twentieth-century paradox: "identifying and combating evil without bringing on the annihilation of all that is good." Hanson warns against a totalizing perspective, like that evident in Hollywood renderings of the horrors of war such as *Saving Private Ryan* without any sense of underlying purpose and ensuing moral complexities. There is a difference, embodied in Western notions of a "just war," between wars that were "amoral, poorly conducted, or waged for reasons that did not justify the commensurate sacrifice" and wars fought precisely *against* evil in the form, for example, of death and destruction during so-called peacetime. Hanson faults a fascination with disembodied "discourse," in part, for the "sheer lifelessness of the present environment in American academia." Words, apart from facts and deeds, give a truncated version of the past, which fails to do justice to complex realities. Counting the dead, an attempt to get the facts straight and a central contribution of historians of war, is a form of respect we owe the dead and contributes to a deep grasp of the reality of war as tragedy, "not melodrama."

Paul Rahe's essay similarly looks at an aspect of the past he considers widely ignored in today's academic climate. The "arrogance," as he puts it, of modern social science imposes "alien paradigms" on all past eras, leading it to dismiss the importance of popular opinion in forming political communities and thus bringing about change. Dominant theories now take an overly narrow view of causality—a central preoccupation of the historically-minded—by seeing all ideas as resulting from "crude passions and material interests," a point of view that ranks social class in all cases as more important than political conditions. Rahe urges the excavation of ancient political science as a more subtle guide than such determinism to recognizing the importance of the ideas of entire populations in historical development, a philosophical standpoint that bridges the "modern distinction between materialism and idealism" and points to a possible integration of social and political history.

In a similar turn toward the wisdom of the ancients, Donald Kagan would have us recover a broader sense of the multiple functions of education. Like other authors in this volume, Kagan observes the triumph of a "relativism verging on nihilism" and connects it in part to a severely diminished sense of the purposes of education. Giving a brief chronology of central changes in liberal education since ancient times, he sees the current form as, sadly, most closely resembling that deemed appropriate to the education of the elite, emphasizing the social tools its members need to appear well rounded and to be easily accepted in polite society. This form of education stresses the making of appropriate friends above the acquisition of extraneous knowledge. Any sense of the relation between learning and the freedom and self-governance of individual citizens, the joys intrinsic to learning, the importance of character formation, and preparation for careers useful to society has all but disappeared. In fact, a result of this diminished vision of education is the loss of "common intellectual ground" that allows for rich conversations in wider society—which Kagan sees as a main element of education—and a concomitant loss of connection and obligation to society itself.

In the final essay of this section, Edward Berkowitz further explores the consequences of particularism—in the form of a celebration of diversity for its own sake instead of genuine learning—and the vanishing of any conception of a shared history. The emphasis on ethnic difference, in this context, helps erode the ideal of social integration and the sense of worthy institutions that embodied it, such as the settlement house. Historians are directly implicated in this state of affairs, Berkowitz asserts, for, while the role of unifying the populace is up to politicians, scholars' actions do have public ramifications. Losing "their sense of proportion," he thinks, historians have turned too far inward to pursue the latest fashions, often comprehensible only to themselves, embracing a false dichotomy of whole peoples as "good guys and bad guys." Taking their legitimate "oppositional" role too far, they help reduce trust in all institutions and any source of commonality. While hardly asking for an end to historians' healthy propensity toward debunking, Berkowitz does raise the question apparent in so many of the essays in this volume, of whether that role has raised new blinders in the form of a new kind of conformity.

As these essays illustrate, sifting carefully through the past and present for what we should keep and what we should retain, or what we should believe and what we should doubt, is not only more challenging but more helpful than assuming a uniform posture of debunking for its own sake. The courage to make such difficult distinctions and judgments is, after all, part of a larger obligation we owe not only to those who have lived before us, but to posterity.

CHAPTER 11

CONFESSIONS OF AN ACCIDENTAL (OR PERHAPS OVERDETERMINED) HISTORIAN

Leo P. Ribuffo

RECENT CONTROVERSIES WITHIN our profession almost require a reflective historian to contemplate two questions: to what extent *should* personal beliefs and value judgments affect the writing of history, and to what extent *have* personal value judgments affected the history each of us has written? We can begin to address the first question by examining some of the statements often heard from nonhistorians. In the first instance, the speaker, usually an undergraduate in his or her teens or early twenties, declares, "I wasn't even *born* when Truman was president, so how do you expect me to know what happened?" In the second instance, the speaker, often a retiree auditing my class, declares, "I was *there* when Truman was elected, and he wasn't the kind of president you say." Although superficially at odds, these two statements share a common presumption: that personal experience provides the best starting point (and perhaps ending point) for understanding the past.

We can leave for another occasion the question of whether this presumption has primal roots in human nature, American individualism, or a contemporary "culture of narcissism." It is sufficient here to note that the presumption seems especially honored in discussions of history compared to other kinds of inquiry. Even the most recalcitrant undergraduate would hesitate to declare in astronomy class that never having been to the dark side of the moon, he could not say for sure whether it is cold up there. Nor do patients in coronary care units protest, "Doctor, how should I know if my arteries are clogged? I've never been inside them."

Not only is the elevation of personal experience above other sorts of evidence commonplace when "everyman" and "everywoman" think about the past, but this attitude also affects molders of opinion. At best, our recalcitrant astronomy student would be recruited for a Jerry Springer Show on adolescents with attitude, and the coronary care skeptic might join a recent returnee from Jupiter on a late-night radio call-in. On the other hand, my student who proclaims his ignorance of the Truman era has a shot at prime time and the "style" section of a major metropolitan newspaper. Indeed, on anniversaries of events that the mass media deem memorable, journalists eager to show "how much things have changed" (their central metaphysical premise) descend on young men and women who, fulfilling their ritual role, declare that Hiroshima or Selma or Woodstock or Watergate mean nothing to them because they "weren't even born." Older folks fare better in these rituals because, like my contentious retirees, they can claim to have been "there," and they fare particularly well if their "there" is judged to be the best "there." No critical interpretation of Truman stood a chance as long as Clark Clifford survived to repeat stories so stylized that even he could not recall when he actually remembered the events in question. And Students for a Democratic Society will bulk larger than George Wallace's 9.9 million votes as long as Todd Gitlin holds his place as gatekeeper of the history of the "sixties."

As Carl Becker emphasized before I was *even born,* there is no unbridgeable gap between the everyman or everywoman who "manages, undeliberately for the most part to fashion a history, a patterned picture of remembered things said and done in past times and distant places," and the historian who works longer, harder, and more systematically to make sense of the past.[1] Furthermore, as Warren Susman stressed—and I was *there* to hear him—rigorous theory sometimes represents the intellectuals' formalization of hunches growing in the grassroots. Still, the gap between historians and nonhistorians remains wide, and bridges are few and far between.

Simply put, despite diverse specialties, varied moral sentiments, and divergent political opinions, historians usually share common approaches to the past that do not characterize most other human beings, including comparably educated, better paid, and more powerful human beings. This claim may sound peculiar in an era when noted scholars discern immense methodological—and even moral—differences between practitioners of the "new history and the old," but a glance beyond our insular controversies should sustain the point.[2]

To begin with, historians typically believe that we can more or less understand the past without having been there or having talked to somebody who was. Except for those of us who concentrate on very recent events, this belief is an occupational imperative since most of the people we study are dead. Yet those of us who can conduct interviews, and even those who listen raptly to aging presidential aides or campus rebels recognize, at least in theory, that Todd Gitlin and the Vietnam War prisoner of war occupied different "theres," and that memories often are confused, formulaic, or self-serving. Such wariness, the staple of a methods seminar for first-year history graduate students, may seem obvious to historians, but journalists, documentary filmmakers, and political scientists easily develop immunity to it.

Furthermore, most historians still believe not only that we can more or less figure out what individuals and groups *intended* by their words and deeds, but also that it is important to do so. Few of us examine the Bill of Rights as ten "texts" without authors, ratifiers, or legislative histories. To be sure, some attributions of intent are easier to make or more consequential than others. We may never know what one government official, customs clerk Herman Melville, intended when he wrote about the whiteness of the whale; perhaps, as some literary critics tell us, we should not much care. But we can infer with certainty—and relief—that another government official, President Ronald Reagan, intended a joke when he said, "I am pleased to tell you I have signed legislation to outlaw Russia forever. We begin bombing in five minutes."[3] Then too, historians typically continue to believe not only that the socially constructed time period called Tuesday comes before the socially constructed time period called Wednesday, but also that this sequence makes a difference. Thus, while puckish literary critics trace the "influence" of twentieth-century poets on eighteenth-century poets, no historian maintains that Japan bombed Pearl Harbor in December 1941 to retaliate for the American bombing of Hiroshima in August 1945.

Finally, though our profession contains some opportunists and charlatans, most historians try to understand past events with atypical seriousness of purpose. Even if such earnestness derives from socialization and habit rather than from high ideals and methodological sophistication, it nonetheless separates us from other people whose jobs require some interpretation of the past. A constitutional lawyer might well argue passionately before Judge Smith on Tuesday that most authors and ratifiers of the First Amendment intended to protect obscenity and then argue passionately before Judge Jones on Wednesday that they did not. Indeed, she might continue this process through a long, lucrative series of Tuesdays and Wednesdays without wondering which interpretation was true, let alone whether the question of truth made much historical sense. Nor would many attorneys question this behavior, since, according to their (more explicit) professional code, lawyers are supposed to serve their clients without necessarily finding out, in Leopold Ranke's famous phrase, "what essentially happened."[4] The (less explicit) standards of conduct among historians differ significantly. Although two or three major interpretative shifts per career are often construed as signs of enhanced maturity, any historian who persistently alternated between incompatible interpretations would be considered a fool or a charlatan.

My purpose is not to denigrate the everyman, everywoman, everystudent, everycritic, and everylawyer who stand on the other side of the intellectual gap sketched here. Nor do I suppose that "learning to think like a historian" is harder than "learning to think like a lawyer" (as lawyers often proudly describe their education) or like an operatic tenor or like a quarterback. Least of all do I want to imply that the ways in which most historians think about the past constitute a "science." Rather, regarding our relationship with nonhistorians, I recommend the advice of an artist, abstract expressionist painter Robert Motherwell. Motherwell thought that there was no more reason to expect the average person to understand modern art than to expect him to understand higher mathematics. So, too, with history.

Members of our profession who believe that historians should spread the true faith, uplift the masses, or defend intellectual standards in an age of grunge culture may be appalled by this analogy, especially if they find modern art boring, dangerous, or incomprehensible. As someone who likes and occasionally understands modern art (with a little help from my friends who create it or write about it), let me assure you that the lessons I draw from Motherwell's advice are less elitist than might be feared. I am not denying that most people can do a better job of thinking like historians (or like abstract expressionists). All they need in our case is a little help from historians, a commitment of time and energy, and, perhaps most important, a willingness to reconsider cherished beliefs. But no matter what we historians do, even those Americans who possess an above average interest in the "patterned picture of remembered things said and done in past times and distant places" are unlikely to commit much time and energy, or risk many cherished beliefs. Rather, most will continue to prefer history as a mildly instructive entertainment. Accordingly, on Saturday afternoons they will curl up with William Manchester's chronicle, *The Glory and the Dream,* rather than such substantial fare as Bernard Bailyn's *The Ideological Origins of the American Revolution* or Gabriel Kolko's *The Triumph of Conservatism.*

Cultural critics who lament America's alleged decline into grunge are so outraged by this sort of laziness that they cannot resist concocting glib historical arguments to fight the trend. Yet there is no good reason for anyone to be surprised, let alone outraged. From time to time historians themselves use the life's work of others as nothing more than mildly instructive entertainment. I confess. After scolding lawyers and journalists for wasting their time on mere chronicles, I tune in Metropolitan Opera broadcasts as background music or indolently watch football games without pondering the techniques of competing quarterbacks. Placido Domingo and John Elway could rightly regard this behavior as outrageously superficial. Saturday afternoons at the National Gallery of Art require greater intellectual energy, yet artists are hardly surprised that I still understand the Spanish Republic itself better than I understand Motherwell's "Elegy for the Spanish Republic."

In short, most historians share both special ways of thinking about the past and unusual respect for what historian Warren Susman called the "pastness of the past" that is absent from most other people, and understandably so. This conclusion could be used to justify many divergent responses from our profession (a much abused term I choose deliberately and with perverse affection), responses that include sloth, apostasy to journalism, and intensified efforts to increase the historical understanding of quarterbacks, operatic tenors, and abstract artists, among others. None of these positions lacks adherents among historians and all retain some visceral appeal for me personally, but they are not my chief concern here. Rather, I submit that because professional historians share so many rare and worthwhile approaches to the past, we should treat one another with greater *respect* and *tolerance* than is customarily the case. Accordingly, my answer to the question—How much should a historian's personal beliefs and value judgments affect his or her scholarship?—is simple and unequivocal. As much as he or she wants.

Fellow historians who have known me a long time may protest that I did not always associate myself with such professional ecumenicalism. Perhaps some of them recall my fondness for Barrington Moore's admonition that we must never underestimate spite as an engine of intellectual progress. They may even believe that my standards have been eroded by excessive exposure to Placido Domingo, John Elway, and Robert Motherwell. Let me reassure them that ecumenicalism need not compromise sound doctrine.

Respect for fellow historians does not necessarily entail admiration or even agreement. It does require a presumption that others are thinking, researching, and writing in good faith, a willingness to consider arguments on their own terms before offering alternate "frames of reference," and an obligation to paraphrase those arguments fully and fairly in the process of criticizing. Nor does tolerance require the ritual celebration of "diversity" that now characterizes our profession; often it requires the opposite. At all times it demands the admission that valuable ideas may sound peculiar at first hearing, that ideological or methodological adversaries are capable of valuable insights, that eccentricity and spitefulness are no bars to brilliance, and—especially—that there is no one best way to write good history.

Thus defined, ecumenicalism seems to me consistent with what I have always hoped the study of history would be, even when, in typical human fashion, my own behavior fell short of my highest values. From one perspective, then, it represents the formalizing of notions that have been growing in my mental grassroots since my sophomore year in college, when I first learned that systematic thought improves our understanding of the past. From another perspective, however, this ecumenicalism grows out of temperamental traits that go back even further.

Elaboration requires a transition to a second question: to what extent have personal beliefs and value judgments affected my own historical writings? Since the medium is at least part of the message, my own reminiscences will be stylistically ecumenical. On the one hand, methodological traditionalists should be pleased to find chronological narrative, contextualist intellectual history, and footnotes. On the other hand, postmodernists should be pleased to find allusions to popular culture, self-indulgent references to notable acquaintances, and an unstable text subject to multiple interpretations, some of which may have been subverted by the "author." There are even allusions buried in the subtext that connect this memoir to the great tradition of *kvetchy* intellectual autobiography. Those who have known me a long time may complain that my recollections are as stylized as Clark Clifford's or Todd Gitlin's. And the author himself is unsure whether his workaday philosophy of history is primarily the product of contingency or totally overdetermined.

Insofar as my books and articles are known, they are known for the empathic examination of historical oddities: for example, Americans who anticipated the imminent arrival of the Antichrist; the minority among them who expected the Antichrist to lead an international Zionist conspiracy; and a president, Jimmy Carter, whom many citizens viewed in terms of what even his own campaign manager called the "weirdo factor." This reputation, though not the sum of my professional aspirations, is altogether fitting. Since adolescence I have been interested in and often sympathetic to weirdos, or, to put the point in intellectualspeak, political dissenters, cultural rebels, and social deviants. An old friend, psychobiographer Peter Carroll, once suggested that my interest in *religious* weirdos represented an unconscious attempt to reconcile my father's Italian-American Catholicism and my mother's eclectic WASP Protestantism. Since I have written similarly about Ronald Reagan, I cannot reject this interpretation out of hand. Yet, at least in my stylized rendition, social class played a larger role in my intellectual development than faith or ethnicity. My father was a public school janitor and my mother a "pink collar" worker. Thus I grew up during the fifties in an amorphous zone between the working class and the lower middle class. This background is atypical among historians of my age cohort and, with the decline of generous fellowships, probably even rarer in the next generation.

According to autobiographical convention and the prevailing methods of our profession, I should now relate my heroic struggle, perhaps inspired by a youthful reading of Karl Marx's *Grundrisse,* to rise from poverty to a professorship. Unfortunately for autobiographical convention, there was neither poverty nor much struggle, and I have never read the *Grundrisse.* Participating in a working-class and lower-middle-class trend now disdained by most historians of the fifties, my family moved from a decaying, racially and ethnically diverse neighborhood in Paterson, New Jersey, to a bland (but still ethnically diverse) suburb across the Passaic River called Fair Lawn. Thus, again I confess, I grew up safe and well fed. I did not sew on buttons in a sweatshop but mixed milkshakes (technically, soy shakes) at a lackadaisical McDonald's in the days before fish sandwiches and Vatican II, when hungry Catholics asked us to violate company policy and cook toasted cheese sandwiches on Fridays.

Fortunately for this text, and perhaps also for my understanding of history, all was not well in Fair Lawn. Mine was among the poorest families in town, and by the time I reached high school in 1959, I had begun to resent the greater affluence of my classmates. Some of them drove their own cars, had visited Disneyland or even Paris, and would be able to afford Ivy League colleges. Occasionally, too, I was scorned by teachers or fellow students as the son of a janitor. Safe and well fed—usually too well fed—I nonetheless felt economically out of place. Moreover, mine was among the least "intellectual" families in Fair Lawn. Although I loved the Landmark histories and Signature biographies for teenagers and often browsed through political memoirs and muckraking journalism, I did not read a weighty adult book, except for the obligatory freshman *Julius Caesar* and sophomore *Macbeth,* until my senior year in high school (Somerset Maugham's *Of Human Bondage*). Having subsequently encountered Dwight Macdonald's writing, I can now dismiss Fair Lawn's adult "intellectuals" as middle brow bourgeois. In the early 1960s, however, I envied families that received Time-Life books each month and did not have to acquire their encyclopedia by the week at the A&P.

Had I been as well read as the best high school minds of my generation, I might have discovered that I was suffering from "status anxiety." Yet this discovery would not have changed my behavior, which was to celebrate myself as an outsider and to sympathize with other outsiders. Probably I was an overdetermined outsider. Not only did my precarious class position push me in that direction, but I was also near-sighted, intermittently overweight, the survivor of a parental break-up at age ten, and, as Peter Carroll might emphasize, a migrant among theologically incompatible Sunday schools in an era when Americans were supposed to be either "Protestant, Catholic, [*or*] Jew."

It did not take much to be a self-conscious outsider at Fair Lawn High School. Perhaps life was very different in Cambridge, Madison, and Berkeley, but in Fair Lawn, 1961–1962, my senior year, still qualified as the "fifties" by every standard except the decimal system. Even the putative hoodlums resembled Fonzie in *Happy Days* more than Marlon Brando from *The Wild One.* Moreover, lacking an aptitude for legally removing, let alone stealing, hub caps, I would have been an incompetent juvenile delinquent (or "primitive rebel," for those readers who prefer a more subversive discourse).

Rather, I hung out with other status anxious outsiders of vaguely intellectual pretension. We listened to Odetta and Olatunji records, discussed Vance Packard's debunking portraits of American life, occasionally read *The Realist* magazine, and attended a scatological lecture by the editor, Paul Krassner. We also demonstrated our heightened sensitivity by drinking beer illegally at the Bleeker Street Tavern in Greenwich Village instead of the Suffern, New York, bars preferred by jocks and cheerleaders. In addition, I was a fellow traveler, though not a *Howl*-carrying member, of the high school bohemian set, kids who quoted Dostoevsky, Shaw, and Ferlinghetti as well as Allen Ginsberg, and who called themselves "hippies" before the term was nationalized. And I told my senior year English teacher that I admired the male protagonist in *Of Human Bondage,* a judgment she pronounced "sick."

If I had been among the best minds of my high school generation, I might have discovered Malcolm Cowley and Kenneth Burke's analogous "innocent rebellion" in suburban Pittsburgh before my *mother* was even born. As an overdetermined outsider, however, I would have missed the bemused tone in *Exile's Return* and inferred instead that Cowley and Burke had been my precursors. En route to the Bleeker Street Tavern, I did see that there were more outsiders of vaguely intellectual pretension than I had supposed.

Indeed, the adolescent suburban secession of the fifties did fit into a venerable American pattern. As was the case with the "innocent rebellion" of the first decade of this century, it involved inchoate left-of-center politics.[5] During my senior year at Fair Lawn High School, I wrote a research paper on William Jennings Bryan, whom I liked a lot even before I discovered that he, too, had suffered from status anxiety. In the process, I traveled back across the Passaic River to use primary sources for the first time—microfilm of the

Paterson Daily News stored at the Paterson Public Library. I discovered that I loved to do research in old stuff.[6] Sometimes, waiting for the bus back to Fair Lawn, I bought a copy of the *Weekly People* from the Socialist-Labor newspaper box incongruously located by the Paterson City Hall. I also sent away for Socialist Labor Party (SLP) literature, which the party dispatched along with an organizer who showed up at my suburban doorstep much to my mother's horror. In my pantheon of old socialists, however, SLP founder Daniel De Leon appealed much less than Eugene Debs. When my senior year history teacher selected three students to speak for the presidential candidates of 1912, I insisted that Debs, too, must be represented—by me.

Nevertheless, compared to the devout Stevenson Democrats, not to mention the "red diaper" babies among the Fair Lawn secessionists, I lacked ideological rigor and commitment. Viewed in reified retrospect, I was a young "cold war liberal" who excitedly asked Norman Thomas for his autograph and excitedly distributed campaign literature for John Kennedy in 1960. Still, I felt less fervor than eclectic curiosity. I also collected Nixon campaign paraphernalia and then developed an anthropological interest in the so-called radical right. In 1962 the Young Americans for Freedom held their first major rally, at Madison Square Garden in New York City. While my fervent friends picketed the event, I wandered around collecting a glorious array of weird pamphlets. Moreover, with the possible exception of the gifted agitator Mark Lane, no one at the liberal counter rally sounded as interesting as the far right weirdos they were picketing. Later I organized a trip to a New York rally sponsored by Fred Schwarz, head of the Christian Anti-Communism Crusade. Schwarz proved to be a disappointingly bland agitator. Yet, already savoring fine distinctions on the far right, I noticed that he deflected charges of anti-Semitism by having the band play "Milk and Honey," a popular Broadway show tune about the founding of Israel.

Eclectic curiosity aside, I was insufficiently secular to fit into the cosmopolitan liberalism or incipient radicalism of the early 1960s. Although I had ceased migrating among theologically incompatible churches, I remained interested in religion and, if I had then known the category, might have called myself a "cultural Catholic." Certainly political or ideological positions rooted in religious faith were not automatically suspect. In 1960, my high school biology teacher, J. Leslie Campbell, did something that now would be unconstitutional but which, at the time, seemed enlightening if unusual. Campbell spent one class session questioning the Darwinian premises that apparently undergirded the rest of the course. I say "apparently" because, even though I attended public school during the educational golden age now celebrated by Lynne Cheney, Diane Ravitch, and other cultural conservatives, all I can remember, aside from the anti-evolution session, is drawing amoebas with colored pencils and killing my hydra with chow mein from the cafeteria. Apparently without disabling classmates bound for medical school, Campbell moved me to think about the limits of science. Viewing the film *Inherit the Wind* shortly thereafter, I enjoyed the iconoclastic character modeled on H. L. Mencken, yet found the Bryan character's opposition to Darwinism at least worthy of empathy.

Although status anxiety precipitated my teenage rebellion, Beardian economic factors kept it innocent. I was determined to go to college in order to "get a good job"—perhaps as a high school teacher. Thus I never crossed the line between outsider and troublemaker. My status-anxious heart still quickens when I recall the advising session in which my junior high guidance counselor, my parents, and I discussed whether I should take French and algebra, or "shop" and business math. Since my grades and test scores were at least respectable, I would have been routinely tracked to college prep courses if my family had been unambiguously middle class. But the guidance counselor, who knew my father the janitor, had his doubts. Finally we agreed to give it a try. At roughly the same time my social studies teacher was making a distinction I found unconvincing, between other countries, which had social classes, and the United States, where there were merely different income levels.

Prudence characterized my response to the Fair Lawn red scare of 1961, an event that suggested for the first time that history could happen to me and my friends as well as Bryanite farmers. History in this case was represented by the House Committee on Un-American Activities (HUAC). Under sustained attack for the first time in fifteen years, HUAC made a movie, *Operation Abolition,* about opponents who had jeered the committee in San Francisco and were then arrested, beaten, and dragged down the steps of city hall. When the film, an inept piece of propaganda that mischaracterized all the protesters as Communists or their dupes, reached the Fair Lawn American Legion hall in early 1961, some of the hippies showed up to protest. At the next screening in town, the president of the Teen Age Republicans made the bizarre charge that much "un-American activity" flourished at Fair Lawn High School.

What followed was characteristic of small scale red scares during the Cold War era. As contending forces mobilized, the question of Soviet Communism versus American democracy merged with petty local animosities and issues of less than world historical significance: for example, the refusal of one hippie to salute the flag; the use of J. D. Salinger's book, *The Catcher in the Rye,* in an English class; and the presence of the word "womb" in the high school newspaper. The result was a characteristic red scare mixture of tragedy and absurdity. One school board member died of a heart attack while defending student patriotism, four teachers (including the proponent of Salinger and "womb") were investigated by the school board, and a candidate for Miss Fair Lawn declared that all students should salute the flag. The summer after my senior year, having little else to do, I wrote a brief history of this local red scare, which I deposited (and which may still rest) in the high school library.

In September 1962 I entered Rutgers University where, according to the convention of intellectual autobiographies, I was supposed to have had an intellectual awakening comparable to a religious "conversion." Perhaps I would have experienced one if I had followed Norman Podhoretz to Columbia University. More likely I would have been shattered, since my prior conception of college life derived largely from 1930s movie musicals and television shows with Ray Milland and Ronald Colman as tweedy professors. Given this naiveté, Rutgers was the best place for me. There were enough smart students to facilitate late night talk about the meaning of life but not so many that I had to work very hard. And several professors differed significantly from Milland and Colman in age, demeanor, and accent.

The history department was full of wonderful campus characters and their peculiarity probably influenced my choice of a major as much as my interest in the subject. During my sophomore year, Professor Lloyd Gardner urged me to consider applying to graduate school. Although law school continued to linger in my consciousness for two years, Gardner's suggestion was instantly appealing. When I raised the question of money, he said that fellowships were readily available. In 1963 it seemed extraordinary that I could actually get paid to learn about history and make even more money by teaching history to others. It still does. But Beardian economic factors alone do not explain my choice of a career. I also liked the prospect of someday becoming a wonderful campus character myself.

But not that much of a character. My beau ideal of a historian was still Arthur Schlesinger, Jr., who advised the president and appeared on television. College teaching looked like a great job but I hardly thought of myself as an intellectual, a term I associated with pretentious creeps majoring in English. During my junior year, I signed up for American intellectual history *despite* the title because the legendary Warren Susman taught the course. The class was, to use a Susmanism, special. Never had I imagined that American history contained *so many* weirdos or that a professor could enjoy them as much as I did. Indeed, he said that Bryan had shown greater intellectual honesty than his opponents at the 1925 Scopes "monkey" trial. Nor was Susman the only Rutgers historian with an empathic eye for odd beliefs and behavior. Although historian Eugene Genovese paid altogether too much attention to fertilizer, his favorite weirdo, George Fitzhugh, was sufficiently spectacular to compensate for reading Lewis C. Gray's *History of Agriculture in the Southern United States to 1860.*

If I had been among the most serious minds of the suburban secession, I might have appreciated that several of my teachers were on the cutting edge of historiography. Lloyd Gardner taught revisionist diplomatic history and invited his mentor, William Appleman Williams, to speak at Rutgers. Despite Gardner's influence, I continued to believe until my senior year that President Kennedy had rightly confronted the Soviets during the Cuban missile crisis. In a junior year seminar on slavery, Genovese started talking about something that sounded like "hedge-EM-ony." After a few minutes I realized I had seen this word in print but mistakenly assumed that it was pronounced with a hard *g* and an accented first syllable.

According to an Italian Marxist named Antonio Gramsci, Genovese explained, ruling classes retained power not only by monopolizing force but also, or even primarily, by convincing others that their values were the best values. This notion seemed sensible enough but hardly extraordinary because that was how jocks and cheerleaders dominated suburban high schools. Little did I suspect that I was present at the birth of a buzz word or that I was participating in the intellectual equivalent of buying Xerox stock when it was sold door-to-door. Indeed, with both Genovese and Gramsci's biographer John Cammett on the faculty, Rutgers was probably the western hemispheric center for hegemony studies in the early 1960s.

Perhaps I would have behaved differently in Cambridge, Berkeley, or Madison, but in New Brunswick, New Jersey, in 1964 I felt no need to *read* Gramsci, which probably was a wise decision, as I find his work opaque even now. Indeed, most of my Marx came secondhand through the heterodox appropriations of Gardner, Genovese, and Susman. But I did read—and love—William James, John Dewey, and others who led the pragmatist "revolt against formalism" in the late nineteenth and early twentieth centuries; some of their intellectual offspring, especially Reinhold Niebuhr and C. Wright Mills; and their trans-Atlantic counterparts, especially Max Weber and George Sorel. Sigmund Freud and Karl Mannheim followed in due course. As this essay shows, I especially liked James's notion that our ideas mesh with our personal temperaments and Dewey's notion that the ways intellectuals think need not differ qualitatively from the ways everybody else thinks. The dual issues of "historicism" and "relativism" also fascinated me. Yet, for reasons I still cannot explain, the absence of philosophical absolutes never bothered me (though I could see why their erosion virtually disabled James, Weber, and Jane Addams). Like Dewey, perhaps, I both found the collapse of "formalism" liberating, and also exaggerated humanity's capacity to "reconstruct" plausible philosophies and build decent societies instead of sliding into nihilism or vicious versions of absolutism.

The subject of my senior honors essay, called a Henry Rutgers thesis, allowed me to explore weirdos, relativism, and philosophical absolutism. A textbook had mentioned Lawrence Dennis as the "intellectual leader of American fascism" during the 1930s and, knowing no more, I set out under Susman's guidance to figure out my latest weirdo. I was surprised to discover that virtually everything written about Dennis and the far right during the Depression was wrong. It was one thing for me to accept the historicist position that interpretations vary with time, place, and circumstance, and another to see over and over again that living *professors* who had published *books* could not escape their own biases. Yet the evidence seemed indisputable that, contrary to the scholarly consensus, Dennis resembled John Dewey and Edward Bellamy more than Adolf Hitler and Benito Mussolini; that he was vindictively prosecuted by the liberal Roosevelt administration with the enthusiastic support of the left; and that even respectable "isolationists" were smeared during what I called a Brown Scare. I presented these arguments in what was, depending on the frame of reference, either the worst Henry Rutgers thesis in the university's history or the best Henry Rutgers thesis ever written in three weeks.

Clearly, my senior year, 1965–1966, brought many distractions, but only one had world historical significance: escalation of the Vietnam War. Once again it appeared that history could happen to me. This realization did not fully sink in until the summer after my graduation in 1966 when I took the "war boards" to secure a graduate school deferment. Nonetheless, I had opposed the war from the moment it entered my consciousness on a regular basis. That moment came in April 1965 when I attended a teach-in dominated by Rutgers historians, including Susman, Lloyd Gardner, and Genovese. Despite their trenchant analyses, I initially considered the war a mistake rather than the logical result of American foreign policies from at least the late 1940s. In 1964 I was treasurer of the Rutgers Young Citizens for Johnson (a post I accepted because the chairman was my friend and because I wanted to meet girls, as we called them in those days, at intercollegiate conferences and the Democratic National Convention in Atlantic City). Unenthusiastic about Lyndon Johnson, I cheerfully played the role of Barry Goldwater's champion when the Rutgers debate team discussed the election at a local high school. In my heart I knew he was wrong, but in my heart, too, I was still a Cold War liberal.

Much as Adolf Hitler inadvertently convinced a generation of social scientists to embrace Franz Boas's critique of pseudoscientific racism, Lyndon

Johnson inadvertently convinced me and many others in my generation to accept a broad critique of American foreign policy. By early 1966, I was a full-fledged Cold War revisionist. In Berkeley, Cambridge, or Madison, I might have been moved to read Lenin on imperialism; in New Brunswick, New Jersey, I contented myself with Charles Beard, Norman Thomas, and other "isolationists" from the 1930s.

Although less volatile than Berkeley, Cambridge, and Madison, New Brunswick was not devoid of excitement as the social-cultural fifties turned into the social-cultural sixties. For the second time, I lived through a red scare. The central issue of the 1965 gubernatorial campaign was Professor Genovese's speech at the April teach-in. Republican candidate Wayne Dumont, supported by Richard Nixon, wanted Genovese fired because he had "welcomed" a Vietcong victory. In this red scare, I mixed participation with observation, guiding through the student government a resolution that defended Genovese's right to his opinions.

Although standard histories of the era suggest otherwise, everyday life continued during the sixties. For me everyday life meant attending Yale graduate school in American studies. Yale had the most renowned American history faculty in the country. My classmates included future winners of the Turner, Craven, Bancroft, and Pulitzer prizes. Nor was professional distinction confined to historians. Erudite professors of literature were pioneering structuralist and poststructuralist criticism. My contemporaries in the law school, affected by the lingering eddies of legal realism, already expected to redirect American government. Some of them—Bill Clinton, Hillary Clinton, and their friends—have now done so. Indeed, recalling celebrated accounts of Paris in the age of Picasso, Stein, and Hemingway; or New York in the age of Kerouac, Podhoretz, and Motherwell, I am tempted to compose a memoir/monograph called *New Haven in the Age of Clinton, Paglia, and De Man.*

All of the facts in the preceding paragraph are accurate, but the conclusion—that Yale constituted a lively intellectual community during the sixties—is nonetheless misleading. Perhaps no one in my generation entered graduate school with greater expectations and then felt greater disappointment. Influenced by Gardner and Susman's tales of Madison in the 1950s, I naively anticipated lively, creative discussions with professors and students who were trying to figure out "what essentially happened" in the past. Instead, there were few ideas, rampant pretentiousness, and institutionalized suspicion of enthusiasm. To be sure, my sour reaction may have been the product of status anxiety. After years in remission at Rutgers, this social-psychological malaria began to give me the shakes soon after I arrived in New Haven.

Yale in 1966–1967 was the strangest place I had ever seen. Having read Vance Packard and C. Wright Mills, I understood in principle that genteel, educated WASPs ran the country, but never had I seen so many of them in one place. Nor had I ever seen so many people of any race, ethnic group, gender, or sexual orientation exude such a sense of entitlement. At Yale in 1966 many professors and some students did look and sound like Ronald Colman and Ray Milland even though they had been born in the United States. One historian asked the ethnic origin of my last name and seemed distressed by the answer that it was Italian (which should have been obvious to a resident of New Haven). Even John Kasson, my first WASP friend, spoke so seriously of living the "life of the mind" that I was in turns energized, amused, and terrified.

Yale had its virtues, not the least of which was that it was not Khe Sanh. It was not even Harvard or Columbia, where graduate students not only competed for faculty attention in tense and tedious seminars, as we did, but also lost their fellowships if they faltered in the competition. As early as 1966, there were other outsiders with wacky, often conflicting ideas about life and history, and our ranks grew larger as the mere chronological 1960s turned into the "high sixties" (1968–1972). Don Worster, a former boy evangelist, questioned the convention that American society was becoming secular. Jim Green celebrated southwestern socialists in his essays and his attire. Mike Sherry and I discussed the virtues and vices of Franklin Roosevelt over and over and over again. Susanna Barrows, Carol O'Connor, Ellen Dwyer, and Sarah Stage taught me to respect women's brains and women's history. Mills Thornton exemplified intelligent, ethical conservatism. Larry Powell showed that good scholarship and passion for social justice could go hand in hand. Dave Pace, a premature postmodernist, warned against biographies that traced a teleological development from infancy to eminence or infamy. Henry Abelove urged me to read *more* Freud, lest I slip into the worst vice of American social thought, *neo*-Freudianism. Citing Peter Berger and Thomas Luckmann's *The Social Construction of Reality,* long before that book's title became a cliché, Bob Schulzinger emphasized the virtual impossibility of writing history. By 1968, there was even one junior faculty member, Bruce Kuklick, who came from a working-class background, criticized American foreign policy, and wore jeans but no tie. From these wonderful campus characters I received most of my education at Yale.

Most important for getting a good job (a major concern of mine even during the high sixties) one senior faculty member turned out to be a kindred spirit. Sydney Ahlstrom's manic energy reminded me of Red Buttons rather than Ronald Colman or Ray Milland, and his knowledge of weirdos spanned continents and centuries. Under Ahlstrom's direction, I recycled my old interest in the far right of the 1930s into a doctoral dissertation. The standard interpretations, which dismissed personal anguish as mere status anxiety and reduced intricate theology to evidence of a "paranoid style," seemed weaker than ever. Ultimately, my effort to explain *how* and *why* orthodox interpretations fell short involved more than the life of the mind. The high sixties forced almost everyone to rethink their conceptions of deviance and dissent. And by 1970, though the pervasive sense of entitlement remained undiminished, Yale itself overflowed with dissidents and deviants.

Even at the time, however, I felt like a deviant among revisionist students of deviance. While other young scholars were rediscovering good deviants—heroic peasants, noble artisans, and prescient Cold War critics—I was trying to figure out what made bigots tick. Clearly the subject fitted my temperament as an overdetermined outsider who found villains more interesting than heroes. Why sip tea with social gospelers at Yale Divinity School when you can eat fried chicken with the nativist Gerald L. K. Smith and contemplate the meaning of America at the base of the Christ of the Ozarks? Furthermore, during the high sixties, when Richard Nixon won the presidency and George Wallace received 9.9 million votes, I thought it important to explain villains to the virtuous. By 1970, almost everyone I knew who was pursuing the "life of the mind" exuded virtue, according to prevailing cosmopolitan standards, but everyone in the rest of my life did not. I was related by blood and affection to people who voted for Nixon and Wallace. Despite my best efforts, virtuous friends rarely understood that the label "racism," which superseded "status anxiety" as the preferred reductionist shorthand, failed to encompass the texture of working-class and lower-middle-class fears.

The year of my birth, 1945, as well as my working-class/lower-middle-class origins made me an outsider during the high sixties. I had admired Daniel Bell's essay, "The Mood of Three Generations," since my first reading at Rutgers.[7] Three or four years later, I concluded that a version of his generational analysis applied to me and some of my friends. Writing in 1960, Bell described his own generation, by which he meant leftist intellectuals from the 1930s who became Cold War liberals during the 1950s, as "twice born." That is, they had moved in twenty years from "chiliastic" dreams of social transformation to practical advocacy of incremental reform. In my own case, I had moved in five years from *de facto* acceptance (despite my adolescent claims to outsiderism) of many dominant American attitudes to skepticism or outright rejection. Unlike many others who reached adulthood on the cusp of the sixties, I made this transition with relative ease. Yet there were enough strains to give me a sense of having changed significantly.

This feeling of being "twice born" was reinforced by my contact with Yale undergraduates from late 1968 onward. I began to teach my own seminar on American social thought in 1969 and became a full time faculty member, with the modest title of acting instructor in history and American studies, the next year. Although my students were only four or five years younger than I, they were "once born" dissidents and deviants. Unlike myself, most had never as young adults trusted their government, thought marijuana a dangerous drug, rushed to end a date by the 1:00 A.M. curfew for girls, considered abortion a sin, questioned interracial romance, or discussed the propriety of marrying women who were not virgins. My views moved leftward on all of these issues, but the *rationale* for my former beliefs remained perfectly intelligible. To most of my students, however, these seemed as incomprehensible as other cultural shards from "Consciousness II," as Yale Law Professor Charles Reich designated the chief intellectual currents from the industrial revolution to the high sixties.[8]

If I had been at a more volatile campus in Cambridge, Ithaca, or Chicago, I might have been vulnerable to the viruses of neoconservatism or neoliberalism that affected such contemporaries as Elliott Abrams and Michael Kinsley. I suspect, however, that my visceral hostility to the privileged would have provided immunity. In the relatively placid world of New Haven, I responded to the high sixties by performing modest good deeds and honing my sense of the absurd. I served as a poll watcher for Eugene McCarthy, George McGovern, and Hank Parker, the first black candidate for mayor of New Haven. I told my students that they could improve the United States without leading a guerrilla band into the Berkshires. I worked hard at my teaching and more or less upheld intellectual standards. We drank a lot of beer in my seminar on the history of American radicalism, and students occasionally arrived stoned or just flipped out—it was hard for a Consciousness II type like myself to tell. But, unlike Professor Reich, I never accepted a loaf of home-baked bread for academic credit.

Absurdity at Yale peaked in 1970, when the local trial of Bobby Seale, accused of murdering a fellow Black Panther, precipitated a student strike (shrewdly co-opted by Yale President Kingman Brewster), an uneasy alliance between Panthers and campus radicals, and a massive demonstration on the New Haven green during May Day weekend. Dutifully participating in debates at the graduate student "collective," I argued that the Panthers certainly deserved a fair trial, but that they might also be guilty as charged. This position placed me decidedly to the right of center. Dutifully attending meetings of history and American studies graduate students and faculty, I encountered distinguished scholars who believed that the United States now resembled the Weimar Republic, a popular motif of the day, especially among "twice born" intellectuals of Daniel Bell's generation on their way to becoming thrice born neoconservatives. My alternate interpretation of the

May Day strike as a manifestation of homegrown American radicalism prompted one eminent European historian to call me "paranoid" (little did he know that paranoia was my business). Since my modest campus good deeds went largely unappreciated, I fell back on savoring the proliferating array of wacky pamphlets, speeches, and rumors. I tried unsuccessfully to spread a surreal rumor of my own, that on May Day a giant monkey would climb Sterling Memorial Library carrying Mrs. Brewster.

By 1972, when the high sixties were dribbling to a close, I had haphazardly acquired both a "good job" as assistant professor of history at Bucknell University and a worldview. During the next twenty-five years, my job moved two hundred miles southward, but my worldview has remained essentially in place. Simply put, I am a Deweyan pragmatist with considerable respect for what William James called the "fringes" of consciousness; a cultural relativist who nonetheless thinks that some explanations, beliefs, and actions are better than others; a Niebuhrian who understands that it is not always easy to decide which explanations, beliefs, and actions are better than others; and an unreconstructed working-class McGovernite who would like to vote for a left rooted in American realities (but who most recently has had to settle for Ralph Nader). Sometimes deliberately and sometimes inadvertently, this conglomeration of coherent ideas, Jamesian "overbelief," and amorphous hopes affects everything I have published, including my two books, *The Old Christian Right* and *Right Center Left.*[9] Moreover, I am embarrassed to admit that I continue to expound on far right and nativist movements even though everything I say merely updates or fine tunes an argument first presented in *The Old Christian Right* sixteen years ago—an argument which itself was intellectualization of my adolescent hunch that even the ideas of weirdos must be studied seriously. Indeed, I am so embarrassed that I will stop addressing these subjects as soon as the historical profession admits that I was correct all along.

Anyone whose *kvetchy* intellectual autobiography slides over two and a half decades in one paragraph, as I have just done, stands vulnerable to the charge (often leveled at Henry Adams) that he has something to hide. To deflect such spiteful revisionism, I can add that some old interests have deepened and new ones have appeared. As before, friendship, personal temperament, status anxiety, and Beardian economic factors intersected in these developments. My wife, Diana Rodriguez, has opened my eyes to the Third World in general and Latin America in particular. I owe my belated interest in art to Lee Fleming, a Washington, D.C., critic, and to her parties in the 1970s, where I alone, quaking with status anxiety, could not distinguish between Modigliani and Motherwell. To continue to earn a living, I convinced the George Washington University history department that I was as much a political and diplomatic historian as an intellectual historian. Ultimately convincing myself, I began a book on Jimmy Carter's not-so-weird presidency, a project that proceeds at my usual, glacial pace. My service as treasurer of a tenants' association during a grueling fight over condominium conversion, the most Beardian experience of my adult life, underscored the importance of "bringing the state back in" to social analysis a decade before many fellow historians noticed the limits of heroic mobilizations by "the people." My colleagues at GW, Bill Becker and Ed Berkowitz, subsequently provided theoretical and empirical support for this hunch.

Retention of my "cusp of the sixties" worldview in the 1990s leaves me an outsider, albeit a comfortable outsider, among historians of the United States. In my ecumenical view, both broad studies of hegemonic "mentalités" and narrow studies of "race, class, and gender" *can* constitute two kinds of good history. According to prevailing professional norms, however, these genres constitute the two best kinds of history. Neither genre fits my temperament. Indeed, devotees of both typically ignore or caricature issues that interest me: the nitty gritty of electoral politics, formulation and implementation of government policy, and the beliefs of men and women who reject "progressive" assumptions. When generalizing about the whole United States, moreover, they typically slight explanatory factors I consider essential, especially religious faith and the surrogate religion of nationalism, and exaggerate the degree to which the countless protests and rebellions in the American past reveal an almost-realized radicalism rather than an ideologically inchoate and often transient anger.

Moreover, I am less convinced than the profession at large that recent borrowing from postmodern philosophy and literary criticism improves our understanding of the perennial issues of historicism, cultural relativism, and the problematical nature of the words we use. Perhaps these borrowings signal little more than an ephemeral appropriation of the latest chic vocabulary (much as references to status anxiety were *de rigueur* when I entered graduate school). If postmodern philosophy and literary criticism were necessary to remind American historians that evidence does not speak for itself and that we need to think about what we are doing when we claim to speak for it, then we should be grateful for the lesson. Yet this lesson has long been readily available in the clearer formulations of many "modern" thinkers, including William James, Dewey, Weber, Mannheim, and the old "new critics" of the 1950s. Indeed, the current heightened sensitivity to the persuasive, deceptive, or controlling nature of language may be an instance in which the hunches of everyman and everywoman are ultimately formalized by intellectuals. During the course of this century, for example, reformers slightly left of center needed no training in linguistics to adopt the popular buzz word progressive, to substitute liberal when progressive started to sound old-fashioned or un-American, and to return to progressive when the "l word" lost popular favor.

Whatever the initial benefits, the losses from the "linguistic turn" in historiography are at least as great as the gains. American historians have become so concerned with methodological problems associated with literary criticism that they now pay insufficient attention to equally valuable ideas available from economists, sociologists, and political scientists. Furthermore, in tandem with the vogue of local social history, this excessive worry about the validity of the texts we read and write has narrowed our range of vision. After all, if we hesitate to say that a page or a paragraph or a sentence is in some sense true, how can we risk generalizing about whole countries over decades or centuries? Yet sorting out change and continuity over time is what professional historians have always done best. Everyman and everywoman will continue to want broad panoramas of things said and done in past times and distant places. If we do not provide them, others less respectful of the pastness of the past will.

Finally, a tendency toward glib moralizing from a left liberal or radical perspective has affected American historical writing for the worse. Perhaps, having spent so much time trying to make far right villains comprehensible rather than merely deplorable, I am too touchy on this point. Moreover, much of the glib moralizing needs to be understood as a defensive response to the so-called culture wars in which some historians have enlisted and many others seem on the verge of being drafted. In this "war," which is better described as the latest cultural shouting match to define a normative American way of life, prominent conservatives, in a typical exaggeration of the consequences ideas have, accuse a generation of once born radicals of not only lowering intellectual standards, but also of corrupting the young.

Although understandable as a response to these attacks, especially since many come from ideologists who have never seen the inside of an archive, our profession's insular defensiveness does more harm than good. In particular, defensiveness has produced proliferating moral *assertions,* about the virtues of the "new" histories as well as about past heroes and villains. These assertions come at the expense of moral *argument* in which historians examine their own personal beliefs and lay out explicit rationales for their value judgments. Perhaps most important, glibly moralistic history undermines our efforts to increase the historical understanding of lawyers, quarterbacks, operatic tenors, and abstract artists, among others. Persons who were not even *born* in past times and distant places tend to regard those who were as at least slightly weird and perhaps morally inferior simply because they looked, sounded, and acted differently from current norms. Glib historical moralists reinforce the smugness of the here-and-now instead of helping to show why people looked, sounded, and acted differently there-and-then. If historians do not do this, who will?

In a sense, these reservations about current trends merely formalize my disappointment that the professional life of the mind has turned out to be much less playful than I have always wanted it to be. I have never gotten over my youthful vision of professors and students arguing together in friendly fashion about what the past essentially was. I want more controversy in the study of American history, not less. Yet my contrarian complaints here constitute neither a declaration of cultural war nor a prophecy of intellectual doom. Indeed, another generation of accidental or overdetermined historians is probably already on the way to challenge the current orthodoxy.

Notes

1. Carl Becker, *Everyman His Own Historian: Essays on History and Politics* (1935, reprinted Chicago: Quadrangle, 1966), 245.
2. Gertrude Himmelfarb, *The New History and the Old* (Cambridge, Mass.: Harvard University Press, 1987).
3. Raymond L. Garthoff, *The Great Transition: American-Soviet Relations and the End of the Cold War* (Washington, D.C.: Brookings, 1994), 159–60.
4. Peter Novick, *That Noble Dream: The "Objectivity Question" and the American Historical Profession* (New York: Cambridge University Press, 1988), 26–31.
5. On the "innocent rebellion," see Henry F. May, *The End of American Innocence: A Study of the First Years of Our Own Time 1912–1917* (Chicago: Quadrangle, 1964), 219–329.
6. For readers who missed the subtext connecting this essay with the great tradition of *kvetchy* intellectual memoirs, this is it! As in Alfred Kazin's *Starting Out in the Thirties* and Norman Podhoretz's *Making It,* the author travels across a body of water (in this case, the Passaic River) to find intellectual excitement in the metropolis (in this case, Paterson rather than Manhattan).
7. Daniel Bell, *The End of Ideology: On the Exhaustion of Political Ideas in the Fifties* (reprinted 1962, Cambridge, Mass.: Harvard University Press, 1988), ch. 13.
8. Charles Reich, *The Greening of America: How the Youth Revolution is Trying to Make America Livable* (New York: Random House, 1970).
9. Leo P. Ribuffo, *The Old Christian Right: The Protestant Far Right from the Great Depression to the Cold War* (Philadelphia: Temple University Press, 1983), and *Right Center Left: Essays in American History* (New Brunswick, N.J.: Rutgers University Press, 1992).

CHAPTER 12

LIVING IN THE SCOTTISH RECORD OFFICE

Deborah A. Symonds

THERE IS SOMETHING in the experience of research that defines the historian. It is humbling, refining, and tempering, although not, at least in my experience, as obvious as a conversion. Nonetheless, the effect of the research experience reminds me of a nineteenth-century French popular print in which bad husbands are dropped into a large chemical apparatus, coming out the other end quite literally converted to good husbands. This strikes me as an excellent graphic metaphor for the process, which for bad husbands, bad wives, bad partners of all sorts, and historians, takes many years; but for historians, at least, the process does indeed have its roots in the empirical experience of the archive, record office, and library.

In 1974 I was briefly locked into the main library at Edinburgh University one night, a victim of my Yankee unfamiliarity with the late sunlight at that latitude. Engrossed in a card catalog in a library in which everything up to and apparently including the incunabula was in open stacks, I sat hunched over a tall desk until the lights went out, and I slowly understood from the slanting light and utter silence that I was alone. The library, relatively new, had glass walls, and after not too long I caught the attention of a night watchman outside, who let me out. I was sorry to leave, and even after twenty-four years I remember the regret I felt as I made my way down the steps into George Square. Those cards hardly constituted the kind of primary research I intend to write about here, but that was the first time I had been so caught up that I understood that what I was doing was more important to me than my carefully cultivated air of worldliness and competence, the armor of a wet-behind-the-ears graduate student in a new country. I left some of that feigned arrogance behind me as I walked out of the library, shedding it almost absentmindedly.

Ten years later, having turned from literary history and folklore to history, I returned to Edinburgh, a city I have never been able to leave easily since I first set foot in it. Working in Register House until it closed at 4:45, I slowly became accustomed, not to the imposing monumental architecture of the neoclassical Adam building, with its rotunda and its flocks of law clerks and genealogists, but to how quickly I forgot them once my books were delivered. At the risk of arrant romanticization, I am inclined to argue that historians must hold the original documents of whatever they study, look at the paper, and smell everything. Only by coming face to face with surviving documents, seals, letters, maps, accounts, and receipts can one, I believe, fully weigh the meaning of terms like intention, falsification, and truth.

All of them are hard to evaluate, not just truth, which so often comes in for a drubbing these days. A colleague of mine, an earnest and serious scholar, illustrated this current attitude toward truth a year or two ago by saying (as well as I remember) that we in the history department should stop lying to our students, for there is no knowable past, and hence no past within human comprehension. This strikes me as an unbearably sad position to take in relation to the universe and to the past, reeking of a desolation that is more familiar to me in Rimbaud, before World War I, or in Wittgenstein in the 1920s. That this attitude should reappear in the late twentieth century, when the influx of material in history alone, about all sorts and conditions and kinds of men and women suggests quite the opposite—that the past is becoming increasingly knowable, in all its damnable and glorious complexity, and even inanity—strikes me as perverse. And it also suggests that, once the Donation of Constantine was discovered to be a forgery, historians who pondered Laurentius Valla's detective work had no choice but to face the full intricacy and irony of their position. In other words, face value—itself a telling phrase—dissolved a long time ago, but not into nothingness. What lay behind that face was research: more papers, more questions of face value, but ultimately the possibility of corroboration amounting to reasonable proof. To paraphrase Wittgenstein, survivor of the trenches: what we cannot speak about, and must pass over in silence, or contemplate in an agony of theory, seems to me, currently, to be greatly outweighed by what we can, have, and must discover and discuss.[1]

But let me go back to Register House, past the guards and the notices about unattended packages and security, past the cloakroom and the old man with several teeth missing, who for years greeted me every morning with,

"Go get 'em, sunshine." The Historical Search Room lies up a cast iron staircase, off a balcony that circles the rotunda, through large double doors that cannot be opened silently. Inside, as in many another archive, are rows of desks, surrounded by bookcases that run up to a high ceiling. Men in uniforms who have worked here for years take slips of paper out of a basket, whisper to each other, and push carts full of bundled papers, bound volumes, and boxes of loose papers in and out of the room. In almost complete silence, papers are distributed to the numbered desks, and you get what you ordered.

For the sake of simplicity, all I will argue here is that history, whatever it may become, begins from the materials of history, and that it is in confronting these materials that questions of belief, intention, falsification, and truth have to be confronted and resolved. Theory comes later, after one has decided what one is, in fact, at the most empirical and scientific level, theorizing about, and how one's own biases dance at the edge of every apparently objective pool of light. In this case, to return to the story, what I had ordered was a volume of circuit court records, from the West Circuit, including Glasgow and surrounding counties, covering the period from September 18, 1767, to May 29, 1769. These volumes traveled with the judges from the High Court of Justiciary who rode the circuits, and probably to make travel easier, they were much smaller than the volumes used by the court in Edinburgh. They were carried in saddlebags, and written in, probably often, by bleary-eyed clerks. This particular volume, JC 13/16, is covered in dried leather, and smells of dust and old paper. I dare say that my friends who are more obliged to critical theory might call this description of an old book as "old" a delusion, an imposture, a facade of some sort. I am willing to call it an old book. The cover does not matter much, and my most immediate, personal, and ingrained response to it, because I am allergic to dust, is to sneeze.[2]

What is in JC 13/16, on its unnumbered pages, is much more important. In this instance, I find something I was not looking for, but which holds my attention. Agnes Dugald, widow of a deceased "coallier," or collier from Campsie, is indicted for murder and denies the charge, which is that she had cut the throat of her own young daughter, near a hedge on the banks of the Clyde, a river just west of Glasgow. Several witnesses heard her confess, and although she later denied the charge in court, she was convicted and hanged. This is clearly no great matter of state, and this brief report of the incident might stand as a small footnote to some larger, but perhaps not much larger, matter in social history. But what I want to discuss is not whether this is important, or how, but something simpler—how one verifies and evaluates this story. Working with court records might seem a sort of escape from the problem, given that the testimony is, simply, the testimony on which the jury had to base its decision. But people lie in court, sometimes because lying comes naturally to them, and sometimes because as good lawyers know, ordinary people confuse direct observation with their own presumptions, and tell stories with implicit conclusions that are not proved, but only suggested by what they have observed.

What follows is not only a small part of Agnes Dugald's story, but also a record of how I worked with the case to find these people, corroborate what they said, understand how the court members heard and questioned their testimony, and expand the slender story left on a few pages of paper into something with implications. The first witness called, William Rutherfurd, was an apothecary or druggist in Glasgow, "aged thirty and upwards," and unmarried. He was probably called first by the prosecutor, Cosmo Gordon, because he had seen much of what there had been to see, and because he was respectable, in the sense that he had a profession, and a medical one at that. Rutherfurd said that "time and place libelled [named]" he had been walking along a footpath with Walter Stirling, a merchant from Glasgow. They came across the body of a child lying face down near the path, and one or both of them turned the body over; it was probably Rutherfurd, for he remembered saying to Stirling, after perceiving the wound, that "the Murderer can be at no great distance." Rutherfurd then went to the end of a nearby hedge, found a boy herding cows, and asked if anyone had passed by. The boy "pointed out a Woman at a considerable distance," and added that she "had just murdered a Child." At this point Rutherfurd gives us the first clue to where this has taken place, near a road or path running west of Glasgow, along the northern bank of the Clyde. Members of the court would have known this already, for it would have been part of the indictment presented at the beginning of the trial—but that indictment, contained in a long list of the court's business in that county, the Porteous Roll, was a separate document, which may or may not now survive among the small papers of the court.

In that indictment, the prosecutor, Gordon, would have tried to draw up both an exact and a general description of the crime, clear enough that it would justify, as it was noted in this court journal, taking the case to trial: "Cosmo Gordon . . . [c]raved the Lords would find the Indictment relevant & Remitt the Pannel [accused] & Indict. to the knowledge of an Assize [jury]." But the indictment is not here for us to consider, for, to save time, the court clerk had only written, in the place on the page where the indictment would have been written in by the High Court clerk, had this trial taken place in Edinburgh, "(Here record the Indict)." So we are left, without the Porteous Roll, to infer what we can from the various testimonies that do survive in the document we have in hand.

And Rutherfurd's testimony probably tells us as much as the prosecutor would have known. Rutherfurd then said that "the Woman at that time was walking pretty fast up the River towards Anderstown [*sic*]." At that point he ran after her, was joined by another man along the path, and they "laid hold of her." They were then near a brewery in Anderston, at that time west of Glasgow, but soon to be engulfed by the city's growth. Since there were cows, a hedge, and a pleasant footpath by the river just west of Anderston, the town itself was probably still a hamlet, given that breweries were often located near sources of fresh, clean water.[3] Rutherfurd and the other man, James Cleland, then looked at her. Rutherfurd said that she had her hands under her apron, and that "having called upon her to show her hands they found them covered with a good deal of Blood." At that, he and Cleland and "several others" took Dugald back to the body, where Rutherfurd seems to have taken charge. Specifically noting, probably in response to a question by a magistrate or lawyer, that he had never seen Dugald before, he reported that he stood her in front of the dead child, and asked "How she could be guilty of so barbarous a Murder upon her own Child for by that time he had learned that she was the Mother of the Child." Before we consider what answer she was able, or willing to make, let us consider the clause "whom he had never seen before." There are at least two reasons why members of the court would have wanted to know what his relationship to Dugald was. He may have had some ax to grind, some private wish to see her implicated; or he may have come looking for her because a rumor had spread in her neighborhood, suggesting that violence was imminent. In this case, Rutherfurd was unconnected, and the court would have known that he was responding chiefly to what he saw, without any preconceived hatred or suspicion of Dugald.

What he and the others now heard Dugald say was that "they gard [caused] her do it for that the Elders had threatened to put her into the Correction House and upon that account she had taken revenge upon her own Child."[4] Whether she managed to express herself so clearly at this point, or whether some of the words were Rutherfurd's, her meaning was plain enough. In trouble, powerless against the elders of the church, perhaps recently widowed, and possibly having been chided for not taking care of the child, she took out her anger on the child. In general, a woman who murders her daughter when threatened with a stay in a house of correction is not a good woman, and the elders may have had reason to harass her. But Dugald's problems might have been averted had her husband lived. Then, she might have raised that daughter, and lived out her life without the infamy of murder and hanging, married to a collier in a rural parish about ten miles north of Glasgow. Life proved too much for her, but whether because life was becoming harder, or because she was particularly weak we cannot know from her life alone. Although the child seems to have been the focus of this dispute, in ways we can no longer fathom, there is simply not enough in this particular record to allow us to understand much of her and the elders' motivations.[5]

But to continue with Rutherfurd, who spent little time recounting Dugald's misery, and more on his own direction of the investigation, we must return to the path running west from Anderston. While the small crowd stood around the body, Rutherfurd asked Dugald, "with what Instrument" she killed the girl, but Dugald would say nothing. Since she had already virtually confessed to the murder, her initial refusal to acknowledge the knife she later admitted using suggests that she did not want to see it, or perhaps believed, since people hold to odd scraps of legal information in crises, that she could not be hanged without the knife. So she was led back along the road towards Anderston, only to be met there "by a number of Women who threatened to strip her." These women were possibly her neighbors, gathering as the story of the child's murder spread, and perhaps well enough aware of the conditions of Dugald's life to have seen it coming. Confronted by them, Dugald then immediately said that "she cut the Child's throat with a knife" and that she had put the knife in the hedge, by the body. At that, several people went off to find the knife, found it, and brought it back. Rutherfurd saw it, as a word inserted in the record makes clear, and he apparently stayed to see Dugald led off to prison on a warrant from the sheriff.

Having given his version of the morning's murder, Rutherfurd was asked to look at Dugald, whereupon he blurted out, "She is the woman that committed the Murder as above described tho he did not see the Murder committed but from the Circumstances above Deponed to [stated] did believe her to be the Murderer of the aforesaid Child." Rutherfurd then signed his testimony with an expert hand, and tasteful flourishes, the mark of a thoroughly literate witness, and quite possibly a man who was not nervous in court. Nonetheless, he was held to that clear distinction between what he had seen and what he presumed. We can push our understanding of his nice handwriting and general mastery of the situation a little further by considering that he probably enjoyed the rising social status of apothecaries in general, who were moving from the role of tradesmen to prescribing doctors in this period.[6]

From Rutherfurd's companion, the merchant Walter Stirling, we learn a little more of the story—and that Stirling wanted little to do with the bloody business. The clerk summarized a good deal of what Stirling said, under the heading of "agrees with the previous witness," and he concluded his summary with the words, "the woman's being seized upon by Rutherfurd," so we can assume that Stirling was not anxious to take any credit for Dugald's apprehension. But Stirling, working off stage, was the man who left the probable bedlam of the crime scene to tell a Mr. Weir, the sheriff substitute, that a warrant was needed, and he also found out Agnes Dugald's name "from another woman at the Riverside." Stirling, for whatever reason, had little taste for the business, but he was competent enough to find a name, and find the sheriff's representative. And his testimony reinforces the possibility that the women who gathered knew Dugald, and saw themselves as women with some stake in how women behaved and how children were treated in their community. It also suggests that Dugald did live in or near Anderston at the time of the murder, about ten miles south of the parish of Campsie, where her husband had been a miner, and where she presumably also had lived.

To understand where she had come from and where she lived at the time of the murder requires attention to place names mentioned in testimony, and maps, gazetteers, and patience. Places change. Villages were moved, towns and cities, especially Glasgow at this time, grew rapidly, and people moved. Anderston survives now on maps of central Glasgow as Anderston Quay, and as an area at the west end of Argyle Street. The cow pasture and hedge are probably somewhere under the quay, and under a major bridge across the Clyde. Given this probable total obliteration of the Anderston that Dugald knew, my colleague's complaint, that there is no knowable past, is an oddly positivist one. History is not about buildings, or for that matter about the physical presence of people, but about what they did. And what they did leaves, often enough, more records than we might want. The collieries of Campsie produced, by 1835, a village that housed hundreds of people who worked in the mines, an alum works, and a printfield. The village, first called Newtown of Campsie, eventually became Lennoxtown, and it was probably somewhere in this area that Dugald and her husband had lived, even though the Newtown was not built until 1785. But change in Campsie may well date from the 1760s because increased demand for coal was disrupting the industry at that time.[7]

In Dugald's story lies more than an individual tale. It is both a single text, one instance of a few pages in one volume of records, and part of a network of records that corroborate and constantly enlarge her very small story. If we continue with it, since there is more, we find the testimony of the cowherd, Robert Craig. He was "betwixt thirteen and fourteen years [and] unmarried," and a servant to a manufacturer in Anderston. He had spoken to Dugald as she walked west from Anderston at six or seven o'clock in the morning. She asked him how far west he was taking the cows; he said "he was not going very far West." She and the child then continued to the west until, still within his sight, they "came to the Hedge which runs up from the River to Lansfield," and disappeared around the west side of it. Half an hour later, she returned, and he remembered that she "was then Sighing & weeping, and She said to him, That She had murdered her own Bairn." Then she began walking back the way she had come, and shortly after, Rutherfurd and Stirling came up to him. He told them what he knew, and they went chasing after her.

Craig also went to look at the child's body, apparently when Dugald was brought back by Rutherfurd, for the cowherd seems to have been specifically asked if the child who was killed was the same child who had accompanied Dugald. He said that "from the size of the body & the Cloaths it appeared to him to be the same Child." He had also heard her confess to Rutherfurd "& the other persons present, that She had murdered her own Child." And he did add something new—that Dugald, made to face her child, "appeared to be in Distress & cried out Oh! her innocent Baby." That this observation was offered virtually at the end of his testimony tells us that what sounds like damning evidence to modern ears was of less interest to the court, the members of which really wanted to confirm details of time and place, physical evidence of blood, and Dugald's movements. It may also tell us that the older men at the scene, taking their responsibility seriously, and perhaps somewhat shaken themselves, had less leisure to remember emotions. But the young cowherd, with less to do, could watch and remember what seemed to be less salient detail.

Craig's testimony was peripheral rather than central, confirming and embellishing what Rutherfurd had established, but he also confirmed necessary details, such as observing blood on Dugald's hands and apron after—but not before—the body had been found, and Craig was the only person who had seen her just before she and the child disappeared behind the hedge. What members of the court wanted to know was that she had not gotten bloody earlier, perhaps from slaughtering an animal, and that she had not sent her child down the road, only to be charged with the death of some other. Circumstance could delude reasonable people, and both the defense lawyer and the judge or judges presiding generally did their best to separate evidence from assumption. The care with which testimony was taken down also shows, in the last line of Craig's statement, where the clerk has written in "One word in the Eight line of this Deposition delete before signing." The word taken out was "Child," which had been replaced by the word "Girl." No word was ever changed, or additions made, without explanation and signatures, so that the completed record stood as it was taken down, and later emendations were impossible. It was careful work for the most part, in a case that, though horrible, was of no great importance—it was not a matter of state, nor were any legal precedents being set.

The last witness was George Andersen, a wright from Glasgow, who had been working at the brewery near Anderston that morning. He too remembered that Dugald and the child had been heading west, but he had paid no attention to them until he saw her returning without the child and heard "a Cry of Murder." He, along with Rutherfurd, James Cleland, and perhaps others, actually seized Dugald, and went back to the body with her. There, Andersen said, "he saw her sitt [*sic*] down by the Child, wailing & confessing herself to be the Murderer." And he too was asked about the bloody hands, but said that he had looked at her only after the body had been found, when everyone who had seen her could confirm that she had blood on her hands and apron. After that, he had no more to say, and the only mystery left would seem to be why, given what the witnesses had to say, and her own confessions at the scene, she denied the murder.[8]

While I have been typing out this narrative of one morning in the life of Agnes Dugald, William Rutherfurd, and all the other witnesses, I have been thinking about the implications of my stubborn belief that these things happened, more or less as the witnesses have recalled them, and my belief that I can confirm many elements of the testimony, such as the location of Anderston, the existence of coal miners in Campsie, the rising status of apothecaries in the late eighteenth century, and the vulnerability of lone women with children. Then again, we will probably never know whether Dugald was a victim, a nasty wretch, or something in between; we cannot know from the evidence we have why the elders of the parish threatened to put her in a house of correction. She could have been a hapless migrant, a widow turned prostitute, or a decent woman made desperate by her husband's death.

As I write this, I recognize that I am far more interested in the story that has emerged—and not entirely from my construction of it, but from a logical mapping of this information against other information—than I am in the problems that other people will have with my taking Agnes Dugald, and all the others, to be any more than a sort of shadow cast by those ever-active agents, discourse, and text. Living some years now after the death of the author, and history's turn toward the methods of literary criticism, I find little of the new language, hell-bent as its authors are on abstractions and jargon, convincing. I prefer Dugald's tale to reading that "a broad clash of stories and categories of sexual and gender difference produced a highly influential if contested cultural narrative . . ."[9]

I prefer Dugald because some shreds of free will and responsibility and human agency are visible in her story, while in all those abstractions and passive constructions, to paraphrase a bit of Foucault, language masters humans.[10] To put this another way, the literary critics, in their various disciplinary manifestations, have burnt all the bridges between the signifier and the signified, the word and the thing, the words "Agnes Dugald" and a once-living Agnes Dugald. If we were to read the trial record in JC 13/16 through that lens, it would become a text in which, as others have said, only ideology is real.[11] Ideology is real, but it does not exist in isolation from its original human proponents, and has no purpose apart from the material realities of life. And so I think we know something about Dugald, Rutherfurd, Stirling, Craig, Andersen, and the crowd of women in Anderston, although what we know is very little, and what we make of it another matter. Nor do I think that this is a matter of faith; rather, I think it is the product of hard work done to confirm, corroborate, and make connections in other records. One might, well beyond the few books and maps I have used here, find records of Dugald's marriage, the birth of the child, the husband's death, Rutherfurd's shop, the elders' complaint, the fortunes of miners in Campsie, local customs of policing, and the growth of Glasgow—if one wished to pursue this case, and had time, and knew where to look, and got lucky.

And there was one other person who sat in that courtroom about whom we know a great deal. Several years passed before I noticed, among all the signatures that follow the testimony of each witness, one in particular, that of Henry Home. Home, whose handwriting looks slightly stiff and small, as if he might have been arthritic, was about seventy on that day when Dugald was found guilty and sentenced to hang. We know him better as Lord Kames, a man at the center of the Scottish Enlightenment, a legal scholar and agricultural writer who, along with Adam Smith and John Millar, came to be known as a Scientific Whig.[12] Firmly committed to the exercise of reason, although no friend to women, Kames may well have been the person who pressed Rutherfurd and every other witness to separate what he had seen from what he assumed he had seen, thereby guaranteeing that Dugald would be condemned on the basis of sound evidence. I suspect that the ideology at work here was chiefly a good dose of Enlightenment faith in reason, exercised self-consciously by men intent on upholding the principles that lay behind Scottish justice.

And so I sit here, no longer in Register House, trying to conjure up the person I know as Kames as he observes Dugald and all the witnesses produced against her. The scene I imagine reminds me of Adam Smith's notion of sympathy, which Kames would have known well by the time of the trial. One sentence from *The Theory of Moral Sentiments* is enough to recall Smith's profound sense of the connectedness of human life, despite the constraints of individual consciousness: "The compassion of the spectator must arise altogether from the consideration of what he himself would feel if he was reduced to the same unhappy situation, and, what perhaps is impossible, was at the same time able to regard it with his present reason and judgment." Not many lines later, Smith added, "We sympathize even with the dead." I understand Smith's human sympathy in a way that I cannot understand the densely layered abstraction of what is called theory these days, and I appreciate sympathy as a moral imperative as well. With that, and with Dugald behind the hedge, I will have to content myself.[13]

Notes

1. Ludwig Wittgenstein, *Tractatus Logico-Philosophicus,* trans. D. F. Pears and B. F. McGuiness (London: Routledge & Kegan Paul, 1961), 151. Not simply to antagonize other friends, I am using the word *silence* in this paragraph to stand for not only silence, but also for certain aspects of contemporary theorizing, which seem to me not to clarify through generalization, but to damn the material world into oblivion through literally boundless abstraction.
2. Thanks are due to the Keeper of Records of Scotland for permission to quote from records held by the Scottish Record Office, hereafter noted as SRO; for Agnes Dugald see SRO JC 13/16, West Circuit Court record for September 18, 1767 through May 29, 1769. All subsequent references are to this volume, the pages of which are unnumbered. The SRO is now The National Archives of Scotland.
3. See Drew Easton, ed., *By the Three Great Roads* (Aberdeen: Aberdeen University Press, 1988), 47–48, on the "charmed circle" of wells surrounding Edinburgh, the basis of the brewing industry there.
4. *Gard* is a past tense form of gar, gare, or gere, given as northeastern, and supposedly obsolete since the seventeenth century in the meaning used by Dugald; see *The Concise Scots Dictionary* (Aberdeen: Aberdeen University Press, 1987), 225–26.
5. More of the story might survive in the parish records, specifically in the minutes of meetings of the parish elders, although these survive randomly. The elders were responsible for discipline, both religious and, rather broadly, moral. This particular situation, with elders having the right to send people to a house of correction, is rather unusual, although a tradition of local discipline, without calling on magistrates and the court, was typical; see Joy Cameron, *Prisons and Punishment in Scotland from the Middle Ages to the Present* (Edinburgh: Canongate Publishing Ltd., 1983), 57. As for the parish of Campsie, Dugald may have lived near the later site of Newtown of Campsie, later Lennoxtown, at the center of mining; see W. Douglas Simpson, *Stirlingshire,* Cambridge County Geographies Series (London: Cambridge University Press, 1928), 54–59 for a description of the region's mining, and Lennoxtown; and also Robert and William Chambers, *The Gazetteer of Scotland* (Edinburgh: Thomas Ireland Junior, 1835), 2: 712.
6. See Bernice Hamilton, "The Medical Professions of the Eighteenth Century," *The Economic History Review,* second series 4:2 (1951): 141–69.
7. For the map showing the quay, see Reginald J. W. Hammond, ed., *The Complete Scotland* (London: Ward Lock Limited, 1975), map between pages 136 and 137. There is a growing literature on Scots coal miners, who were unfree laborers in the seventeenth and eighteenth centuries; see the first chapter of Alan B. Campbell, *The Lanarkshire Miners: A Social History of Their Trade Unions, 1775–1974* (Edinburgh: John Donald Publishers Ltd., 1979). On Lennoxtown and the date of development, see T. C. Smout, "The Landowner and the Planned Village in Scotland, 1730–1830," in *Scotland in the Age of Improvement,* edited by N. T. Phillipson and Rosalind Mitchison (Edinburgh: Edinburgh University Press, 1970), 73–106, esp. 104, and the map facing 103.
8. Her denial was probably the product of a criminal court system that provided defense lawyers at no cost to the poor, and that traditionally expected the best lawyers available to take on the most miserable clients. Competent defense lawyers more than once embar-

rassed prosecutors, and the constant presence of an alert and sometimes brilliant defense guaranteed that the prosecution had to make a good case. So Dugald's lawyer had probably urged her to deny the charge, if not to save herself, at least to ensure that the case made against her was sound and carefully presented.

9. See Lisa Duggan, "The Theory Wars, or, Who's Afraid of Judith Butler?" *Journal of Women's History* 10, no. 1 (1998): 9–19. Despite the example I drew from it, the article is a useful attempt to discuss what the author refers to as the "theory wars."
10. See Brian Palmer, *Descent into Discourse: The Reification of Language and the Writing of Social History* (Philadelphia: Temple University Press, 1990), 25. Much of my thinking in these latter paragraphs improved when I read Palmer, and Catherine Clement, *The Weary Sons of Freud,* trans. Nicole Ball (New York: Verso, 1987).
11. For the reference to ideology as the only reality, see Joyce Appleby, Lynn Hunt, and Margaret Jacob, *Telling the Truth about History* (New York: W. W. Norton & Company, 1994), 203.
12. On Lord Kames, see Peter Stein, "Law and Society in the Eighteenth Century," in *Scotland in the Age of Improvement,* edited by N. T. Phillipson and Rosalind Mitchison, 148–68; and the standard biographies, W. C. Lehmann, *Henry Home, Lord Kames, and the Scottish Enlightenment: A Study in National Character and the History of Ideas* (The Hague: Martinus Nijhoff, 1971), and I. S. Ross, *Lord Kames and the Scotland of His Day* (Oxford: Clarendon Press, 1972).
13. For both quotations, see Adam Smith, *The Theory of Moral Sentiments,* ed. D. D. Raphael and A. L. Macfie (Oxford: Clarendon Press, 1976), 12. Smith's theory was originally published in 1759. And for understanding that some things are not recoverable, I am indebted both to Ludwig Wittgenstein's *Tractatus,* and more practically to Margaret Spufford, *Contrasting Communities* (London: Cambridge University Press, 1974).

CHAPTER 13

WRITING THE HISTORY OF PRACTICE

THE HUMANITIES AND BASEBALL, WITH A NOD TO WRESTLING

Bruce Kuklick

In recent years philosophers have analyzed social endeavors they call practices.[1] I shall illustrate the structure of the many kinds of practices and their history by contrasting baseball with the humanities. For baseball, with a little help from wrestling, can shed a light of special clarity on the human sciences.

A practice is a coherent and complex form of cooperative human activity, with a history and standards of excellence. In trying to meet those standards, practitioners achieve specified goals. Tick-tac-toe is not a practice, nor is planting carrots, bricklaying, nor throwing a baseball skillfully. The professional game of baseball is, and so are farming and architecture. So also are inquiries of physicists, philosophers, historians, literary critics, and classicists, and the creative writing of novelists.

There are two kinds of goods to be gained from baseball, as from all practices, external and internal. Suppose I want to teach an athletic seven-year-old boy to play baseball. He has no desire to play baseball, but he does like candy. I tell him that if he plays ball with me every day, I shall give him fifty cents worth of candy. Time goes by, and he stars on my little league team—for fifty cents worth of candy per game. As coach of the team, I even promise him more candy if the club wins the championship. Thus motivated, he plays and plays to win. But so long as the candy alone is motivating him, he has reason to help his team cheat. Yet we can hope that a time will come when he finds in things specific to baseball a new set of reasons for playing, which might be described as the desire to develop a set of physical aptitudes, a kind of strategic imagination, and a competitive intensity. They might make him want not just to win but to excel. If he then cheats, he will be defeating himself.

External goods, like fifty cents worth of candy, are contingently related to practices by the accident of social circumstances. For grownups who play baseball professionally, external goods include prestige, status, money. Alternative ways of achieving these goods always exist; the practice is never the only way to gain them. In contrast, internal goods can be gained solely by engaging in the practice. They can be identified and recognized only through participation in the practice or by learning systematically what goes on in it. We may say that Jackie Robinson was a superb base runner; or, if you want to know about baserunning, look at how Robinson stole home in the 1955 World Series against the New York Yankees; or, if you want to learn about playing shortstop, watch Ozzie Smith of the St. Louis Cardinals.

Similarly in the humanities, training consists of an apprenticeship in which one learns the craft. Graduate students may work with a group of exceptional practitioners—Berkeley classicists or Yale critics. The culmination of graduate school is study under a mentor who, ideally, knows how to do "it." Someone says, "I did my degree with Stanley Fish," or describes someone as "an Edmund Morgan student."

The competition for external goods differs from the competition to excel, which results in internal goods. The more external goods one person has, the fewer there are for others. This is necessarily true of power and fame and contingently but inevitably so for money. Excellence is also limited in baseball: just one person will be batting champion. But when internal goods are gained, the whole community interested in the practice benefits. All of baseball celebrated Joe DiMaggio's hitting streak of 1941.

Practices require technical skills. But what is distinctive about a practice is that, over time, the skills transform and extend the internal goods of the practice. Entrance into a practice means entrance into a relation not only with contemporaries but with those who came before, particularly with those whose accomplishments have extended the reach of the practice to the present. That is, practices do not have fixed goals for all times—say, the scoring of a single run through strategically placed hits, as baseball was played from 1900 to 1920. The history of the practice transmutes its goals. Babe Ruth's home runs led us to "big inning" baseball, in which the object is to overpower the opposition with one strong time at bat and put your team so far ahead that momentum shifts decisively to its side. Practices may change without decay.

All colonial American historians must still confront Perry Miller's studies of the Puritans, just as Miller had to confront his teachers, Kenneth Murdock and Samuel Eliot Morison. C. I. Lewis's *Mind and the World-Order* (1929); Rene Wellek and Austin Warren's *Theory of Literature* (1949); and Thomas Kuhn's *Structure of Scientific Revolutions* (1962) altered the ways students in various disciplines understood their craft. Lewis changed the standards of clarity in American philosophy; Wellek and Warren shifted the focus of criticism from context to text; and Kuhn discredited certain ways of doing the history of science.

Although I cannot here analyze the concept of practice exhaustively, let me elaborate some of its dimensions. Baseball provides an extreme case of the proposition that disputes over the evaluation of quality in any practice occur within narrow limits. Like all games, baseball has rules, which the humanistic practices do not. But not all games are practices. Monopoly is not. And not all practices have rules. They do have traditions, norms, standards of workmanship. There are no rules for building houses and various ways of doing so; but architects might judge a building to be well made or a design to be flawed. Architects can be wrong, but we would be foolish not to consider their advice.

Those who start to play baseball will never learn to pitch, or even to appreciate good pitching, unless they acknowledge that others know better than they how to throw a fastball. In practices the authority of standards rules out relativism for both the practitioner and the student. Practitioners are tested by a tradition from which they must learn if they learn at all. Mark McGwire understood that Babe Ruth and Hank Aaron had set the goals for consistent power hitting, and in examining McGwire's career, we do the same. To appreciate Sandy Koufax as a left-handed pitcher, we need to look at the pitching of Lefty Grove, Carl Hubbell, Warren Spahn, and Steve Carlton.

Would-be-novelists who think they can rely on inspiration and raw talent to write a great novel are misguided: they have to learn the craft. Most first novels are poor, and most novelists fail. Some literary critics have fundamentally misunderstood the nature of practices in urging that the choice, say, between Hortense Calisher and Jane Austen is like that between hoagies and pizza. Do we really need to take this seriously? The eating of hoagies and pizza does not constitute a practice. With such choices, who would bother to write a novel? Or do criticism? Appraising the quality of novels is not simply a matter of taste.

Discussion and argument do occur in a practice. In the 1950s the Yankees, Giants, and Dodgers produced stellar center fielders. In New York City no disputes were more ferocious than over who was the best—Mantle, Mays, or Snider? To some, debate over canonical texts in the humanities suggests that no literary work is better than any other. Others demand that certain texts be held inviolate. Similar conundrums do not lead to such confusion in baseball whenever an "all-time team" is considered. Every expert has his own nine greats, but everyone agrees that Babe Ruth was more valuable than assorted journeymen or even star outfielders. To deny that Jane Austen is simply better than most novelists is a joke. Either we recognize that practices impose norms, or we cannot understand practices at all. But, debates over the merits of competing canonical reading lists or all-star teams are not very interesting; there are many other questions to ask.

What is the relation of practices to virtues? Virtues are acquired human qualities that help us to obtain goods internal to practices, and the lack of such virtues prevents our obtaining these goods. In a practice, we have to subordinate immediate gratification; listen carefully to discussion of our deficiencies; and be honest in dealing with the facts. A practice requires certain relations among its practitioners, and the virtues are those qualities that, like it or not, define our relation to those people. The virtues emerge in practice and form its background. Virtue is what sportswriters are getting at when they talk about a ballplayer's "work ethic." In the 1988 World Series fans honored Orel Hersheiser of the Los Angeles Dodgers for humming "Praise God from Whom All Blessings Flow." They valued him for his skill but also for his humility and grace under pressure. When Kirk Gibson, who could barely walk, homered in the first game of that series, he limped into history because people responded to his grit, courage, and determination.

Different virtues accrue to different practices. The virtues associated with twentieth-century American philosophy are perhaps limited to certain kinds of analytic intelligence tied to the study of logic and mathematics. Historians may be solid, even plodding, honest, if uninspired. Classicists and students of ancient languages display the historians' virtues at an extreme: they are doggedly precise and have an infinite capacity for taking pains. Most "new wave" theories in the humanities have had little impact on Assyriology in the United States. The enormous substantive weight of learning required for the mastery of ancient texts has narrowed the intellectual scope of students of cuneiform. The virtues of Assyriologists are not those of imagination and synthesis. Conversely, it is a nice question whether fascination with theoretic questions goes hand in hand with insubstantial learning. Overall, the virtues of a practice are embedded in the character of its practitioners, and different practices produce different modal characters with different virtues.

Consider the connection within practices between external and internal goods. The New York Yankee franchise does not exemplify baseball, nor does the history department of Yale University exemplify history. Practices should not be confused with institutions. Chess, physics, and medicine are practices; chess clubs, labs, and hospitals are institutions. Institutions are characteristically intertwined with external goods—in obtaining the money and other necessities essential for the existence of the practice. The Yankee franchise, one of the social bearers of the sport, rewards and punishes with external goods—fame, status, power, money. This is the distinction writers and fans have in mind when they say they are tired of reading about contract negotiations and assorted scandals and, instead, want to read about the game—about what transpires, on, not off, the field.

There is nothing wrong with many external goods. Most are worth having, and the administrators of institutions linked with a practice have a clutch of genuine moral commitments themselves. No practice can survive unsustained by institutions; in the real world virtue is not its own reward. If a practice is to prosper, practitioners must find a way to mesh their interests with the interests of nourishing institutions. Institutional managers negotiate the way the wider values of a culture relate to the practice. Yet, while a thriving practice depends on its ability to attract institutional protection, the viability of the institutions depends on people's concern for the practice. In the early 1950s, the Philadelphia A's were a subpar team. People stopped caring about the baseball of the A's—the team lacked internal goods—and in 1954 the franchise that allocated external goods went out of business.

Since practices and institutions and internal and external goods are intimately linked, we dare not compartmentalize on-the-field and off-the-field behavior. The competitiveness of a practice's institutions for external goods has a tension-laden relation to the practice itself. The creativity and ideals of the practice are vulnerable to the acquisitiveness of institutions. The virtues of a practice—the character of its practitioners—may help practitioners resist the power of institutions that could undermine a practice. Historians will locate changes in the practice in the interchange between the practice and institutions over time.

There are numerous examples of stress between external and internal goods. The scandal over the sex life of Boston Red Sox star Wade Boggs, for instance, was not extrinsic to fans' grasp of the game. According to all the testimony, one of his liaisons hurt his play and the morale of his club. An understanding of the quality of Red Sox play during the scandal requires a knowledge of the external good Boggs acquired—sexual power over women through his athletic prowess. In the old days managers and owners often tried to stop their ballplayers from having sex on the grounds that it exhausted vital energies and affected play negatively. Leo Durocher, while manager of the Brooklyn Dodgers, once paid prostitutes to spend the night with the pitchers on another club to harm their performance in a critical doubleheader. Dwight Gooden's use of cocaine and Daryl Strawberry's of alcohol provide other examples of dangers that come from external goods. Gooden's interest in unlawful drugs provoked a response from baseball institutions—suspension—that altered his performance. Similarly for Strawberry.

The pressures of institutions and external goods can demean practices: change can be decay. Gambling poses the greatest threat to baseball and other sports. Money is a crucial external good, and the institutions connected to a practice are always adjudicating the boundaries between practitioners and money. Wagering on contests can generate enormous sums for those who know in advance who will win or can determine who will win. Athletes who fix a game attack the heart of the sport, and alter it permanently for the worse.[2] When athletes no longer play to win, the point of the practice *qua* practice is lost. Since the virtues help protect a sport against discredit, the character of practitioners comes to the fore.

Gambling attacks the core virtues of sports and has from time to time debilitated baseball. Prize fighting is a practice that seems almost always subject to the pressure of gambling, which has several times almost ruined boxing. Wrestling, once a professional sport that required great skill, has been transformed by gambling. Some people now think of it as corrupt practice, a kind of vulgar exhibition; others think of it as a peculiar kind of entertainment, cartoons for grownups. Although gambling has turned wrestling into a freak show, distaste for this entertainment-exhibition is ultimately aesthetic.

From the nature of practices let me turn to the writing of their history, beginning with a survey of how we actually do write about baseball history. I shall rely here on some conventional scholarly ideas to present my own views. The principal way to write the history of baseball is to focus on its internal development. The Society for American Baseball Research, a quasi-scholarly group some 6,100 strong, contributes to this endeavor, with a series of publications, including *The National Pastime.* Recent issues of *The National Pastime* were devoted to a study of the 1893 and 1894 seasons of the Globe Stars of Woonsocket, Rhode Island; Honus Wagner's rookie year; the Cincinnati Reds' 1936 spring training in the Dominican Republic; and the calculation of batting averages.[3] To the study of the internal development of baseball, academics have made such contributions as Charles Alexander's admirable biographies of Ty Cobb and John McGraw.[4] Although the priorities of such highly empirical writing remain elusive, it recaptures a part of the past that most historians have ignored—the number of consecutive scoreless innings Cy Young really pitched; the exact date Nap Lajoie started to play professional baseball; what actually happened when Ty Cobb spiked Frank Baker; the average offensive statistics of a Hall of Famer. This sometimes valuable research focuses narrowly, but not merely on the sport. Cobb's personality concerns Alexander, for example; others try to fathom how baseball writers display group bias in Hall of Fame selections. Such concerns are nonetheless made subservient to a better grasp of the sport. Authors assume that they are writing for those who want to learn more about it. This kind of history is not meant to intrigue non-baseball fans: it strongly resembles literary studies of the imagery of T. S. Eliot's poetry; or the comparative study of the romantic aspects of the writing of Goethe, Wordsworth, and Rimbaud; or a history of philosophical skepticism in the eighteenth century.

Social history is the other kind of history that concerns itself with sports. To legitimate an interest in sports, many scholars have investigated the sociology of sport or the way in which sports reveal important aspects of American society. Neil J. Sullivan's *The Dodgers Move West*[5] argues that the relocation of the Brooklyn franchise illuminates urban politics. Andrew Zimbalist's *Baseball and Billions* chronicles the changing contours of American labor relations.[6] Stephen Reiss's *Touching Base*[7] relates baseball to Progressive period politics and business. The central concern of such social history is the way in which the game illustrates large features of life in the United States—usually, characteristics of the capitalist system. Francis Couvaris's and Roy Rosenzweig's books on nineteenth-century cities discuss entrepreneurs of leisure and look at how spectator sports, among other recreational pastimes, developed and reconfigured working-class culture.[8] Much of this scholarship, while compelling, constitutes a genre in which the practice is a means for studying something professional historians think is more significant—industrialism or the working class. *The Dodgers Move West* puzzles about its conclusions because, Sullivan writes, we are after all dealing with "a child's game."[9]

Similar studies occur in the histories of intellectual or literary endeavor or "humanistic activity." Ian Watt's powerful tour de force, *Rise of the Novel,*[10] looks at the social conditions in England that nurtured book-length fiction. Watt certainly respects the artistry of the early novelists he writes about, but he insists that peculiar aspects of the changing British economy drive their artistry. A history of the British scientific societies that have supported natural scientific research would be called externalist, as opposed to, say, an internalist history of the development of Newtonian mechanics. Whether one likes or dislikes external history, it is often true that it makes the practice—baseball, novel writing, or natural science—a dependent variable, which alters as a function of certain aspects of society.

There are some obvious similarities between internal and external histories and my understanding of the practice and the institutions that carry it. In understanding practices and their history, should we want a synthesis of the two kinds of histories? Here the model need not be a book like Michael Seidel's *Streak,* a study of Joe DiMaggio's 1941 season that sets the baseball alongside a contemporary narrative of international affairs, the movies, and domestic mores.[11] As common as such side-by-side analyses are, we should prefer a history in which the practice and relevant institutions interact. I have tried to write some of this sort of history myself, embracing the practices of philosophy and theology and the institutions that support them.[12] Baseball should be examined in its social context, but without losing a proper sense of the texture of the practice: its study should reflect a clear sense of the culture that has legitimated it. Most analyses of practices, baseball included, do at least touch on the world outside the practice, while many external studies cannot conceal their interest in the practice itself. Integrated scholarship is a desideratum.

But the interactive model common to exhortations on the need for a combination of internal and external history is not my goal. Hence, I did not begin with the distinction between external and internal but with practices, their organizational transmitters, and the virtues common to their successful pursuit. Writing the history of a practice requires an explicit focus on the virtues that join institution and practice. We can go further than the interactive model. A "social history of practice" offers only the necessary first step. It should be part of an effort to chart the nature of the virtues that a practice—and a culture or subculture—values; the way these virtues change over time; and the way the virtues (and practice) may be corrupted. An exposure of the nature of the virtues in the practice tells us about our values and how our institutions serve or degrade them. These notions about a historical moral philosophy are hardly new, but in the context of an understanding of practices, they can illuminate ideas about baseball and the humanities.

Of the many books on baseball, the one academics prize most is Jules Tygiel's book about Jackie Robinson, *Baseball's Great Experiment.*[13] Its repute, I believe, derives from its focus on race. Tygiel's story illustrates how the race issue revealed virtues in the United States in the 1940s. Robinson exemplifies a peculiar sort of courage, and the supporting cast is suited to a morality play: Branch Rickey, a flawed but essentially decent and powerful white humanitarian; Robinson's enemies, men of the past, on the wrong side of one of the great ethical issues of the century. Tygiel provides a history of American virtue with respect to color.

To focus on virtue, let us reconsider gambling, the great contaminator of sport. In 1919 gamblers and some members of the Chicago White Sox conspired to throw the World Series to the Cincinnati Reds, who did indeed win. The story broke in 1920; in response, professional baseball adopted a new institutional system to eliminate the influence of gambling. The eight White Sox players charged with participation in the fix (the "Black Sox") were banned for life.

The scandal has attracted widespread attention for three-quarters of a century, most recently in the 1988 movie *Eight Men Out.* The movie and Eliot Asinof's book of the same name are about virtue destroyed. The tight-fisted greed of Chicago owner Charles Comiskey alienated his players with mean-spirited ideas about salaries; baseball officials prudently averted their eyes until they could no longer ignore the facts; players made thick calculations; and Kenesaw Mountain Landis, the new "Commissioner" of Baseball, seethed with righteous indignation.[14] A *Chicago Herald & Examiner* editorial declared the scandal as important as such pressing issues as disarmament, world commerce, racial tensions, and prohibition. But it did not identify baseball as a key to understanding politics; rather, it maintained the scandal said something about national character, and that our character would determine our response to the other issues.[15]

Sportswriters have argued that only the commanding adulation shown over the next several years for the young Babe Ruth and his home-run hitting saved professional baseball from extinction. Fans were disgusted by the assault on the honor of the game, and Ruth helped them to forget the Black Sox. A more recent example of gambling and corruption is the case of Pete Rose,[16] an extraordinarily gifted player who starred for the Reds for many years. Toward the end of his career in the mid-1980s, while managing Cincinnati, he got into debt by gambling, and, to extricate himself, he bet on baseball games. Baseball's governors suspended Rose from baseball for life. Since the Black Sox scandal, they had condemned gambling as an offense worthy of severe punishment. The Baseball Hall of Fame in Cooperstown, New York, took steps to see that Rose could never be elected to its select membership.

Even most of the commentators who believe that Rose did bet on baseball deny that his gambling should detract from his achievements on the field, especially since he never bet against his own team. It would be hypocritical, his defenders say, to ban Rose from Cooperstown when other players of doubtful character—they usually cite Ty Cobb—are enshrined. Some have also argued, consistently from their view, that Joe Jackson, the great outfielder thrown out of baseball in the Black Sox scandal, should be posthumously reinstated into baseball and elected to the Hall of Fame.

Yet a compelling case can be made against Rose. He bet on his own team to win, but did not bet all the time. In particular he did not bet when Mario Soto pitched for the Reds. Suppose Rose had a bet on a game subsequent to one in which Soto was pitching. Can we assume that his managerial strategy in the Soto game was unaffected in some measure by his doubts that the Reds could win and that he had a great incentive to win the next game? Almost certainly Rose could not help having his judgment influenced. Not that he did anything as crude as throwing a game. But enmeshed in the world of gambling, he could not just play to win. He compromised the moral soundness of his sport.

This is what A. Bartlett Giamatti, the commissioner of baseball, a former President of Yale and a Dante scholar, was talking about when he banished Rose. He perhaps had a romantic notion of baseball but also a sense of its traditions as a practice; he understood how gambling demeaned it. Giamatti wanted to protect the institutions of baseball and the loyalty of the fans. He saw that people prized what he called the "integrity" of the practice and wanted to be assured that it remained intact.

We may nonetheless put these arguments aside and make a simpler one that recognizes the connection between the practice and the social order. We know that gambling corrupts the virtues of sports. For those who value the beauty of baseball, as Giamatti did, and understand that Rose's actions contributed even in a miniscule way to turning it into something analogous to contemporary professional wrestling, then his punishment was minimal. At the heart of the practice is the character of its practitioners. These nice moral issues, however, are most important to people interested in the sport.

Also intriguing about the Rose affair is the way in which its history tells us something about the structure of the organizations that make baseball viable and therefore tells us something about the values that Americans admire. As a baseball player, Rose became an authentic folk hero. Except for his athletic ability, he was unprepossessing in character and intelligence. But his fearless commitment to successful competition made him an icon. Many liked Rose because he never gave an inch and ultimately prevailed in his quest for an important record, most hits in a career; because he displayed contempt for the upper-middle-class verities associated with gentility; and also because the purveyors of these verities respected him. In many ways Rose resembled Richard Nixon. He had scrambled to the top by giving no quarter and found his support among people who appreciated the role of aggressive resentment in his professional ethos. Americans, however, are ambivalent about the wholeness of their heroes. Rose's unwillingness to concede anything to those who convicted him of gambling—to admit his guilt—was consistent with his character. Some people defended his hard line, but many others yearned for him to confess. They did not want him to beat his breast and weep over his guilt. But they did not like the stonewalling of a Nixon. They wanted a sincere, thoughtful self-analysis, and they promised forgiveness if they got it. Rose did not get this message in his trying appearance on Phil Donahue's talk show.

Rose's downfall revealed complicated links between the working-class commitment to toughness and the more middle-class commitment to respectability. Television exposed these class virtues in the series of visual images it presented the morning Giamatti pronounced judgment. In Cincinnati a camera focused on a crowd of workers—secretaries and hardhats with Styrofoam cups of coffee— who were watching "Commissioner" or "Doctor" Giamatti, the smoothest of smooth Yalies and a Renaissance humanist, expel Rose from baseball. Poor Rose, unable to speak for himself, referred all questions to his New York lawyer, Reuven Katz. The press directed its questions to "Pete," and then to "Mr. Katz," who interceded on behalf of his inarticulate client. This story, which at last pit Rose helplessly against his betters, provided a glimpse of the structure of values in America.[17]

Many intellectuals, including intellectual historians, aware that disciplines change over time, are today reflecting publicly on the nature of the humanities and their role in the world. Let the case of baseball be a guide. Practices change, and the quest for external goods may degrade practices. The character of practitioners may protect practices, but the virtues that insure the probity of a practice are enmeshed in society's dominant constellation of values and power.

In general, significant change in the humanities might come from the impact of external factors—politics—on the practice itself. The humanistic equivalent to gambling might be various forms of cheating: unprepared teaching; falsification in the preparation of manuscripts; partisan evaluation of publications; political appraisals of academic merit; and trimming in the enunciation of scholarly goals. Most universities, journals, and scholarly societies have rules against cheating. Certainly, the view that norms are irrelevant strikes at the heart of what practices are about. The rhetoric of all academic decisions is that of standards.

In the United States the motive for practitioners to cheat would probably be the love of money or prestige, although we should not slight such factors as sexual conduct or substance abuse. Cheating erodes criteria of excellence, although no litmus test distinguishes alteration from erosion, mere change from decline.

No commissioner of humanities authoritatively determines if cheating has occurred or if there is a threat of corruption. But we would expect to see people of little character, whatever their merits as practitioners, become important. Careerism might well become a noteworthy feature of an era of debased humanism, with practitioners hawking their wares, much as Rose cashed in on his fame by selling his signature to collectors of baseball memorabilia. To understand change we cannot assume that any change signals decline, but we can see that some changes are not good.

We have to inspect the core commitments of the individuals who lead the institutions that sustain the humanities, corrupt or intact. Professional baseball has always feared that cheats would destroy the practice—and its institutions—but the debased practice of wrestling, with the social organizations that keep it healthy, is still around. The virtues associated with the intense pursuit of the internal goals of a practice appear higher and purer than those associated with the institutional administrators. But those who run the institutions that sustain the humanities have their own ethical concerns.[18] They try to sustain the enterprise and act to perpetuate it. It would be mistaken to impugn their morality simply because, for example, decisions made at one time could later be judged unfortunate.

The leaders whose role we should examine are people like Giamatti. As president of Yale, he had an important part in maintaining the ecological niche that perpetuates the humanities, although his part was not as central as the one he undertook in baseball. In the humanities and baseball, Giamatti believed in gentility, respectability, and a patrician order. He admired excellence and had an aristocratic disdain for the common. His views were those of more or less patriarchical, educated white males of a certain age. He would, for example, not want literary criticism to resemble wrestling.

Wrestling matches feature made-up, grotesque men and rouged and abnormally developed women, all of whom are acrobatic and entertaining. There is smirking media coverage by fake sportscasters. Sham contests ostensibly pit "goodies" against "baddies." In actuality there is only play-acting, which, ironically, demonstrates that in deformed practices the virtues, while maximized for their drawing power, have lost all meaning.

Notes

1. See Alasdair C. MacIntyre, *After Virtue* (Notre Dame, Ind.: University of Notre Dame Press, 1981), whose discussion I have followed closely.
2. A different sort of cheating is the use of performance-enhancing drugs to *win* contests and might be illustrated by the alleged use of steroids by Jose Canseco, formerly of the Oakland A's. This is a topic I am not going to explore, but the problem, though thorny, seems less serious to the integrity of a practice than "taking a dive."
3. See *The National Pastime:* 7, no. 1 (spring 1988), 8–9 (on the Woonsockets); and 6, no. 1 (winter 1987), 11–17 (on Wagner), 22–27 (on the Reds), and 68–74 (on batting averages).
4. Charles C. Alexander, *Ty Cobb* (New York: Oxford University Press, 1984), and *John McGraw* (New York: Oxford University Press, 1988).
5. Neil J. Sullivan, *The Dodgers Move West (*New York: Oxford University Press, 1987).
6. Andrew Zimbalist, *Baseball and Billions* (New York: Basic Books, 1992). A similar book, covering all professional sports is James Quirk and Rodney D. Fort, *Pay Dirt* (Princeton, N.J.: Basic Books, 1992).
7. Stephen Reiss, *Touching Base (*Westport, Conn.: Greenwood Press, 1980).

8. Couvaris, *The Remaking of Pittsburgh: Class and Culture in an Industrializing City, 1877–1919* (Albany: State University of New York Press, 1984), 124–31; Rosenzweig, *Eight Hours for What We Will: Workers and Leisure in an Industrializing City, 1870–1920* (Cambridge, Mass.: Harvard University Press, 1983), 172–79, 182–85, 226–28.
9. Sullivan, *Dodgers Move West,* 219.
10. Berkeley: University of California Press, 1957.
11. Michael Seidel, *Streak: Joe DiMaggio and the Summer of '41* (New York: McGraw Hill, 1988).
12. See *The Rise of American Philosophy: Cambridge, Massachusetts, 1860–1930* (New Haven: Yale University Press, 1976) and *Churchmen and Philosophers: From Jonathan Edwards to John Dewey* (New Haven: Yale University Press, 1985).
13. New York: Oxford University Press, 1983.
14. Eliot Asinof, *Eight Men Out: The Black Sox and the 1919 World Series* (New York: Henry Holt Publishers, 1963). More revealing is Victory Luhrs, *The Great Baseball Mystery: The 1919 World Series* (South Brunswick, N.J.: Scarecrow Press, 1966).
15. Quoted in Asinof, *Eight Men Out,* 274.
16. On Rose see Ira Berkow, "Rose's Story Comes up Blank," and "Charlie Hustle Wears a New Suit," both in the sports section of the *New York Times,* November 5 and 27, respectively, 1989; and George F. Will, "Foul Ball," *New York Review of Books,* June 27, 1991.
17. James Reston, Jr., *Collision at Home Plate: The Lives of Pete Rose and Bart Giamatti* (Lincoln, Neb.: University of Nebraska Press, 1997).
18. A penetrating discussion of these issues can be found in Stuart Hampshire's *Innocence and Experience* (Cambridge, Mass.: Harvard University Press, 1989).

CHAPTER 14

THE DILEMMAS OF THE CONTEMPORARY MILITARY HISTORIAN

Victor Davis Hanson

Confess: it's my profession
that alarms you.
This is why few people ask me to dinner,
Although Lord knows I don't go out of my way to be scary.

—MARGARET ATWOOD
"THE LONELINESS OF THE MILITARY HISTORIAN"

HISTORIANS OF WAR often go to great lengths to deny their craft. How odd that when we remember that our first historians, Herodotus and Thucydides were recorders and analysts of wars. Apparently to write of anything other than warfare simply was not history. Today, some military historians insist they are misunderstood "intellectual historians" who, on occasion, write about things bellicose. Others declare themselves students of "cultural" or "economic" history who sometimes write about war, largely because of its radical alterations of national economies and social mores. In my experience, few military historians freely acknowledge that they study and write largely about killing. Those who do suspect that their colleagues find them scary. As they do.

The general public loves to read about war and to watch military documentaries and movies from a safe and suburban distance. Go to any major bookstore and compare the World War II or Civil War sections with that, say, of classical antiquity. The former may cover an entire aisle, the latter at best a few shelves. In an age of peace and prosperity not seen in Europe since Gibbon's much heralded reign of the Five Good Emperors at Rome, complacent contemporary readers want to know about the savagery of war: from the hardware of destruction to the reasons some men fight well while others do not; from morbid curiosity about wounds to simple appreciation of valor and sacrifice under fire.

Contemporary writer Tom Clancy's appeal for the suburban male is partly grounded in his minute descriptions of the machines of death and the esoterica of the American military: command structure, acronyms, military bases, and new-age weaponry. Scholars as diverse as Stephen Ambrose, James McPherson, and John Keegan have captured an audience well beyond that merely interested in particular wars by giving readers a feel for the smoke and blood of war in general, some idea of why men fought so brutally, and what it was like to do so. Much as the daily dinnerware, public buildings, coins, and gravestones of the classical Greeks were decorated with images of cavalry, hoplite infantrymen, and triremes, our media reflects the public's macabre fascination with war, sensing its futility, barbarity, and undeniable heroism and sacrifice.

Most contemporary military historians who shy away from acknowledgment of their craft teach at universities, where they face various dilemmas. Despite Americans' interest in war, American society in general and the academic community in particular increasingly accept the post-Enlightenment idea of war as unnatural and inevitably evil, and thus, through education and proper understanding, preventable. Hence the rise of peace studies programs, implicitly dedicated to the idea that proper therapeutic training can inculcate the techniques of "conflict resolution": two reasonable parties, properly sensitized and educated, can avoid war and come to a rational compromise. Indeed, during the International Year of Peace in 1986, a global panel of scientists declared scientifically incorrect the idea that our species is innately bellicose, due to either our genes or to the evolutionary process of natural selection. Those who think differently are ignorant, militaristic, or simply unbalanced.

This utopianism is a relatively recent and un-Hellenic notion. Even Kant remarked that a war conducted with order and respect for the rights of combatants "has something sublime about it, and gives nations that carry it on in such a manner a stamp of mind only the more sublime the more numerous the dangers to which they are exposed, and which they are able to meet with fortitude." Philosophers as diverse as Heraclitus and Plato called war "the king of everything" and peace "but a parenthesis" in the normal state of relations among peoples. Athenians like Aeschylus, Socrates, and

Thucydides, themselves veterans of combat, deplored the stupidity of particular wars that were amoral, poorly conducted, or waged for reasons that did not justify the commensurate sacrifice in lives and national treasure—the perverse occasions, as Herodotus reminds us, when fathers bury sons rather than sons fathers; or the impoverishing state of affairs that Hesiod called "a curse from Zeus."

Still, these same Greek poets had no illusions about the need for defense, uniformly recognizing the necessity of wars for combating aggression or thwarting malignancy, whether the rise of Athenian imperialism, the spread of Spartan hegemony, or invasion by would-be Persian enslavers. In the Greek view, many people in the world, and for that matter states themselves, are not always nice or rational. They take with force what they desire until they are stopped with force. Vegetius's commonly quoted, "Let him who desires peace, prepare for war" [*Qui desiderat pacem, praeparet bellum*], is a loose adaptation of what Thucydides wrote eight hundred years earlier, when he made the Boeotian general Pagondas say the only way to have peace with the neighboring aggressive Athenians was for his countrymen always to be ready for war.

The twentieth century changed that traditional Western acceptance of just wars to preserve family, home, and culture. The classical idea that a long peace at any cost created decadence, effeminacy, and a commercial rather than spiritual citizenry—best phrased by Juvenal, but reiterated by Kant and Hegel—could not survive the ghastly reality of the World War I killing fields of the Somme and Verdun. Indeed, between classical antiquity and the present age lie the trenches of World War I, the carpet bombing of World War II, the death camps, and the apocalyptic threat of World War III. Thus, intellectuals have been quick to point out the senselessness of trench warfare, the needless destruction of Dresden, and the sheer absurdity of Mutually Assured Destruction. Rarely have they couched that reproach in the Hellenic spirit of criticizing unwise tactics and unnecessary strategies within a necessary conflict against Prussian militarism or fascist and Soviet totalitarianism.

A Greek might have argued to the man at Thermopylae that it was not smart to fight. He likely would not have argued that King Leonidas was decapitated for a senseless cause or that a quarter million Persians could be rebuffed by good will and reason, or that the carnage of Xerxes' Immortals and the Spartan royal guard was, as all killing in war is, obscene. Thucydides probably believed the expedition to Sicily strategically unsound and the executions at Melos reprehensible, not necessarily that Athens was wrongly fighting for its survival against Spartan oligarchy and its coalition of Dorian states. Euripides' *Trojan War* is a lament about the unnecessary barbarity of war and the needless destruction of civilian lives, but Euripides hated the Spartans as much as any Athenian hoplite in the ranks.

In the late twentieth century, the great task of the military historian is to return to the Hellenic practice of identifying stupidity, barbarity, and tragedy in needless battles, not necessarily to condemn war as uniformly wrong or immoral. Dresden was probably unnecessary, but bombing the German cities and the Nazis' means of production shortened the existence of the Third Reich. Hiroshima may not have been wise—it was surely savage to incinerate women and children—but total war against Japanese fascism was a noble and obligatory struggle. Rather than merely expressing horror over those burned alive, though we must surely document such carnage, military historians, given the strategic and spiritual landscape of the times, should explain what alternatives were available to end the rule of the Japanese militarists and their bloodletting in China and the Pacific: More firebombing of the Japanese mainland? An invasion of Japan itself? More Okinawa-like island hopping? Stern reprimands and offers of a six-month truce? A negotiated settlement that left the Japanese government intact?

Historians, rather than voicing easy condemnation of war's brutality, must appreciate the dilemma of twentieth-century man: he has had fewer ways to resist contemporary evil cheaply and painlessly, whether in the form of Hitlerism, Stalinism, Maoism, which together murdered some one hundred million people, or the terrorist thug and bomber, without in the process destroying the prosperity and tranquillity of the modern Western life that we hold so dear. Inherent within this failure to solve the twentieth-century paradox of identifying and combating evil without bringing on the annihilation of what is good lies the seeds of modernism, existentialism, and postmodernism—of despair itself.

Saddam Hussein is evil, granted; but we do not wish to see on television any more scenes like the ghastly remains of incinerated looters on the "Highway of Death." So we cease our hostilities, spare the Republican Guard, and allow him to butcher thousands of Shiites and Kurds in the weeks following the Gulf War—rotting corpses we hope we shall not see on the six o'clock news or read about in the morning papers. Hussein is evil, but in the post-Gulf War period of prosperity, we resent spending treasure and lives to guard his air space constantly. Hussein is evil, but we wish to believe that once we leave Iraq, he will not really manufacture poison gas and biological agents to attack our cities.

We do want to avenge the Lockerbie bombing of innocent airline passengers and the murder of civilians in American Embassies in Africa, but in a world of instant communications and instantaneous electronic piety, we fret that our retaliation may be either too brutal and too indiscriminate, or in itself bring on more terrorist acts. So we often do nothing and seek to frame that nothing in the general Enlightenment idea that we are somehow beyond war, and our enemies are not so much our moral as our intellectual inferiors. Even the worst terrorist who vows to murder us is seen as more ignorant than evil. Afraid that we ourselves may kill—or die—we often allow killers to kill as long as their killing is kept distant and to a tolerable minimum.

We as a public have largely lost the age-old Western notion, noted by Plato, that the great wrong is not so much in committing evil, as in allowing it to go unpunished. We have forgotten the Greeks' notion that conflict rarely is a choice between obvious good and evil, but between that which is mostly bad and that which is surely better. Amid such a relativist cultural landscape the contemporary military historian somehow is made to feel his topic is an aberration, a vast tragedy of senseless killing. Indeed, in a proper world there would be no wars, and no need for the military historian to try to make sense of them.

Thus, post-Vietnam peace studies rejects the idea that war is not only inevitable, but often necessary and desirable to stop great evil. The disappointment of Steven Spielberg's *Saving Private Ryan* arose from the inability to show the audience the purpose for those first thirty minutes of mayhem on Omaha Beach: namely, that by June 1944, there were few ways of stopping the evil of the Nazi state other than landing in Europe and literally marching into Germany to kill or capture a murderous cadre. Each day the Allies went eastward was one day less that the death camps operated. *Saving Private Ryan* has the unintended result of almost suggesting that the carnage on D-day was, like the floating limbs and heads in *Jaws,* senseless and without purpose, rather than recognizing that there were few alternatives to retaking, both concretely and morally, inch by inch, the European continent that had been transmogrified into the bastion of a new barbarism. If only the producers would have given us a brief hint that all those severed heads, limbs, and entrails on D-day were for a noble purpose, a brutal inauguration of a 337-day, thousand-mile march to destroy Nazi Germany, which was demonstrably a far different—and far more evil—nation than England and America.

It is not just the mood and fashion of the times that makes contemporary military history suspect. A second dilemma arises from the simple absence among military historians of any personal knowledge of war itself. Few who write about war have seen it, and thus tend either to ignore its horrors, or, worse, display a grotesque interest in mayhem per se from the safety of the library carrel and faculty lounge, the academic counterpart of the paintball-gun weekend warrior or video addict glued to the severed arms and decapitated heads of the latest offering from Nintendo.

Military history itself originated as a purely Western enterprise of Greek military veterans. Thucydides, the exiled admiral, wrote as a direct result of the punishment that followed his failed leadership at Amphipolis.

His descriptions of the plague and the execution of schoolboys at the tiny hamlet of Mycalessus are horrible but never gratuitous. Oozing boils and speared animals serve his larger purposes of illustrating what man is indeed capable of once the veneer of civilization has been stripped away. Xenophon, veteran of the expedition of the Ten Thousand into Persia, composed his *Hellenica* largely as a chronicle of Sparta's wars against the Persians and other Greeks; he surely was an eyewitness to some of the greatest carnage in Greek history. When he remarked that the battle of Coronea (394 B.C.) was "like no other of our time," he had seen his Spartan friends "crash against the Thebans front to front; as both sides threw up shields against shields, they pushed, battled, died, and were killed." An otherwise obscure battle in the backwaters of Boeotia is enshrined in history because an eyewitness who knew bloodletting created a picture of the unbelievable slaughter of shock warfare. Its killing truly was unlike any the historian had witnessed or participated in.

Even abstract thinkers, like Socrates or the authors of military handbooks like Aeneas Tacticus, the obscure general from Stymphalus, were themselves veterans of warfare. The participant in battle or the eyewitness to killing has established a tradition in the West that the man who has seen killing firsthand, even done it himself, has somehow earned the moral capital to write about larger questions of tactics and grand strategy. We think not of the tradition of the careerist Caesar and the inauguration of the military memoir for propagandistic purposes or as an apologia for past campaigns, but instead of the battle veteran as chronicler of events rather than his own career—a Xenophon, Liddell Hart, General Fuller, Winston Churchill.

Yet because of the increasing distance between the academic and the muscular classes that staff the all-volunteer, mercenary armies, and because of the sheer absence of large wars in the West in the last half century, it is unlikely that the contemporary military historian knows or will know much, if anything, about what war is really like. The great World War II historians of the United States' army, such as a Forrest Pogue or Martin Blumenson, who at least served in the American army in the age of combat, probably will not be replaced. Of the military historians of antiquity, the generation who served in World War II, a W. K. Pritchett or N. G. L. Hammond, are now in their nineties. In short, we who write about hoplite killing of the ancient world have not been in war, or even served in an army at all.

Why does this matter? All military historians retain their moral capital only through graphic description or at least explicit acknowledgment of the carnage, avoiding the extremes of titillating with blood and guts or turning killing into a soulless, antiseptic enterprise. For Thucydides, Pericles' decision to evacuate Attica must invoke the picture of a plague-ridden city, with starving women and children fighting over biers on which to burn their loved ones. That picture must be presented as part of the larger tactical, strategic, and cultural consequences of his decision to abandon Attica, a strategy that cost the life of Pericles himself. For Livy, Cannae is not just an ingenious pincer movement that traps a consular army and frees the way for Hannibal to run wild in Italy for the next decade, but an occasion on which fellow Romans were sliced to death with hand weapons at the rate of six hundred legionnaires a minute.

The modern academic historian, without military experience, then, must recreate the gore he has never seen in the flesh, and yet recreate it for a larger purpose beyond the macabre interests of his readers. Long ago, Aldous Huxley warned us of the amorality of losing sight of the battlefield:

> The language of strategy and politics is designed . . . to make it appear as though wars were not fought by individuals drilled to murder one another in cold blood and without provocation, but either by impersonal and therefore wholly non-normal and impassable forces, or else by personified abstractions. . . . Accordingly, when we talk about war, we use a language which conceals or embellishes its reality. Ignoring the facts, so far as we possibly can, we imply that battles are not fought by soldiers, but by things, principles, allegories, personified collectives, or (at the most human) by opposing commanders, pitched against one another in single combat. For the same reason, when we have to describe the processes and the results of war, we employ a rich variety of euphemisms. Even the most violently patriotic and militaristic are reluctant to call a spade by its own name.
>
> "Words and Behavior" in *Collected Essays* (New York: Harper, 1958) 246–48.

Other problems confront the contemporary military historian besides his being out of place in an ideological age or dismissed as a nerdy war-gamer with vicarious interests in that which he studiously avoids in the concrete. In the era of multiculturalism and political correctness, it is difficult to talk in anything but general terms about the rise of the West. True, some historians have noted that the story of Western arms from Salamis to the Gulf War is largely the story of Western military primacy: the technology, the values, and the capital of Europe when applied to the battlefield tend to make the West as dominant in the arts of killing as in its cultural, economic and political spheres. Indeed, by 1914 the West controlled eighty-five percent of the world's territory. While imperialism is today an embarrassment to Western powers, its twin legacy of global capitalism and entitlement democracy is sweeping the planet as effectively as did the British navy of the past—and it is backed by the ability of Western powers to strike instantaneously and without danger at almost any country in the world.

In the present age, non-European countries have anchored their defense in the realm of Western military technology, tactics, and organization. Few doubt that European-style armies, if they seek to make war decisively and completely, can literally defeat any adversary they wish. Iraq may have more tanks than France, themselves constructed either in the West or on Western designs, but few doubt that France could defeat Iraq. Only through vast purchases of Western motorized armor could Iraq overwhelm Yemen or Afghanistan. Quite simply, a nation enjoys security to the degree its military is Westernized, technologically and organizationally. Contemporary Western military dominance exists precisely because of a long tradition of applying uniquely Western ideas about organization, science, religion, and cultural flexibility to the battlefield.

Herein the military historian faces the challenge to explain Western prowess in an environment that interprets the rise of the West mostly as imperialist or colonialist. High-school students learn that the villainy of Westerners from the Crusaders to Cortes to the Afrikaners rests upon their use of superior technology to slaughter peace-loving, more natural indigenous peoples. In short, global military history emerges as an explication of how the culture that began in Greece and Rome inextricably ended up where it is today. That story ultimately is one of Europeans' superior military practice to ensure the expansion of Western influence across time and space, a truth that sorely bothers a great many professors who either deny or lambast Western "exceptionalism."

Many social scientists in the universities implicitly see the history of war as the history of European dynamism used for largely evil purposes. Or the critic cites exceptions to Western military dominance as if they were the rule—the sack of Constantinople, the defeat of the Crusaders, Vietnam—to nuance a valid generalization. But every military historian must confront the story of civilized war as the story of a gradual dominance of Western arms. In academic terms, this is the explanation for the racism, sexism, economic exploitation, and colonialism that comprises much of the current university curriculum in the social sciences, an ideology that has turned tragedy into melodrama. To be a military historian means being an unwitting explicator of the frightening lethality of Western arms, a burden few wish to undertake.

The sheer lifeless environment of academia in America today further challenges the military historian. Contemporary ideology, with its fascination with rhetoric and discourse, tends to train scholars to look at history more by what was said than what was done. To be avoided is the easy target of postmodernist and literary theorists, who fortunately have little influence on military scholarship. It is, after all, difficult to envision incinerated bodies as a linguistic "construct," or the March 11, 1945, B-29 fire raid on Japan as a "narrative effect." Inasmuch as military historians rightly see their craft as an appendage to larger cultural history, they often adopt premises and suppositions clearly unsupported by what they find on the battlefield. As military historians, we often forget that the study of war, through its sheer antithesis to pretense, provides a corrective to much of the naiveté, romance, and nonsense of contemporary historical writing. When military historians ask how many were killed and why, they often arrive at conclusions far different from those advanced by others. Consider two examples of how a concentration on matters purely military can provide a radically different picture of historical events once we see that military history looks not at what is said or supposed, but at the unalterable facts of the battlefield: the number of dead and the reasons they died.

An example from the ancient world compares Periclean Athens with the little-known fourth-century democratic federation of Boeotia, which reached its zenith with the career of the obscure Theban general Epaminondas (371–362 B.C.). The former we associate with the Parthenon, Athenian tragedy, and cultural renaissance, the latter with a brief political florescence in an agrarian outback of Greece. The warmaking of each state tells a radically different story. Athens waged war two out of three years in the fifth century, the great majority of those campaigns to extend its imperialism. Pericles's entire democratic ideology became inseparable from his efforts to kill for Athenian imperialism. Thucydides has him announce to the Athenian *ekklêsia:* "For what you hold is, to speak somewhat plainly, a tyranny; to take it perhaps was wrong, but to let it go is unsafe," an admission also shared by his arch rival, the demagogue Cleon. At Athens, firebrand and statesman alike acknowledged their maritime empire as probably amoral and yet essential for the material well-being of the Classical Athenian state. The body count supports their belief.

Scholars rarely tell us that more Greeks died fighting against Athens than all those killed in the Persian Wars. Yet, contemporaries were well aware of the Athenian massacres at Scione, Melos, and Euboea; their brutal enslavement of Samos; and their attempted conquest of democratic Sicily. While modern historians may argue that the Parthenon really was not financed from the blood of others, the ancients, who counted corpses, at least believed Pericles' temples on the Acropolis to be dividends of a rapacious and murderous policy of imperialism. Despite the recent hoopla of celebration (1993 was the 2,500-year anniversary of the founding of Athenian democracy),

Periclean Athens, if the sheer number of those it killed are any indication, was the most murderous state in the history of Greece, finally unwinding after waging (and losing) a murderous twenty-seven-year war against Spartan oligarchy.

In contrast, Epaminondas and his Boeotians freed the states of the Peloponnese and asked for no tribute. They mustered nearly 70,000 allied Greeks, a huge march of truly democratic ideals; invaded Sparta; devastated a land sacrosanct and untouched for 600 years; ravaged the estates of the elite; humiliated the Spartan army; and continued westward to free the 200,000 helots of Messenia—in a single year destroying what Athens could not in twenty-seven. They fought and defeated Sparta to free, not enslave, others. In that campaign of 370–369 B.C., few Spartans or Boeotians were killed amid the greatest transformation in the history of the Greek city-states. In lieu of a Samos enslaved or a holocaust on Melos, the Boeotian army left behind free, fortified cities of Megalopolis, Mantinea, and Messenê that would prevent resumption of Spartan hegemony.

Indeed, Epaminondas attached no preconditions to his assistance to other Greeks. He executed no Greek who chose to resist his overtures. He dismantled the entire three hundred-year system of Spartan apartheid in four months at less than perhaps one thousand casualties in campaigns that involved thousands on both sides. How odd that Athens, whose sophisticated culture enslaved or killed thousands of freedom fighters on Euboea, Aegina, Samos, Scione, and Melos, we venerate as the paradigm of democracy, whereas we largely ignore the fourth-century democratic Boeotians, who mobilized communities hundreds of miles distant to decide their own affairs. The battlefield tells a different story than the monuments on the acropolis.

After the Persian Wars (490 B.C.; 480–479 B.C.), Athenian imperial democracy, unlike the army of Epaminondas, never fought again for reasons other than imperialism or narrow sectarian interests until its citizens joined the Thebans at Chaeronea in the eleventh hour of the city-state. Their respective wars against Sparta show that Epaminondas' Thebes, not Periclean Athens, was the true exemplar of democratic battle prowess in the ancient world and did more than any other state in the millennium of classical antiquity to enhance freedom. A good way to assess the comparative morality of Athenian democratic imperialism and rural Boeotian democracy is to tally the respective balance sheets of the innocent Greeks butchered at the hands of each.

The same wide gulf between rhetoric and deeds has prevented an accurate assessment of the American General George S. Patton, a warmaker who talked of killing, but whose skill and celerity once again saved, not expended, lives on both sides. Patton loathed Grant's idea of the "terrible arithmetic," which lay at the heart of the reasoning of generals Dwight D. Eisenhower and Omar Bradley, who apparently chose to wage war steadily and soberly. In their view, greater American manpower and supplies eventually would ensure that in such barbarous frontal assaults as those in the Hurtgen and Ardennes forests, the Germans would crack first.

In their memoirs, both Eisenhower and Bradley fell into the classical fallacy of seeing the successful end as proving the wisdom of prior means. They dismissed criticism of "what might have been" on the grounds that the Allies won ahead of their projected schedule anyway, as if the Allied victory justified their conservatism in restraining the impetuous Patton at Falaise, Brest, the Seine, the Lorraine, the Bulge, and near Prague. They assumed that a careful advance was more circumspect than a rapid envelopment. In fact, their conservatism, not Patton's boldness, cost thousands of unnecessary casualties. Once more, for the military historian, those killed, not what was professed, tell the real story. Two-thirds of all allied casualties in the liberation of northern Europe took place after the Third Army had raced five hundred miles and was stopped in sight of the German border.

Patton, the uncouth and blustering bigmouth, not his superiors, emerges as the real humanitarian, for, in contrast to his peers, he believed he could wage a war so mobile, flexible, and lethal that the Americans never would need to rely exclusively on their superior human reserves, and, in fact, would suffer far fewer casualties than the Germans. When George Patton started up the Third Army on August 1, 1944, Allied progress in Normandy was forty-five days behind the rather timid Overlord timetable. But in just thirty days of Third Army operations (at D-day plus seventy-nine days), Patton had not only caught up with the planned schedule, his men were now in France actually far to the east of where they were slated to be at D-day plus ninety days. In the nearly two months of warring under Bradley and British general Bernard Montgomery, the Allies had advanced no more than twenty miles from the beaches. By the end of the first thirty days of Third Army's deployment, the Americans were nearly four hundred miles away from the French coast, approaching Verdun and barreling forward less than a hundred miles from Germany itself.

Again, the obscenity in Patton's mind was a complacent war of static fronts, huge numbers of men engaged in rear echelon tasks, commanders ensconced hundreds of the miles to the rear, dreary communiqués: war as the daily cranking, bureaucratic mill that inevitably would grind the Germans up first. Eisenhower and Bradley took no chances that they might lose the war, and in the process lost thousands of GIs in the Bulge and at the Siegfried line. Patton took every risk he could and thus saved thousands more. Eisenhower and Bradley were promoted and deified, Patton was ridiculed and relieved in the same manner the firebrand Epaminondas was put on trial after destroying the Spartan slave state.

The loudmouth Patton chose to race his troops to the rear of the German opponents; the judicious Bradley and Eisenhower chose to advance lock step in a broad frontal and bloody assault. Patton stomped, swore, bullied, and acted hysterically as his men endured unimaginable savagery; Bradley and Eisenhower appeared reasoned and restrained as their men, too, endured unimaginable savagery. History can judge which is the appropriate moral public stance of the respective commanders.

Patton's order to close the Falaise Gap would have led to lives saved, not lost. Scholars today argue over who allowed it stay open, not over the wisdom of leaving it open. They argue over whether it would have ended the war in the West; they do not doubt that its effect was enormous. In all such speculations, Patton alone cannot be blamed. Had he been left alone in Brittany, Brest would have been captured much earlier and American troops released for the drive eastward. I know of no historian who believes that Patton should have advanced more slowly to the coast, or that he should, as the Allied master plan mandated, have devoted more of his divisions to clearing the peninsula. Patton's superiors ignored his plan to cut off retreating German forces on the far bank of the Seine, and those very Germans returned to kill Americans in the winter of 1944–1945. From what we know of German defenses in the Lorraine in late August and the success of American tactical air forces, it is hard to see how a supplied Patton would have been destroyed while crossing the Rhine in late summer 1944. Controversy rests only on how far Patton could have advanced into Germany without eventually being surrounded. We know, of course, the horror that continued in the death camps from September 1944 to May 1945. The Germans regarded Patton's idea to cut the Bulge off at its base as the preferred course of action. No serious American historian disagrees, and none blames Patton for the safe retreat of the Panzers to the Rhine. A near half century of communist suffering in Prague should have settled the argument over the wisdom of stopping Patton's half-million-man army at its outskirts.

We associate Pericles with culture and art, Eisenhower and Bradley with sobriety and competence. But if we look to the battlefield—those killed, those saved, those freed—the obscure Epaminondas and the seemingly mad, obnoxious, and often repulsive Patton are the real humanists. Military history, then, in the sense of a radical narrowing of focus on the number of dead, and the conduct that saves lives while achieving victory for a just cause, can lead to radically unorthodox appraisals. Epaminondas did more than any Athenian zealot to destroy Spartan apartheid, and the most die-hard, antifascist could not match Patton's destruction of Nazi military power.

Tragically, such architects of humanity remain either unknown or misunderstood. Epaminondas warrants little mention in Greek history textbooks, and Patton is caricatured as a dangerous zealot wisely kept on a short leash by the more circumspect Eisenhower and Bradley. In no large part, that misapprehension exists because when we look at war, we too often listen to what is said rather than examine what was done on the battlefield; or we feel uneasy with the rhetoric of the enthusiastically bellicose; or in retrospect, we rue the destructiveness of Western armies and warriors whom we sent to save us in the first place.

Military history can do a great service for history at large, for its currency is honesty, a truthfulness engendered by the ultimate sacrifice of human life that transcends all pretension and rhetoric. Military historians, who most often count the corpses of history, should teach us that war is an unfortunate, horrible event that will not disappear—and perhaps should not, for it is often the last available mechanism to destroy evil and save the lives of those who otherwise are doomed. Indeed, the military historian must learn to acknowledge without apology that there are far more evil things than war: Hitler's slave state executed or worked to death more than the *Werhmacht* killed on the battlefield; Stalin wiped out more Russians before, than Hitler did during, World War II; and Mao caused the deaths of more Chinese after the war than the Japanese did during it.

We who write military history and who for the most part have no experience either with war or armed service must acknowledge without qualification the great historical responsibility of Western military prowess, a military practice that will either save or destroy the globe. To claim that the West was and is not militarily superior, or that its preponderance of arms has characteristically been used to accomplish evil, is not so much an easy lie as a betrayal of historical integrity.

Most of all, as military historians, we must at times ignore great art and culture, pay no attention to legend and romance, and if need be, give only secondary credence to kind and competent men in history. Instead, we must seek the reasons men fought, and estimate how many were killed and how many saved. If we do all that, we will not be ashamed of military history, but learn that it is properly the preeminent discipline, the frequent corrective, of all historical study. It alone is the story of the ultimate human sacrifice. So it is no accident that for the Greeks, history begins as, and in some sense remains, the story of war.

CHAPTER 15

ARISTOTLE AND THE STUDY OF HISTORY: A MANIFESTO

Paul A. Rahe

Suppose that we were to define what it means to be a people [*populus*] not in the usual way, but in a different fashion—such as the following: a people is a multitudinous assemblage of rational beings united by concord regarding loved things held in common. Then, if we wished to discern the character of any given people, we would have to investigate what it loves. And no matter what an entity loves, if it is a multitudinous assemblage not of cattle but of rational creatures and if these are united by concord regarding loved things held in common, then it is not absurd to call it a people; and, surely, it is a better or worse people as it is united in loving things that are better or worse. By this definition, the Roman people is a people, and its estate [*res*] is without doubt a commonwealth [*res publica*]. What this people loved in early times and what it loved in the ages that followed, the practices by which it passed into bloody sedition and then into social and civil wars, tearing apart and destroying that concord which is, in a certain manner, the health and welfare [*salus*] of a people—to this history bears witness. . . . And what I have said concerning this people and concerning its commonwealth, this also I should be understood to have said and thought concerning the Athenians, the rest of the Greeks, . . . and the other nations as well . . .

—AUGUSTINE[1]

Iris Murdoch, in her novel *The Nice and the Good,* introduces readers to John Ducane, a wealthy, remarkably fastidious, forty-three-year-old bachelor civil servant. In delineating his character, she offers observations on his favorite pastime that might serve as an appropriate introduction to any inquiry into the past, especially the distant past:

> The immense literature about Roman law has been produced by excogitation from a relatively small amount of evidence, of which a substantial part is suspect because of interpolations. Ducane had often wondered whether his passion for the subject were not a kind of perversion. There are certain areas of scholarship, early Greek history is one and Roman law is another, where the scantiness of evidence sets a special challenge to the disciplined mind. It is a game with very few pieces, where the skill of the player lies in complicating the rules. The isolated and uneloquent fact must be exhibited within a tissue of hypothesis subtle enough to make it speak, and it was the weaving of this tissue which fascinated Ducane.[2]

Iris Murdoch's remarks on Roman law and early Greek history could be applied to history generally. The evidence for life before the immediate past is not just scanty; it often reflects a bias, the nature and depth of which modern researchers are ill placed to discern. They find themselves in the position of children eager to reconstruct a vast jigsaw puzzle, aware that the great majority of the pieces are missing and many others broken, who then discover, to their great dismay, yet another, perhaps graver deficiency: They have no notion of what the puzzle would look like if pieced together.

Thus, classical antiquity poses an almost insuperable obstacle to the modern understanding. As Alfred Zimmern acutely observed with regard to ancient Hellas:

> We must imagine houses without drains, beds without sheets or springs, rooms as cold, or as hot, as the open air, only draughtier, meals that began and ended with pudding, and cities that could boast neither gentry nor millionaires. We must learn to tell the time without watches, to cross rivers without bridges, and seas without a compass, to fasten our clothes (or rather our two pieces of cloth) with two pins instead of rows of buttons, to wear our shoes or sandals without stockings, to warm ourselves over a pot of ashes, to judge open-air plays or lawsuits on a cold winter's morning, to study poetry without books, geography without maps, and politics without newspapers.[3]

But we must do much more, for the difficulty posed by the ancient Greek polis and the Roman civitas is largely conceptual. Few terms coined for the political experience of the West in the last two hundred years can help make sense of the regimes of classical antiquity. The scientific and technological revolutions, the Enlightenment's popularization of philosophy and the concomitant emergence of ideology, the foundation of representative democracy, and the development of capitalism—events that decisively shaped the republics of modern times, have altered the range of political options so radically that much of antiquity seems almost unrecognizable.

This profound transformation has not escaped notice. In 1816, Thomas Jefferson commented:

> So different was the style of society then, and with those people, from what it is now and with us, that I think little edification can be obtained from their writings on the subject of government. They had just ideas of the value of personal liberty, but none at all of the structure of government best calculated to preserve it.... The introduction of this new principle of representative democracy has rendered useless almost everything written before on the structure of government; and, in a great measure, relieves our regret, if the political writings of Aristotle, or of any other ancient, have been lost, or are unfaithfully rendered or explained to us.[4]

About twenty years later Alexis de Tocqueville advanced an even more general claim when he tried to compare the republics of Greece and of Rome with those in America. Of the attempts to judge the one by the other and to predict events by considering what had occurred two thousand years before," he said, "I am tempted to burn my books in order to apply none but novel ideas to so novel a condition of society."[5]

Jefferson's and Tocqueville's remarks on ancient political thought and modern politics apply to the application of modern paradigms to ancient circumstances. It makes little sense to ask whether the Lacedaemonian regime was totalitarian or liberal. It was, properly speaking, neither. In its heyday, Sparta was never subject to a tyrant—least of all to a tyrant in command of a party animated by a revolutionary ideology, intent on imposing a particular worldview on the populace, and willing to employ terror to snuff out political and cultural dissent. Nor was classical Lacedaemon an open society in which the citizen could live his life as he pleased, free from external restraint and respect for public order. Like the regime described in Jean-Jacques Rousseau's *The Social Contract,* the Spartan polity was simultaneously a closed society and a participatory democracy.[6]

A measure of the chasm that separates the republics of antiquity from those of recent modernity is our difficulty in understanding how a polity that denied its citizens any rights against the community could concurrently foster their participation in its governance. The Americans who founded the first great liberal democratic republic, acutely aware of this possibility, witnessed the decay of a world akin in certain decisive respects to that of the ancients, and they self-consciously proposed an alternative to classical republicanism. They were ideally situated to profit from the institutional political science established by Machiavelli and Hobbes and developed in various ways by Harrington, Neville, Locke, Trenchard, Mandeville, Montesquieu, Bolingbroke, Hume, Blackstone, Adam Smith, and de Lolme.[7] The men who launched the American Revolution and founded America's governments distinguished between ancient and modern regimes with a modicum of precision, and they thereby encouraged us to achieve that critical distance required for an attempt to understand antiquity in its own terms.

A word of caution: The institutional political science of early modern Europe and revolutionary America cannot readily provide "a tissue of hypothesis subtle enough" to elicit fully intelligible speech from "the isolated and uneloquent" facts available to the student of antiquity. In stressing the formative influence of political institutions, their political science was broader than and superior to the modern social science devised by such figures as Karl Marx, Max Weber, and their disciples. No one can accuse John Adams, Thomas Jefferson, James Madison, or Alexander Hamilton of underestimating the degree to which political architecture shapes civil society and the classes and social groupings within it. But, like recent social science, the institutional political science of early modernity is reductionist at heart.[8] Both are predicated on the questionable assumption that what Machiavelli once called "the effectual truth of the matter [*la verità effettuale della cosa*]" is the truth, the whole truth, and nothing but the truth.[9] Both presuppose that Machiavelli's distinguished English disciple the marquis of Halifax said all that really needs saying when he observed, "Men's resolutions are generally formed, by their appetite or their interest," and then added, "Reason is afterwards called in for Company, but it hath no Vote."[10] Institutional political science and contemporary social science both tend to dismiss opinion as a matter of secondary concern and treat what Augustine called "concord regarding loved things held in common" largely as a reflection of social and political arrangements rather than as the element that constitutes civil society and grounds its many institutions.[11]

Historians do have much to learn from comparative ethnography and political science, but they cannot readily derive what they need most from the homogenized products of contemporary social science. To the extent that they succumb to the reductionism that reigns in the social sciences, their history becomes a pack of tricks played on the dead. The method systematically applied by most modern students deconstructs and reduces historical phenomena in a fashion that disarms the past and obscures its true character. These disciplines, which pretend to be impartial, are actually deeply partisan. Behind their studied neutrality lies an arrogance unchecked because unremarked. For what poses as a rejection of all ethnocentricism is, in fact, an ethnocentricism fully victorious: Contemporary researchers are taught to take for granted that the people they study were deeply wrong, above all else because they were unaware of their own ethnocentricism—because they failed to recognize that the beliefs they professed and for which they were sometimes willing to die were self-serving, arbitrary, and nonsensical.[12]

Whether the social scientist takes as a mentor Marx, Freud, Weber, Durkheim, or some lesser figure, he seeks, typically, to "explain" his subjects' words and deeds by tracing them to crude passions and material interests. As a consequence, much of what now passes as scholarship attempts, more or less unconsciously, to debunk the past and to legitimate the trends of the last two hundred years. By rendering familiar and banal what was once thought noble and sublime, historians deprive the past of anything but antiquarian interest. If, for example, "the fundamental vectors of Athenian society" were simply "the needs for food, shelter, security, and conflict resolution," as one distinguished classical scholar has recently argued, Athens would be a proper subject for idle and self-congratulatory curiosity alone, for little more than the accident of circumstance would distinguish the ancient Greek citizen from the modern bourgeois, who could justifiably take considerable pride in the remarkable material advances of the intervening centuries.[13]

In the midst of the Cold War, a number of Marxist historians, to their great credit, displayed an awareness of some of the weaknesses inherent in a narrow and unenlightening species of class analysis.[14] Many then spoke of "false consciousness" or resorted to Marx's distinction between "a class-in-itself" and "a class-for-itself" and unwittingly confessed that, for all practical purposes, a class without class consciousness is no class at all.[15] But only a very few took the final, fatal step and joined with Antonio Gramsci in emphasizing the "hegemony" of the ruling class and acknowledged that "once an ideology arises it alters profoundly the material reality and in fact becomes a partially autonomous feature of that reality." The ablest and most resolute of these historians tacitly abandoned anything recognizable as a "theory of class determinism"; and then, largely unawares, they approached a purportedly outmoded and virtually forgotten, pre-Machiavellian species of political analysis that recognizes the partisan character of all class rule but gives opinion its due.[16]

Well over a century ago, John Stuart Mill touched on the critical feature of all political life. One of the conditions of "permanent political society," he observed, "has been found to be, the existence, in some form or other, of the feeling of allegiance, or loyalty." Mill knew that this feeling "may vary in its objects," and that it "is not confined to any particular form of government." But he insisted, "Whether in a democracy or in a monarchy, its essence is always the same; viz. that there be in the constitution of the State something which is settled, something permanent, and not to be called in question; something which, by general agreement, has a right to be where it is, and to be secure against disturbance, whatever else may change." Mill thought self-evident the "necessity" for "some fixed point: something which men agreed in holding sacred; which, wherever freedom of discussion was a recognised principle, it was of course lawful to contest in theory, but which no one could either fear or hope to see shaken in practice; which, in short (except perhaps during some temporary crisis), was in the common estimation placed beyond discussion." To be sure, Mill explained, no community could be "exempt from internal dissension," and inevitably "collisions" would occur "between the immediate interests and passions of powerful sections of the people." But nations and peoples have generally weathered these storms precisely because, "however important the interests about which men fell out, the conflict did not affect the fundamental principles of the system of social union which happened to exist; nor threaten large portions of the community with the subversion of that on which they had built their calculations, and with which their hopes and aims had become identified."[17] Mill's insight echoed the fundamental premise of premodern political science, which had its origins in classical antiquity and came to fruition while trying to make sense of the ancient Greek polis.

Political science emerged in the fifth century B.C., when Herodotus traveled about the eastern Mediterranean and the Black Sea, investigated the *nómoi* (customs, habits, and laws) of Hellenes and barbarians, and reflected on those of each nation with an eye to its *politeía* (political regime). At the end of the century, Thucydides used his history of the great war between the Athenians and the Spartans to depict an epic contest between different republican regimes and to analyze the strengths and weaknesses of each. In a similar spirit of inquiry, Xenophon interpreted the Persian monarchy. Plato pioneered the study of political psychology in the rise and the decay of the different regimes. Aristotle brought regime analysis to full maturity, applied it to an assortment of the polities that then existed, and left it as a legacy to the great Greek and Roman writers who recorded so much of the little we know about the ancient world, and who tried to make sense of the changes that took place.[18] Modern scholars must turn to these authors to piece together the jigsaw puzzle of ancient history from the little surviving evidence, and they must use the conceptual framework provided by ancient political science as a tool to weave "a tissue of hypothesis subtle enough" to coax intelligible speech from "the isolated and uneloquent" facts now available.[19]

Except in matters of religion, ancient political scientists did not ignore public opinion, explain it away, dismiss it as false consciousness or mere ideology, or interpret it simply as a product of the historical process. Typically, they accorded the views of ordinary men a respectful hearing and showed that, when considered as a systematic whole, they point beyond themselves to something nobler and more intelligible. In fact, doing justice to popular opinion became a principal goal of ancient political science. Thus, the modern political science of Hobbes and his successors, like the modern physical science of Descartes and his admirers, aims to achieve a quasimathematical certainty and categorically rejects opinions "vulgarly received."[20] Aristotle customarily began with a careful consideration of *éndoxa* or "reputable opinions." He understood the task of political science as identical with that of science in general as understood by Plato: both aimed at making sense of the ordinary man's perceptions and at showing their relation to general principles.[21]

Because they respected the opinions of ordinary men, the ancient political theorists understood that the articulation of humanity into nations and political communities is of fundamental importance and has greater weight than its articulation into economic and social classes. They further understood that they were attributing more influence to the political regime than to the tyranny of circumstance. They did understand the severe limits imposed on human freedom by the need to eke out a living, and they paid careful attention to the formative influence of specific political institutions. But they considered both of these factors secondary to the general character or spirit of the political regime. Though much separates Plato from Aristotle, on this fundamental point they agreed that an understanding of the ancient Greek polis requires attention to two propositions: (1) The political regime (*politeía*), rather than economic or environmental conditions, largely determines what one acute ancient observer called "the one way of life of a whole polis" and another dubbed "the city's soul." (2) Education in the broadest and most comprehensive sense (*paideía*) is more important than anything else in deciding the character of the regime.[22]

Aristotle suggests in *Politics* that common education (*paideía*)—and nothing else—turns a multitude (*plêthos*) into a unit and constitutes it as a polis, and he insists that the regime (*politeía*) defines the polis. Though apparently in contradiction, the two statements are equivalent. Thus, Polybius's celebrated discussion of the Roman *politeía* is, in fact, a discussion of the *paideía* accorded the ruling element (*políteuma*) at Rome—similarly, Xenophon's account of the Persian *politeía.* For Polybius and Xenophon, certain opinions reign within a given community because their advocates have consolidated dominion and persuaded themselves and their subjects of their right to rule as men who, in speech and deed, have achieved preeminence in honoring those very opinion.[23]

The ancients were tougher-minded than today's putative realists. They insisted on the primacy of *paideía,* but recognized the strong case for institutional balances and checks. While judging human affairs from the perspective of the best regime, they conceded that, in politics, one must nearly always settle for the lesser evil. They harbored no illusions about the normal behavior of human beings. They knew that ordinary, uninstructed human desire tends to be insatiable, and they acknowledged that most people who enter politics do so for money and material advantage. Consequently, they took for granted that the justification advanced by the *políteuma* within any *politeía* would, in some measure, be partisan, partial, and self-serving.[24] Notwithstanding a sober appreciation of human weakness, they regarded the partisan character of the *politeía* as of secondary importance.

This needs emphasis: The ancients never doubted that people could be both self-serving and public spirited. La Rochefoucauld may have been the first to remark, "Hypocrisy is an homage that vice renders virtue," but he was hardly the first to recognize the fact.[25] And, as a great disciple of Machiavelli, he would doubtless have conceded that vanity normally dictates that opinions at first hypocritically embraced should come to be cherished sincerely. The marquis of Halifax justly asserted that, while a "good man, for his own sake, will not bee guilty of hipocrisy, . . . for the sake of the world, hee will not discourage it in others." Hypocrisy, he continued, really is "a Paradox; It is rayled at, and deserveth it; yet doth more good to Mankind, than the best of the vertues they commend." Otto Hintze hit the nail on the head when he observed that "man wants to have a good conscience when he pursues his vital interests; and in pursuing them he develops his powers fully only if he is conscious of simultaneously serving purposes higher than purely egotistical ones."[26] That hypocrisy and self-delusion are needed to mask the partisan character of the political order is a sign of man's innate generosity and capacity for impartiality, for they are the dark shadows cast by the tension within human nature between the desire for private advantage and a genuine public-spiritedness.

In pondering the character of a political community, Plato's Thrasymachus was at least partially correct in thinking that, within every regime, political justice embodies "the advantage of the stronger." But primacy goes to the insight inherent in Polemarchus's conviction that justice is inseparable from the friendship grounded in a common, cooperative pursuit of the noble and the good. For even if the political community consists of a gang of thieves, it will quickly fall apart if unsustained by some such vision of the whole. Sir Lewis Namier missed the point when he remarked that in politics, "What matters most is the underlying emotions, the music, to which ideas are a mere libretto, often of very inferior quality."[27] An opera, to be effective, must have music and words sound the same theme, and the same may be said for emotions and ideas in politics.

The modern distinction between materialism and idealism makes little practical, political sense. To decide who is to rule or what kind of people are to share in rule and function as a community's *políteuma* means to determine which of the competing claims are authoritative. And that means to decide upon the qualities to be admired and honored, what is considered advantageous and just, and how happiness (*eudaimonía*) should be pursued. This decision—more than any other—determines the *paideía,* which constitutes "the one way of life of a whole polis." This decision may be a matter of chance. Nations and peoples often stumble on what Burke called "establishments" and J. S. Mill called that "something" in their constitution "which is settled, something permanent, and not to be called in question." Even Alexander Hamilton conceded that few if any societies have ever established "good government from reflection and choice"; most, if not all, have been "destined to depend, for their political constitutions, on accident and force."[28] But, as the ancients fully recognized, where circumstance usually predominates, it does so either because citizens have been overwhelmed by the sheer momentum of events or because they have managed affairs ineptly. Then the resultant drift allows fortune to function as a lawgiver in the distribution and disposition of the polity's offices and honors, which determines the city's *paideía*. What remains essential from the vantage point of Plato and Aristotle is that circumstance need not predominate. Thus, ancient political science stresses the limits of human mastery, while it presupposes the possibility of statesmanship.

With Iris Murdoch, I am arguing for an attempt to "complicate" and alter the rules of the scholarly "game." To meet what is just in the penetrating criticism leveled at social history by distinguished scholars who often oppose each other's views on other matters, we need to incorporate much of what passes today as social history within political history, which should in turn be understood in a much more comprehensive fashion than is now the norm. This project requires that we make central to historical research the political regime and its ruling element and the "loved things held in common" that animate both.[29] In sum, I would suggest that Aristotle offers a peerless framework for the study of the past. There is no better way to make sense of how human beings come to fashion their lives in political communities.

Notes

1. In citations, I have used the standard abbreviations for classical texts provided in *The Oxford Classical Dictionary,* 3rd ed., ed. Simon Hornblower and Antony Spawforth (Oxford: Oxford University Press, 1996). Where appropriate, the ancient texts and more recent works are cited by the divisions and subdivisions employed by the author or introduced by subsequent editors (that is, by book, part, chapter, section number, paragraph, act, scene, line, Stephanus page, or by page and line number).
2. Iris Murdoch, *The Nice and the Good* (London: Chatto and Windus, 1968), 165.
3. Alfred Zimmern, *The Greek Commonwealth,* 5th ed. (Oxford: Clarendon Press, 1931), 215.
4. Letter to Isaac H. Tiffany on 26 August 1816, in *The Writings of Thomas Jefferson,* ed. H. A. Washington (New York: Taylor and Maury, 1853–55) 7: 31–32.
5. Consider Alexis de Tocqueville, *De la démocratie en Amérique* 1.2.9, in Tocqueville, *Oeuvres, papiers et correspondances,* ed. J.-P. Mayer (Paris: Gallimard, 1951–), 1:1 316, in light of Robert P. Kraynak, "Tocqueville's Constitutionalism," *American Political Science Review* 81 (1987): 1175–95.
6. The connection between classical Sparta and the regime imagined by Rousseau is particularly evident in the famous chapter in *The Social Contract* dealing with the legislator: see *Du contrat social* 2.7, in Jean-Jacques Rousseau, *Oeuvres complètes,* ed. Bernard Gagnebin and Marcel Raymond (Paris: Gallimard, 1959–69), 3:381–84.
7. See Paul A. Rahe, *Republics Ancient and Modern: Classical Republicanism and the American Revolution* (Chapel Hill: University of North Carolina Press, 1992), 231–541.
8. For a brief exposition that brings out the reductionist character of this new political science, see Albert O. Hirschman, *The Passions and the Interests: Political Arguments for Capitalism before Its Triumph* (Princeton: Princeton University Press, 1977), 9–113.
9. Machiavelli, *Il principe* 15, in Niccolò Machiavelli, *Tutte le opere,* ed. Mario Martelli (Florence: Sansoni, 1971), 280.
10. See Halifax, *Miscellaneous Maxims,* in *The Works of George Savile, Marquis of Halifax,* ed. Mark N. Brown (Oxford: Clarendon Press, 1989) 3:422.6–12.
11. August. *De civ. D.* 19.24. For a recent study that illuminates the difference between ancient and modern political science, see Harvey C. Mansfield, Jr., *Taming the Prince: The Ambivalence of Modern Executive Power* (New York: Free Press, 1989).
12. See Herbert J. Storing, ed., *Essays on the Scientific Study of Politics* (New York: Holt, Rinehart, and Winston, 1962).
13. John K. Davies, *Wealth and the Power of Wealth in Classical Athens* (New York: Arno Press, 1981), vii.
14. For the inadequacy of Marx and Engels's analysis, see Richard F. Hamilton, *The Bourgeois Epoch: Marx and Engels on Britain, France, and Germany* (Chapel Hill: University of North Carolina Press, 1991).
15. See, for example, G. E. M. de Ste. Croix, *The Class Struggle in the Ancient Greek World: From the Archaic Age to the Arab Conquests* (Ithaca, N.Y.: Cornell University Press, 1981), 19–69, 81–98 (esp. 60).
16. See, for example, Eugene D. Genovese, "Materialism and Idealism in the History of Negro Slavery in the Americas" and "On Antonio Gramsci," *In Red and Black: Marxian Explorations in Southern and Afro-American History* (New York: Pantheon Books, 1971), 23–52, 391–422 (esp. 32, 40, 406–9).

17. Mill, "Coleridge," in *Collected Works of John Stuart Mill,* ed. John M. Robson et al. (Toronto: University of Toronto Press, 1963–91) 10:117–63 (at 133–34). See Mill, *A System of Logic,* 8th ed., 6.10.5, in ibid., 8:922–23.
18. See Leo Strauss, *The City and Man* (Chicago: University of Chicago Press, 1964), 139–241, esp. 236–41. Cf. Moses I. Finley, "The Ancient Historian and His Sources," *Ancient History: Evidence and Models* (London: Chatto and Windus, 1985), 7–26 (at 18, 26).
19. Cf. Ste. Croix, *Class Struggle in the Ancient Greek World,* 409–52. In contrast, see Harvey C. Mansfield, Jr., "Marx on Aristotle: Freedom, Money, and Politics," *Review of Metaphysics* 34 (1980): 351–67.
20. Cf. Thomas Hobbes, *Elements of Law Natural and Politic,* 2nd ed., ed. Ferdinand Tönnies (London: Cass, 1969), 1.13.3, with René Descartes, *Discours de la méthode,* 1–6, and *La recherche de la vérité par la lumière naturelle,* in Descartes, *Oeuvres et lettres,* ed. André Bridoux (Paris: Gallimard, 1953), 879–901.
21. See Arist. *Top.* 100a18–101b4 (esp. 100b21–23), *Eth. Eud.* 1216b26–1217a18, 1235b13–18, and *Eth. Nic.* 1145b2–7. The stated principle of Aristotle is entirely in keeping with the practice of Socrates in the Platonic dialogues, cf. Pl. *Phd.* 96a–100b. See also Leo Strauss, *The Political Philosophy of Hobbes: Its Basis and Its Genesis* (Chicago: University of Chicago Press, 1952), 142–45; Ronna Burger, *The Phaedo: A Platonic Labyrinth* (New Haven: Yale University Press, 1984), 135–60; Seth Benardete, *Socrates' Second Sailing: On Plato's Republic* (Chicago: University of Chicago Press, 1989); Harold Cherniss, "The Philosophical Economy of the Theory of Ideas," *American Journal of Philology* 57 (1936): 445–56; and Martha Craven Nussbaum, "Saving Aristotle's Appearances," *The Fragility of Goodness: Luck and Ethics in Greek Tragedy and Philosophy* (Cambridge, Mass.: Cambridge University Press, 1986), 240–63.
22. For definitions for the term *politeía,* see Schol. Pl. *Leg.* 1.625b and *Isoc.* 7.14. This explains the prominence of *paideía* as a theme in both *The Republic* and *The Laws:* cf. Pl. *Resp.* 2.376c–4.445a, 6.487b–497a, 7.518b–541b, 8.548a–b, 554a–b, 559b–c, 10.600a–608b with *Leg.* 1.641b–2.674c, 3.693d–701b, 4.722b–9.880e, 11.920a–12.962e.
23. Cf. Arist. *Pol.* 1263b36–37 with 1276a8–b15. Cf. Polyb. 6.19–58 with Xen. *Cyr.* 1.2.15. And see Pl. *Ep.* 7.336d–337d.
24. See Pl. *Leg.* 3.691d–692a, 693a–b in light of 3.691c–d, 692b, 9.874e–875d, and note Aristotle's discussion and critique of "the techniques [*sophísmata*] of legislation": cf. *Pol.* 1297a14–41 with 1307b40–1308a2. See also Arist. *Eth. Nic.* 1109a28–35 and *Pol.* 1280a7–1284b34, 1296a22–32, 1318a17–26, 1318b1–5; and see Pl. *Leg.* 11.918a–920a (esp. 918d–e), 689e–690d, 4.712e–715b, and 8.832b–c.
25. François, duc de La Rochefoucauld, *Réflexions ou sentences et maximes morales: Édition de 1678,* no. 218, in La Rochefoucauld, *Oeuvres complètes,* ed. L. Martin-Chauffier and Jean Marchand (Paris: Gallimard, 1964), 432. For an earlier statement of the same point, see Montaigne, "De l'utile et de l'honneste," *Les essais de Michel de Montaigne,* ed. Pierre Villey and V.-L. Saulnier (Paris: Presses Universitaires de France, 1978), 790.
26. Halifax, *Miscellaneous Maxims,* in *The Works of George Savile, Marquis of Halifax* 3:370.21–371.8. Otto Hintze, "Calvinism and Raison d'Etat in Early Seventeenth-Century Brandenburg," *The Historical Essays of Otto Hintze,* ed. Felix Gilbert (New York: Oxford University Press, 1975), 88–154 (at 94).
27. Cf. Pl. *Resp.* 1.338d–339b with 1.331d–335e, and 1.348b–352d. Lewis Namier, "Human Nature in Politics," in *Personalities and Powers* (New York: Macmillan, 1955), 1–7 (esp. 4–5).
28. See, for example, Pl. *Resp.* 8.543c–9.592b and *Leg.* 3.689e–701b, 4.712b–715d. For Hamilton, see Alexander Hamilton, James Madison, and John Jay, *The Federalist,* ed. Jacob E. Cooke (Middletown, Conn.: Wesleyan University Press, 1961), 3 (no. 1).

29. August. *De civ. D.* 19.24. On social history, see Elizabeth Fox-Genovese and Eugene D. Genovese, "The Political Crisis of Social History: Class Struggle as Subject and Object," *Fruits of Merchant Capital: Slavery and Bourgeois Property in the Rise and Expansion of Capitalism* (Oxford: Oxford University Press, 1983), 179–212; and Gertrude Himmelfarb, "'History with the Politics Left Out,'" *The New History and the Old* (Cambridge, Mass.: Harvard University Press, 1987), 13–32.

CHAPTER 16

WHAT IS A LIBERAL EDUCATION?

Donald Kagan

WHAT IS A LIBERAL education and what is it for? In our time, in spite of the arguments over core curricula, canons, and multiculturalism, the real encounter is avoided and the questions ignored. From Cicero's *artes liberales* to the *trivium* and *quadrivium* of the medieval schoolmen, to the *studia humanitatis* of the Renaissance humanists, to Cardinal Newman's *Idea of a University,* to the attempts at common curricula in the first half of this century, to the chaotic cafeteria that passes for a curriculum in most American universities today, the concept has suffered from vagueness, confusion, and contradiction. From the beginning the champions of a liberal education have thought that it seeks at least four kinds of goals.

One was an end in itself, the achievement of that contemplative life that Aristotle thought was the greatest happiness; knowledge, and the acts of acquiring and considering it were the ends of this quest, and good in themselves. A second goal was to shape the character, the style, the taste of a person, to make him good himself and better able to fit well into the society of others like him. A third was to prepare him for a useful career in the world, one appropriate to his status as a free man. For Cicero and Quintillian this meant a career as an orator that would allow a man to protect his private interests and those of his friends in the law courts and to advance the public interest in the assemblies, senate, and magistracies. The fourth goal was to contribute to the educated citizen's freedom. The ancients thought that free citizens should be not ignorant and parochial but learned and cosmopolitan; they should not be ruled by others, but must take part in their own government; servants specialized in some specific and limited task, but free men must know something of everything and understand general principles without yielding to the narrowness of expertise. The Romans, in fact, claimed all these benefits as the products of a liberal education. To achieve their goal the recommended course of study was literature, history, philosophy, and rhetoric, gleaned from an informal canon of authors generally thought to provide the best examples in all respects.

It was once common to think of the medieval university as a place that focused on learning for its own sake. Recent studies, however, have made it clear that the medieval universities, whatever their commitment to learning for its own sake, were also institutions that trained their students for professional careers. Graduates in the liberal arts earned a license to teach others what they had learned and to make a living that way. Some studied the liberal arts to prepare for careers in medicine, theology, and law, and for important positions in church and state.

The seven liberal arts of the Middle Ages consisted of the *trivium* (grammar, rhetoric, and logic) and the *quadrivium* (arithmetic, geometry, astronomy, and music). The discovery and absorption of Aristotle's works in the twelfth century quickly led to the triumph of logic and dialectic over the other arts. They were the glamour subjects of the time, believed to be the best means for training and disciplining the mind and to provide the best tools for successful careers in both church and state. The dominant view of knowledge and truth was that they both already existed. They needed only to be learned, organized, and harmonized. There was nothing still to be discovered; knowledge and truth had only to be systematized and explained. The great summas of the twelfth century and after set out to do exactly that and, with their help, an ambitious scholar could hope to achieve some semblance of universal knowledge. They believed that this was good in itself, for to the medieval mind God was the source of all truth, and to comprehend truth was to come closer to divinity. Thus, there is something to the claim that scholars of the Middle Ages prized learning as something intrinsically good. But they also placed great value on the practical rewards of their liberal education, and rightly so, for their logical, dialectical, mathematical, and rhetorical studies were the best available training for the clerks, notaries, lawyers, canons, and managers so badly needed in the high Middle Ages. Missing from the list of benefits claimed for the liberal education was the training appropriate to the free gentlemen sought by the Romans, but this ideal of the classical world had no real place in medieval society.

That ancient goal of the liberal arts had great appeal, however, for the humanists of the Renaissance. Typically citizens of the newly flourishing city-states of northern Italy, they made a conscious effort to return to the ideas and values of the classical age. As Christians they continued to study the church fathers but rejected the commentaries and summas of the medieval schoolmen and went directly to the sources themselves, applying the powerful new tools of philological analysis. Their greatest innovation and delight, however, was the study of classical texts by the pagan authors, whose focus on the secular world and elevation of the importance of mankind appealed to them. Their idea of a liberal education, the *studia humanitatis,* continued to include grammar and rhetoric from the old curriculum but added the study of a canon of classical poets, historians, and political and moral philosophers. They thought these studies delightful in themselves but also essential for achieving the goals of a liberal education: to become wise and to speak eloquently. The emphasis was on use and action: the beneficiary of a humanistic liberal education learned what was good so that he could practice virtue. The varied and demanding life of the Renaissance city-state led to a broad definition of the qualities needed for a successful and good life, one that increasingly resembled the ancient view.

Castiglione's *Book of the Courtier,* aimed at educated noblemen living in ducal courts, set forth the ideal of the well-rounded man who united in his person a knowledge of language, literature, and history with athletic, military, and musical skills, all framed by good manners and good moral character. These qualities were thought to be desirable in themselves, but they would also be most useful to a man making his way in the courts of Renaissance Italy. The civic humanists, chiefly citizens of the republic of Florence, applied the humanistic education in a way that suited their own experience. They wanted it to train good men for public service, for leadership in the cultural and political life of their city. Such humanists as Colluccio Salutati, Leonardo Bruni, and Poggio Bracciolini served as chancellors of Florence, defending it against aggression with the skills and abilities perfected by their training. They also found time to write histories of their city intended to celebrate its virtues and win for it the devotion of its citizens, a no less important contribution to its survival and flourishing.

For the Italian humanists, as for their classical predecessors, freedom still meant the ability to control one's own life, to dispose of one's own time, to put aside concern for gain and to devote oneself to the training of mind, body, and spirit for the sake of higher things. No more than the ancients did the humanists think that liberal education should be remote from the responsibilities and rewards of the secular life of mankind. Their study, to be sure, pursued a knowledge of virtue, but that knowledge was aimed at virtuous action in the public interest, and such action sought fame as its reward.

The idea of liberal education came to America by way of the English colleges and universities, where the approach of the Renaissance humanists gained favor only in the eighteenth century. In Georgian England, "Humane learning came specifically to mean the direct study of the most renowned classical texts, and especially those authors who were literary figures."[1] But the English version of a humanistic liberal education selected only some elements from the program of the Renaissance humanists and rejected the others. There was little interest in the hard training that turned philology into a keen and powerful tool for the critical examination of primary sources and the discovery of truth. Nor was liberal education meant as preparation for an active life of public service. It was the education of one of Castiglione's courtiers rather than one of the civic humanists' chancellors. The result was an education that suited English society in the eighteenth century, one where the landed aristocracy was still powerful and where connections and favor were very important. A liberal education was one suitable to a free man, who, it was assumed, was well born and rich enough to afford it. It was to be a training aimed at gaining command of arts that were "liberal," "such as fit for Gentlemen and Scholars," as a contemporary dictionary put it, and not those that were servile—"Mechanick Trades and Handicrafts" suited for "meaner People."[2] It was an education for gentlemen, meant not to prepare its recipients for a career or some specific function, but to produce a well-rounded man who would feel comfortable and be accepted in the best circles of society and get on in the world. It placed special emphasis on preparing young men to make the kind of educated conversation required in polite society.

The universities continued with the old Aristotelian curriculum centering on logic and religion. Their main contribution to the current idea of liberal education was to give their students the opportunity to make the right sort of friends, and "Friendship," as one schoolmaster put it, ". . . is known to heighten our joys, and to soften our cares," but, no less important, "by the attachments which it forms . . . is often the means of advancing a man's fortunes in this world."[3]

Such an education prized sociability. It took a dim view of solitary study aimed at acquiring knowledge for its own sake, which was called pedantry, a terrible term of abuse at that time. Pedants were thought to be fussy, self-absorbed, engaged in the study of knowledge that was useless. We find fathers writing to warn their sons at the university against the dangers of working too hard and becoming pedants, ruining their health, and damaging their social life. Education was meant to shape character and manners much more than intellect. The universities, with their cloistered atmosphere, were seen by some to be irrelevant, useless, and even damaging to the social goals and the economic advantages that English gentlemen sought for their sons in the age of Enlightenment.

The first decade of the nineteenth century brought a great change to English universities. The number of undergraduates entering the universities grew rapidly, with young scholars full of intellectual energy and boldness. If their energies were as untapped, their interests as undirected, their leisure as copious as in the past, who could tell what dangers might befall? The response of the university faculties was to revive a medieval device that had fallen into disuse—competitive examinations. These examinations had the desired effect, absorbing the time and energy of the undergraduates and turning their minds away from dangerous channels. For most students a liberal education came to mean the careful study of a limited list of Latin and Greek classics, with emphasis on mastery of the ancient languages, but it was now justified on a new basis, not the Humanism of the Renaissance: this kind of learning cultivated and strengthened the intellectual faculties. Commissions investigating Oxford and Cambridge in the 1850s concluded that, "It is the sole business of the University to train the powers of the mind."[4] This new definition, the limited curriculum, and the examination system that connected them soon came under attack from different directions. The growth of industry and democracy led some critics to demand a more practical education that would be "useful" in ways that the Oxbridge liberal education was not. It would train its students for particular vocations, on the one hand, and on the other, it would provide the expertise the new kind of leaders needed in the modern world. At the same time, very different critics complained that the old values of liberal education had been undermined by the sharply limited classical curriculum, the sentence-parsing and fact-cramming imposed by the examinations. Liberal education, they insisted, must not be narrow, pedantic, one-sided—in short, illiberal. It must be useful in more than a pragmatic sense; it must train the character and the whole man, not merely the mind. Still others argued that the restless, tumultuous, industrial society of the nineteenth century, increasingly lacking agreement on a common core of values, needed leaders trained in more than style and manners. Liberal education must become general education, including languages, modern as well as ancient, literature, history, and the natural sciences. In the words of one writer, "A man of the highest education ought to know something of everything, and everything of something."[5] This was a call for a new "universal knowledge." Its advocates urged broadening the field of learning to include all that was known, and synthesizing and integrating the information collected by discovering the philosophical principles that underlay it all. As one Victorian put it, "The summit of a liberal education . . . is Philosophy—meaning by Philosophy the sustained effort . . . to frame a complete and reasoned synthesis of the facts of the universe."[6]

The new universal education remained intellectual and academic, not practical and professional. It was, therefore, attacked as useless, but its champions insisted that although it was not *merely* useful, it was useful nonetheless. Cardinal Newman was the most famous proponent of the new program, but he resisted the idea of usefulness entirely. "That alone is liberal knowledge," he said, "which stands on its own pretensions, which is independent of sequel, expects no complement, refuses to be informed (as it is called) by any end, or absorbed in any art, in order to present itself to our contemplations. The most ordinary pursuits have this specific character, if they are self-sufficient and complete; the highest lose it, when they minister to something beyond them."[7] Newman's intention was to resist the pressure on the secular side from those who wanted chiefly practical training and on the religious side from those Irish Catholics (for his remarks were prompted by the creation of a new Catholic university in Dublin) who wanted what amounted to a seminary. Newman was an intellectual, an academic, and an Aristotelian, and he defended the ancient idea of the value of learning and knowledge for their own sake at a time when the tide was running against it, as it usually does. The result was the same one that befell King Canute. In the last decades of the century, Newman's idea of knowledge for its own sake and the whole concept of universal knowledge for the purpose of philosophical understanding were swept away by a great educational tidal wave from across the channel, chiefly from Germany. Originality and discovery now became the prime values. The idea of the university as a museum, a repository of learning, gave way to the notion that it should be dynamic, a place where knowledge was discovered and generated. Scientific method and the new values were not confined to the natural sciences but were applied to the old humanistic studies, as well, with good results. The new methods and the new zeal for research invigorated the study of history, literature, and theology, and even the classics, symbol of the old order and chief target of reformers.

These gains, however, exacted a price. The new knowledge required specialization, hard, narrow training at the expense of broad, general education for the purpose of philosophical understanding, at which the advocates of "universal knowledge" had aimed. Champions of the new order, therefore, changed the definition of liberal education. A famous Oxford classical philologist put it this way: "The essence of a liberal education is that it should stand in constant relation to the advance of knowledge. Research and discovery are the processes by which truth is directly acquired; education is the preparation of the mind for its reception, and the creation of a truth-loving habit."[8] He believed that knowledge obtained by rigorous research would produce truth and that only truth could lead to morality. Research, therefore, would provide a new basis for morality.

That required the application of scientific method to all subjects which, in turn, demanded specialization. Science and social science kept creating new fields and subfields, all of which had equal claim to attention and a place in a liberal education, since all employed the correct method and all claimed to produce new knowledge and truth. No one dared to rank subjects according to an idea of their intrinsic value or their usefulness. Practitioners in each field came to have more in common with their fellow investigators in other universities than with their colleagues in other fields at their own. Both they and their students became more professional in their allegiance and in their attitudes. The distinction between a liberal and a professional education became ever more vague, and some denied that there was any. Although these developments were well under way at the end of the last century they seem to me to be the forces that have shaped our own universities and remain influential today.

I have rehearsed this inadequate capsule history of the idea of a liberal education, first, because such knowledge is good in itself, but also because I think it may be a useful basis for examining the status of liberal education today. When I ask which of these images of liberal education most resembles what passes by that name in American colleges today, I come to conclusions that surprise me. It seems to me that the education provided at a typical liberal arts college today comes closest to achieving the goals sought by English gentlemen in the eighteenth century. To be sure, success in that world did not require any particular set of studies or any specialization, for the graduates could look forward to a comfortable life supported by their landed estates. Otherwise, I am sure the training then would have contained some equivalent of our modern departmental major. In most other respects our curricula today, with their lack of any set of subjects studied in common, the lack of agreement on any particular method of training the mind, the lack of a culminating examination testing the acquisition of a body of knowledge, and the emphasis on well-roundedness, defined only as the opposite of narrowness and achieved by taking a few courses in some specified number of different fields—all these fit the eighteenth-century English model nicely.

If we examine the full reality rather than only the formal curriculum, the similarities seem even greater. I submit that in America today the most important social distinction, one almost as significant as the old one between gentle and simple, is whether or not one has a college education. Within the favored group finer distinctions place a liberal education as opposed to a vocational or merely professional one at the top of the social pyramid. Graduates of the more prestigious liberal arts colleges are most likely to gain the best positions and to marry the most desired partners. The fact that each year there are at least seven applicants for every place in the freshman classes of such colleges at a cost of more than twenty-five thousand dollars each year for four years shows that this is widely understood. Apart from any preprofessional training they may obtain, successful applicants gain about the same advantages as those sought by young Englishmen from their less formal eighteenth-century education. They sharpen useful skills in writing and speaking, they pick up enough of subjects thought interesting in their circle and of the style of discussing them to permit agreeable and acceptable conversation. They learn the style and manners to make them comfortable in a similarly educated society. They learn and absorb the political attitudes favored by the group they are entering. They have excellent opportunities to make friends who may be advantageous to them in later life. The practical task of learning to make a living is largely left to professional schools and on-the-job training.

Other objectives, I think, are less well served. The search for general, universal knowledge and for the philosophical principles on which it may be based has long since been abandoned. It might be thought, at least, that those values produced by the study of the natural sciences, of research, and of scientific method flourish in today's version of liberal education; I mean the rigorous training of the mind, the inculcation of a "truth-loving habit," and the universal triumph of the scientific method. I don't think that such a goal for liberal education was ever adequate; nevertheless its achievement would be worth a good deal, but I do not think our modern versions of liberal education achieve even that. In liberal arts colleges today the study of mathematics and the natural sciences is separated from other studies in important ways. The hard sciences are committed to rigorous training of the mind in a single method, the scientific one. Teachers of science continue to believe in the cumulative and progressive character of knowledge and in the possibility of moving toward truth. Students who major in these subjects are likely to acquire the method and to share these beliefs. While teachers and students are interested in the practical uses of science, I think many of them come to value learning and knowledge as good in themselves, although their scope is often limited. These are all good reasons, apart from those of practical necessity, for encouraging the serious study of natural science for all students. Even so, only a minority of students in liberal arts colleges major in mathematics or natural science. In some places students who do not major in these subjects are required to study neither; in others there is a minimal requirement that rarely achieves the desired goals.

Nor do I think that most modern attempts at liberal education sufficiently encourage students to pursue learning and knowledge as a serious and valuable contribution to their own lives. The absence of a core of common studies limits the possibility of taking learning seriously and making it an important part of life. Students follow different paths, read different books, ask different questions. They have no common intellectual ground. The result is to impoverish conversation and the thought that can arise from it, acknowledged since the time of Socrates as perhaps the most potent form of education. Serious talk on serious subjects based on shared knowledge is difficult, since the knowledge that comes from learning is scattered and specialized and thus unavailable to serve as the substance of important discussions. Belief in the intrinsic value of learning is diminished, since what each student has learned in courses is peculiar to himself or herself and not truly available for critical discussion. It is merely "academic," confined to forgotten papers and examinations, playing no part in the serious consideration of real issues and problems. If there were a general agreement on a body of knowledge worth learning, one that all educated people could share, and one, therefore, that could readily serve as the basis for serious discussion of important questions and might, thereby, yield wisdom, there would be a far greater chance of success than there is today.

The greatest shortcoming, I believe, of most attempts at liberal education today, with their individualized, unfocused, scattered curricula, and ill-defined purpose, is their failure to enhance the students' understanding of their status as free citizens of a free society and the responsibilities it entails. To my mind, liberal education is inconceivable outside a free society. Every successful civilization must pass on its basic values to each generation; when it no longer does so its days are numbered. The danger is particularly great in a society such as our own, the freest the world has known, whose special character is to encourage doubt and questioning even of its own values and assumptions. Such questioning has always been and remains a distinctive, admirable, and salutary part of our education and way of life. So long as there was a shared belief in the personal and social morality taught by tradition, so long as there was a belief in the excellence of the tradition and institutions of the nation, and so long as these beliefs were communicated in the schools, such questioning was also safe. Our tradition of free critical inquiry counteracted the tendency for received moral and civic teachings to become ethnocentric complacency and intolerance and prevented patriotism from degenerating into arrogant chauvinism. When students came to college they found their values and prejudices challenged by the books they read, by their fellow students from other places and backgrounds, and by their teachers.

I suggest to you that the situation is far different today. Whatever the formal religious attachments of our students may be, I find that a firm belief in traditional values is rare. Still rarer are an informed understanding of the traditions and institutions of our country and their roots in the more remote past and an appreciation of their special qualities and virtues. The admirable, even the uniquely good elements are taken for granted as if they were universally available, had always existed, and required no special effort to preserve. All shortcomings, however, are quickly noticed and harshly condemned.

Our society is judged not against the experience of human societies in other times and places, but against the Kingdom of Heaven. There is great danger in this, for our society, no less than others now and in the past, requires the allegiance and devotion of its citizens if it is to defend itself and progress toward a better life. In my experience, however, traditional beliefs have not been replaced by a new set of beliefs firmly set on different traditions. Instead, I find a cultural void, an ignorance of the past, a sense of rootlessness and aimlessness, as though not only the students but also the world were born yesterday, a feeling that the students are attached to the society in which they live only incidentally and accidentally. Having little or no sense of the human experience through the ages, of what has been tried, of what has succeeded and what has failed, of what is the price of cherishing some values as opposed to others or of how values relate to one another, they leap from acting as though anything were possible, without cost, to despairing that nothing is possible. They are inclined to see other people's values as mere prejudices, one no better than another, while viewing their own inclinations as entirely valid, for they see themselves as autonomous entities entitled to be free from interference by society and from obligation to it.

Because of the cultural vacuum in their earlier education and because of the informal but potent education they receive from the communications media, which both shape and reflect the larger society, today's liberal arts students come to college, it seems to me, bearing a relativism verging on nihilism, an individualism that is really isolation from community. Each one resembles, as Aristotle put it, a single checker apart from a game of checkers. The education they too often receive in college these days, it seems to me, is more likely to reinforce this condition than to change it. In this way, too, it fails in its liberating function, in its responsibility to shape free men and women. Earlier generations who came to college with traditional beliefs rooted in the past had them challenged by hard questioning and by the requirement to consider alternatives. They were thereby unnerved, and thereby liberated, by the need to make reasoned choices. The students of today and tomorrow deserve the same opportunity; they, too, must be liberated from the tyranny that comes from the accident of being born at a time when and in a place where a particular set of ideas is current. But that liberation can come only from a return to the belief that we may have something to learn from the past. The challenge to the relativism, nihilism, and privatism of the present can best be presented by a careful and respectful examination of earlier ideas; such ideas have not been rejected by the current generation but are merely unknown to them.

When today's students have been allowed to consider the alternatives they, too, can enjoy the freedom of making an informed and reasoned choice.

The liberal education needed for the students of today and tomorrow, I suggest, should require a common program of studies for all its students as part of the full curriculum. That would have many advantages, for it would create an intellectual communion among students and teachers that does not now exist. It would also affirm that some questions are of fundamental importance to everyone, regardless of his or her origins and plans, that we must all think about our beliefs, our responsibilities, and our relationships with one another and with the society in which we live. The program to meet these goals should include the study of mathematics and science, of literature, philosophy, and history (in which I include the history of the arts and sciences) from their beginnings. It would be a study that tries to meet the past on its own terms, examining it critically but also respectfully, always keeping alive the possibility that the past may contain wisdom that can be useful to us today. It would include moral and civic goals among its purposes, critically and seriously examining the beliefs discussed, private and public, personal and political. Such an education would show the modern student times and worlds where the common understanding was quite different from his and her own—where it was believed that human beings have a nature and capacities different from those of the other animals, that their nature is gregarious and can reach its highest perfection only by living a good life in a well-ordered society. It would reveal that a good society requires citizens who understand and share its values and accept their own connection with it and dependence on it, that there must be mutual respect among citizens and their common effort both for their own flourishing and for its survival. Students enjoying such an education would encounter the idea that freedom is essential to the good and happy life of human beings but that freedom requires good laws and respect for them.

Aristotle rightly observed that in matters other than scientific, people learn best not by precept, but by example. Let me conclude, therefore, by making it clear that the colleges that claim to offer a liberal education today and tomorrow must make their commitment to freedom clear by their actions. To a university, even more than to other institutions in a free society, the right of free speech, the free exchange of ideas, the presentation of unpopular points of view, the freedom to move about and make use of the university's facilities without interference, are vital. Discussion, argument, and persuasion are the devices appropriate to the life of the mind, not suppression, obstruction, and intimidation. Yet for more than three decades, our colleges and universities have permitted speakers to be shouted down or prevented from speaking, buildings to be forcibly occupied and access to them denied, student newspapers to be seized and disposed of, speech codes that enforce approved opinions to be imposed, and various modes of intimidation to be employed with much success. Most of the time the perpetrators have gone unpunished in any significant way. Colleges and universities that permit such attacks on freedom and take no firm and effective action to deter and punish those who carry them out sabotage the most basic educational freedoms. To defend those freedoms is the first obligation of anyone who claims to engage in liberal education.

The history of the human race shows that liberty is a rare flower and that societies in which freedom has flourished have been few and short-lived. There is no reason to take freedom for granted, for its seems to require both good fortune and careful cultivation to have any chance at all. We seem to have lost sight of the most basic and noblest purpose of liberal learning: to pass on to each new generation the heritage of freedom and to provide each man and woman with the knowledge needed to understand, cherish, and protect it. If liberty is to survive we must demonstrate our commitment to it in both word and deed. Most important of all, we must provide our children with an education shaped by the purpose of creating citizens of a free society who will love liberty, who will understand the discipline and sacrifice needed to preserve it, and who will be eager to do so.

Notes

1. Sheldon Rothblatt, *Tradition and Change in English Liberal Education* (London: Faber and Faber, 1976), 43.
2. Rothblatt, *Tradition and Change,* 25.
3. Quoted in Rothblatt, *Tradition and Change,* 62.
4. Rothblatt, *Tradition and Change,* 130.
5. F. W. Farrar, *Essays on a Liberal Education* (London: MacMillan and Co., 1867), 87.
6. Farrar, *Essays on a Liberal Education,* 140.
7. Cardinal John Henry Newman, *On the Scope and Nature of University Education* (London: J. M. Dent & Sons, Ltd., 1915), 103.
8. Henry Nettleship, quoted in Rothblatt, *Tradition and Change,* 169.

CHAPTER 17

THE DEATH OF JANE ADDAMS

Edward Berkowitz

WE LIVE IN A very uncertain age in which no one group seeks responsibility for governing the behavior of another. This age is unlike the end of the nineteenth century, when social workers like Jane Addams took it upon themselves to settle among the immigrant poor and assist in the process of Americanizing them. Addams respected the differences among the ethnic groups living on the edge of downtown Chicago and wanted each in the neighborhood around Hull House to maintain pride in its heritage. Still, she regarded it as her business to acclimate them to American life, to transform them from foreigners into Americans. She had no doubt that it was the American culture that should predominate and that the ultimate goal was integration, not segregation.

The immigrants who lived in the cities of the late nineteenth and early twentieth centuries inhabited an ethnically diverse world. Yet they could depend upon the kindness of strangers such as Jane Addams and on the aid of institutions that consciously sought to downplay their differences in the interest of establishing a common American identity. Not only the settlement houses but also the schools and even the city governments assisted in the effort.

Today we have lost those mediating institutions. Modern immigrants, including the millions of African Americans who have come from the South to settle in the North, must cope on their own. The goal of integration no longer seems tenable or even desirable. Some intellectuals even go so far as to encourage diversity for its own sake.

Originally published in a slightly different form in *The Word & I,* January 1997.

Among those who consciously seek to heighten the differences among Americans are the academic historians who write books in celebration of various ethnic and racial groups. These academics have largely abandoned the effort to construct a common history of America that applies to all groups and both genders. In the process, they have contributed to the loss of the common myths and symbols that once brought us together.

What the Academic Historians Are and Are Not

There is a tendency among disgruntled conservatives to see the behavior of academics as undisciplined or self-indulgent. The academics may well be self-indulgent in the sense of being romantic, but they are far from undisciplined.

Many academic historians look to the past to recover the possibilities that they no longer see in the present. Hence, they celebrate the world of the preindustrial artisan who could make his own way without depending on the dollars-and-cents generosity of a large corporation; they scour the historical record for evidence of African American accomplishments, hoping to refute today's racists who feel that, when all is said and done, blacks are inferior to whites. In other words, they use the past to liberate themselves from some of the dreary aspects of the present, an escape from reality that is inherently romantic.

Despite this romantic streak, today's academic historians, particularly the ones who have gotten their jobs recently, are an industrious lot. They have been through hell, participating in a dismal job market, suffering the humility of one-year jobs in which they have been asked to teach more than their share and in which they have never gotten to enjoy the security that is the academic trade-off for inadequate salaries. Those who have somehow crossed the line and gotten a tenure-track job still have to publish a great deal—much more than their senior colleagues—if they ever expect to reach the nirvana of tenure. Nor is it easy to publish, since the market for academic writing is far from hospitable. Financial pressures have forced most academic presses to cut back significantly. As a result of all these market forces, the younger academics inhabit a Darwinian world in which the pressure to succeed is intense.

These younger academics often work harder and always at lower wages than their contemporaries who have elected to become doctors, lawyers, or stockbrokers. Traveling on their own nickel, they journey to obscure historical archives and borrow money to photocopy historical documents. They steal time to write their books and articles in the face of constant demands from students who expect to be treated like privileged consumers, to receive lectures illustrated by video clips, and to gain the benefits of informal psychotherapy designed to put the occasional bad grade in the right emotional light. These same wage slaves who minister to their students write more material each semester for lectures alone than many full-time writers produce in a year. Having taken care of their classes, they still need to keep a large stock of metaphors handy for their books and articles, the only pieces of their writing that the profession will see, and then beg publishers to put them in print.

It would be expecting too much of these scholars to think that they could take intellectual risks. Instead, they seek to expand the existing academic literature in a way that does not offend any of the elders or the powerful gatekeepers who peer-review their books and articles. Essentially, they replicate the current literature by churning out pieces on artisans, women, and blacks, all keyed to the heroic tone of the recent literature.

Profession over Public

As numerous commentators have noted, the academics have paid a price for their relative isolation from the intellectual mainstream. That price is public indifference to their work. The public watches historical documentaries on television with fascination. War stories and biographies have become staple fare on such cable networks as The History Channel and Discovery. The movie *Nixon,* while an overwrought and self-consciously arty film, nonetheless reminds us that the public once shared a common set of political images. Most members of the World War II generation could close their eyes and picture Alger Hiss, the Checkers speech with Pat sitting primly on the side, the first debate between swarthy Dick and Palm Beach Jack, and the venomous "last" press conference.

The nostalgia for the nation's shared military and political experiences lingers. To confirm this fact, one need only go the local Borders bookstore. There one will find high piles of books by David McCullough and Doris Kearns and loads of books on Kennedy and Nixon, not to mention volume after volume about this military campaign or that.

Not so in academia, however. Within the academy, military history remains a small and unpopular specialty. Political biographies, particularly of dead white men, can be a scholar's one-way ticket to Palookaville. As a result, the academics have lost their hold on the public imagination, if they ever had it in the first place. That means that academics talk largely to one another in conversations that have become increasingly rarefied. They babble on about the "maternalist welfare state" and other matters of no public interest.

I do not mean to paint a cartoon of academia. Some of the conversations pack real intellectual punch. More to the point, there are countervailing trends within the history profession. Students appear to want courses in military history, and academic administrators realize that institutional survival depends to some extent on responding to student demand. Hence, one sees job advertisements for military historians. Political history, the story of presidents and political parties, appears to be making a comeback, at least as judged by the enthusiastic responses to panels on that topic at the last three meetings of the Organization of American Historians.

For the moment, however, there is still far more academic work being done on the student counterculture of the 1960s than on the development of the Republican party in that decade. Historians have lost their sense of proportion. One could therefore dismiss academic history. It is marginal to contemporary concerns, leftist in a conservative age, and fatally flawed by a strict form of political correctness that inhibits the formation of well-nuanced judgments about the past. In an age when we need history to tell our national story and bring us together, the historians instead contribute to our national sense of alienation. They facilitate our disengagement from politics (why bother to vote when males, WASPs, or some other form of the power elite inevitably dominate?). They heighten our sense of futility about solving national problems (why try to reform welfare when America is a racist country that will never give inner-city blacks a chance?).

An Oppositional Profession

One could dismiss academic history, but, as Richard Nixon might have said, that would be wrong. I think the common criticism misses the point because it fails to take the development of the history profession into account. Historians have always been oppositional. That is the very nature of the enterprise. The first professional historians—who worked in the early graduate schools such as Johns Hopkins, Wisconsin, and Harvard—consciously rejected the work of the genteel amateur historians who had celebrated the rise of America. Using what they believed to be a scientific history that took a hard look at the evidence and employed social science theory, these early historians, such as Charles Beard and Frederick Jackson Turner, tried to replace myth with what they regarded as realism. Their picture of America highlighted conflict. They portrayed an America of regional and class conflict: Turner recognized that the values of the frontier were not those of the eastern seaboard; the Civil War, according to Beard, was the second American revolution, a struggle between two forms of economic organization. Indeed, it was Beard who insisted upon an economic interpretation of the Constitution itself. This form of progressive history held sway from the early twentieth century well into the 1930s. In the 1940s and 1950s, a revisionist school of history arose that consciously tried to revise the teachings of the progressive school. To be sure, contemporary conditions influenced the tone of this history. Historians educated by the G.I. Bill, the first in their families to go to college, could hardly have contained their delight at finding themselves in tenured positions at Ivy League institutions. Hence, they found it natural to celebrate the accomplishments of America. In contrast to the Marxist theory with which many had flirted in the 1930s, they discovered it was the absence of conflict, not conflict itself, that demanded comment. Despite the enormous ethnic diversity of America, things had turned out well, thanks to a pragmatic blend of government intervention and basic American values.

To a large degree, however, these consensus historians took their intellectual agenda from the historians preceding them. In that sense, they were oppositional to the prevailing professional wisdom, if not to the common societal wisdom. They found it necessary to reexamine Beard on the Constitution, Turner on the frontier, and U. B. Phillips on the nature of the slave plantation. In this last area, the change in the established narrative was the most complete. Where progressive historian U. B. Phillips had tended to downplay the harshness of slavery, postwar historian Kenneth Stampp, writing in the era of Brown v. Topeka Board of Education, highlighted its cruelty.

Continued prosperity facilitated still another shift in the historian's outlook, beginning in the 1960s. With so many jobs available, as there were in the mid-1960s, younger historians could afford to challenge some of the opinions of their elders and still end up employed. The prosperity also hastened the younger historians' progress toward tenure and with it a modicum of editorial independence. Hence, a more critical historical voice developed in the 1960s. Once again conflict replaced consensus as the prevailing mode of explanation. It now became necessary for the new historians to reverse the findings of their elders.

The generational break was not quite as sharp in this round of revisionism as in the break between progressive and consensus history. The reason was that some of the senior historians—such as Columbia's Richard Hofstadter, who was the most brilliant and influential of the lot—were having second thoughts of their own about the progress of America.

By the end of the 1960s, the run of optimism that had conditioned American life in the postwar era appeared to be waning. Stories about racial relations, for example, could no longer have the same optimistic tone after the Watts riots of 1965 that they had had before. As the 1960s slowly blended into the 1970s, integration looked to be a dead issue. Nor did it seem that America's many domestic problems could be solved, particularly after the dependable engine of economic growth ground to a halt in the middle of the 1970s. The conflicts between white and black, rich and poor, East and

West that had been obscured by the consensus historians suddenly became visible again.

Furthermore, the government could no longer be so easily viewed as an agent of reform. Instead, it was regarded as a force for repression. In contemporary lingo, it was the agent, both at home and abroad, of the imperialist exploitation of people of color. Histories needed to be written to reflect those "facts," and they were.

A Gendered Past

In the course of undermining the consensus historians, the neoprogressive historians of the 1970s discovered the issue of gender, which became a new and significant source of division in American history. Before this decade, historians had simply regarded the family as a cohesive unit. They looked across families, not within them. As a consequence, it mattered if a family were, say, Italian, but the internal dynamics of Italian families received almost no attention. In the era of women's liberation, historians developed an interest in trying to uncover the role of women within the family. That led to a more general project to write on the history of women.

Here was a potentially vast field to which a growing history profession might turn its attention. As the once abundant job market shrank in the 1970s, the field of women's history emerged as one of the few growth areas within the profession.

There was a natural constituency for women's history that fed the boom in gender studies. Women entered graduate school in the field of history in record numbers and received a significant share of the waning number of jobs. Many of these women chose to specialize in women's history and thus to reinterpret the major issues of American history in terms of gender.

In time, women's history became a much larger field of endeavor than the previous cutting-edge field of African American history. There was a simple reason for this: Women greatly outnumbered blacks in the profession and in the student bodies of American universities. They constituted a majority of the population, making them, in the peculiar manner of academia, a very potent minority.

By the 1980s, women's history had become the largest single specialty within the historical profession (although the data are quite elusive on fields of specialty). Each summer, women historians met for a conference that featured more sessions and more participants than did the annual meeting of the American Historical Association. Women began to occupy positions of influence within the historical profession. That meant that a large component of the history profession took as its mission the creation not of general American history but of gendered American history. Stories that were once written without reference to gender now highlighted that theme.

Social Security as Battered Symbol

The field of social-welfare history provides a good example of the general phenomenon. Once concerned with the growth of government programs and public institutions such as hospitals, the field became a subset of women's history in the 1980s. In place of consensus-era monographs that celebrated the achievements of the welfare state, one began to find books that criticized the "inequality" in the welfare state. That meant that our welfare programs favored men over women. "How did welfare . . . become a metonym for women's inequality?" began one such book, as if everyone shared this particular assumption. "Gender and culture were the axes of early twentieth-century welfare policies," the book asserted.

Indeed, the example of social-welfare history can serve to highlight how changes in the history profession have undercut the unifying power of national symbols. Hofstadter once wrote of the cleansing power of reform to rid the body politic of the evils of a particular era. To be sure, there was a destructive and intolerant strain of reform that was represented by the Populists at the end of the nineteenth century, with their anti-Semitic denunciations of Jewish money power, and by Joseph McCarthy and his followers in the middle of this one, with their disregard of free speech. More enduring and representative were the reforms of the Progressive Era at the beginning of the century and of the New Deal. They provided just enough income redistribution and other adjustments to preserve our American system of free enterprise and democracy.

One of the key elements of the New Deal was the 1935 passage of the Social Security Act. A large and complicated act, it nonetheless produced an important and enduring program that Americans came to call Social Security. At first regarded as a serious threat to freedom, Social Security emerged as a valuable part of the American consensus by the 1950s. It was a pragmatic piece of reform in which the government acted in concert with the people to preserve capitalism. It was a form of self-help, since individuals contributed to their own security, but it was also a form of government aid.

No one looked too closely at the actual terms of the program. Instead, it became a symbol of American ingenuity and pragmatism, a way of incorporating the federal government in the American myth of free enterprise. Historians hastened to celebrate this particularly American version of the welfare state. Arthur Schlesinger, another of the brilliant consensus historians, devoted a great deal of space to Social Security in his much read and respected history of the age of Roosevelt. Economists also gave their blessings to Social Security. Nobel laureate Paul Samuelson wrote a widely circulated *Newsweek* column in which he praised Social Security for the sense of community it helped to create. He called Social Security our "most successful" program. "Social insurance makes sense," he added, "because we are all in the same boat."

Then along came the neoprogressive historians, who saw fit to deconstruct Social Security. One line of inquiry held that blacks were systematically excluded from Social Security and, when included, given the short end of the stick. This line of reasoning gained so much credence that it became commonplace to observe that the Social Security Act of 1935 was a racist conspiracy.

To be sure, there was something to this view. The original Social Security program did not cover farm workers or domestic servants, occupations with a large concentration of black workers. Whether the exclusions reflected practical administrative difficulties or the racist desires of Southern legislators to maintain the existing labor market was a difficult matter to decide. Despite the uncertain nature of the data, the neoprogressives did not hesitate to read their modern preoccupation with race back into the minds of 1930s policy makers. Surely, they argued, the legislators of the 1930s were acting with racist motives in excluding blacks.

In their haste to label the actions of New Deal policy makers racist, the historians overlooked some key facts. Between 1935 and the present, the Social Security program has been improved. In the 1950s, those years of the great consensus, Congress agreed to expand Social Security coverage to include nearly everyone in the labor force. Furthermore, the program contained a feature in its benefit formula that allowed poorer workers to receive a greater return on their Social Security investments than richer workers. This feature tended to work more often to the advantage of blacks than whites. No matter, Social Security remained a racist conspiracy in the eyes of the historians.

Next came the feminist critique of Social Security. One line of criticism compared the relatively generous Social Security program with relatively stingy welfare programs like Aid to Families of Dependent Children (AFDC). Branding Social Security a masculine program and AFDC a feminine program, the critics observed that our social-welfare system discriminated against women. Another line of criticism pointed to the unequal treatment of women in the Social Security program itself. Widows received only three-quarters of a benefit, not a full benefit. By rules established in 1939, a widow had to be sixty-five before she could receive even these less-than-full-scale benefits. Younger widows suffered. If a single woman and a married man contributed an equal amount to the Social Security system, chances were that the married man would receive more for his money.

Here again, historians cast their modern conceptions of the family back on the past, and they ignored the fact that, because of differential mortality rates, a considerably greater number of women received Social Security benefits than did men. No matter, Social Security was flawed.

The historical criticism fed a more general leftist belief that what America really needed was a guaranteed income that went to everyone, whether or not a person worked. By hoping for this income, historians indulged their romantic notion that fundamental reform was possible in a system geared to incremental change.

The desire for ideological purity was not limited to the left side of the political spectrum. Even as liberals criticized Social Security for not going far enough, conservatives condemned the program for going too far. In the 1970s, in particular, the program faced real financial peril, because stagflation had the effect of lowering revenues (tax receipts) and raising benefits (which were indexed to inflation). It was a recipe for financial disaster.

Conservatives hastened to point out that the notion of Social Security as a passive piggy bank was a myth and had always been a myth. Instead, the government collected taxes and used those taxes to pay the benefits of current beneficiaries. The program was not really insurance. It was just another tax-and-spend program that existed at the government's whim. It did not greatly contribute to the nation's savings rate.

Worst of all, conservatives noted, the program functioned like a Ponzi scheme. The first investors received windfall profits. Legislators used early surpluses in the program to liberalize benefits. In time, however, the bills came due; the number of beneficiaries rose while the number of taxpayers declined. The returns on a person's Social Security investment fell until one could do better investing in private securities than in Social Security. For the baby boomers, the largest age cohort in the population, the consequences of the Ponzi scheme were particularly dire. Social Security might go broke just as it became their turn to receive benefits.

As a result of these criticisms from the left and the right, public faith in Social Security began to crumble. A 1991 public opinion survey indicated, for example, that more than half of the respondents between 18 and 64 believed there would not be enough money in the Social Security trust fund to pay their benefits. What had once been a reassuring symbol of societal stability emerged as just another maligned entitlement program. Historians, who with their sympathy for minorities and other disadvantaged groups might have been expected to rally support for Social Security, instead emerged as some of the program's most vocal critics. In this instance the historian's interest in race and gender triumphed over the affirmation of New Deal social reform.

One does not often think of Social Security as an important national symbol, yet clearly it is. The program serves as one of the mediating institutions that has replaced Jane Addams's more hands-on approach to helping the poor. Historians have felt no great obligation to boost Social Security any more than they have felt an obligation to laud other institutions that help to bind the country together.

The Deconstruction of Everything?

The present generation of historians has abandoned the belief that there are national institutions or symbols that are, in effect, above criticism. In this regard, modern historians have come to resemble their predecessors who also sought to undermine intellectual complacency.

Recent developments in historical analysis only underscore the general trend. Historians talk less of events and more of texts. In this postmodernist view, something that is apparently real emerges instead as a construction. Diseases, once dreaded entities with the power to kill, are now merely social constructions. So, for that matter, is the Civil War. In this view, there is no such thing as a fixed event. The past is what historians make of it. In this regard, Gertrude Himmelfarb has written with dismay of one historian who urges young historians "not to become 'fact fetishists' like some of their elders."

I do not think that deconstruction means the end of the world. Instead, we should view the moves toward cultural history and deconstruction as the next turns of the professional wheel: the means by which new textual historians attempt to overturn the work of the old neoprogressive historians. It is about time for something new to emerge.

I would urge those who view the work of academic historians with dismay to remember that what passes for history has as much to do with the state of the history profession as with the state of the world. That need not necessarily be bad. We need a group of people whose role it is continually to revise our received wisdom about the past. Historians, as I have stressed, are oppositional by their very nature.

At worst, historians risk becoming irrelevant. If one believes that a market for ideas exists, then society has natural protection against the outrages of modern historians. When the ideas presented by historians stray so far from the popular wisdom that people no longer recognize the past from the historian's description of it, then historians will lose their audience. Students vote with their feet, state legislators with their hands. Both are in a powerful position to affect the size of the history profession. So are publishers, who have only limited money to subsidize the more esoteric of historical endeavors. In today's market, academic history has indeed become a marginal enterprise, making it even harder for hardworking historical practitioners to find work.

At their best, however, historians open up new vistas on the past. It is not the role of the historian to support myths about the superiority of the American people any more than it is the place of the historian to transform all women and blacks into heroes. I think it is nonetheless possible for historians to people the past with women and blacks and to write about women and blacks as people, not as supermen and superwomen. For historians are at their best when they sift through the primary evidence and find out new things about old events. Since the advent of professional history, the best history has adopted a critical tone toward the past. Myths require the willing suspension of disbelief, and historians have, if anything, developed a heightened sense of disbelief.

To be sure, we need institutions that rise above our current fragmentation. We need contemporary counterparts of Jane Addams who can devote their lives to bridging ethnic and racial differences and who have a vision for America. But I would not count on the historians' support for this effort. We have to rely on our politicians for inspirational leadership, I am afraid. It is the burden of historians to debunk the actions of politicians and to transform politicians from heroes into ordinary beings. For in the end, we need historians not to boost national self-confidence or reinforce our national myths but rather to come along after the fact and tell us what happened.

PART IV

AN EDUCATIONAL MISSION: STANDARDS FOR THE TEACHING OF HISTORY

During the past decade, the theoretical conflicts among historians over the nature and value of history have spilled over into conflicts over the teaching of history in the schools. It is a rare professor of history who has not fretted about college students' woeful lack of historical knowledge, and the evidence suggests that professorial complaints reflect a good deal more than perennial crankiness. As Diane Ravitch notes, the most recent National Assessment of Educational Progress (1995) reported that "57 percent of high school seniors scored 'below basic' in their knowledge of American history." In 1998 in Virginia, high school students took a comprehensive test, which 97 percent failed. Nothing suggests that students elsewhere would perform significantly better.

The essays in this section engage the problem of teaching history, specifically in response to the debate over the drafting and implementation of national standards. By the 1980s, concern about the widespread historical ignorance of young Americans was attracting attention, and toward the end of the decade it prompted the National Endowment for the Humanities, the Department of Education, and other groups to support a project to reverse the trend by devising national standards for history. None doubted the magnitude of the challenge or the impossibility of satisfying everyone. But few foresaw the violent reaction that exploded in 1994 in response to the release of the draft of the standards. Diane Ravitch has been an important participant throughout, from her position in the Department of Education as one of the original sponsors of the project and as a participant in the ensuing debates. Here, she traces the specifics of the reaction and counterreaction.

At the heart of the controversy two radically different views of American history confronted each other. The original drafters had sought to ground history education in social history, with special attention to the voices and experience of groups that had traditionally been ignored. Their political agenda emerged clearly from the tendency of the standards to focus upon Native Americans, African Americans, women, and other "marginalized" groups at the expense of "great men," political, military, and intellectual leaders. The leading professional associations, Ravitch notes, encouraged this agenda, although only the American Historical Association intervened directly in a successful effort to dictate the outcome. The AHA threatened to withdraw its support for the entire project, Ravitch writes, "unless language according special recognition to Western civilization in the criteria for world history standards was revised."

The heated public conflicts over the standards, most dramatically captured in the Senate's ninety-nine to one vote to condemn them, focused upon these political and ideological questions, which Walter McDougall and John Diggins take up in their essays. Both protest the depth of the anti-Western and anti-American bias that pervades the standards, which offer no inkling of why people from around the globe may seek to emigrate to the United States, much less why the economic, political, and technological accomplishments of the Western world may inspire emulation elsewhere. Like other critics, McDougall and Diggins call attention to the standards' tendency to privilege the experience and values of non-Western peoples of various political inclinations. McDougall points to the resulting absurdities such as the invitation to view Gengis Khan "through the eyes of a papal legate, whose cultural biases pupils are told to discern." The example captures the pervasive anti-Western bias that also emerges in the standards' silence about the Aztec practice of human sacrifice or the existence of slavery among non-Western peoples, including Africans. McDougall takes the standards' treatment of religion as symptomatic of a general attitude toward any ideological conviction the authors do not approve. Apparently to avoid criticizing non-Christian religions, the authors treat religion "as ethics—ethics betrayed, moreover, as soon as believers attribute them to a transcendental source."

The greatest furor, however, concerned the standards' presentation of American history. Many fumed that the Sierra Club received more mention than George Washington, the Ku Klux Klan, and Ulysses S. Grant, who initially received none. John Diggins traces the ways in which the politically slanted social history that the standards embody results in the systematic neglect or discrediting of most of the people and events that had been taken to embody American ideals of greatness. The authors of the standards, he notes, defend the significance of the study of history on the grounds that "knowledge of history is the precondition of political intelligence," and he takes sharp issue with the politics they promote. Diggins charges the standards with uncritical celebration and promotion of those on the bottom of the social heap, notably Native Americans, African Americans, and women. In so doing, he insists, they miss the ways in which African Americans and women at times valued the accomplishments and legacy of the white male elite and sought to participate in their development. Diggins further reproaches the standards for their failure "to demonstrate how those at the bottom take shape as a political force, gain consciousness of their own interests, and win some measure of freedom as a result of obtaining the power in order to alter the conditions of life."

Both McDougall and Diggins acknowledge the value of including new groups in the main historical narratives and pay special attention to the claims of women's history. The only grounds for objecting to the introduction of substantial attention to women's history, McDougall writes, is if the subject becomes "a fig leaf for ahistorical ideology." Unfortunately, however, he finds that the standards "invariably invite students to conclude (or be told) that sexual roles were always a function of patriarchy backed by theology." In this context, it is clear that politics, not the expansion of focus, is the real bone of contention. Yet even the politicization of the standards cannot fully account for their failure—and the sorry cost of that failure for the future of historical education in the United States.

If anything, Diggins pays more attention to the standards' treatment of women's history, and he sharply criticizes their ideological presuppositions, not least for failing to credit the ambitions and accomplishments of exceptional women. The standards' real problem, he writes, "lies in their theoretical floundering in radical categories of thought that possibly preclude women from naming the problem that has no name—the problem of freedom and its inextricable relation to power." He especially deplores the tendency always to associate women with community life and collective action. This "disdain against all that is exceptional and outstanding" merely confirms the extent to which women's history remains in servitude to men's history. Thus does ideology foreclose the possibility of recognizing exceptional women and the importance of their contributions to American history.

In the end, Ravitch maintains, all who participated in the sponsorship, drafting, and criticism of the standards bear some responsibility for the stalemate that has ensued. Both Ravitch and Sean Wilentz argue that, notwithstanding the standards' palpable failings, their discrediting exacerbates rather than alleviates the main problems in history education, which begin, they insist, with its dwindling presence in the curriculum. They caution that, in our squabbles over which history should be taught, we are ignoring the greater danger, namely that no history will be taught. Wilentz outlines the progress of social studies during the twentieth century, demonstrating that increasingly it is replacing history in the curriculum. Initially, the social studies movement had benefited from distinguished leaders, including John Dewey and W. E. B. DuBois, who sought to introduce social texture into history. Today, however, social studies views itself as a substitute for history and justifies its claims to preeminence by the need for the curriculum to embody respect for diversity, teach problem solving, and enhance the self-esteem of students. Social studies teachers belong to a powerful lobby that has consistently discouraged a renaissance of historical education in any form, but especially in a form that focuses upon the historical development of institutions, the contributions of political leaders, and the changes in intellectual and religious life. In this perspective, Wilentz concludes, the collapse of the project to adopt national standards for history heralds the virtual disappearance of history from our schools and, hence, from public consciousness.

Ravitch and Wilentz leave no doubt that the most important battles lies before us. Like others throughout the historical profession, they view primary and secondary education as a major responsibility for the profession as a whole, including those who teach in colleges and universities. Should we fail to attend to the fate of history in the schools, we will make ourselves complicit in its certain demise.

We have no reason to assume that the heated debates over the implicit politics and ideology of historical narratives will dissipate in the foreseeable future, but if historians allow themselves to place them above all other considerations, we are likely to discover that we have thrown the proverbial baby out with the bath. For if we do not seriously attend to the challenges of basic history education we will condemn our profession and ourselves to futility and irrelevance. And we can ill afford to settle for the cynicism that dismisses both sides in the debate as equally flawed. We all know that each generation rewrites the history it has inherited to conform to the exigencies of its specific situation. We also know that no compelling revision can totally erase previous accounts, for the previous ways of telling the story are themselves part of our history. At a minimum, we should acknowledge that the history of the United States as a nation merits a central place in the education of its citizens, much as the history of France, China, Brazil, or Nigeria merit—and receive—a central place in the curricula of the schools of each country. McDougall reminds us that an intellectual elite's cynicism about its nation's history "is a sure-fire sign that a nation is losing the will to sustain itself. A people's history is the record of its hopes and travails, birthright and education, follies and wisdom, and all else that binds it together. A nation grown cynical about its own history soon ceases to be a nation at all." Just as, we might add, an academic discipline grown cynical about its basic educational responsibilities soon ceases to be a profession.

CHAPTER 18

THE CONTROVERSY OVER NATIONAL HISTORY STANDARDS

Diane Ravitch

IN THE FALL of 1994, an explosive controversy began in the pages of the *Wall Street Journal.* The former chairperson of the National Endowment for the Humanities, Lynne V. Cheney, wrote a blistering critique of national standards for the teaching of American and world history that her own agency had underwritten during her tenure. In the months and years that followed, charges and countercharges have been exchanged by partisans in an extraordinary instance of prolonged public attention to the content and teaching of history. I would like to consider what happened, why, and with what consequences for the teaching of history in the schools of the United States.

Anyone who hopes to understand his or her own life, as well as to comprehend events in society and the world, must have a firm grasp of history. Educated people recognize the necessity of teaching young people why the past matters and how it influences our understanding of the present. Yet there are precincts within the education profession in which history is disparaged as nothing more than a bunch of names and dates about long-ago events and dead people, therefore not especially interesting or relevant to today's young. Some leaders of the social studies field say that they want to teach "critical thinking," not "content"; or they say that since no one knows which knowledge is true, it is best to concentrate on teaching students how to look

---

Originally presented before the American Academy of Arts and Sciences, April 9, 1997.

things up. Such attitudes help to explain why American students have for a long time displayed an abysmal ignorance of history.

I must acknowledge my own interest in the events surrounding the national history standards. Since the mid-1980s, I have been an advocate of improved history education. I helped to write a new history-centered curriculum, which was adopted by the California Board of Education in 1988. A book I coauthored in 1987 with Chester E. Finn, Jr., *What Do Our 17-Year-Olds Know?,* described the results from the first national assessment of history, which showed that large numbers of high school juniors did not know important things about American history. Some two-thirds, for example, did not know in which half-century the Civil War had taken place, and even larger proportions could not identify the Scopes trial, the Progressive Movement, or Jim Crow laws. After the book appeared, I helped to organize the Bradley Commission on History in the Schools and the National Council for History Education.

I was also assistant secretary in the United States Department of Education from 1991 to 1993, when the department awarded grants to groups of scholars and teachers to develop voluntary national standards in science, history, geography, civics, English, the arts, and foreign languages (mathematics standards had already been developed by the National Council of Teachers of Mathematics). The grants were processed by the Office of Educational Research and Improvement, which I headed, and I enthusiastically supported this initiative.

Both the National Endowment for the Humanities and the U.S. Department of Education awarded funding for the history standards project. The organization that received these dollars was the National Center for History in the Schools at the University of California at Los Angeles. This center was established with Lynne V. Cheney's strong encouragement when she was chairperson of the NEH. The center and the NEH signed a cooperative agreement that gave NEH the authority to review and approve all of the center's products before they were published. The center was selected to coordinate the development of history standards because Cheney liked its work; its leaders then enlisted every significant organization with an interest in history and social studies to participate in the proposed standard-setting project. Hundreds of scholars and teachers collaborated in the standard-writing process.

All of the principals involved in this effort sincerely wanted to see good national history standards. Those of us at the Department of Education did; Lynne Cheney did; the leadership at the UCLA Center did.

And yet things went horribly wrong.

Lynne Cheney's first salvo against the history standards appeared in October 1994, only days before the draft standards themselves were officially published. She indicted the standards as a paradigm of political correctness that emphasized race and gender while ignoring traditional heroes, and that magnified the failings of American society while belittling its accomplishments. She complained that the document mentioned Senator Joseph McCarthy and McCarthyism nineteen times; mentioned the Ku Klux Klan seventeen times; mentioned Harriet Tubman six times; but left out Paul Revere, Robert E. Lee, Thomas Alva Edison, Alexander Graham Bell, and the Wright brothers. She objected to double standards that romanticized non-European cultures, pointing to a teaching example that expressed admiration for the architecture and agriculture of the Aztecs while overlooking their practice of human sacrifice; she contrasted a teaching example that encouraged students to admire "the achievements and grandeur of Mansa Musa's court" in Africa with another teaching example that proposed a mock trial of John D. Rockefeller for amassing too much wealth.

In the days and weeks after Cheney's preemptive strike, conservative talk-show hosts excoriated the standards as a menace to the republic, historians debated their merits, editorialists opined pro and con, and a spokesman from the Clinton administration issued a statement pointing out that the standards had been funded by the Bush administration. The U.S. history standards were attacked for political bias; the world history standards were assailed for minimizing the importance of the West. There will surely be books written detailing the charges and responses, and I will not attempt to do that. The volume of outrage was sufficient to provoke the U.S. Senate in January 1995 to pass a resolution disapproving the history standards by a vote of ninety-nine to one. Later that year, Secretary of Education Richard Riley firmly distanced the Clinton administration from the controversy, saying, "This was not our grant. This is not my idea of good standards. This is not my view of how history should be taught in America's classrooms."

The draft standards were vigorously defended by the leaders of the historical profession; Gary Nash, a prominent historian who had overseen the writing of the standards as director of the UCLA Center, was president of the Organization of American Historians; he insisted that the attacks were aimed not just at the standards but at an entire generation of historical scholarship.

In the midst of this extraordinary polarization, a few voices of moderation contended that the standards should be revised, not abandoned. The late Albert Shanker, president of the American Federation of Teachers and a strong proponent of national standards, was critical of the standards for their negativism and their failure to place democratic ideals at the center of the nation's history, but he appreciated that they called for "substantive and demanding" history in the schools. He argued that the draft standards should be rewritten and improved. And thanks in part to his urging, this is what happened.

Early in 1995, the revision process began, sponsored by the Council for Basic Education. The CBE convened two panels of historians, one to review the draft U.S. history standards, another to review the draft world history standards (I was a member of the American history panel). Historians of widely divergent views participated on the CBE panels, which were a model of democratic discussion and professional responsibility. The panels noted that the project had defined excellent criteria for standards, and that most of the problems stemmed from the project's failure to meet its own criteria. The panels called attention to the standards' inadequate treatment of economics, science, medicine, and technology as well as their tendency to portray technological changes in terms of their negative social impact. The world history panel discounted the charge that the standards had denigrated Western civilization, but noted prejudicial language in which Europeans "invade" other countries, while similar actions by non-Europeans are described as "expansion" rather than "invasion."

The panels commended the UCLA Center for the rigor of the standards and pointed out that "the majority of the documents' shortcomings are in the teaching examples." In the U.S. volume, the teaching examples—which occupied far more than half of the text—gave the misleading impression of a national curriculum, that is, detailed specifications of what was taught and, in some cases, how it was to be taught; furthermore, these teaching examples tended "to dwell on the country's shortcomings" and conveyed "a disproportionately pessimistic and misrepresentative picture of the American past." Further, in their effort to draw attention to those who had been underrepresented in the past, the teaching examples were "unbalanced in the other direction, giving the appearance of a curriculum that pays little attention to political history." A relatively small but significant number of these examples violated the project's own criteria about the importance of avoiding presentism and moralism in teaching history; some examples posed loaded or leading questions that expressed political bias.

Gary Nash and his colleagues at the UCLA Center responded professionally and enthusiastically to the CBE report. Language that was flagged as politically biased was revised or eliminated. All twenty-five hundred or so teaching examples were dropped; these teaching examples, not the standards themselves, had prompted most of the criticism, and many readers confused them with the standards.

When the revised standards were released, the controversy largely subsided. Some critics, unappeased, continued to insist that the standards were unacceptable, but after the egregious excesses that fueled the original controversy were removed, the public battle receded. This is more or less where matters stand today: a standoff, an uneasy silence, a controversy that has left the headlines but not the hearts and minds of those who were in the trenches on both sides.

Stepping back from the melee, I would like to express some tentative judgments about what happened and why it matters still.

First, Gary Nash was right when he argued that the attack on the history standards was an attack on an entire generation of scholarship. The original history standards—especially the standards for U.S. history—reflected the significant influence of those social historians who have used race, class, and gender as lenses through which to view the past (although it must be said that many contemporary social historians have pursued other lines of inquiry). These ideas assumed unusual prominence in the standards, far more than most Americans can recall from their own history courses in high school and college. To be sure, American history should no longer be taught without attention to the experiences and achievements of previously neglected groups and individuals, but the decisive shifting of the balance toward the *pluribus* in the U.S. standards document prompted concern that the *unum*—the common civic ideas and values that unite us as a nation—would now be neglected.

Additionally, in the wake of Vietnam, political assassinations, and Watergate, many of the younger generation of historians derided any celebration of the nation's past, especially of the sort that used to be typical of high school textbooks. Consequently, historians have discovered new heroes among previously neglected groups, but have cast a hypercritical eye toward traditional heroes, whose failings now seem to loom larger than their accomplishments. The historian Stephen Ambrose complained that the annual meeting of the Organization of American Historians in 1993 had sessions on "black, Indian, Hispanic and other minority history, gay and lesbian history, and multicultural history," but not a single session marking the two-hundred fiftieth anniversary of Thomas Jefferson's birth. He concluded that this was probably a good thing, since "had there been a session, it almost certainly would have been on whether or not his slave Sally Hemings was his mistress and mother of some of his children," or on Thomas Jefferson "the slaveholder and racist."

Second, it is important to note the adversarial role played in the history standards project by representatives of the American Historical Association, who warned that their organization would quit the project unless language according special recognition to Western civilization in the criteria for world history standards was revised. Whether the membership was aware of these views is not clear, but they were forcefully expressed in several letters by the

AHA's deputy director and the vice-president of its teaching division. A few other organizations agreed with the AHA, but no other organization threatened to withdraw support for the consensus process if its views did not prevail. The leaders of the UCLA Center disagreed, but ultimately the confrontational style of the AHA staff prevailed. The UCLA center's council revised the offending language in order to preserve the project. Once made, however, this decision conveyed the impression that the standards project was ambivalent about acknowledging the distinctive European contribution to American and world history.

Third, defenders of the standards mistakenly insisted that few reputable historians objected to the standards, thus implying that only racists and yahoos were on the other side. Nash's codirector warned me that my reputation would suffer if I criticized the standards because only racists, anti-Semites, and the far right were doing so; this refusal to brook any criticism was not the stance one expects from those responsible for writing national standards. In fact, a number of reputable historians criticized the standards, including Walter McDougall of the University of Pennsylvania, David Kennedy of Stanford, Elizabeth Fox-Genovese of Emory, Sheldon Stern of the John F. Kennedy Library, and John Patrick Diggins of the City University of New York. Arthur Schlesinger, Jr., objected that the U.S. standards failed to credit the European origins of "the formative American political ideas—democracy, representative government, freedom of speech and the press, due process, religious toleration, human rights, women's rights, and so on." While applauding the standards' attention to the history of those who had previously been slighted, Schlesinger worried that the standards had embraced the *pluribus* at the expense of the *unum,* a concern that I shared. Although the documents' own criteria declared that standards for U.S. history should reflect "both the nation's diversity . . . and the nation's commonalities" and develop understanding of "our common civic identity and shared civic values," it seemed to me that the original draft of the standards did little to promote understanding of either "the nation's commonalities" or its "common civic identity and shared civic values." However, when the revised standards were released in April 1996, Schlesinger and I jointly endorsed them in an article in the *Wall Street Journal.* We concluded that the revised standards were "rigorous, honest, and as nearly accurate as any group of historians could make them."

Fourth, even after the revisions were released, some die-hard critics continued to attack the standards as though nothing had changed, while some defenders continued to insist that the original standards were flawless and that the revisions were only cosmetic. In this bitter debate, reasonableness went out the window early on, and some adversaries never wanted to find a workable compromise.

Fifth, the overall effort to develop national standards became hopelessly hobbled by partisan politics in Washington. Originally, there was supposed to be a nonpartisan panel to review and evaluate proposed national standards, to consider criticisms, and to recommend revisions. The Goals 2000 legislation authorized a review panel in 1994, but it became ensnared in politics, and President Clinton never appointed its members. In 1995, Congress abolished the nonexistent review board. So, those who wrote voluntary national standards had no external agency to review their work; critics had no place to direct their comments; the authors of the standards were put in the inappropriate position of deciding which critics to attend to; and documents that should have been treated as provisional drafts were wrongly presented and wrongly perceived as finished standards. All in all, it was a messy and failed process, which left no avenue for sober public evaluation of the proposed national standards.

The story does not end happily, because in many states and school districts, the controversy over the national history standards reinforced the position of those who prefer to stick with social studies and to steer clear of history altogether. Consider some of the standards that have been promulgated in the past two years.

In Illinois, the 1996 draft standards for history include the following: "Assess the long-term consequences of major decisions by leaders in various nations of the world, drawing information from a variety of traditional, electronic and on-line sources." Vaguer still, "Compare and contrast varying interpretations of major events in selected periods of history." Another example of a standard lacking in content: "Analyze the impact of major human-generated events that affected a wide segment of the world's population in the 20th century." Such statements provide no guidance for teachers, students, textbook publishers, or test developers.

In Wisconsin, history is only one of ten thematic strands in the social studies. The state's history standards lack any specificity and refer to events in sweeping and meaningless terms. High school seniors will be expected, for example, to "analyze differing historical and contemporary viewpoints within and across cultural regions and political boundaries." They are supposed to "analyze the economic, social, and political changes in response to industrialization and urbanization in the nineteenth and twentieth centuries." Each local school district is left to decide how to interpret the meaning of these vague statements.

In Minnesota, middle school students will be expected to "understand historical events and contributions of key people from different time periods." Nothing is defined; no events, no issues, and no individuals are identified as especially worth knowing.

The significance of statements like these is clear: those who think history is boring are still in control, still believing that it is possible to teach "critical thinking skills" without content or knowledge. But experience shows that when states do not require the study of history and do not establish clear content standards describing what should be taught and tested, history often is replaced by nonhistorical social studies. This occurs not because of a lack of popular interest in history, but because pedagogical leaders long ago decided that young people would be more attracted to current events than to history. One consequence of such views is that fifty-three percent of those now assigned to teach history in American schools have neither a major nor a minor in history. In my view, there should be national history standards that identify the ideas, issues, events, and individuals about which there is broad consensus. The best argument for national standards is that the central facts and issues in American history are the same regardless of whether one is a student in Anchorage or Key West, in Dallas or Detroit, or for that matter, in Paris or Tokyo.

The issue, in my view, was never whether to have national history standards, but rather whether national standards should be created by a deliberative public process, or should continue as implicit standards, controlled by the serendipitous requirements of textbook committees in three or four major states. We seem to be back where we started, having taken a circuitous route that involved lots of bruises, injuries, and split lips.

But we are not really back where we started. Historians and the public learned something about one another. Some historians seem to think that a large sector of the public is made up of ignoramuses who don't appreciate and refuse to defer to expert knowledge, and some members of the public seem to think that historians are elitists, contemptuous of the views of ordinary people.

Is this chasm necessary? Was this controversy inevitable? Perhaps—given the wide gulf between the politics of the majority of the historical profession and the politics of the larger public—it was. Surely conflicts were bound to arise in any effort to reach agreement about the history that should be taught to our children. Yet it does seem that there was at least the possibility of a middle ground, a path that was not taken. On one side, the standards' authors asserted that the history standards had revolutionized the study of history, opening up for study the experiences of groups that had previously been left out. On the other side, critics asserted that many of today's social historians disdain America and belittle its traditional heroes.

Perhaps there could be no middle ground between those who want a critical view of our nation's history and those who want a history that inspires love of country. But if we set aside those who hold the most extreme views, those who want the schools to teach students only the dark side of American history and those who want the schools to teach only the bright side, there is a reasonable middle ground. That reasonable middle ground requires that we acknowledge the importance of race, ethnicity, class, and gender in history while also paying due heed to important historical figures like Washington, Franklin, Jefferson, and Edison. Why not weave together both approaches and add new faces to the pantheon of American heroes?

It is also important for historians to realize that the critical perspective appropriate for university students may not be appropriate for children in elementary and secondary schools. According to the "criteria for the development of standards" produced by the UCLA Center, one of the purposes of history education in the schools is to "contribute to citizenship education"; this is not usually a goal of historical studies in the university. When citizenship education is a goal, then history education must teach not only how to think critically, but also which ideas and experiences unify our nation and which ideals and individuals deserve our admiration and respect.

The drafters of the history standards thought that they had satisfied the need for heroes by such statements as "analyze the character and roles of the military, political, and diplomatic leaders who helped forge the American victory [over the British]." Why not identify which military, political, and diplomatic leaders achieved historic significance? Why not name those whose signal accomplishments were unusually important in American history? Whether to examine the lives of specific leaders is not simply a question of heroes or no heroes: biography is an excellent way to learn history.

In an article written for the *William and Mary Quarterly,* Gary Nash acknowledges that the drafters of the standards "consciously tried to temper the great man theory of history." They believed that students were likelier to be involved in politics and community affairs if they saw ordinary people as shapers of important historical events. Yet, it does not seem necessary for those who write national or state standards to decide whether historical agency comes from above or below, from the elites or the masses; youngsters need to learn both about great individuals—many of whom were ordinary people who did great things—and also about the way events and social movements were influenced by ordinary people who did not become famous.

In the same essay, Nash notes that the new scholarship embodied in the history standards attempted "to prick the nation's conscience while serving as an antidote to the flag-waving, jingoistic, self-congratulatory history that was the standard fare of textbooks for generations." This reevaluation of the American past, he says, was intended to "remedy the malign neglect or vicious treatment of African and Native American history," but he observes that there has also been "a tendency to romanticize those previously denigrated or to overlook the dark side of peoples previously ignored while seeming to reserve criticism mostly for the European colonizers." Nash writes that the original version of the national history standards shows the influence of scholars who wanted to "analyze American history in a more penetrating way," while helping their students "appreciate and recognize the achievements and struggles of minorities and non-western peoples." Nash anticipates that "as thesis leads to antithesis and then to synthesis, self-correction in a mature profession has certainly been taking place." He predicts that in years to come, another generation of scholars will produce new history standards, reflecting new understandings. It certainly was not the intention of the Department of Education nor the NEH to commission a rewrite of American history or to empower any particular political agenda; the intention was to identify the fundamental understandings about the past that students need to know.

The debate over the national history standards has certainly produced lots of thesis and antithesis. We have not yet seen much in the way of synthesis. This is a sort of political tragedy that might be called "Murder on the Orient Express." If you remember the Agatha Christie whodunit, everyone on the train had a motive and opportunity to kill the victim. When the crime was finally solved, it turned out that everyone had done it.

This too is a case in which everybody done it:

The historians done it, especially those who failed to understand that some of their most controversial decisions—especially their inattention to the commonalities that define American nationality and our shared civic culture—were questions of political ideology, rather than issues of scholarship.

The critics of the standards done it, especially those who made false and inflammatory charges about the standards, as well as those who refused to help in the process of revision and continued to condemn the standards after they were revised.

The social studies field done it, because it has long treated history as a discipline that is not interesting to most young people and seen its own role as shapers of students' political and social attitudes rather than as teachers of history, geography, and civics whose responsibility is to enable students to reach their own judgments.

I done it too. I accept responsibility for not having insisted—when the contracts were negotiated in my office at the U.S. Department of Education—that the consensus process include a significant representation of public members from the very beginning. Participation by journalists, civic leaders, legislators, parents, and others who were neither historians nor teachers might have ensured that the standards passed the "barbershop test" before they were released to the public. The "barbershop test" has been suggested by Shirley Malcom of the American Association for the Advancement of Science as a metaphor for a forum where ordinary citizens discuss public policies that affect them. In a democracy, expert views are never the sole determinant of public policy. The consensus process for the national civics standards did include non-experts, and the document was warmly received. For those who would shape public policy, the lesson is, either public engagement at the beginning of the process or public trial by fire later.

In the end, we all done it, because we bear collective responsibility for the education of the next generation. So far as history goes, the next generation doesn't know much. The latest National Assessment of Educational Progress, released in late 1995, reported that 57 percent of high school seniors scored "below basic" in their knowledge of American history. "Below basic" is as low as it is possible to go on this exam. These youngsters will be voters in a year or less. They will probably never study history again after high school.

The distinguished historian Bernard Bailyn recently said that high school history teaching must do two things: First, it must give students the "basic structural lines to large-scale historical narratives—basic information, so they know that there was an English Civil War, that Rome follows the great era of Ancient Greece, that neither Germany nor Italy was a nation until the nineteenth century, that Napoleon follows the French Revolution and that what he did was related to it, etc." And second, it must "fascinate high-school students with history—get them excited about it, show the fascination of events, personalities, and outcomes; emphasize the drama and personal interest of it all—so they see that this is something that can be vitally, intrinsically interesting to them, and not something dull."

These seem to me to be the right goals for history education. To judge by the results of the national assessment of history, we are currently not achieving them.

I continue to believe that we need national history standards. Like Arthur Schlesinger, Jr., I would be pleased if students today knew even half of the content in the UCLA Center's national and world history standards. I will be even more pleased when the synthesis that Gary Nash predicted becomes a reality; when history in the schools ceases to be a battleground between warring ideologies; and when educators agree with Bernard Bailyn that history education must give the younger generation a basic structure of historical knowledge and inspire them with enthusiasm for learning more.

If our recent arguments about teaching history speed that day, then the struggles and controversy of the past few years will have been worthwhile.

CHAPTER 19

THE NATIONAL HISTORY STANDARDS

John Patrick Diggins

IN MOST COUNTRIES the study of history is inseparable from the spirit of the nation. The United States is the exception. Here the discipline of American history, as taught in colleges and universities, seems to exist in a state of separation that is as proud as it is fierce. Between many professors and much of the public, there are, as the divorce courts put it, "irreconcilable differences."

The bitter controversy was set off in November 1994 by the announcement that National History Standards (NHS) had been adopted. These guidelines for state education departments are not mandatory for the nation. The NHS were produced by the National Center for History at the University of California at Los Angeles. The Center was founded by the National Endowment for the Humanities (NEH) in 1992 after reports of low test scores revealed students' woefully inadequate knowledge of American history. Critics, such as Lynne Cheney, who as director of the NEH, supported the project, later objected to a document that devoted so much time to multiculturalism and other politically correct subjects and so little to the study of important events and significant political leaders and scientists. A few history professors also protested, but the two leading academic organizations, the American Historical Association and the Organization of American Historians, strongly endorsed the NHS. The U.S. Senate voted overwhelmingly to condemn them.

In response to the criticisms, the NHS committee released a revised document in the spring of 1996. The revision makes concessions by sprinkling

---

Originally published in *The American Scholar,* Autumn 1996, 65:4.

the document with paeans to patriotism, begrudgingly mentioning some important leaders, and dropping a revealing, and most embarrassing, passage pertaining to the Cold War. The changes satisfied many former critics, who have since announced their support for the revised document. But the changes represented no serious reconsideration on the part of NHS director Gary Nash, history professor at UCLA. Years earlier, in *Red, White, and Black: The Peoples of Early America*, Nash complained of the "historical amnesia that has blotted out so much of our past," leaving us with "a white-oriented hero-worshipping history," when we should be studying how non-Europeans were "actively and intimately involved" in determining the course of America's development. That Nash still adheres to that view became clear soon after the new report was released. That evening he went on National Public Radio and defended the earlier version, acknowledging that this version was his preference and his passion and claiming that the critics were mainly nonacademics such as Rush Limbaugh and Oliver North. Nash's colleague at UCLA, Professor Joyce Appleby, then president-elect of the American Historical Association, took the same position. "I was very pleased with the original one," she told the press. "Lynne Cheney is not a professional historian. You couldn't name more than five historians who would criticize them."

How many historians support or criticize the NHS would be important only if truth lies solely in numbers. The first version of the NHS deserves close scrutiny not only because it was endorsed by professional historians' associations, but because it also reflects the state of American historiography as it incorporates the viewpoints of many scholars. The categorical assumptions remain in the second version even though the "teaching exercises" in the first version have been dropped in the latter, as though the review panel that went over the first document sought to bury the evidence without addressing the director, who himself had veto power over the composition of the panel's membership. Indeed, Nash's theory of American history, spelled out in *Red, White, and Black*, reads like a parable of the Fall:

> Throughout the colonial period European observers stood in awe of the central Indian traits of hospitality, generosity, bravery, and the spirit of mutual caring. Indians seemed to embody these Christian virtues almost without effort in a corner of the earth where Europeans, attempting to build a society with similar characteristics, were being pulled in the opposite direction by the natural abundance around them—toward individualism, disputatiousness, aggrandizement of wealth, and the exploitation of other humans.

The Indian as sinless Christian and the paleface as acquisitive predator—this *Dances with Wolves* scenario would have students believe that America existed in a state of Edenic innocence. Could America have become what it became and remain in that state? But the first settlers blew it, and American civilization stands condemned. "Are we," asked the French historian Marc Bloch, "so sure of ourselves and of our age as to divide the company of our forefathers into the just and the damned?" Apparently so.

It is curious why the NHS's critics endorsed the new version. Except for the Cold War, the second version offers little improvement over the first and, in fact, reiterates many of its questionable assumptions. History is still presented as a therapeutic tool meant to promote the self-esteem of all students, especially those whose history has yet to be told; hence, the NHS aims more toward the promotion of cultural appreciation than toward the teaching of historical understanding. In both the older and revised versions, there is little understanding of the nature of power and, as a consequence, of the meaning of freedom based upon the specifically Anglo-American tradition of natural rights. "In the beginning," wrote John Locke, "all the world was America." Locke saw America as a kind of second chance where life could start anew, free of the oppressions that have characterized world history. The NHS has America beginning where Locke saw the world ending in stagnation.

History from Below

Gary Nash has put much time and effort into the NHS's development, and he has admirably held his own ground when taking abuse from different groups, particularly those in Oakland, California, that were demanding that his textbook be changed this way and that for reasons of ethnic politics. Nash is one of the rare professors seriously concerned about the education of America's children. In recent years the late Allan Bloom shared that concern, and before him so did philosopher John Dewey. Yet the orientations are strikingly different. Where Bloom thought that students should look back to classical texts of antiquity, and Dewey thought that they should look forward to encounters with experience, Nash thinks that students should look down, all the way down, to discover the realities of class.

Nash represents the now-prevalent school of thought known as the "new social history." Embracing the study of women, minorities, and the working class, social history fixates on "history from the bottom up," on the forgotten, the unfortunate, and on subaltern peoples who have been excluded for cultural as much as for class reasons. Social history, or at least that which bears its mark on the NHS, has little use for individuals as pathbreakers, great men as leaders, heroes as movers and shakers, civilization as in any sense preferable to undeveloped cultures, and universal values as more important than particular customs and practices. Philip Curtin, an NHS member, made this clear to the press. "In the older fashion it was like the great man theory, where you study the great man. You studied great civilizations. But you left out a lot of places that weren't great civilizations but were part of the human experience." What is not great seldom rises to the top, and, thus, true history is that which resides at the bottom and must be studied to see when and how whatever is there might break forth from below so that the last can come first. Whether or not the meek shall inherit the earth, the forgotten will now have their rightfully central place in history textbooks.

Few previous historians—Jules Michelet is one of the notable exceptions—approached history with such romantically unexamined assumptions about agency from below, assumptions that characterize Nash's scholarship. Karl Marx, who saw industrial workers as transforming themselves into a conscious proletariat, recognized that such a possibility lay in the future while the past continued to weigh like a "tumor" on the brain of the living. Even Antonio Gramsci, in academic circles the most influential Marxist of the twentieth century, saw history as a cultural phenomenon that amounted to a struggle for hegemony at the higher reaches of society. So, too, the great black historian W. E. B. Du Bois. "Was there ever a nation on God's fair earth civilized from the bottom upward?" asked Du Bois. "Never; it is, ever was, and ever will be from the top downwards that culture filters."

Whether history is studied upwards, downwards, or sideways, it is questionable whether the values the NHS's authors seek to inculcate in students can be derived from the knowledge they want students to learn. Can the meaning and value of citizenship, once the province of the older political history, be based on the new social history?

Why study history? "The reasons are many," the NHS advises, "but none are more important to a democratic society than this: *knowledge of history is the precondition of political intelligence.* Without history, a society shares no common memory of where it has been, what its core values are, or what decisions of the past account for present circumstances." Such learning is indispensable to the "*public citizen*" as well as to the "*private individual.*" Why? "Historical memory is the key to self-identity, to seeing one's place in the stream of time, and one's connectedness with all humankind." History also enables one to cope better in facing the present. "By studying the choices and decisions of the past, students can confront today's problems and choices with a deeper awareness of the alternatives before them and the likely consequences of each."

Willing Backwards

Bearing such pronouncements in mind, consider the following from the third paragraph of the opening page:

> What is required is mastery of what Nietzsche once termed "critical history" and what Gordon Craig has explained as the "ability, after painful inquiry and sober judgment, to determine what part of history [is] relevant to one's current problems, and what [is] not," whether one is assessing a situation, forming an opinion, or taking an active position on an issue.

After informing the readers of his books that colonial Amerindians enjoyed the Christian traits of succor and caring, it is surprising to hear NHS director Nash cite as an authority on history the German philosopher Friedrich Nietzsche, who saw Christianity as a "slave morality" that spelled submission and defeat to any group practicing it. Even more awkward is that the NHS started off with Nietzsche's view of the value of studying history when his point was also the wisdom of not studying it.

Nietzsche advised truly historical students to avoid exhausting themselves in either preserving, honoring, or lamenting the past. What one needs to know about history is when to remember it and when to forget it. Nietzsche contrasted "critical" history to "monumental" and "antiquarian" history precisely to teach how the past is to be overcome. "Critical" history is for the sufferer in need of liberation. But rather than dwelling on victimhood, the student "must have the strength . . . to shatter and dissolve something to enable him to live." How will it benefit the masses of humanity to be told that their ancestors were slaves, indentured servants, desperate farmers, harassed grandmothers, abused children, exploited uncles, failed merchants, drunken sots, and other species of the flesh? "Become who you are," exhorted Nietzsche, who reminded us that "the will cannot will backwards." Since history is irrevocable and nothing can be done about it, the students' vision of the past can only "turn them towards the future," where freedom and knowledge of who we are become an act of self-creation and not an object of historical discovery.

Had the NHS used Nietzsche's advice correctly, history "from the bottom up" would go belly up. Running through the NHS is a kind of ethnic determinism at odds with Nietzsche's Emersonian passion for freedom. What one needs to know, wrote Nietzsche, is "how to grow out of oneself in one's own way," and to do so by opening the mind to "the most foreign." The

NHS rests on the dubious assumption that education requires reducing the foreign to the familiar by way of concentrating on one's own ethnic roots—as if one grows backwards and one's inherited and hereditary nature is to be accepted with the finality of fate.

The NHS declares that we can obtain a "deeper awareness" about everything we need to know in the present by "studying the choices and decisions of the past." Nietzsche taught us that history serves, as does philosophy, to sadden, to make us aware that the past is indeed a "painful inquiry," as Gordon Craig put it, because the hurts and injuries of earlier times cannot be re-addressed and the human masses who suffered such a fate are the last people to study for their "choices and decisions," since people themselves seldom were in a position to make the decisions that determined their lives. Marx once distinguished the "kingdom of freedom" from the "kingdom of necessity" to make us aware of the harsh conditions hindering humanity in the various stages of history where people were subjected to the will of rulers and had no claim to sovereignty. Until the NHS came along, no one suggested that we can appreciate the value of freedom by studying the "choices and decisions" of a premodern past where the possibility of choosing and initiating, of enjoying alternative visions of life, and of having the power to act upon such visions had yet to be born among those living under the yoke of necessity. To study the past on the terms that the NHS offers is not to understand it but to seek revenge upon it and falsely to will backwards when true freedom and responsibility call for facing forwards.

The "Great Convergence": Anthropology Replaces History

The urge to avenge history hits the reader squarely in the face when he is confronted by the title: "Era I. Three Worlds Meet (Beginnings to 1620)." American history no longer begins with Christopher Columbus and the age of exploration; it now begins with "the first peopling of the Americas some 30,000 years ago." Then in the late fifteenth century a "great convergence takes place among European, African, and North American peoples." The curtain of American history rises not only with the arrival of Christian Europeans but with the prior presence of North American tribes and the existence of Islamic kingdoms of West Africa. Why the overreach? "Students will not grasp the collision of cultures without understanding the extensiveness and complexity of the societies of pre-Columbian America and West Africa."

The multicultural emphasis of the NHS made the new casting of American history serve the perceived present needs of a multiethnic society. What the NHS authors were up against is understandable. The "standards for United States history should reflect both the nation's diversity exemplified by race, ethnicity, social and economic states, gender, region, politics, and religion and the nation's commonalities. The contributions and struggles of specific groups and individuals should be included."

Fair enough. But what does a nation's present diversity have to do with the claims of a past "convergence"? Apparently none of the members who sat on the panel reviewing the first version of the NHS challenged that thesis, which actually first appeared twenty years earlier in Gary Nash's *Red, White, and Black*. Yet the latest scholarship indicates that between Spanish conquistadors and Mesoamericanos there was no "convergence," there was no coming together, because profound differences existed not only in language and communication but in concepts of time and history and attitudes toward death. The three cultures described by NHS did not so much converge as bypass one another by means of exclusionary classifications and tragic misperceptions.

Now it could well be that students should learn the views of others whose ways of life are foreign to their own ways of looking at things. But such a curriculum may have more to do with anthropology and ethnology than history, with disciplines not necessarily concerned with how the natural and social world came to be altered and transformed. At times it seems the NHS is more interested in having students appreciate differences than in having them analyze dynamics as the prime movers of progress. Cultural understanding is a worthy exercise, but it may have no bearing on teaching students how to think historically.

R. G. Collingwood made us aware that to know is to know the causes of things, and to know the causes is to know the motives that led to the choices and decisions that brought forth change and produced the conditions that made people freer. With its emphasis on premodern cultures, the NHS teaches little about freedom as the study of that which is volitional, self-determining, and purposeful, that which initiates change and thus is original and unprecedented rather than continuous and repetitive. An ethnological history that concentrates on culture rather than on events scarcely suggests even a note of tragedy, since primitive societies seldom embrace openness to the play of possibilities. The Mexican writer Octavio Paz questioned whether the pre-Columbian world could even be subjected to historical analysis based on temporal significance. "Meso-American civilization negated history more completely" than even China in preferring symbolic, atemporal thinking to the disruptive road to change, Paz writes. "From the Mexican high plateau to the tropical lands of Central America, for more than two thousand years, various cultures and empires succeeded one another and none of them had historical consciousness. Meso-America did not have history but myths and, above all, rites."

The NHS introduction emphasizes that "without historical knowledge and inquiry, we cannot achieve the informed, discriminating citizenship essential to effective participation in the democratic processes of government and the fulfillment for all our citizens of the nation's democratic ideals." One would think that the NHS would have begun with countries from which democratic ideals sprang. Instead it had—and still has in the revised version—students studying past cultures whose people reproduced their own bondage to rites and rituals.

The NHS continually proclaimed that the value of studying the past is to understand the present better. Given the NHS materials, it is difficult to see how we are to understand contemporary reality historically. "The broader context of American history," we are told, "avoids provincialism and drives home the point that the English, as latecomers to the Americas, were deeply affected by what had already occurred in the vast regions of the hemisphere."

"Affected," perhaps; "deeply," doubtful. Those of us who, many, many years ago, managed to stay awake in grammar school, will remember that the Plymouth Colony pilgrims were grateful to the Wampanoag Indians for offering corn and teaching them techniques of growing and hunting. The NHS also asks students to consider the "expert" ways Native Americans played European powers against one another, which recalls James Fenimore Cooper's description of certain warrior tribes as "forest Machiavels." But the Indians' knowledge of nature and their bravery in battle comprise only half the story, which, treated uncritically, becomes utter romance and turns itself over to Hollywood.

As in the latest Hollywood films, the NHS depicts history in Manichaean terms, with spirit and harmony all on one side and the aggressions of the dreaded white man on the other. Thus evil inhabits only one of the three cultures in the convergence scheme, and even here it emerges as a result of alleged economic deprivation rather than moral deficiency. The Western colonists' mistreatment of Indians and enslavement of blacks is duly emphasized, but not so much as the "sin" of greed and exploitation and the temptation to render invisible the human objects of property in order to escape guilt, the terms with which Abraham Lincoln condemned slave owning, but more as a benign aspect of "land hunger," as though the New World suffered from a scarcity of elbow room.

Meanwhile, the two other cultures enjoying the convergence are, despite all the puffs about their rich "extensiveness and complexity," rather simple and certainly innocent. One searches hard for any mention of tribal massacres, enslavement of captives, starvation, ritual sacrifice, illiteracy, genital mutilation, female infanticide, death by stoning for being unfaithful, and the absence of the plow, the wheel, and a tradition of political rights—in short, the brutal, degraded status of women and the complete acceptance of patriarchal domination as part of the natural order of things.

In failing to look squarely at the ugly underside of nonwhite history, the NHS has been depicted as a "radical" document out to subvert traditional American values in favor of third-world cultures. Actually, in several respects, the NHS is quaintly conservative in a religious sense, which, from a Nietzschean perspective, can only guarantee that "history from below" will keep people below.

First, its emphasis on the "convergence" asks students to appreciate stable cultures of lineage, unchallenged standards, filial authority, village identity, and totemic solace, all alien to America's liberal values but perhaps not radically subversive, except to early American Calvinists and their antiauthoritarianism and the individual believer burdened by real intellectual complexities. The NHS also prefers studying the peoples of the past who endured history rather than used their lives in ways today's students might identify with strength and success—a tendency that perhaps proves, as Claude Lévi-Strauss has noted, that both Christianity and anthropology express the "remorse" of the West in the face of inexorable change.

Is change always and everywhere a good thing? The answer can only be relative to one's values and preferences. At the turn of the century, Max Weber dealt with this issue in a passage he wrote after returning from a trip to the United States. He compared the Indians who lived in the Salt Lake area to the Mormon migrants who arrived later. Judging which culture was "well or poorly adapted," he noted, is a matter of personal preference and cannot be based on any objective criteria considered authoritative. Some may be impressed by the Mormons' achievements in transforming the land; others may disapprove of the effects of such achievements and "prefer the desert and the romantic existence of the Indians. No science of any kind can purport to be able to dissuade these persons from their respective views."

If the NHS had taken such a position, we could appreciate the authors' effort to avoid cultural egocentricity and anachronism. But the NHS invites us to look at societies different from our own to persuade us of their moral superiority.

The Indian: Extinct Aristocrat or Incipient Capitalist?

The NHS is awash in Indian lore. Students are asked to study "Native American values and beliefs. How are symbols in origin stories such as wood, rock, rivers, corn, and squash used to explain migration, settlement, and interactions with the environment?" Every child likes to play Indian, and even risqué adults are delighted to find out that some tribes smoked pot. But the NHS is deadly serious about getting students to grasp the culture and environment of Native Americans:

> Marshal specific evidence from such Native American societies as the Hopi and Zuni cultures of the Southwest, the Algonkian and Iroquoians cultures of the Northeast Woodlands, and the earlier Moundbuilders and Mississippian cultures of the Ohio and Mississippi valleys to develop a historical argument on such questions as the following: *Were Native American societies such as the Hopi and the Zuni different in their agricultural practices, gender roles, and social development from the 15th-century peasant communities in Europe? To what extent did the striking differences between Native American societies reflect different phases of the agricultural revolution in the Americas? To what extent did they reflect different geographical environments and resources available to these societies?*

Historians have traditionally dealt with the rise and fall of civilizations. But in the NHS, Native Americans neither rise nor fall as students are asked to concentrate not on actions and events, but on the fixed conditions of differing environments. We are told that Native Americans had "complex" patterns of this and that, but where it all led goes unmentioned. What Max Weber knew and Alexis de Tocqueville analyzed, students subjected to the NHS will never learn.

"I have said before that I regarded the origins of the Americans, what I have called their point of departure, as the first and most effective of all the elements leading to their present prosperity," wrote Tocqueville. "When I consider all that has resulted from this first fact, I think I can see the whole destiny of America contained in the first Puritan who landed on these shores. . . . One must never forget that."

Tocqueville recognized that America's liberty and prosperity derived from her Puritan heritage, and this recognition, which he would have no one forget saddened him deeply when he observed the status of Indians in America. Tocqueville was in America at the time that controversy erupted over the removal of the Cherokees from their land in Georgia. He commented critically on the dispossession of a tribe that had "created a written language and established a fairly stable form of government." The Creeks and Cherokees "have assuredly displayed as much natural genius as the European peoples in their greatest undertakings." But other observations left him distressed. "The natives of North America consider labor not only an evil, but also a disgrace, and their pride fights against civilization almost as obstinately as their laziness." It was not the "environments and resources available" to them that explained the Indian's historical position, as the NHS contends. It was their macho culture of hunting and warfare. "No Indian in his bark hut is so wretched that he does not entertain a proud conception of his personal worth; he considers the cares of industry degrading occupations; he compares the cultivator to the ox plowing a furrow and regards all our crafts as merely the labor of slaves."

In Tocqueville's observations, the Indians lacked the very Protestant work ethic that was rapidly transforming America, and their refusal to change their ways spelled their doom. How does the American historian treat this issue? James Axtell, a leading historian on the subject of Native Americans, treats it as cultural misunderstanding. "From the descriptions of the first settlers, the Indians have been branded with an indelible reputation for laziness and lack of industry." While Indians would expend "energy and thought on various tasks," working "laboriously" in systematic toil offended them, Axtell admits. He cites one young missionary who observed of the Shawnees: "The savage state has always been unfavourable to the female. The superior strength of the man is used, not in protecting and lightening the burdens of the weaker sex, but in depressing them. But men are *ashamed* of all kinds of labour. . . . Such is the pride of these lazy lords of the wilderness." Axtell hastens to refute such descriptions by citing another report denying that squaws were treated as slaves. But he has no doubt that Indians were falsely "branded" as lazy and that the white man was simply too culturally conditioned to see the reality of a foreign species of humanity. "Bred, like all people, to an ethnocentric world view, the English saw what they expected to see in Indian life."

Tocqueville did not expect to see what he in fact saw among the "red races" of America. "How odd it is that the ancient prejudices of Europe should reappear, not along the European populations on the coast, but in the forests of the New World." Tocqueville was surprised to discover the Old World's aristocratic disdain for labor reappearing in the woods of America. It was not that Indians were "primitive" that worried him but that they were "noble," too proud to stoop to toil and too caught up in ancestral memory as their only identity. He judged the Indians with the same verdict he judged his own aristocratic ancestors and tragically recognized that both were doomed to extinction.

Yet Tocqueville may not be the last word on this long elusive subject. Whenever white men and Indians met, according to the historian John Demos, they invariably met on terms of "exchange," with natives coveting English tools and blankets and pilgrims in need of canoes and slain deer. French Jesuits also noted the Indian desire for things and objects, although more in sorrow than in satisfaction. According to one account, when "black robes" would hold up the crucifix in an attempt to bring the message of Christianity, Indians wanted to exchange it for pelts. They didn't want to be converted; they wanted to trade.

Such accounts can only be upsetting to those historians who insist on believing that premodern societies were innocent of anything other than what E. P. Thompson called "a moral economy," or a cooperative system of provision and mutual welfare. Indians, it seems, were well into, to use Marx's language, "commodity fetishism" and "exchange relations," phenomena supposedly only characteristic of modern industrial society. What Adam Smith called the "propensity to truck, barter, and exchange" seemed to be part of the Indian mentality. Were, then, our first authentic Americans also our first capitalists? Their reluctance to engage in productive labor may have kept them apart from an emerging market that, in Fernand Braudel's words, "spells liberation, openness, access to another world." But their disposition to exchange and circulation may help explain how in recent years some Indians have left the reservation to start up gambling casinos to beat the white man at his own game.

"Remember the Ladies"

If people have been left out of American history because of their non-Western ancestry, women have been left out of that same history despite having been born into a Western culture that valued literacy, political rights, and the work ethic. The challenge of doing women's history has stumped the best of minds. In *The Second Sex*, Simone de Beauvoir wrote seven hundred pages of excellent analysis, only to conclude that women had neither an event-making history nor a sense of sisterhood that transcended class and nation. But years earlier, in *Woman as Force in History*, Mary R. Beard insisted that the story of women could be found if students turned to hitherto unexplored sources. Beard also perceived that the fate of women depended upon the Western idea of equality, and, although she did discuss John Locke, she seemed unaware of Locke's role as the first philosopher to challenge the idea of patriarchy. But even with the legacy of Locke, which made women the rightful heirs to political rights, history written by men relegated the other sex to oblivion. Why this systematic exclusion of our mothers, sisters, wives, daughters, aunts, nieces, and mistresses?

The obvious answer is that traditional history emphasized politics, statecraft, wars and revolutions, the rise and fall of empires, the formation of government—in short, the spectacle of power and the relations of forces struggling for dominance and leaders capable of transforming events into history. Such is not the stuff of social history, and even Catherine the Great is disqualified owing to her title, while Eleanor Roosevelt was allowed to make an appearance provided that she left tea parties to head for the coal mines (she has been dropped from the revised NHS). In explaining how women have had no significant place in the "master narratives" of history, the new social historians seldom address the question of power but instead turn to rhetoric and its representations.

The current explanation for the absence of women in written history blames the very function of re-presenting, and hence the "French turn" to poststructuralist theory to insist that past linguistic representations rendered women invisible, marginalized, repressed, out of sight, and, hence, out of mind. Mistaking the effect for the cause, historians conclude that the absence of women was a matter of rhetorical strategies rather than of power realities and that the notion of gender is a construction waiting to be deconstructed.

It is curious that American women scholars have seized upon the writings of Frenchmen and have turned to male constructions to find out about female constrictions. "The woman who is known only through a man is known wrong," warned the historian Henry Adams, the hero of Mary Beard's book. The lost status of women perplexed Adams, who wrote the little-known address, "Primitive Rights of Women." Adams questioned the commonly held view that marriage originated in purchase or capture and in the cult of patriarchy that subordinated women throughout history. His belief in sexual equality could hardly be based upon his skepticism of democracy; instead he sought to redefine feminine dignity in nature itself. "The idea that she was weak revolted all of history," he observed of the opposite sex; "it was a paleontological falsehood that even a Euocene female monkey would have laughed at." Yet history complicated matters. "Women had been supreme," he wrote in the *Education*; "in France she still seemed potent, not merely as a sentiment but as a force; why was she unknown in America?" At a dinner one evening, Adams turned to the person next to him and asked whether there was a possible explanation as to why "the American woman was a failure." Without a moment's hesitation, she shot back: "Because the American man is a failure."

Adams knew that history is the study of power and the play of forces that seek to possess it. Such an approach to history is by no means a masculine monopoly, as indicated in the writings of Antonia Fraser, Jeane Kirkpatrick, and Seyla Benhabib. But the field of women's studies and the new social history that have shaped the NHS pay attention only to the distaff side of Adams's family.

Thus, the NHS asks students to "analyze how women's quest for new roles and rights for their gender" can be seen in Abigail Adams's well-known letter to John Adams written in 1776:

> Remember the Ladies, and be more generous and favourable to them than your ancestors. Do not put such unlimited power into the hand of husbands. Remember all Men would be tyrants if they could. If particular care and attention is not paid to the ladies we are determined to foment a Rebellion, and will not hold ourselves bound by any laws in which we have no voice, or representation.

Can one use this single letter as emblematic of "women's quest for new roles and rights"? According to Edith B. Gelles's biography, *Portia*, there is no evidence that the First Lady had such intentions in mind. "Abigail," writes the author, "disapproved of women who breached the prevailing code of female behavior." If Abigail was not advocating new roles and equal rights, and hence was no precursor of modern feminism in questioning motherhood and wifehood, what was poor John to remember when he was asked to remember the ladies?

Throughout the NHS, students are continually asked to examine the "role" women played in a given episode in the past. This emphasis on role-playing helps us understand that we are creatures of society's expectations. In feminist theory, becoming aware that the self is socially constituted is liberating in that gender can now be seen as something constructed rather than as an essential aspect of nature. Since women as a social creation are "constituted discursively," the task of the historian, advises Joan Scott, is "to interrogate the processes of their creation." One would think, then, that women would partake of an Emersonian view of the self as "aboriginal," with the potential to be self-reliant and as autonomous as possible. But the idea of a self-made woman capable of resisting determination from without is anathema to feminist history.

Thus, whether it is because the NHS sees the individualistic self as "bourgeois" and too close to capitalism, or whether feminists prefer to see women in the past acting through groups as a source of strength, in the document, action is generally presented in a given social framework, and women appear to be compelled to engage life collectively. Such an approach to history, wherein human acts take on meaning only by external reference to society, may be incompatible with the NHS's goals of teaching "political intelligence" and the values of freedom. As François Furet has emphasized, "political history is primarily a narrative of human freedom" involving "the thought, choice, and actions of men. . . . Politics is the quintessential realm of chance, and so of freedom." Social history, in contrast, deals with patterned structures and roles, often so determining that "society speaks and acts autonomously. According to this view, social agents simply enact their society's rules of operation and reproduction without knowing that they do so, and enjoy no other freedom than the possibility of entertaining the illusion of freedom." Or, as Denise Riley put it in *"Am I That Name?": Feminism and the Category of "Women" in History*, to treat women as a social phenomenon carries many of the same deterministic implications as treating gender as an aspect of nature. In the past not only biology but society too, Riley notes, had "horribly circumscribed" women as a fixed category. In *Three Guineas*, Virginia Woolf describes society as a "conspiracy": "You shall not learn; you shall not earn; you shall not own." Does such a female mind need to be told that she had been "constituted discursively"? Must women be reduced to a role?

With little attention to events, social history seems indifferent to change, progress, and some examples of successful achievement that can distinguish the dominant from the dominated. Social history, reigning unquestioned, could well be death to young women's imaginations. Women's history only betrays its servitude to men's history by continuing a common disdain against all that is exceptional and outstanding. Consider what students could learn if the new social history allowed intellectual history a voice of its own, giving women a place in the American mind, particularly women who could do as they chose and were "great" precisely because they dared to be different.

It was a woman who first discerned the logical contradictions of Calvinism (Anne Hutchinson), who first earned a living as an author (Hannah Adams), and a million dollars as an entertainer (Lotta Crabtree), who first brought Goethe to America (Margaret Fuller), who first assaulted plantation slavery by allegorizing it (Harriet Beecher Stowe), who first saw the implications of evolutionary biology for her sex (Charlotte Perkins Gilman), who first wrote a Flaubertian novel on the silk cage of domesticity (Kate Chopin), who first poeticized the "soft eclipse" of woman by the requirements of wifehood (Emily Dickinson), who first made us aware of the environment's ecological fragility (Rachel Carson), who first appreciated modern art (Gertrude Stein) and supported it (Peggy Guggenheim) and turned it into landscape realism (Georgia O'Keeffe), who first took up music to make Parisian society swing (Josephine Baker) and bring tears from the soul (Bessie Smith) and make an aria vibrate with the beauty of black spirituality (Leontyne Price), who first went back beyond modern America to understand human relations (Margaret Mead), and who first showed us that the American Revolution succeeded because it had no need to address the "social question" of human misery and class oppression (Hannah Arendt).

Remember the ladies indeed!

History through a Bottomist

NHS director Gary Nash has spent much of his academic career writing a history at complete odds with Arendt's thesis. In *The Urban Crucible: Social Change, Political Consciousness, and the Origins of the American Revolution* (1979), a study of the seaport cities of Boston, Philadelphia, and New York, Nash argues that previous scholars have tried to explain the American Revolution while ignoring such social realities as "mass indebtedness, widowhood, and poverty." Nash succeeded in that book in making us aware of pockets of social distress in American society, but his insistence that the study of history is the study of "popular collective action" began to sound like a marching street chant from the sixties, as though "We Shall Overcome" had joined with the music from *Les Misérables.* Nash did uncover some rumblings from below, but he was never quite able to connect his data to the outbreak of the Revolution—which brings to mind Trotsky's remark that if poverty explained revolution, there would be a revolution every day. Yet Nash continues to believe that the truths about the past are down there to be found at the lower depths of society and that it is history "from the bottom up" that will redeem America. Downtrodden humanity not only endures history, it is "actively and intimately involved" in making it. Gary Nash is a bottomist.

In the early part of the century, Carl Becker informed us about a dual revolution taking place at the time of the Revolution, a struggle for home rule and a struggle to see who shall rule at home. Yet neither Becker nor Nash addresses the central issue of Arendt's thesis in *On Revolution*: that it was absence of social misery and class oppression that explains why the American Revolution succeeded in realizing liberty and institutionalizing freedom in the Constitution and why all other subsequent revolutions failed to do so. What Arendt called "the social question" is mentioned neither in the Declaration of Independence nor in the writings of Tom Paine or others who sought to see America liberated from British rule and who did not want to transform social relations from top to bottom and turn society upside down.

Nash's effort to describe the Revolution as a radically transforming event explains why students were asked in the NHS to see the event as a possible "civil war" consisting of "multiple movements" and has them dwelling on the Shaysites, Paxton Boys, Regulators, and "Whiskey Rebels." Social historians seek to highlight struggle from below and any possible challenges to authority wherever they may be found, and this search for "oppositionalist" impulses characterizes the second version of the NHS as well as the first. It is endemic in much of historiography. But while the bottomists bloom in the profession, will students be prepared to understand the nature of a revolution when asked this question:

> How have the ideas that inspired the American and French Revolutions influenced the 20th-century revolutions in Mexico, Russia, China, Cuba, and Vietnam? How have Americans viewed these modern revolutions?

The choice of these countries is puzzling yet revealing. As Franco Venturi has shown, in the eighteenth century, the American Revolution reverberated in Holland, Sweden, France, Spain, Turkey, Prussia, and Russia. In the twentieth century, with the exception of Mexico, all other revolutions were inspired by a Marxist-Leninism that had no use for the liberal doctrines of the American or French revolutions. Marx once praised the United States as "the highest form of popular government, till now realized," only to change his mind and declare the American republic "the model country of the democratic imposture." Trotsky formulated the "law of combined development" to convince comrades that Russia could skip the liberal stage of history that America enjoyed in the eighteenth and nineteenth centuries. What Fidel Castro thinks of the American Revolution should perhaps not be repeated to schoolchildren.

No Knowledge of Power, No Understanding of Freedom

In defending Nash, the sociologist Todd Gitlin has argued that while the NHS looks to history as "explanation," its critics are only interested in "veneration." Both sides, it seems to me, ask for uncritical veneration and differ only concerning where it should be directed: from the top down or the bottom up. Gitlin also charges that the critics have missed two essential points in the new way of looking at American history. "First, traditionally American history was mainly the history of power, and power was white, male, and elite. (What else could it have been?) But the new standards carried a sense that history was also a struggle against power."

Can people obtain power if they do not have a *Machtpragma*, exercise in the use of power? In *The Urban Crucible*, Nash writes:

> It was not political power itself that the laboring classes yearned for, but an equitable system in which they could pursue their modest goals. . . . Yet their periodic excursions into "radical" politics, in order to either conserve the corporate community or to pry open the doors of opportunity in the new entrepreneurial age, had a cumulative effect. A sense of their own power grew as their trust in those above them diminished and as their experience expanded in making decisions, exercising leadership roles, and refuting those

> who were supposed to be wiser because they were wealthier. Hence factional politics intensified.

Neither Nash nor anyone who writes history "from the bottom up" can deal with power if his or her presuppositions about "class consciousness," the announced theme of *The Urban Crucible*, preclude describing workers as having a drive toward it. Nash would have us believe that his urban workers challenged the authority of and deference to the merchant and gentry classes as the Revolution approached and the acts of the British Parliament fell heavily on the poor. But Nash is also convinced of another theme running through the NHS: that the presence of class antagonism is itself evidence that social classes are of differing characters, with each having its own system of values and those at the bottom bearing no trace of whatever may be above them; hence no envy, resentment, or acquisitiveness born of emulation; no need for respect and mutual recognition from the "wiser" and "wealthier"; no desire to prevail and dominate; and, seemingly, no interest or passion that demands to be gratified. "The urban lower order formulated distinctly different points of view from the ones held by those above," insists Nash.

Simone Weil, who closely and despairingly studied French factory workers, came to the opposite conclusion. "It is difficult to see how their world springs up from the masses, spontaneously, to be the opposite of the system that formed, or deformed, them." Tocqueville and Lincoln also saw what Nash and the NHS either deny or miss seeing. In societies undergoing change and liberalization, they pointed out, situations of subordination are temporary as wealth circulates and status is in transition; thus as the servant can move into the class of the master, and so desires to move upward, he is no more different from the master than the artisan is from the merchant and perhaps even the laborer from the capitalist.

Nash is only one of hundreds of historians who teach students that the working class has its own "distinct set of cultural values" and that its sense of "class solidarity" stands in opposition to the classes above. Once again Du Bois seems wiser than those white scholars. "Why," asked Du Bois, "should we assume on the part of unlettered and suppressed masses of white workers, a clearness of thought and a sense of human brotherhood, that is sadly lacking in the most educated classes?" Rarely can such historians as Nash prove the existence of this alleged "class consciousness," and, thanks to the recent research of Simon Middleton, we now know that the colonial-era worker was no different from the incipient capitalist in being competitive, in lusting after contracts, and in bringing lawsuits against fellow workers. *The Urban Crucible*, whose thesis about class runs through the NHS like a red thread, so misleads students about the nature of power and the character of the working class that it invites an irresistible Nietzschean analysis of the genealogy of pseudomorality. The impotence of the "lower order" becomes virtue, its satisfaction with the simple things of life becomes goodness, and its historical inability to rise to dominance becomes innocence. Where is the challenge to power?

The notion that intensified factional strife is itself tantamount to power, or even to the "struggle against power," is more an act of hope than a feat of history, an illusion that the powerless possess the secret of power by virtue of not wanting to possess it through pursuing wealth and that power is derivative of simple action rather than strategic organization and location. Such sentiments smack of the "participatory democracy" of the sixties—an ethos innocent of how power eludes people because it can only assert itself by excluding others in ways that make domination and participation incompatible.

Would that the NHS did show students how history can teach us about the many meanings of power and how to struggle against it. How to resist power and tame it became the theme of the *Federalist*, a brilliant document that receives almost no attention in the NHS. Hannah Arendt absorbed those essays as a profound meditation on power, citing Madison, who said that politics and knowledge of power comprise "the greatest reflection on human nature." The hapless students subjected to the NHS will know nothing about power to the extent that intellectual history becomes not a means of analyzing ideas but instead a therapeutic tool for promoting cultural identity. Consider the following question asked in the World History Standards:

> Read excerpts from Machiavelli's *The Prince* and compare his understanding of "realpolitik" with earlier writers like Kautilay and the Qin Legalists such as Han Fei. Could Machiavelli have been influenced by these earlier philosophers?

Note that students are asked not to grasp what Machiavelli was saying but to show that he was not so original and that his ideas may have come from non-Western sources. Whether or not these exotic-sounding authors knew the secret of power, some Chinese thinkers believed that holders of power could be trained to be sages endowed with moderation and benevolence. A far cry from Machiavelli, who didn't read Chinese.

Bottomists deceive themselves. For all their incantations of "class formation," social historians have yet to demonstrate how those at the bottom take shape as a political force, gain consciousness of their own interests, and win some measure of freedom as a result of obtaining the power in order to alter the conditions of life. As Marx himself noted, in countries that are experiencing liberalization and modernization, the dynamic of history is not from the bottom up but from the top down. "Liberation from the point of view of the bourgeoisie—competition—was the only possible way during the eighteenth century to open up the individual to a new career for freer development." The NHS director depicted America's becoming individualistic as a violation of Christianity when almost every other thinker saw individualism as the natural outcome of Protestantism. "Capitalism's ceaseless striving toward the general form of wealth," wrote Marx in the *Grundrisse,* "drives labour beyond the limits of its natural paltriness [*Naturbedürftigkeit*], and thus creates the material element for the development of the rich individuality which is as all-sided in its production as in its consumption." Marx reminded readers of the *New York Daily Tribune* of what goes unacknowledged in the NHS: that "capital is productive" and that the "bourgeois period of history" is as creative as it is necessary. In the London *Times* in 1857, Marx delighted in describing the despair of a West Indian plantation owner who could not get his slaves to work hard. Marx looked to the culture of capitalism to liberate existence from natural necessity by introducing ambition and industriousness.

Every major nineteenth-century thinker (Tocqueville, Marx, and Weber, among the giants) saw America as having broken away from feudal Europe, while the NHS insists that America must be understood as having "converged" with premodern civilization. But the ultimate validity of the NHS turns on its interpretation of America's political founding, which Nash interprets as a social historian and articulates in *The Urban Crucible.* As a result the standards document perpetuates many of the false claims about the American Revolution that Bernard Bailyn has so learnedly challenged: the Revolution transforms social relations and overthrows the "old regime"; it eliminates widespread suffrage restrictions that supposedly suppressed democracy; ends deferences and class structures; and, above all, "reinforces the belief of critics of late twentieth-century liberalism that the modern capitalist world, with its inequities, dominated by the ethic of possessive individualism, is a repudiation, a reversal, not the fulfillment, of the communitarian idealism of the original, true, American Revolution." The spirit of seventy-six represented none of these things. "Nor," Bailyn continues, with the thesis of Nash and other social historians in mind, "have the efforts to locate the roots of the revolution in progressive impoverishment of working-class protest succeeded."

But they have succeeded in the NHS, where working-class protest parades itself through the text until it seems as though the only meaning of history lies in the shouts coming from the streets. In the NHS, 1968 lives!

What Happened to George Washington?

The NHS reads more like a prison house of group categories than an analysis of freedom based on natural rights and power as individual growth and self-development. It is also straddling an embarrassing incompatibility in thinking it can teach the values of freedom and at the same time insist that history is the sole locus of one's identity. "Historical memory is the key to self-identity, to seeing one's place in the stream of time, and one's connectedness with all humankind. We are part of an ancient chain, and the long hand of the past is upon us—for good and for ill—just as our hands will rest in our descendents for years to come." The first sentence is psychologically questionable, the second historically debatable.

With all the emphasis on "one's place" and "one's connectedness," the NHS refused to acknowledge that people in the past had no say about the place where they found themselves and the culture into which they were born. "A culture is a system of prejudgment," writes Ernest Gellner. "Social institutions and culture are seldom chosen: they are our fate, not our choice." The multicultural bias that runs through the NHS presupposes that the identity of each ethnic group originates in its respective past culture, and hence the purpose of history is to find that identity through memory. Yet Franklin, Jefferson, Emerson, Margaret Fuller, William James, Ralph Ellison, and other American thinkers show us that whatever is worthwhile in life is not inherited but chosen, not derived from fixed antecedents but created from new challenges. "To be free," wrote Ortega y Gasset, "means to be lacking in constitutive identity, not to have subscribed to a determined being, to be able to be other than what one was." Rather than helping people free themselves from the past, the NHS traps them in their ethnic differences, and in so doing makes a virtue out of diversity at the expense of American history and the possibility of a common curriculum that will enable students to identify with something other than themselves.

Is it really in keeping with the meaning of America to insist that we are products of the "long hand of the past" and "our hands" will rest on those who follow us? It is difficult to see America, a liberal culture that has always been under the "dominance of the foreground" (George Santayana), turning to the background for identity and adhering to tradition and custom. However Native Americans may have oriented themselves, a nation of immigrants seldom looks back, and imported slaves rarely desire to go back. The Founders themselves rejected historical precedent when formulating "a new science of politics." Jefferson declared that the "earth belongs to the living," and he would have been appalled at the idea that the "hands" of the present generation should rest on the shoulders of the future; Emerson urged not backward but "onward thinking"; Lincoln believed Americans must "disenthrall" themselves from the past, "and then we shall be saved."

But Lincoln, whose tragic sense of history resembled Nietzsche's, also believed that we must know when to forget the past and when to remember it. Thus he lamented that the "mystic chords of memory" might fade away, falling silent like fallen oaks. He had in mind the "glory" of the Revolution and the "towering genius" of George Washington.

In the first NHS version, the name *Washington* is mentioned twice; once when students are asked to construct a dialogue between him and an Indian chief, and again when students are asked to couple two leaders in order to compare them, a strange fate for a figure in history who was once regarded as incomparable. The revised NHS also mentions him twice, again as a "leader" and also a "founder," no doubt to satisfy its patriotic critics who want their heroes back on the pedestal. As long as the NHS prevails, whether the first or even the second version, students will never know the stature that Washington once commanded, not only in the United States but in South America and in Europe. For more than a century, Washington remained the supreme symbol of political virtue among such leaders as Simón Bolívar, José Martí, and others who did not want to see their own revolutions deviate from the promises of freedom and end up with some form of Bonapartism. Lord Byron, a man of the left who devoted his life to the cause of freedom, taking on "Tory scoundrals" in England and the "barbarian" Holy Alliance on the Continent, aptly described the stirring memory of the man who has disappeared from American history:

Where may the wearied eye repose
  When gazing on the Great;
Where neither guilty glory glows,
  Nor despicable state?
Yes-one-the first-the last-the
        best-
The Cincinnatus of the West,
  Whom envy dared not hate
Bequeathed the name of Washington,
    To make the man blush there was but one!

Why did the NHS refuse to allow students of history the knowledge, pleasure, and inspiration that might be obtained from "gazing on the great"? Whether or not great leaders shape the course of history and actualize the spirit of an age is a philosophical riddle. But the NHS was so biased in its selection and emphasis, and in such gross violation of even its own standards, that it seemed oblivious to the very advice it offered. History, the NHS announced, "trains students to detect bias, to weigh evidence, and to evaluate arguments, thus preparing them to make sensible, independent judgments, to sniff out spurious appeals to history by partisan pleaders, to distinguish between anecdote and analysis."

A curious statement coming from a document that can neither distinguish history from anthropology nor "detect bias" in its own contrived curriculum with its "spurious appeals" to redemption from below and afar. This deep self-deception remains as characteristic of the revised NHS as of the first version. Thus one can only wonder if students will ever be aware of how and why progress took place in history. Noting that history stagnates when the individual feels powerless, Bertrand Russell wrote:

> There has been in recent times a dangerous tendency, not unconnected with totalitarianism, to think only in terms of whole communities, and to ignore the contributions of the individual. But consider: some man or men invented the wheel, but in the American continent it was unknown until the white man introduced it. Probably it was not one man who made the invention, but several men, starting from round logs used as rollers; however that may be, the difference that these men made to civilization is immeasurable. The need of individual genius is shown by the fact that the Mayas and the Incas, though in some ways highly civilized, never hit upon the simple invention. The difference between our world and the world before the industrial revolution is due to the discoveries and inventions of a small number of men; if by some misfortune, a few thousand men of exceptional ability had perished in infancy, the technique of production would now be very little different from what it was in the 18th century. Individuals can achieve great things, and the teacher of history ought to make this clear to his pupils. For without hope nothing of importance is accomplished.

In rejecting such wise words as nothing more than "the great man" theory imposed by "a white-oriented hero-worshipping history," the NHS deprives us of both hope and history itself.

CHAPTER 20

CLIO BANISHED? BATTLES OVER HISTORY IN THE SCHOOLS

Sean Wilentz

THE FIERCE BATTLE over the proposed national history standards for America's schools may well be remembered as one of the high points (or, more likely, one of the low points) in the culture wars of the 1990s. Even now, more than two years after a revised set of rigorous standards won broad assent from history educators, some of the belligerents still nurse bad feelings. On the right, some of the most vociferous critics of the standards have never made their peace with the improved version and have stuck to objections that have grown increasingly far-fetched with the passage of time. On the left, meanwhile, the developers and defenders of both the original and the revised standards are still loath to discuss the profound historical deficiencies in the original proposal on such pivotal topics as the Cold War, and how those deficiencies contributed to the contretemps.[1]

Yet for all of the attendant harsh rhetoric and headline-grabbing, the History Standards controversy may prove far less consequential for the future of history education in this country than will a far less publicized series of fights over the teaching of history and social studies in the nation's schools. Although it was heavily freighted with political opportunism, the attack on the History Standards was essentially concerned with what sort of history should be taught to our children. Almost completely lost in the shuffle has been a momentous and continuing debate over how much history, of any kind, should be taught.

To an alarming degree, public educators around the country do not believe that history is a fundamental academic subject. Instead, they would require students to learn updated versions of the old mishmash known as "social studies," taking up current events, world cultures, and related matters, with curricula that feature little historical content. These educators, including some state superintendents of public education, like to pose as courageous progressives who want to liberate our schoolchildren from the tyranny of rote instruction and the misbegotten worship of dead heroes. But if they have their way, the historical illiteracy of today's young Americans will only worsen in the generations to come.

Professional scholars ignore this threat—to their great peril. Unless they are the parents of school-age children, college and university historians generally are clueless about history's banishment from the schools. We lament that our undergraduates, even in the best institutions, seem remarkably unprepared when it comes to basic historical knowledge. We note, along with the rest of the educated citizenry, the shocking results when high-school students are tested on matters as simple as when the Civil War or the Great Depression occurred. Depending on our viewpoints, we blame the bad news on everything from the deleterious influence of television and video games to a supposed waning of public appreciation for the past. At either end of the political spectrum, old prejudices get redeployed: Whereas hard-line conservatives are apt to fault—what else?—the '60s counterculture for the current historical illiteracy, multicultural leftists snarl about the hegemony of white male privilege.[2] That is, we blame everything except the demonstrable decades-old decline in American history education.

The origins of this mess date back to the Progressive Era and its immediate aftermath. Inspired by the so-called "new history" of James Harvey Robinson and others, educators began looking for ways to teach history to youngsters in a more comprehensive and "useable" way than traditional methods allowed, embracing the history of social and economic development as well as of politics. These early efforts had the merit of expanding the potential of historical instruction. In the 1920s, for example, a widely used secondary school textbook, *An American History*, by Columbia University historian David Muzzey, became the bellwether of the new departure by bravely and intelligently challenging the conventional schoolroom filiopiety and complacency—and came under heavy fire from alarmed superpatriots. In the 1930s, however, the controversial textbooks of Harold Rugg, who was not a historian but a professor at Columbia Teachers College, took matters a dangerous step further by trying to embed history in a grander system of social knowledge, thereby slighting the distinctive qualities of historical inquiry. Even more troubling, meanwhile, was the rise of something called "social studies" in some of the nation's black colleges, a field designed by well-meaning paternalists as a practical alternative to history for students they deemed unprepared for the rigors of historical studies. (Of this alternative, W. E. B. Du Bois remarked that it encouraged young blacks to "dream dreams of cornbread and molasses.")[3]

By the late 1960s, advocates of social studies (no longer confined to the black colleges) transformed themselves from a group of advocates into a formidable power within American public education, led by progressive ideologues who berated the study of history as little more than fact-grubbing. As the social studies establishment consolidated its power within the nation's education schools and curriculum committees, college and university historians abandoned what had once been a strong professional interest in the state of history teaching at the primary and secondary levels. Contacts between professional organizations like the American Historical Association and teachers' groups, above all the National Council for the Social Studies, became sporadic. Although history continued to be taught in the schools, it increasingly became restricted to high-school advanced placement courses open to the brightest students in the more privileged areas of the country. The masses got social studies.

Only in the late 1980s, with the odd convergence of a few concerned historians (some liberal, some conservative) and George Bush, the self-declared "education President," did matters begin to change. Around the country, state departments of education discovered to their distress that history requirements in most schools had dwindled to trivial levels. While state officials fretted and began undertaking revisions, a National History Task Force, under the direction of Lynne Cheney, head of the National Endowment for the Humanities, began discussing the possibility of constructing a set of voluntary national standards for history instruction from the kindergarten through the twelfth grade. In what later proved an ironic match, the task force gave the job of devising the standards to the liberal-minded National Center for History in the Schools, based at the University of California at Los Angeles under the directorship of Gary Nash. After two years of work, the history center's proposals were ready to see the light of day, when Cheney—displaced by the Clinton victory in 1992—unleashed a blistering surprise attack on the project in *The Wall Street Journal,* initiating the great two-year History Standards debate.

That debate was only the beginning. Even in their revised and improved form, the national history standards were really just suggestions; federal officials could not force states to live up to them. Therefore, since 1996, the action has shifted to the state level, where boards of regents and departments of education have been trying to implement calls for new and exacting standards in all areas of primary and secondary instruction. The terms of debate have shifted here, as well, from what types of historical subjects should be taught to whether much history should be taught at all. As soon as efforts to establish state history standards began, proponents of social studies, including the National Council for the Social Studies, took the offensive. Some of them claimed that the proposed reforms were Eurocentric—a curious charge, in view of the struggles over alleged multicultural biases in the National Standards, from which many state efforts take inspiration. Others claimed that the reforms demanded too much both of students and (more tellingly) of the large numbers of social studies faculty members, who are inadequately prepared in history. In some states, notably Wisconsin, proposals to revamp the teaching of social studies around a core historical narrative met with stiff resistance from state education officials, who said that such plans ran counter to the approved social studies approach and threatened local control of school curricula. Above all, the social studies supporters asserted that the reforms would unfairly elevate the discipline of history—what one leading social-studies educator has derided as "pastology"—in a disguised attempt to turn back the clock to an America of white-bread smugness and memorized facts.

Such criticisms might be valid if the study of history were the same today as it was eighty years ago, when the social studies movement got underway. Back then, history teaching was, indeed, a narrow enterprise, dedicated to drumming names and dates into schoolchildren's heads, and limited to the chief political and diplomatic episodes of the past. But the field of history has changed dramatically. Formerly neglected aspects of the past, including the history of women, and of racial and ethnic minorities, have come to occupy a central place in historical research and instruction. Emphasis now falls not simply on the recitation of facts (a necessary chore, pace progressive dogma), but also on the interpretation of facts and primary documents. Social studies, meanwhile, has mutated into a catchall field, blending bits and pieces of the different social sciences with an emphasis on "process" and practical skills rather than on content and historical knowledge. Or, in the words of one of its advocates, James L. Barth of Purdue University, "Social studies is the interdisciplinary integration of social science and humanities concepts for the purpose of practicing problem solving and decision making for developing citizenship skills on crucial social issues."[4]

Beneath such boilerplate descriptions lurks a fundamental disregard of history as a vital subject. To be sure, social studies programs may instruct students in historical events, like the Protestant Reformation or the American Revolution. But those events assume importance only to the extent that they have relevance to our own world—to aid in "decision making . . . on crucial social issues." The pastness of the past is lost—and with it the humanizing lesson that people in history, although every bit as intelligent as ourselves, thought and lived in ways very different from our own. Areas of history that cannot be easily connected to current priorities inevitably are neglected. Diverse ideas and cultures are reduced to one-dimensional subjects or "factors," divorced from their sources and their historical lineage. Furthermore, the teaching of crucial facts, such as when the Bastille fell, is demoted in favor of teaching abstract concepts. Thus students may learn nothing about the presidency of Abraham Lincoln except as it pertains to the persistence of racism in the United States.

Today's history-minded reformers, led by the National Council for History Education, do not deny the importance of teaching students how to evaluate the issues that confront contemporary society. They contend, however, that this goal is best reached by teaching the discipline of history, not by relentlessly turning the past into a mere prologue of the present. Interdisciplinary efforts have merit, but only after students have mastered the various disciplines in question. That means instructing students in world history and American history, as well as geography and government (or civics). To combine that instruction from the start with a hodgepodge of anthropology, sociology, and economics—that is, to sustain social studies as we know it—is to deprive students of the building blocks they need in order eventually to study those other fields. It is also to lull students and parents into the belief that the schools are teaching advanced social science fields effectively.

Advocates of more demanding history standards have gained some ground. In 1995, Virginia's Board of Education, supported by Governor George Allen and the American Federation of Teachers, adopted strenuous learning standards in history, geography, and economics, from kindergarten through high school, making history the integrative core of the proposed curriculum. An equally impressive curriculum framework in history and social science has been proposed for Massachusetts, and similar reforms have been debated in California, Connecticut, New Jersey, and other states.

Still, approval of these reforms is far from certain. Predictably, the social studies lobby has impugned the reformers' political motives, attacking the curriculums as tools for reactionary fact-grubbers and mindless patriots.[5] Early signs of welcome change have in some cases run into difficulty. In my home state of New Jersey, for example, curriculum reformers campaigned for two years to Governor Christine Todd Whitman, the state legislature, and the Department of Education, to revise their draft curriculum standards for social studies in order to include more specific material on United States and world history. Yet after a string of missed deadlines and broken promises, nothing substantial changed. In February 1998, a study for the Fordham

Foundation evaluated the history content in the social studies core curriculums of thirty-seven states and the District of Columbia, and ranked New Jersey's standards at the very bottom. Six months later, the American Federation of Teachers, for the second year in a row, announced that New Jersey's standards "are so vague that they have little value," and specifically criticized the state for failing to "include specific U.S. history or world history content." Only since then, thanks to the reformers' persistence, has a more substantive historical framework for social studies standards appeared in New Jersey.[6]

The real issue here is not one of right and left, as the social studies lobby contends. It is whether history, as it now is taught and studied, ought to be a key element of schooling in the United States. However benevolent its origins, traditional social studies education has outlived its usefulness—with the sad result that most of today's schoolchildren are ignorant of the most basic information about their own country's past. Professional historians, who have a larger stake than most in reversing this trend, can make their greatest contribution by educating themselves about the situation in their states and localities, and by joining forces with the beleaguered forces for reform.

Notes

1. For a fuller discussion of these matters, see my review of Gary B. Nash, Charlotte Crabtree, and Ross E. Dunn, "History On Trial: Culture Wars and the Teaching of the Past," in *New York Times Book Review,* November 30, 1997, 28, 31.
2. For a review of these matters, albeit one that is uninformed about efforts to combat such trends, see Christopher Hitchens, "Goodbye to All That: Why Americans Are Not Taught History," *Harper's Magazine,* (November 1998): 37–47.
3. Du Bois quoted in Don Johnson, "Reclaiming History Education: Historians and the Social Sciences, a Troubled History," unpublished paper, courtesy of Professor Johnson.
4. Quoted in Sean Wilentz, "The Past Is Not a 'Process,'" *New York Times,* 20 April 1997.
5. See, for example, Alan Singer's remarks on history teaching in *OAH Newsletter* (August 1997): 3, 12.
6. For details, see John Pyne, "What's Happened to History in the Social Studies Curriculum?: New Jersey: A Case Study," *History Matters,* 11 (December 1998), 1, 7. For the most recent developments, see Hank Bitten, "A New Curriculum Design for New Jersey: Implementing the *Social Studies Framework," History Matters,* 11 (May 1999), 5–6.

CHAPTER 21

WHOSE HISTORY? WHOSE STANDARDS?

Walter A. McDougall

THE NATIONAL STANDARDS Project, conceived under George Bush, born and reared by Bill Clinton's *Goals 2000: Educate America Act*, and nursed with $2.2 million from the National Endowment for the Humanities (NEH) and the Department of Education, took sick the moment the November 1994 election returns were in. Conservative critics had claimed that the standards*—two volumes of outlines and study guides for the teaching of, respectively, world and U.S. history in grades five through twelve—were an abomination designed to indoctrinate young people in anti-Americanism. Riding this wave, Republican senators Robert Dole (Kansas) and Slade Gordon (Washington) then introduced amendments that would have forbidden the use of federal funds for implementation of these standards, and required that any future recipients of such funds "have a decent respect for United States history's roots in Western civilization."

In the event, the Senate settled on a resolution, rather than a law, condemning the standards. It passed on January 18 by a vote of ninety-nine to one, the lone dissenter, Democrat Bennett Johnson (Louisiana), holding out for tougher action.

Originally published in *Commentary,* May 1995, 36–43.

*National Center for History in the Schools, *National Standards for World History: Exploring Paths in the Present* and *National Standards of United States History: Exploring the American Experience,* Charlotte Crabtree and Gary B. Nash, project codirectors (University of California at Los Angeles, 1994).

Does this mean that the national history standards are dead? As a federal guide to state school boards, perhaps. But the fact remains that the standards reflect a consensus of the historical profession on what and how children should be taught. Indeed, they reflect what our children are *already* taught in schools across the country, and are sure to influence future authors of textbooks as well. If liberal academics suffer at all from this affair, it will result not from the Senate's wet blanket, but from their own triumphalism in publicizing what had heretofore been a quiet conquest of America's schoolrooms.

Among critics of the standards, Lynne Cheney, former head of the NEH and thus the person who, ironically enough, had assigned management of the project to UCLA's National Center for History in Schools, fired the first shot in this latest battle of the culture wars. Imagine, she wrote in an October 1994 *Wall Street Journal*, an outline of history that pays more attention to the founding of the Sierra Club than to George Washington. Or that invites students to celebrate the "grandeur" of Mansa Musa's West African kingdom while focusing its discussion of Europe on persecution, imperialism, and the slave trade. Or that makes seventeen references to the Ku Klux Klan but only one to Ulysses S. Grant, the man who saved the Union, and none to Thomas Edison, who changed the fundamental relationship between man and nature. In Cheney's view, the standards "save their unqualified admiration for people, places, and events that are politically correct"; she judges that the project went off the rails because revisionist historians took heart from the 1992 election of Bill Clinton and "iced out" those with more traditional views.

Following Cheney, columnists like Charles Krauthammer, Patrick J. Buchanan, and John Leo, and historians like John P. Diggins and Elizabeth Fox-Genovese, complained that the standards denigrate Western civilization and always depict non-Western ones in a favorable light. They adduced more examples: the standards invite students to appreciate Aztec "architecture, skills, labor system, and agriculture," but ignore the Aztec religion of human sacrifice; depict Genghis Khan through the eyes of a papal legate whose cultural biases pupils are told to discern; ask students to indict John D. Rockefeller; assess Ronald Reagan as "an agent of selfishness"; and contrast the ecological virtue of Native American culture with Europeans' rapacious industrialism.

For their part, defenders of the standards accused conservatives of forming an opinion on the basis of a few "howlers" so often repeated that one had reason to ask whether the critics had really read the volumes. "Even a cursory look," wrote Jon Wiener, "suggests that the assault by Cheney and Co. was flawed." Wiener saw no "preferential treatment of women and minorities." Perhaps Washington's and Edison's names do not appear where one might expect, but students could hardly avoid them while doing assignments on the American Revolution and great inventors. In any case, counting references proves nothing, since the *most* mentioned name turns out to be Richard Nixon's. (One need not wonder why.)

William H. McNeill, a revered dean of world historians, denied "anti-Western bias," and insisted that our children need to know about our "global past" and the "variety of peoples and groups that played a part in the development of the U.S." Finally, the *New York Times* accused critics of misrepresentation: "Liberal bias creeps into, perhaps, a couple dozen of the 2,600 sample lessons."

How can a responsible citizen judge this artillery duel? One way is to take the word of the columnist whose politics most resemble one's own, but to do so means simply reinforcing one's prejudices. The opposite response is to say, in effect, "a pox on both your houses." After all, history has no epistemology comparable to the natural sciences; it is a function of selection and viewpoint, and hence can never be wholly objective. Moreover, each generation rewrites history according to new information, methodologies, and its own search for a "usable past." So why not declare, with Tolstoy, that history is "a collection of fables," or with Mark Twain that it is just "fluid prejudice"?

Why not? Because cynicism, unfortunately, is a sure-fire sign that a nation is losing the will to sustain itself. A people's history is the record of its hopes and travails, birthright and education, follies and wisdom, and all else that binds it together. A nation grown cynical about its own history soon ceases to be a nation at all.

So I concluded that in order to form a discriminating opinion of the standards, I must read them in their entirety and attempt to come to grips with not only the political but perhaps especially the educational issues they raise. Having done so, I ask my critics in turn to consider the substance, and not just the source, of what follows.

The two books of standards begin with almost identical chapters describing the purpose of the overall project. On the first page a tension erupts between two italicized reasons why history matters: first, because "*Knowledge of history is the precondition of political intelligence*"; second, because "*History is the only laboratory we have in which to test the consequences of thought.*"

The first formula, though undeniable, is almost an invitation to teachers to abuse classroom instruction as a ploy to help children make "intelligent" political choices. The second formula is a corrective, inasmuch as the consequences of ideas have so often been terrible. The test of the standards is thus whether a healthy tension is maintained between the two formulas, or whether in fact the lessons are long on "presentist" allusions and short on the perils of ideology. We shall see.

The introduction also describes the skills that students ought to acquire. Historical memory is labeled the key to our connectedness with all humankind. History should teach us to see matters through others' eyes, without requiring that we approve or forgive. Standards should be demanding, and promote active questioning rather than passive absorption. Standards should be applied to *all* students equally; no "dumbed-down" curricula that deny equal opportunity to large numbers of children. Standards should be rooted in chronology and teach students to apprehend patterns and cause-and-effect relationships. Standards should strike a balance between broad themes and specific events. Standards should impart the values of rigorous scholarship such as evaluation of evidence, logical argument, interpretive balance, comparative analysis, comprehension, and "issues-analysis and decision-making." Finally, students should apply these "thinking skills" to their own lives in order "to detect bias, to weigh evidence, and to evaluate argument, thus preparing them to make sensible, independent judgments, to sniff out spurious appeals to history by partisan pleaders, and to distinguish between anecdote and analysis."

Who could not applaud a school that trains children—*all* children—in all these ways? But what are the chances any school could do so? Consider asking high school students not only to read their homework assignment with a modicum of understanding but then to do the following with it:

- Identify the source of a historical document and assess its credibility.
- Contrast the differing values, behaviors, and institutions involved.
- Differentiate between historical facts and interpretations.
- Consider multiple perspectives of various people.
- Analyze cause-and-effect relationships and multiple causes.
- Challenge arguments of historical inevitability.
- Compare competing historical narratives.
- Hold interpretations of history as tentative.
- Evaluate major debates among historians.
- Hypothesize the influence of the past.

This splendid instructional guide for a dissertation defense is what the standards aim to require of all fifth to twelfth graders, including those we used to regard as in need of remedial help or as underprivileged. In practice, this curriculum would overtax the capabilities of most *teachers,* not to mention pupils, with the result that 90 percent of the students would flunk, or else (more likely) 100 percent would pass, under the "Wizard of Oz" syndrome.

("You're just as smart as anyone else," the Wizard said to the Scarecrow. "The only thing you don't have is a degree.")

Diane Ravitch has argued that the notion of standards does not mean "dragging down the students at the top, but expecting more of all students, especially those who are in the bottom half." But insofar as that equality plank is invoked to abolish "elitist" segregation of advanced students from those who are variously "challenged"—indeed, the notion that history should nurture self-esteem among women and minorities informs the standards throughout—one has reason to wonder whether the standards will have the impact Ravitch desires.

In the world standards, history is divided into eight eras, the first of which covers prehistory up to 4000 B.C.E., the second up to 1000 B.C.E., the third up to 300 C.E., the fourth up to 1000, the fifth up to 1500, the sixth 1450 to 1770, the seventh up to 1914, and the last the twentieth century.

Each era contains a certain number of standards, and each standard is elaborated, in turn, in subheads describing subjects to be covered. Finally, each list of subheads is followed by study lessons deemed suitable for grades five through six, seven through eight, or nine through twelve. The lessons number well over a thousand—a measure, perhaps of their author's determination not to appear to discriminate against any civilization or era.

Few would dispute that American students today need to learn about other cultures. Historians like McNeill were arguing the case for world history long before "multiculturalism" came along. Accordingly, the standards' general guidelines mandate that courses "should treat the history and values of diverse civilizations, including those of the West, and should especially address the interactions among them." But inasmuch as the standards assume that world history will take the place of the old "Plato to NATO" Western Civilization course, it is legitimate to ask, as the critics do, whether the standards "privilege" *non*-Western histories, thereby reversing rather than righting the wrong.

As I worked my way through the eight eras, I did get an impression that the West was slighted. So I made a tally of the 109 subheads, dividing them into columns labeled "Western," "Non-Western," and "Interactive" (which usually entailed relations between "the West and the rest"). I counted the ancient Mediterranean as Western, pre-Columbian America as non-Western and post-Columbian as Western except when Latin America was lumped with the third world. The rest of the rubrics lent themselves to easy triage.

The results surprised me. Western history won out over non-Western by a margin of 43 percent to 35 percent, with Interactive garnering 23 percent. If we award the West a 40-percent share of the Interactive sections, the overall balance is almost 50-50; that is, half the material covers what we think of as Western Civ, and half the rest of the world put together. If, in practice, students are obliged to take only one year-long course in world history, *every* culture would be slighted. But if students spend four or more semesters on world history, as the standards recommend, then the 50-50 division is commendable. It all depends on what is taught about the civilizations and the interactions among them.

One more introductory note. A peculiar feature of the world standards is the labeling of sub-standards as either "core" or "related." On first thought, this technique seems a useful aid for teachers deciding what to stress during precious class time. But on second thought, the curriculum is so all-encompassing that most teachers will probably not pay any attention to related subjects; they will just toss them out with a sigh of relief. And that means genuine loss in the few cases when seemingly indispensable subjects are inexplicably stamped Related.

One such case appears in the standard on Ancient Greece. Athenian democracy (and its "limitations") are core. So, too, is the expansion of Hellenic culture by Alexander the Great. But the "major cultural achievements of Greek civilization" and the Greek wars with the Persian empire are merely related. Thus, students learn (1) that Athenian democracy was flawed (by slavery, class oppression, and patriarchy), and (2) that otherwise Greek civilization is notable only for the militarism that coopted it and set off to rule the world. Is this meant to serve as a "distant mirror" of American history? Perhaps not consciously. But the authors do consciously render as optional all of Greek art, science, and philosophy, the spread of which is why Alexander was important in the first place, as well as the moving tale of Thermopylae, when the West first united to defend itself against an Eastern tyranny—not to mention the birth of history itself in the works of Thucydides and Herodotus.

My suspicion is that the project directors invented the category of Related in order to ease compromise among committee members pressing their own specialties and those determined to keep the standards manageable. "OK, OK," says the weary chairman, "the 'influence of the T'ang Dynasty on Southeast Asia' is in, but only if it's related . . ." At which point the China scholar barks. "Do you have any idea how crucial the T'ang is to Asian history? Besides, Europe got three cores and no relateds last time. If you're going to call the T'ang related, then make early medieval Europe related, too." And so it is.

A second potential source of distortion is the standards' determination to give all cultures equal time. Thus, while the overall balance is defensible, some particular equations seem absurd. Standard 3 in Era 3, for example, covers the rise of major religions *and* empires in Eurasia from 500 B.C.E. to 300 C.E. Does this mean what it says? Are the Roman empire and the first Chinese and Indian dynasties lumped together in a single standard with the origins of Christianity, Buddhism, and Confucianism? Yes! In the meantime, standard 4 is wholly devoted to "the achievements of Olmec civilization," a *core* subject. Such "symmetrical asymmetries" permeate the major standards.

One surprising slight is the deemphasis on the history of ideas. This may not have been deliberate; it may be another perverse side effect of inclusiveness. If everyone is to be covered, then everything *about* everyone cannot be. But to omit huge chunks of philosophy, science, and art not only contradicts the stance against "dumbed-down" curricula, it renders incomprehensible other broad swaths of history. For instance, the standard for nineteenth-century Europe covers nationalism and social movements but labels "technological, scientific, and intellectual achievements" related. Ditto for "new departures in science and the arts . . . between 1900 and 1940." It would seem that the authors do not deem the revolutions in power and work wrought by thermodynamics, chemicals, electricity, internal combustion, modern medicine, and nuclear physics to be central to the task of teaching what the twentieth-century experience is all about.

What is more, a student restricted to core standards might well escape high school without ever being exposed to the ideas of Mill, Marx (he appears once, so do not play hooky that day), Darwin, Nietzsche, Freud, and Einstein. Nor do any of the study plans appear to explain the origins and nature of ideology. How then can students comprehend the relativism and totalitarianism that are defining features of "modern times"? How, indeed, can they "test the consequences of thought," as the standards' introduction promises they will?

According to the *Times,* the real "treasures" are found not in the outline of history but "among the 2,500 assignments that accompany the standards." In fact, many of these "examples of student achievement" are pedagogically silly, whatever their ideological slant. No treasures are buried among the assignments designed to make the classroom "crackle" with mock trials, debates, and play-acting. Such ploys are artificial, time-consuming, and often boring to students not directly involved. Moreover, no one but an expert could "recreate a *tertulia*, or social gathering, held by women leaders such as Maria Josefa Ortiz" without the script being written for him.

Nor are treasures found among assignments that are impossibly difficult for most high-schoolers ("Research the core and periphery thesis of Immanuel Wallerstein"), impossibly time-consuming ("Using books like *The Scarlet Pimpernel* and *A Tale of Two Cities,* assess the accuracy of such literary accounts in describing the French Revolution"), or simply impossible ("Write a dialogue between a Muslim and a Hindu on what they see as the reasons for the spread of Christian missions, what the impact will be on their faiths, and how best to resist the appeals of Christian missionaries"). Crackle, snore, or make things up?

One common criticism of the assignments is that they always look at events from the point of view of the downtrodden and their self-appointed spokesmen. The truth is more subtle than that.

Some sections in which one would expect to encounter a "devil theory" (for example, nineteenth-century European imperialism) are in fact circumspect. Some are bizarre: of the twenty assignments on World War II, five address the Holocaust, three address children, three more address children *in* the Holocaust, and four raise moral objections to *Allied* bombing. Others are skewed: enslavement of Africans and slave revolts are mentioned repeatedly, always in core standards (the Haitian rebellion appears in three separate contexts), but the American abolitionist movement is "related" and slavery in other cultures is not mentioned at all. Still other lessons are deafening in their silence: China's Taiping rebellion—a slaughter on the scale of World War I—is discussed only in terms of "rural poverty," and Communist Chinese purges and famines—slaughter on the scale of World War II—are ignored with the exception of one eighth-grade assignment inquiring after the results of the Cultural Revolution.

So it is true that non-Western cultures are given a moral pass, but with one exception: their treatment of women. If any consistent ideological thread runs through the world standards, it is feminism. Over and over again, whether the subject is ancient Rome, Christian Europe, the Islamic world, China (footbinding gets repeated coverage), India, or Mesoamerica, students are prompted to ask "what obstacles [women] faced," "what opportunities were open to them," "what life choices were available," and "in what ways were women subordinate?"

Nowadays few would argue against the inclusion of hefty doses of women's history so long as the subject is not a fig leaf for ahistorical ideology. But who can doubt that boys and girls are expected to conclude from the above questions that: women have always and everywhere been suppressed; they undoubtedly hated their lot; and the cause of this universal phenomenon was . . . what? Ah, there is the crux of the matter. Was it due to the physical exigencies of child-bearing, or the economic exigencies of child-rearing, in preindustrial societies? Or because a sexual division of labor was taken for granted by most women as well as men? No: the promptings invariably invite students to conclude (or be told) that sexual roles were always a function of patriarchy backed by theology.

Which brings us to religion, another hot button. Perhaps to avoid the risk of offending Bible Belt school districts, the authors do not hold up Christianity for explicit assault, nor do they ridicule other world religions (except in regard to their dogma on women). But close reading reveals some interesting tendencies. Judaism is reduced repeatedly to "ethical monotheism"; the prophets and messianic promise are absent, and Moses is not mentioned by name until a query concerning his place in the Qu'ran. The teachings of Jesus and Paul are likewise described in ethical terms and compared to Buddhism. The Gospel is absent. The defining debate over Iconoclasm in Byzantine history is absent. The role of Benedictine monasteries in the founding of European civilization is "related" (so the "Dark Ages" are condemned to remain dark). The Crusades are treated at length, but not as the belated Christian *counter*offensive they were. The Reformation lessons contain *one* question on the theology of Luther and Calvin. And although Jews appear in various contexts, Judaism as a historical force disappears.

So religion is treated as ethics—ethics betrayed, moreover, as soon as believers attribute them to a transcendental source. It should therefore come as no surprise that the finale—the last assignment in the entire world standards—asks pupils to "define 'liberation theology' and explain the ideological conflicts surrounding the philosophy." The true "end of history": liberation theology! Or is it not a theology but an ideology? Or a philosophy? The confusion about what distinguishes these three categories may be the authors' most chilling shortcoming of all.

In short, the world standards are pretty much what one would expect from a committee. For all their balance between West and non-West, and their laudable stress on cultural interaction, they are too inclusive, difficult, tendentious, or ahistorical. A brilliant, tireless teacher *might* walk an elite class through this material in two or three years. Even then, I doubt whether students could explain why Western civilization became the only universal one; why science, technology, freedom—and prosperity beyond the dreams of Kublai Khan—arose in the West, and not elsewhere; why at length the West fell into a long civil war, and why the totalitarians lost.

Am I then suggesting that students should be taught to honor Western civilization, despite its history of wars and oppression, and despite the contributions of other cultures? I am. The decency of life in the next generation may depend on it.

In the context of American history, the functional equivalent of multiculturalism is "diversity." According to their critics, the authors of the U.S. standards were so determined to celebrate diversity that they ended up, in Diane Ravitch's words, "accentuating *'pluribus'* while downplaying *'unum.'*" The alleged result is a curriculum that goes out of its way to mention the struggles of "marginalized" groups at the expense of what used to be thought the central narrative of American history.

To be sure, the standards' criteria themselves mention the importance of commonalities, but only as an afterthought: "Standards for United States history should reflect both the nation's diversity exemplified by race, ethnicity, social and economic status, gender, region, politics, and religion, and the nation's commonalities." The last include "our common civic identity and shared civic values," "democratic political system," and the (question-begging) "struggle to narrow the gap between [our] ideals and practices." Nowhere do the standards suggest that conflict between equality and liberty is the defining fact of American history.

Having read the criticisms, I expected the authors to give short shrift to politics in favor of social and cultural history. So I did another content analysis. To begin with, the U.S. standards divide our national story into ten eras with the breaks coming at 1620 (arrival of the pilgrims); 1763 (end of the French and Indian Wars); 1801 (end of the Federalist period); 1861 (Civil War); 1877 (end of Reconstruction); 1900 (U.S. emergence as world power); 1930 (onset of the Depression); 1945 (end of World War II); and 1968. These watersheds conform to traditional periodization, and the temporal coverage (with its halfway point at 1877) is also conventional. Each era is then defined by standards (two to four, in the U.S. case) and sub-standards listing the topics students are expected to master.

I totaled the 91 sub-standards according to both field (political, social, economic, and so on) and "group focus" (women, Native Americans, white males), splitting some standards in half when they focused on two groups or relations between them. It turns out that nearly 60 percent of the sub-standards cover politics and foreign policy, and traditional material, all told, comprises about 65 percent of the book. Not bad.

But let us turn the equation around: is not 35 percent a generous portion to attribute to the implicitly unique experiences of women and racial minorities, especially when virtually no space is devoted to the unique experiences of Irish, Germans, Italians, or Jews? My own sense is that, while issues of "race, class, and gender" probably are overrepresented, the basic political narrative is still there. So the question hinges again on what "spin" it is given.

The spin is spun on the first page of the first standard, when fifth and sixth graders are asked to compare Native American ideas on "how the land should be used" with those of Europeans. In the seventh and eighth grades, students ask whether Native American societies were "primitive" at all, or whether they had not in fact "developed complex patterns of social organization, trading networks, and political culture." The true answer to this false dichotomy is: yes, the Amerindian tribes had social conventions, trade, and politics—what human beings do not?—but, yes, they were primitive and certainly just as capable of aggression toward aliens (and one another) as any other race. But that is not the answer suggested for Native Americans, or for West Africans, who are likewise celebrated for their high culture and "attitudes toward nature and the use of the land."

Enter Columbus. Now, Spanish and English practices toward Amerindians and Africans are ugly pages of history that need to be read. But they need to be read *as history*, which is to say that students need to enter the heads of the historical actors. Imagine you were a sixteenth-century Spaniard who happened upon an Aztec temple bristling with horrific idols and priests carving out the living hearts of men. Would you have any doubt that you had stumbled on to Satan's own kingdom? Can you imagine the carnage if the *Aztecs* had managed to equip themselves with galleons and guns and sailed off to Portugal or West Africa? That Europeans were greedy hypocrites goes without saying. The crime against history is for the authors to pretend that non-Western cultures were somehow pristine.

Why the pretense? The answer appears explicitly in the introduction to Era 2: while learning about European decimation of Native Americans and enslavement of Africans, "students should also recognize that Africans and Native Americans were not simply victims, but were intricately involved in the creation of colonial society and a new, hybrid American culture." In other words, the spin is there to raise the self-esteem of minority students: yes, you are victims, but you also have great value. And to raise the consciousness of white students: you owe much, in both senses of the word, to people of color.

The historiography of self-esteem also demands a pecking order. I was surprised at first that the standards follow their indictment of the Spaniards with assignments questioning England's "black legend" about the evils of Catholic Spain. Then I understood: Hispanics, too, are victims, so long as their accusers are WASPs.

The standards on the American Revolution have been the subject of particular acrimony. One accusation—that they do not pay attention to the colonists' struggle to "bring forth a new nation"—is not borne out. There is plenty of material on the Revolutionary War and Constitution. What strikes me as idiosyncratic is how *Tory* it is. Students are repeatedly asked whether the English Parliament's position on taxation was not in fact reasonable, whether the colonies' resistance was really justified, how a Loyalist would have viewed the Intolerable Acts, whether a break with England was inevitable.

A conspiracy theorist might see here a bias against liberty. But the real flaw in the treatment is, once again, ahistoricity. Thus, four of the five sub-standards covering the Revolution's effects deal with the contributions and frustrations of slaves, Native Americans, and women. As the introduction explains, the Revolution "called into question long-established social and political relationships—between master and slave, man and woman, upper class and lower class, officeholder and constituent, and even parent and child—and thus demarcated an agenda for reform that would preoccupy Americans down to the present day." And so, "students need to confront the central issue of how revolutionary the Revolution actually was."

Well, how revolutionary was it? To be sure, women in revolutionary America were not given the vote. But in how many countries could *anyone* vote in 1776 or, for that matter, 1876? The slaves were not freed. But where else in the world did anguished debate over slavery occur at that time? The authors seem surprised by all that was commonplace, and take for granted all that was rare. So they ask students to seek explanations for the wrong data. It should not be surprising that eighteenth-century Virginia planters owned slaves. What is striking is the fact that these rustic colonials wrote the Declaration of Independence, Constitution, and *The Federalist Papers,* and made advances in self-government and human dignity that amazed and shook the Atlantic world.

Finally, what "agenda" was it that the standards say was "demarcated," and by whom? The nature of the "agenda" is no mystery, because it reappears in every later era. For the 1801–61 Era, the leitmotif is a quotation from Emerson: "What is man born for but to be a reformer" (as if no "reform" could possibly have negative consequences). Students are told to discover the "predecessors of social movements—such as the civil-rights movement and feminism" in the "attempts to complete unfinished agendas of the revolutionary period." The introduction to the Civil War warns against placing "[t]oo much stress on the unfinished agenda . . ." The one for the early twentieth century instructs students to be "fascinated with the women's struggle for equality . . ." The introduction to Era 8 concedes that "World War II deserves careful attention as well" because it "ushered in social changes that established reform agendas that would occupy the United States for the remainder of the 20th century." The introduction to Era 9 instructs teachers that post–World War II history "will take on deeper meaning when connected to the advent of the civil-rights and feminist movements that would become an essential part of the third great reform impulse in American history." Finally, the introduction to Era 10 "claims precedence" for the "reopening of the nation's gates to immigrants" and the "struggle to carry out environmental, feminist, and civil-rights agendas." Not surprisingly, given this abiding *agenda,* the "last word" in the U.S. standards is this: "Evaluate the effect of women's participation in sports on gender roles and career choices."

If, then, the U.S. standards are not grossly imbalanced in terms of coverage, they do explain the "deeper meaning" of American history in terms of minority and female struggle versus white male oppression. This is the *gnosis* a pupil must grasp to get good marks. Europeans braved the unknown to discover a new world, only to kill and oppress. Colonists carved a new nation out of the woods, only to displace Native Americans and impose private property. The "Founding Fathers" (the term has been banished) invoked human rights, only to deny them to others. Businessmen built the most prosperous nation in history, only to rape the environment and preside over a structure that put workers in misery.

Nowhere do the standards suggest that when aggrieved minorities have demanded justice, they have appealed to the very civic and religious principles bequeathed by our nation's architects. Nowhere do they suggest that women and minorities have striven not to overthrow what white men had built, but to share more abundantly in it. Nor do they mention that most women, most of the time, have identified with their fathers or husbands as farmers, clerks, or laborers, Democrats or Republicans, Southerners, Northerners, or Westerners, Protestants, Catholics, or Jews.

In most lessons women are just women, blacks are just blacks. Only once does an apparent reference to men as just men appear, in a question imagining the damage done to workers' self-esteem by unemployment during the Depression. But even then the gender-neutral term "heads of households" is substituted. Apparently there were no *men* in America's past. So who was oppressing women all those years?

I was especially skittish when I read the sections on foreign policy, expecting a neo-Marxist critique of American imperialism. In fact, the treatment of nineteenth-century diplomacy—the tale of Manifest Destiny—is instructive and balanced. The standards even pass up the chance to ridicule the War of 1812, one of the sillier episodes in American history, and they present a balanced portrait of the origins of the Mexican War. The section on the Spanish American War says too little about its roots in the Cuban revolt, but exposes students to a range of opinions on the U.S. colonial episode.

How strange, then, that a negative spin enters the text with Woodrow Wilson. First, students are invited to conclude that American neutrality was a sham. Then students are asked to explain why Americans dedicated to "'making the world safe for democracy' denied it to many of their citizens at home, actively prosecuted dissenters, and violated the civil liberties of nonconformists." Finally, Wilson's Fourteen Points are introduced for the purpose of asking whether he lived up to them when he intervened in

Russia, whether Germany was cheated when it agreed to an armistice on the basis of them, and whether they contributed to the failure of the Treaty of Versailles.

These are all legitimate issues. But they betray an ahistorical double standard that judges American *motives* by the most saintly ideals, while excusing or ignoring other nations' *deeds* on the grounds of necessity or differing values. Setting aside the question of accuracy, is it wise to teach gradeschoolers that Wilson was foolish or hypocritical to proclaim democracy, disarmament, self-determination, free trade, and a League of Nations to a war-ravaged world? Maybe the authors are just too eager to teach subtleties better saved for college. Or maybe they mean to answer *yes,* lest a new generation be seduced by patriotic rhetoric into new Vietnam-style crusades.

It gets much worse. The seventh- and eighth-grade standards for World War II say *nothing* about the nature or ideologies of the fascist regimes, but do ask students to assess American blame for going isolationist, and to consider the causes of American tension with Japan dating back to 1900. Thus prepared, ninth to twelfth graders will have no trouble answering, "Why did Japan set up the Co-Prosperity Sphere?" and whether the U.S. oil embargo was "an act of war" precipitating Pearl Harbor.

The four high school lessons on the conduct of the war cover (1) the Anglo-American delay in opening a second front and the Soviet role in defeating the Axis; (2) the Allied failure to respond to the Holocaust; (3) the extent to which Norman Rockwell's illustration of the Four Freedoms is an accurate portrayal of the American image; (4) the decision to use the atomic bomb. What are students to conclude when all their lessons call into question *Allied* conduct?

As for the standards on the effects of the war, these include questions on women workers, internment of the Japanese-Americans, the anti-Hispanic "zoot-suit" riots, the wartime contributions of African, Mexican, and Native Americans, and two more on the internment of the *nisei.* Millions of mothers and wives of servicemen, not to mention the (overwhelmingly white male) veterans themselves who risked their lives to destroy fascism, may wonder why there is no room for them.

The Cold War, defined as the morally neutral "swordplay of the Soviet Union and United States," is important not because this nation sacrificed for four decades to contain another totalitarian empire, but rather

> because it led to the Korean and Vietnam wars as well as the Berlin airlift, Cuban missile crisis, American interventions in many parts of the world, a huge investment in scientific research, and

> environmental damage that will take generations to rectify. It demonstrated the power of American public opinion in reversing foreign policy, it tested the democratic system to its limits, and it left scars on American society that have not yet been erased.

Accordingly, the lesson plans make no mention of Soviet expansion, or Soviet and Chinese totalitarianism and mass murder. Instead, one of three questions for grades five through six is about McCarthyism; three of five questions for grades seven through eight are about McCarthyism; and two of three questions for grades nine through twelve are about . . . McCarthyism, while the third asks students how "U.S. support for 'self-determination'" conflicted with "the USSR's desire for security" in Eastern Europe, and whether we threatened the Soviets through "atomic diplomacy."

So instructed, students would be hard-put to explain why the United States, Western Europe, Japan, and ultimately China joined hands in fear of the Soviet Union. So beset by red herrings, students would be easy prey for conspiracy theories linking the Cold War to hysterical anti-Communism or the military-industrial complex.

There may be no such thing as Truth-with-a-capital-T about complicated historical phenomena. But there is such a thing as discernible Falsehood. And the above is an example—with a capital F.

The standards came into existence because of the widespread realization that young people are largely ignorant of history. Now that the project has borne fruit, it is clear that people had different ideas as to what students are ignorant of. A parent of the older generation may be shocked that students do not know our first president. A professor from the sixties generation may be shocked that students do not "know" that the U.S. was at least equally at fault for the Cold War. An avatar of the "new history" may be shocked that students do not know Susan B. Anthony, and would rather discuss MTV.

The codirector of the standards project, Gary B. Nash of UCLA, says his benign purpose was to liberate pupils from the "prison of facts" that make history "boring." But facts are not imprisoning: they are all we have to *liberate* us from the tyranny of deception and opinion, our own as well as others'. Liberals used to believe that: it is terrifying to learn they no longer do. And as for history being boring, the fault for that lies, always, with the teacher. How can you possibly make the French Revolution boring?

Let us be honest. These standards are too demanding for most *college* surveys. They are offensive to all who value the exceptional achievements of the American experiment. They will even fail to advance the cause of the politically correct, and that is because they aim to debunk historical myths that have not been imparted to this generation in the first place. Ghetto blacks and valley girls are not going to have their consciousness raised. They will simply imbibe (or ignore) a new myth concocted by a new "over-thirty" elite.

What is more, the standards' droning critique of white, middle-class American men may provoke an intellectual backlash as earnest (if not as violent) as the student revolts of the sixties. The authors of the standards may not realize this because (I suspect) they are still aiming their arrows at their own parents and teachers from the fifties and sixties. But they are hitting the kids of today between the eyes.

Those kids are bleeding. I see it every semester in my Ivy League classrooms. Graduate students who are ignorant of the bare skeleton of the historical narrative. Honor students who cannot write grammatical English. Average students who cannot write, do not read, and will not think. Or are intimidated. Or handicapped by self-hatred, self-righteousness, second-hand anger, or cynicism. The youth of Athens, corrupted.

My plea to high school teachers is this: Forget the politics—forget *your* politics. Just make sure your graduates can read and write, know some geography, and know when the Civil War happened. For if they do, then college professors will have something to build on. As it is now, we spend much of our time conveying basic facts, correcting writing, and debunking the reverse myths so widely taught in high schools: "No, Mr. Slackoff, we did not drop the atomic bomb on Japan rather than Germany because we were racist. The first atomic test did not occur until two months after Germany surrendered. Meanwhile, do you know what a dangling participle is?"

The battle of standards is part of a larger war: Donald Kagan's fight for Western Civ at Yale; the Enola Gay exhibit at the Smithsonian; the politicization of the American Historical Association, which voted in 1982 to condemn the Reagan defense buildup on the learned conclusion that it would provoke nuclear war. In light of this melee, the notion that nationally mandated standards are wise is mad. I agree with Hanna Gray, president emeritus of the University of Chicago, when she writes that "certification" of a version of history is "contrary to every principle that should animate the free discussion of 'knowledge.'" But she ducks one point. Children will be exposed to one textbook, one teacher. They *will* have standards imposed on them. So the question remains: who chooses?

I have no instrumental solution. But I do know that none will work unless educators remember their calling, which is to impart not attitudes, feelings, or even convictions, but knowledge and wisdom. These are hard to acquire, harder still to impart. But they are what breed success, and success is what breeds self-esteem. That is why the late Carl Becker, whose high school text first hooked me on history, and a liberal at a time when liberals still honored liberty, dedicated his otherwise "Eurocentric" *Modern History*

TO ALL TEACHERS
OF WHATEVER RACE OR COUNTRY
OF WHATEVER PERSUASION
WHO WITH SINGLENESS OF PURPOSE
HAVE ENDEAVORED TO INCREASE KNOWLEDGE
AND PROMOTE WISDOM IN THE WORLD.

PART V

HISTORIANS AT WORK

THE HISTORICAL SOCIETY proceeds with the conviction that the quality of historical scholarship does not depend upon the politics of the historian—that honest, engaging, and illuminating history can be written from different political and ideological points of view. Demonstrably, politics and ideology influence historical scholarship, but they should not trump or supplant the fundamental canons of the historian's craft, which historians of differing perspectives observe. Respect for the canons of the craft does not dictate one or another historical topic or method. A wit once quipped that there are no dull subjects, only dull authors. The same may be said for methods. Respect for diplomatic, military, or economic history does not preclude respect for social or cultural history. Different methods appeal to different historians just as different topics do, and the richest historical understanding depends upon contributions from all of them.

The essays in this section offer selected examples of the variety of topics and methods that engage diverse talents. The relations among the various essays, in the measure that they do relate to each other, derive from the authors' common respect for the evidence and for the relation between the evidence and the interpretation or argument. The essays focus upon different topics and rely upon different methods to propose new perspectives on familiar historical questions.

In "Capitalism and Socialism in the Emergence of Modern America: The Formative Era, 1890–1961," Martin J. Sklar offers a bold interpretation of the symbiosis of socialism and capitalism in recent American history. Sklar argues that during the years in which the large corporate enterprise has become the dominant feature of the political economy, American society "has evolved as a mixture of capitalism and socialism." In Sklar's reading, capitalism and socialism, whether in conflict or in symbiosis, have intertwined across the divides of class and industry, as well as within them. For capitalism needs socialism for stability, while socialism needs capitalism to generate the wealth to support expanding egalitarianism, which in turn depends upon noncapitalist investment in social programs. In combination, socialism and capitalism have joined with liberal democracy to foster a distinct "corporate liberalism." One striking feature of this development lies in the bipartisan support it has garnered, captured in the "continuing glacial leftward shift" of both the Republican and Democratic parties. Few readers will demur from Sklar's choice of Bill Clinton as one of the main leaders of this leftward shift in party politics and political culture, but his choice of Newt Gingrich as the other may strike many as less obvious.

Sklar's essay not merely challenges the instinctive tendency to view socialism and capitalism as inherently antagonistic, but suggests that as corporations expanded their hold on the American economy, they themselves became "as much socialist as capitalist entities." Sklar's arresting interpretation of recent American history as a distinct combination of socialism and capitalism runs counter to the prevailing wisdom that the United States has consistently resisted the lure of socialism. Sklar reminds us of the dangers of taking political rhetoric at face value and of interpreting political culture in isolation from economic and business history. For the engineers of the distinct American combination of capitalism and socialism tended to be precisely those who publicly denounced socialism as a threat to American freedom and prosperity.

Just as a single-minded focus upon ideological considerations has led some historians to posit a natural opposition between socialism and capitalism, so has it led others to posit similar oppositions between religion and science and between women and men. In "Center and Periphery in the History of Science," Miriam Levin challenges these facile assumptions by close attention to the development of scientific education in western New England during the nineteenth century. Part of the confusion, Levin suggests, may be attributed to historians' unfortunate tendency to banish science to the periphery of their concerns. Relocating it to the center of her inquiry, Levin demonstrates that, during the early nineteenth century, it played an influential role in the development of educational institutions for women as well as for men. The career of Mary Lyon, founder of Mt. Holyoke, offers a clear illustration of the way in which scientific education intertwined with the social change attendant upon early industrialization, the early efforts to provide systematic education for young women, and the Evangelical clergy's adaptation to both in the wake of the Second Great Awakening.

Mary Lyon and the teachers of Mt. Holyoke pioneered in an educational project that brought science into women's classrooms, but brought it in under the direct aegis of Evangelical men. These teachers, beginning with Mary Lyon herself, saw no conflict between science and religion, which they took to complement one another as manifestations of God's plan. Nor did the male Evangelical teachers and ministers (frequently the same person) oppose the plan of educating women in science. Indeed, they countenanced and presided over it, normally providing the lectures themselves. The women teachers for their part easily accepted this male leadership, especially since they found that the men retained such decorum with respect to female anatomy that they and their students could discuss the lessons in comfort and without risk to modesty. Above all, however, Levin suggests that the female teachers valued highly their participation in a kind of partnership with the men, which drew them into central intellectual currents of their day.

Levin's essay reveals a world in which scientific education took shape within the Evangelical fold rather than in opposition to it and in which women consolidated their claims to education and to independence in conjunction with men rather than in struggle against them. This world, she argues, is one in which the development of science—and the need for scientific education—ranks as a central, not a peripheral, feature, conjoining the interdependence of industrialization, education, women's changing roles and opportunities, and Evangelical Protestantism.

Sklar's and Levin's essays have an explicitly theoretical cast, although substantial research and careful assessment of evidence figure prominently in their discussions. In "Work in the Moctezuma Brewery," John Womack embeds his theoretical concerns in a lush proliferation of detail. It would be hard to find a better example of what Clifford Geertz calls "thick description," short of a novel by Charles Dickens or Honoré de Balzac. Nothing, however, would be further from the mark than to view Womack's essay as purely empirical. Close readers will rapidly recognize that the profusion of empirical detail itself embodies an implicit commentary upon the practice and possibilities of labor history. After a concise summary of the economic role and significance of the Moctezuma Brewery, Womack turns directly to the process of production. His discussion is characterized throughout by its exquisite precision, whether with respect to quantities produced, forms of bottling, temperatures of brewing and storage, or any of the myriad of tasks that production required. The accumulation of detail in turn creates an aura of immediacy that invites the reader's direct participation. Imperceptibly, the brewery begins to come alive, drawing the reader into its rhythms and imperatives.

The sense of seamless flow, however engaging, can nonetheless deceive. For at strategic points, Womack interjects indications of the theoretical issues he is engaging and elucidating. From the start, we know that the work takes place in a "modern factory" of several large buildings spread across seven or eight acres, although it is left to us to remember that the "modern" in question is 1908. Shortly thereafter, Womack alerts us to other complications, noting that "only in finishing its product did this factory function on a classic factory system." The ensuing descriptions of the work offer constant reminders that modernity in Mexico of 1908 had many characteristics of what we might think of as a "traditional" world. Subsequently, it becomes clear that Womack is evoking a world that, even on its own terms, was torn between old and new. For at Moctezuma, the definitive work of brewing and fermenting "was a combination and succession of mechanical, chemical, and biological operations. However orderly, precise, industrial, it remained the practice of an ancient art."

The masters of this art, the brewmaster and the master mechanic, who made the cold upon which the success of the brewmaster's brews depended, combined in their work both the old and the new. Only upon the word of the brewmaster could a batch of beer be considered "done," which meant that for the workers, both day and night were "irregular, arbitrary, and indefinite." Womack notes the oddity that one of this factory's processes of production, namely fermentation, "required the adoption and development of a life." In a further oddity, the same process required a considerable span of time and could not be rushed. The development of life followed a slow linear trajectory that could not be adapted to the normal pattern of industrial production, simultaneous work on different parts of the final product. Intuitively, linearity suggests modernity—or at least a modern notion of progress—yet that linearity bound the brewery, notwithstanding its modern attributes, to the cyclical patterns of nature. Thus did traditional rhythms inscribe their claims upon the work of the "modern" factory.

Womack's essay abounds in the ironies and ambiguities that enthrall many postmodernist historians who emphasize the "literary turn" in historical studies, but frequently elude social and labor historians. In this case, however, the ironies are not teased from texts by critics and theorists, they abide in the minutiae of the process of production. Only through the most painstaking research that permits a recreation of a previous world in all its particulars can a historian make them visible to us. Lewis Ferleger and Richard Steckel invite us to grasp this problem from the other end, namely through a consideration of the appropriate historical uses of the literary text.

Ferleger and Steckel start from the observation that William Faulkner's dense representation of the nineteenth- and twentieth-century South has decisively colored many people's vision of southern society. Faulkner, they note, consistently offered a picture of Southerners as unhealthy and mal- or undernourished. Throughout his fiction, Faulkner describes Southerners as excessively given to alcohol and tobacco consumption and as variously puny or obese. These descriptions have found an uncritical welcome among the many Americans, southern and northern alike, who willingly view the South as backward, underdeveloped, and unhealthy. Notwithstanding the resilient grip of this picture upon our imagination, nothing in the hard data provides evidence for it.

Ferleger and Steckel guide the reader through the kind of data that permits us to test the plausibility of Faulkner's representation of the South. Their review of available statistics on mortality, diet, per capita income, and related indicators discloses a gold mine of information that social and cultural historians often neglect. On the basis of this data, they demonstrate that during the years that Faulkner evokes in his fiction, southern Americans, black and white, were in as good, if not better, physical condition and enjoying as long, if not longer, lives than their northern counterparts. Furthermore, during the same years, the southern economy was growing more rapidly than the northern, southern men were marginally taller (an important indicator of health) than northern, and many Southerners were still benefiting from the advantages of a largely rural society, namely access to fish, game, and fresh vegetables.

Faulkner, Ferleger and Steckel contend, demonstrably got it wrong. The question remains why. This question rejoins their essay to those of Sklar, Levin, and Womack in a devastating, if muted, critique of ideologically driven or purely relativist theories of history. The case of Faulkner's evocation of the South makes the point dramatically. Ferleger and Steckel evoke the words of another economic historian, William O. Adydelotte, to make the general case that while novels may be helpful for understanding the opinions of an age, they are not a reliable guide to its conditions. Novels "show not the facts of the age, but the mind of the novelist, not social conditions, but attitudes toward social conditions." In this respect, Ferleger and Steckel remind us, "literature influences people's perceptions of the past and the present, as much through inaccuracy as accuracy."

These four essays offer engaging examples of how historians work. More important, they offer compelling evidence that historians can do their work and can do it with theoretical engagement, sensitivity to the diversity of experience and point of view, and attention to the complexity—and more than occasional unreliability—of evidence. By stretching the boundaries of their respective fields, these historians extend to us the promise that history ranks among the most demanding, challenging, and rewarding of crafts. And that those who respect the demands and wrestle with the challenges will extend and deepen our understanding of the past on its terms and hence enliven our imaginations about the possibilities of today.

CHAPTER 22

CAPITALISM AND SOCIALISM IN THE EMERGENCE OF MODERN AMERICA

THE FORMATIVE ERA, 1890–1916

Martin J. Sklar

The period 1890–1916 marked the rise and early development of corporate capitalism as the dominant property-production system or mode of production in the political-economic history of the United States. This same period also marked a great age of reform in social relations, politics, institutions, culture, and thought. Corporate enterprise and social reform have continued their fellow-traveling ever since.

Social change in this period inaugurated an incessant interaction, both antagonistic and complementary, between capitalism and socialism that shaped and reshaped American society in the twentieth century. The continuing corporate reorganization of enterprise and of the national economy has in its essence involved the meshing of capitalism and socialism in an American society distinguished politically by liberal democracy.[1]

Business enterprise, narrowly construed, correlates strongly with the mode of production, broadly construed. As business historians well know, the study of enterprise is necessary, although not sufficient, for an under-

Originally presented at the Fifth International Week on the History of the Enterprise, December 1993. This version is significantly revised.

standing of the rapidly changing society of the modern world. Enterprise as such encompasses not simply business in the narrow sense, not simply profit and loss, organization and technique, input-throughput-output, but broad social relations of property, labor, class, sex, and culture. It encompasses contracts and law, statutes and jurisprudence, modes of consciousness and sensibilities.[2] The rise of corporate capitalism in the late nineteenth and early twentieth centuries may therefore be understood as also representing the early phases of a sociopolitical reconstruction of American society based upon a hybrid of capitalism and socialism in a liberal democracy.

"Capitalism," "socialism," and "liberal democracy" are better understood in historical context, which for immediate purposes refers to relations of property, labor, and class, along with their corresponding social movements and modes of consciousness in the United States from 1890 to 1916. Capitalism has characterized the United States while not a single vote has ever been cast for an American "Capitalist Party." By the same token, the relative paucity of votes for a "Socialist Party" does not mean that socialism has been absent from, or has not been a major characteristic of, American society. Similarly, the substance of liberal democracy is not simply a matter of professing and prescribing, but of evolving institutional and social relations.

"Capitalism" is not simply enterprise for gain which, throughout history, has characterized economic activity of many types, including the socialistic. Rather, a capitalist society and its characteristic property relations consist of widespread money-market relations in which production is generally for market exchange effected by money or monetary instruments as the medium and measure of exchange and as a store of effective demand for, and a legal claim upon, resources, products, and labor. More than this, "capitalism" denotes a society in which not only land, resources, and goods, but also labor power, appear in the market as objects of monetary exchange: labor power as a commodity in the form of wage labor. The prevalent investor-employer-manager function becomes personified in capitalists, property owners engaged in discretionary investment of money, time, and effort for private gain, whereas other basic labor functions appear as propertyless wage earners. Respectively, property owners and wage earners appear as great classes of society. Each exhibits diversity and hierarchy, but wage-earning labor is generally subordinate to capital in authority, power, and wealth in the enterprise and in society as a whole. But the wage laborer accrues payment, liberties, obligations, and liabilities, which differ or are absent from those that characterize those of the slave, the serf, or the self-employed. Wage labor is governed predominantly under principles of commutative justice with largely market-made work incentives. Capitalist property rights and market relations have constantly redefined, expanded, and limited individual rights in accordance with evolving class differences and custom, contractual relations, law, and government structures and functions.

In capitalist relations, principles of liberty and efficiency tend to broaden the sphere of individual initiative and authority as well as equalitarian values and behavior. Simultaneously, on behalf of concurrent principles of property rights and economic development, they tend to range themselves against emergent, ever broader standards of liberty, equality, and social justice. Modern capitalist relations, therefore, provoke crisis-building tensions from multiplying claims of liberty, equality, and development, which manifest themselves in class antagonisms, social movements, currents of thought, and politics. The American liberal democratic political system, with its cognate political culture, demands and usually gets political leaders who can navigate among the rival claims and reconcile them in evolving syntheses, subordinating some to others, or transforming the mixture and pattern of the claims altogether.

Modern socialism historically had its roots in social relations and modes of consciousness within and integral to capitalism, oriented toward (1) applying the principle of self-government, or self-control, to wage earners, not only to employers and the self-employed, in market relations; and (2) adapting market relations to social goals, hence to public policy, as determined not only in the market as such, but also in sociopolitical, or civic, spheres—that is, both in society and in government. It represented the principles of citizenizing the wage earner and civil-izing the economy. These socialist principles cohered with prevalent American political principles associated with republicanism and rooted in the traditions and experiences of the American Revolution; accordingly, they have always enjoyed strong standing in the American grain.

The strengthening of socialist tendencies in modern times has corresponded in the United States with capitalist industrialization. They spread and deepened with the rise of large-scale business enterprise, especially the large corporations that eventually severed the investor, owner, and managerial functions; with such social formations as agricultural cooperatives, modern credit systems, social insurance organizations, and trade unions; and with a growing, diversified wage-earning working class and a growing, diversified managerial and professional middle class. Socialist relations have appeared in political, associational, and contractual activity that seeks to provide an alternative to, or a means of redefining, property ownership. Such activity seeks to make the market socially accountable and responsible through political, social, and economic reordering that regulates, modifies, remedies, or displaces, market behavior and outcomes. It employs social policy determined in some cases contractually, civically, or associationally, and in other cases politically and governmentally—both in spheres in which policy may be determined in principle by socially engaged persons ("one person, one vote") and in market spheres in which policy may, in principle, be determined by dollar holdings ("one dollar, one vote").

Socialist relations have, accordingly, embraced principles of distributive justice to complement and modify principles of commutative justice, so as to conceive and treat workers not simply as "labor" (a market-made factor of production), but as human beings and citizens. In this view, instead of primarily market-made or negative work incentives, workers deserve an increasing weight of socially constituted or positive work incentives and socially "progressive" standards and conditions of living. Socialism, therefore, has corresponded with social relations, law, public policy, standards, and values that assert a broadening conception of human rights and the recasting of property rights and market behavior. These assertions emanate incessantly from such sources as trade unions, social movements, interest groups, churches, civic associations, and electoral activity, as well as initiatives within the business sphere itself. In sum, a citizen-associational stake in society increasingly supplements, refashions, or in some degree displaces the property stake, as an increasingly preponderant authority in society. Associational investment that serves such social goals or needs as health care, pensions, worker compensation, unemployment insurance, day care, occupational safety, and environmental protection significantly complements or constrains discretionary investment directed primarily toward the investors' private gain.

As socialist relations gain strength, associational and governmental investment, based on social goals or public policy, redirects, complements, or displaces discretionary investment for private gain. Capitalists, as society's sole or paramount investing, profit-accruing, enterprise-managing, and surplus-disposing agency, are increasingly regulated, directed, complemented, supplemented, or replaced by other agencies that range from government to public corporations, to trade unions and interest groups, to pension funds, philanthropic foundations, religious bodies, and other civic associations, not to mention groups of stockholders and professional managers within enterprises. Nonprofit sectors of society grow as fields of gainful employment, and along with them gainfully employed activity in social services, in policy formation, in ministering to people's wants and needs, and indeed in inventing and creating new wants and needs. These trends expand the realm of human discretion or freedom, although some of our latter-day tory-radicals denounce them as involving a deleterious "consumerism." Since consumerism is, properly speaking, an essential working-class principle, the abstemious-minded among middle-class intellectuals who disown it, at least in theory, may be less "pro-worker" than they think themselves to be.

As these trends grow stronger, people tend to hold their political leaders and government, rather than business leaders and business enterprise, primarily responsible for a well working and just economy characterized by prosperity, security, opportunity, development, and progress, for the people at large, not merely for the propertied and privileged. Prevalent political thinking, especially in public discourse, affirms the need to reconcile liberty *and* equality, efficiency *and* social justice, as conditions of development, instead of leaving them arrayed in mutual enmity. If the older Whig principle was that dominion or power follows wealth or property, socialism signifies the rise of a new, inverted Whig principle that wealth and income follow power—the power of the ballot, public opinion, law and litigation, civic and political organization.

During the twentieth century, while liberal democracy produced the broad political consensus that permitted and contained persistent class and social conflict, American society has developed along both the capitalist and socialist lines sketched above. With the emergence and development of large corporate enterprise as the prevalent characteristic of the political economy, American society has evolved as a mixture of capitalism and socialism, intertwined, both in conflict and in symbiotic service to one another, on different sides of class and institutional divides, as well as within and across them. Capitalism needs socialism for stability and civic development, and socialism needs capitalism for the wealth creation that generates and supports an ever expanding equalitarianism and noncapitalist investment and labor activity.

The large business corporation itself, representing an evolving mode of production or set of property-production relations, has constituted an embodiment of the mixture of capitalism and socialism.[3] It is a major ahistorically static mistake to think of corporations or business in general as simply capitalist in essential characteristics. The same may be said of trade unions, agricultural cooperatives, credit unions, pension funds, and countless other associations, institutions, and social movements. They all embody the capitalism-socialism mixture in their operations, goals, principles, and values. Socialist relations in modern society promote a democratic politics oriented strongly toward equalitarianism, social goals, and public functions, which become more and more integral to the workings of the economic system *per se.* An economic theory that ignores this civic and political dimension will be found wanting.

"Liberal democracy" as practiced in the United States, refers to a political order in which, in principle, society and not the state, is sovereign: The state serves society. Accordingly, government powers are established and limited by law, as determined largely by representative institutions and decisively enforced by an independent judiciary. This type of political order, with a government and society under the rule of law, recognizes individual liberties and rights embedded in and protected by constitutional and statute law. It restricts individual and social behavior according to law and rejects arbitrary or ad hoc government or party action. In principle, law and prevalent political and juridical thought and practice define the individual as the basic unit of society and the body politic, and rights and obligations remain fundamentally individual, not corporative. In the United States, the principle of positive government, as against state command, has matured within this political order. During much of America's first two hundred years, liberal democracy effectively excluded from citizenship African Americans, women, and others, but it became more inclusive as the twentieth century progressed, especially since midcentury, with the continuing development of corporate capitalism and the capitalism-socialism mix.

Insofar as modern liberalism is a species of "corporate liberalism," it is characterized in the United States by sociopolitical movements with a general outlook oriented toward making corporations and the market system serve the purposes of efficiency, innovation, and economic development, and oriented also toward reformist and socialist efforts at making corporations and the market system serve the causes of equal rights, equal liberties, and equal opportunities. In a broader perspective, "corporate liberalism" refers to the prevalent sociopolitical movements in the United States, which since the early twentieth century have operated incrementally to combine capitalism and socialism with liberal democracy. In so doing, these movements have constructed a vigorous social associationalism in market and civic spheres, and strong positive government, as the effective alternative to an organizational corporatism or a corporate state.

In the United States the historic political development of the last third of the twentieth century was the bipartisan embrace of corporate liberalism and a continuing glacial leftward shift of the Republican party, as well as the Democratic party, and of American society in general. In the 1990s, President William Clinton and House Speaker Newt Gingrich were the outstanding leaders of this bipartisan leftward shift in party politics and the political culture. Hence, the right-wing coup against both was more effective within the GOP: Gingrich is gone, Clinton is not, and the sum total was a further leftward shift.

Consider some implications. Capitalism is not to be equated with "markets" and socialism with "government." Both capitalist and socialist modes of production and their attendant social relations have historically included both markets and government. The large corporation, smaller enterprise, and the market in general are not simply capitalist, and government is not the sole redoubt of socialism. Capitalism is not to be equated with "management" and socialism with "workers." Capitalism and socialism both exhibit class conflict, class complementarity, and analytically distinct, yet historically intersecting, modes of consciousness. Workers, farmers, professionals, intellectuals, reformers, as well as capitalists (investors, employers, owners, managers) have engaged in constructing and affirming capitalism; capitalists as well as workers, farmers, professionals, intellectuals, reformers, and others have engaged in constructing and affirming socialism. Usually, the same people have been engaged in constructing and affirming capitalism and socialism at the same time, whatever their intent.

The older linear evolutionary conception—first capitalism, and afterward (if at all), socialism—does not stand the historical test. Nor does the idea that the two are necessarily and properly mutually exclusive. In much of the Western world, capitalism has generated socialism—supplied its soil and nutriment—and the two have codeveloped both antagonistically and symbiotically. In a similar vein, "communism" (state-command socialism) has generated capitalism and the capitalism-socialism mix in the Eastern world. The mixed or combined mode of production, which has been developing steadily and transnationally, requires a new or substantially revised terminology—a requirement expressed, still rather inadequately or awkwardly, in the frequent references to the modern economy as "the information economy," or "the digital economy," or "the service economy."

Commentators of all hues of opinion, however fiercely independent they may be in other matters, have submitted to a "Leninist cultural hegemony" (*pace* Gramsci) in their equating "true socialism" or "real socialism" with the Soviet-style system of government ownership, state command, managerial authoritarianism, and a vanguard party political monopoly—in effect, also with a populist or millenarian utopia. In this Leninist-Populist captivity, they have equated socialism with a primitive collectivism or "communitarianism" that emerged in thought and social relations in preindustrial, indeed largely premarket, societies in a manner analogous to the equating of capitalism with its less developed mercantilist, preindustrial types. It makes more sense to identify modern socialism, as Marx did, with a society characterized by modern capitalist market development, complex associationalism, and a constitutional-democratic political system.

Liberal democracy ought not be identified exclusively with capitalist, or "bourgeois," society. Although historically originating and developing in bourgeois societies, liberal democracy is transhistorical in character and career. It has developed in correlation with both capitalism and socialism, as they have codeveloped. Hierarchical relations in some spheres (corporations, families, schools, universities, associations, churches) are compatible with, and often constitute the basis of, equalitarian relations in other spheres. The capitalism-socialism mix in the United States and the correlated "corporate-liberal" outlook, have worked to make corporate hierarchies not only serve the purposes of efficiency, innovation, and growth, but also the social goals of equal rights, liberties, and opportunities.

Let me sketch briefly ways in which the rise of modern corporate enterprise about the turn of the century represented the incipient phase in the development of a property-production-market system with capitalist and socialist characteristics. Marx himself assessed this economic change as transitional between capitalism and socialism, but an odd *ménage à trois* of populists, Leninists, and free-marketeers has labeled it "predatory corporate interests" or a "monopoly capitalism," purportedly obstructive alike of economic efficiencies and social justice. These critics have strongly influenced scholars and intellectuals to consider corporate enterprise less a matter of historical institutions to be studied and understood—and shaped and reshaped—than as a matter of Mr. Dooley's (Finely Peter Dunne's) "hideous monsters" to be denounced and destroyed, although "not so fast"—and although they nevertheless seem to endure.[4]

Corporate enterprise represented a shift from individual-proprietary to associational forms of property ownership, and hence a transformation of property relations in substance as well. It represented "private" property "publicly held." Ownership and liability became both widely spread and limited, or socialized. Individuals and associations owned stock, but none of the stockholders, let alone the managers, owned the physical property as such or even intangible assets other than the stock. In intensifying the specialization and division of labor on the basis of their horizontal and vertical coordination or integration, corporate enterprise separated the investor-ownership function from the managerial. It thereby gave practical embodiment to the distinction between the enterprise as a technoeconomic organization, and the enterprise as property. This marked an important departure from the older capitalist unity of investor-owner-manager in the proprietary form of enterprise—a departure immeasurably strengthened by subsequent practice and jurisprudence that subordinated stockholder claims and interests to management discretion, authority, and prerogative. In addition, the large corporation brought into cooperative association hitherto "arms-length" market-competitive or market-exchanging units. By hierarchical coordination or integration, it brought into cooperative relations managerial, professional, technical, and manual labor, office and shop floor, men and women, and especially in the United States, people of diverse racial, national, ethnic, religious, cultural, and regional backgrounds. In such ways as these, the large corporations were socially as well as economically integrative, and hence politically significant along a broad front.

Large corporate enterprise exerted a huge and varied impact not only on its own immediate personnel, but on innumerable persons and whole communities outside it. Contributing to the corporation's impact were the size and complexity of its associational activity, the widespread public ownership of its stock, and its concentrated and extensive market power in buying, selling, and contractual activity. For public opinion—including that of business executives as well as that of political and intellectual leaders—it became "natural" to view the large corporation as no longer representative simply of private property in the older sense, but as property affected with, and embodying, a public character, concern, and interest. The corporate reorganization of the property-production system spurred growing civic and government intervention, regulatory and distributive, in the marketplace at local, state, and national levels. The large corporation brought into play checking and balancing powers within and outside the market, which moved programmatically and psychologically toward patterns of social accountability for both the corporate and noncorporate sectors of society.

The transformation, commonly described as a movement toward oligopoly, may also be designated as a passage from competitive to administered markets. It included a growing capacity of enterprises to manage and regulate investment and supply, and to influence or modify demand so as to adjust supply to demand and make rather than simply take prices, and to target revenue volume and rates of return. This new capacity permitted countercyclical planning by corporate managers to stabilize prices, returns on investment, and employment, at targeted levels, thereby in effect socially intervening to modify and soften the business cycle, which under the competitive regime had been regarded as almost a force of nature beyond human control—a softening trend noticeable from 1898 to 1929.[5]

Administered pricing meant that the enterprise's revenues exceeded replacement and expansion requirements. Surplus funds became available for allocation to other purposes, ranging from acquisitions, new ventures, and reorganization, to advertising and public relations, to worker pensions and other benefits, to philanthropy, research and development, politics, lobbying, and taxes. Prices thus came to carry both enterprise costs and social costs—a "price socialism" through market administration. This transformation could only have transpired without noticeable impoverishment or constriction of noncorporate sectors, because the new hierarchical organization of managerial corporations, combined with new financial, productive, transportation, and communications processes, permitted new efficiencies not attainable under the proprietary-competitive regime—efficiencies manifested, for example, in integrations and standardizations that yielded rising volumes of production and a diversification of products. They yielded significantly higher productivity with a continuing lowering of real costs per unit of output, measured in energy, materials, and labor time, which found expression at both the micro- and the macroeconomic levels in the statistical record for 1898 to 1929 and subsequently.

These new social planning powers of corporate administration, whether or not judged to be class-biased, shortsighted, or unjust in these years, gave business enterprise a social and political significance of a scope and intensity different from that which it had had under the proprietary-competitive market regime. Corporation managers now assumed palpably far-reaching roles and powers in the market, in local communities, and in society at large, which called for social accountability, or in Madisonian terms, effective checks and balances from the civic and political spheres, as well as from within the market and within the corporations themselves. These checks and balances facilitated fair pricing and other kinds of desirable market behavior. They exerted a discipline that a competitive price mechanism no longer provided, promoting innovation and steadily rising efficiency. In the liberal-democratic United States it was hardly possible for government not to "compete" in the exercise of administrative powers through regulatory, fiscal, monetary, and transfer policies. The Madisonian tradition, in particular, validated—indeed mandated—the continuing implementation, extension, improvisation, and refinement, of the mixture of capitalism and socialism. The source of strong government engagement with market relations does not lie in exotic or "radical" doctrine and practice; on the contrary, it is squarely in the American Grain of the "American Science of Politics." Both the mixture of capitalism and socialism and the Madisonian imperative refer, moreover, not only to government-market relations, but to market relations themselves.

The work of Alfred D. Chandler, Jr., and other recent business historians has shown that in the corporate regime, organizational or planned coordination adapts to markets, but also makes markets—shapes and reshapes, creates and invents, displaces and replaces, administers or manages, markets.[6] These relations pertain to the government-economy relation as well as to the internal and external relations of firms themselves. They correspond to what I refer to as a corporate-administered property-production system or a system of administered markets, in which both enterprises and the general economy combine capitalist and socialist characteristics. Corporations and "business" are as much socialist as capitalist entities.

The corporate reconstruction of the economy brought with it a new interplay of "public" and "private" associational authority, governmental and nongovernmental, acting within and upon market relations and subjecting them, with new intensities and demands, to social and political pressures and action. It ushered in a new stage in the history of property-production systems or modes of production. The period 1890–1916 marked the origins and only an early phase of this historic departure. The more corporate capitalism developed, and the more capital accumulation in goods production evolved into what I have elsewhere interpreted as capital disaccumulation, the stronger became the socialist characteristics and trends, manifested in a continuing enlargement and interplay of the spheres of associative governance in both the "private" and "public" sectors.[7]

In this early phase of corporate liberalism, law and the judicial process confronted two major questions: (1) how to permit and at the same time check, balance, and harness the great concentrations of power in the market and in society represented by the large corporations; (2) how to fashion a system of substantial and growing governmental regulation, intervention, and participation in the market without surrendering the principle and practice of society's supremacy over the state—without, that is, embracing a comprehensive system of state command, in short, how to reconcile the modern economy and the capitalism-socialism mix with liberal democracy.

By the late 1880s, Americans were no strangers to significant government efforts to shape or regulate national economic development. They had long experience with the rules and regulations of the national banking system, public land disposal, rivers and harbors projects, land grants for higher education in aid of agriculture and industry, subsidies and land grants to transcontinental railroads, pensions for soldiers and widows, protective tariffs, and the creation and regulation of the money supply. New initiatives that extended and intensified the national government's engagement in economic regulation came in response to a growing regulatory power that had emerged in the market within and among capitalist enterprises, usually in corporate form, first in railroads and then in some manufacturing industries. Proposals for government intervention arose as practical responses to changing market circumstances, which translated rather promptly into political issues in an environment of liberal democracy. "Business" preceded government in the acquisition and development of many regulatory powers.

In railroads and industry, the regulatory power developed by "private parties" through internal growth, functional and product diversification, marketing and contractual strategies, managerial organization, and mergers had several purposes. One of the more important of these purposes—or at any rate an essential effect—was to give business institutions a "social security" against the invisible hand of the competitive market-price mechanism. Economists might call this reducing risk. In part, businesses brought government into the regulatory function to help make their "social security" arrangements lasting and fully effective. In part, the resort to government regulation came from protective efforts of large corporations' competitors, suppliers, customers, employees, civic hosts or neighbors. Government regulation also came from efforts of reformers who feared great market power in restricted or privileged hands and feared its economic, political, and cultural ramifications, and from efforts of reformers who welcomed the new business power, properly harnessed and limited, as a progressive step in the nation's modern development. Government regulation also came from efforts of those like farmers, who would have liked, but by themselves were unable to attain, a power of market social security and who resorted to government to get it. By the 1890s, a diverse and broadly based movement toward government regulation of the economy combined an interest in market security with an interest in making it socially accountable, whether for self-protection or for the general welfare.

The regulatory interest in corporate social accountability strove for a variety of objectives: (1) to provide a replacement for the older competitive investment and pricing discipline to spur cost efficiency, innovation, and growth, and to guarantee fair prices, equitable market behavior, and reasonable returns on investment; (2) to make management operate responsibly toward investors, creditors, consumers, suppliers, distributors, workers, and the public; (3) to secure the confidence of investors—smaller, as well as larger, individual as well as institutional—in the corporation and the stock market, as a safe place for savings and as fair and reliable in the allocation of property income and other revenues; (4) to restrict or guide management practices in a manner consistent with conservation of natural resources and the health and safety of employees and consumers; (5) to make corporate market power work in favor of, rather than athwart, efforts to moderate the business cycle and to stabilize employment, income distribution, and a progressive national development. In the older competitive capitalism, many of these were not governmental concerns; now they were more and more becoming so.

The first major government regulatory measures in railroads and industry, the Interstate Commerce Commission Act (1887) and the Sherman Antitrust Act (1890), along with their judicial and statutory revision and supplements, represented, respectively, the two basic principles of regulation that guided policy-making in these years: state command and positive government. These two principles correlated strongly with what came to be regarded in policy-making as a basic distinction between public utilities (common carriers, energy, telecommunications) and the general economy. Public utilities were considered "natural monopolies," or as uncommonly vital to the public interest, and could be subjected to state command. But the general economy was viewed differently, since its subjection to state command would impair economic efficiency and seriously undermine or destroy society's supremacy over the state. Instead, the general economy should be subjected to the reach of strong positive government, its powers extending, in Woodrow Wilson's words, as far as "experience permits or the times demand," in such manner as to promulgate rules of market behavior, incentives, and inhibitions, but leaving to enterprises the primary and initiating roles as actors in the market, subject to a secondary if substantial governmental regulation.[8] In this way, corporations could be made agents of social policy without discarding the productive and marketing dynamism associated with capitalist enterprise.

This outlook validated and provided a legal framework for new principles and practices of the administered market system that was replacing the older "free (competitive) market" system.

In the 1880s and 1890s judicial decisions relating to common carriers extended substantive and procedural due process protections to corporations, and thereby established a legal framework not only for maintaining investor ownership and protecting an investor's property right to a reasonable return, but also for subjecting common carriers to comprehensive oversight by the Interstate Commerce Commission. Congress then revised and filled out that legal framework as it strengthened and extended the ICC's powers from oversight to comprehensive controls, which ranged from rate setting to investment operations. In 1916, Congress added controls over hours of work, specifically an eight-hour day for railway workers. Comprehensive government control subsequently became the pattern for public utilities in state and local as well as national policy. In mixing public and private authority, the enterprise would serve social policy and goals, while preserving the incentive of associational initiative and gain. Public utility policy thereby applied the principle of state command by attenuating it.[9]

For the rest of the economy, debate focused, first, on whether to permit large corporate enterprise to exercise regulatory power in the market at all, and if so, whether to treat it in effect as a public utility subject in principle to (an attenuated) state command or whether to subject enterprise to a strong, but secondary, government regulation. The older common law tradition on restraint of trade and monopoly had permitted regulatory powers exercised by business enterprise if they did not violate public policy, did not constitute unfair practices or prices, did not unduly injure or impair the public health, safety, morals, or welfare, and did not violate others' legitimate property rights or liberties or improperly prevent them from competing in the market. This left a wide berth for judicial guidance or determination on a case-by-case basis that permitted consideration and affirmation of changing practices with changing circumstances as the market and the economy evolved. The question in jurisprudence and politics became whether the Sherman Act constituted a federal statutory embodiment, or a superseding, of the common law tradition.

From 1897 to 1911, the Supreme Court held that the Sherman Act had superseded the common law, that, therefore, only the federal government could regulate the interstate and foreign market and that the market must otherwise be left to competitive mechanisms.[10] Presidents William McKinley, Theodore Roosevelt, and William Howard Taft declined to apply the Sherman Act to the enforcement of such public policy. Roosevelt viewed large corporations as technologically and economically progressive, although in need of governmental supervision to make them socially accountable. Aware of the inefficiencies of government ownership, he came to advocate application of the public utility principle to large corporations throughout the economy, in effect subjecting them to a state command system of federal registration or license combined with a commission regulation that covered their contracts, investment strategies, market behavior, and, as the state might consider necessary, prices, wages, and labor policies. Roosevelt's proposals sharpened the focus on the larger issues and resulted in their rejection not only by Congress but by some of his own closest political loyalists.[11] In 1911, the Supreme Court, in the "Rule of Reason" decisions in the Standard Oil and American Tobacco cases, reinterpreted the Sherman Act to constitute, in effect, a federal statutory embodiment of the common law. The Federal Trade Commission Act and the Clayton Antitrust Act, both of 1914, combined with the Supreme Court's common law construction of the Sherman Act, established the essential framework of positive government regulation for the general economy that has since prevailed, permitting regulatory powers by business enterprise in the market, but subject to legislated policies, executive commission action, and judicial process and review.[12]

This framework for the mixture of public and private authority became the basis for making corporations socially accountable in a liberal democracy. It was applied generally—for example, to the establishment and design of the Federal Reserve System in commercial banking, the Federal Farm Land Banks in agricultural finance, and as time went on, to much else. It would not be until the 1930s and afterward, that effective attention would be paid to intracorporate accountability in management-labor relations.

In the early years of the twentieth century, before doctrinal rigidities set in, the capitalism-socialism mix found recognition in the thinking and writings of leading public officials, social scientists, and other prominent intellectuals.

In 1913, for example, John Bates Clark, the preeminent American neoclassical, marginal utility economist, stated:

> There are two movements in progress which have so strong a hold on the American people that no political party can hope for success which disregards them. They are both moral and economic in nature, and taken together, they have placed American politics on somewhat the same moral plane which they occupied before and during the Civil War. We may characterize them as the struggles for Socialism on the one hand, and for reform on the other.

Insofar as socialists were utopians, Clark held that they "can always outdo other classes in promising," but as realists "in all probability reformers can outdo them in fulfilling." It was a matter of choosing between a socialist's unrealizable "vision . . . more beatific than any other," and a reformer's "Eden . . . that he can seriously expect to reach," and that "is practicable for all humanity."[13]

At about the same time, Wesley Clair Mitchell, the great pioneer in business-cycle study who was to serve as a principal adviser to Herbert Hoover, both when he was the secretary of commerce and the President, wrote: "The union of self-interest and social service in the economic life of the individual appears on a larger scale in the life of society under the guise of a union of individualistic and socialistic institutions." (Note: "institutions," not merely inclinations, or tendencies, or ideals.) Seeing symbiosis, rather than mutual repulsion or exclusion, between money-market relations and socialism, Mitchell observed, "Production as carried on by a thoroughgoing use of money is in external form an eminently socialistic process. It is conducted by interdependent groups of interdependent individuals." People "can promote their individual interests best by working with others and for others," while at the same time, "they make their own terms, and they are nominally free" to change jobs. "This union of self-interest and social service in the economic life of the individuals, and of individualistic and socialistic institutions in the economic life of society, rests on the use of money as a means of conducting exchanges." Mitchell here, in effect, formulated a principle of the associational and market basis of the mixture of capitalism and socialism. Mitchell highly valued the productive vitality of capitalism, but noted, "The socialist movement is one of the dynamic forces in the present body politic with which everyone must count who seeks to know what is and forecast what will be."[14]

Earlier, in 1896, Henry Carter Adams, the American statistician, economist, and ICC official, wrote:

> Certain it is that association is responsible for an increment of product peculiarly its own. These suggestions are not new. They are, on the contrary, the common thought of socialist writers. . . . To deny the fact of social production, and thus preclude the possibility of a development in the idea of property, is not only unfortunate, but there is no justification for it . . . Individualism does not consist in living in isolation, but rather dwelling in a society of recognized interdependencies. Its development is marked by the regress of self-sufficiency and the progress of association.

Adams accordingly noted that, although "the modern productive process is undoubtedly a highly socialized process," this did not mean that "each individual must be swallowed up in society." In modern society, individualism and associationalism went hand in hand. It followed that John Stuart Mill had brought political economy, in Adams's words, "as far as it was capable of being brought under the eighteenth century concept of property, and the further evolution of industrial theory, as well as the reconstruction of the legal framework of industrial society, must begin with the modification of the concept of property." Significantly, he added, "It is a common law development and not a constitutional change, or a statutory enactment, that is needed."[15]

We tend to forget that Frederick Jackson Turner, the eminent historian who did much of his most influential work during the years 1890–1916, directed his thinking, including his "frontier thesis," to explaining not only how society in the United States differed from societies in Europe, but also how it was similar. In particular, he noted that, from the closing years of the nineteenth century onward, the United States was developing along lines common to those of other industrializing countries, especially those of Western Europe. He sought to explain why in the United States, no less than in Europe, as he wrote in 1891, "The age of machinery, of the factory system, is also the age of socialistic inquiry. . . . We are approaching a pivotal point in our country's history." Twenty years later, he wrote, "The present finds itself engaged in the task of readjusting its old ideals to new conditions and is turning increasingly to government to preserve its traditional democracy. It is not surprising that socialism shows noteworthy gains as elections continue." It may be that Clark, Mitchell, Adams, and Turner understood the United States and its modern course of development better than Werner Sombart, who thought there was "No Socialism in the United States," and better than many professing socialists then and since.[16]

Notes

An earlier, shorter version of this essay, under the title, "Making Corporations Accountable in a Liberal Democracy: The United States in the Modern Formative Era, 1890s–1916," was presented at the Fifth International Week on the History of the Enterprise: Hierarchies, Markets, Power in the Economy: Theories and Lessons from History, Libero Istituto Universitario Carlo Cattaneo, Castellanza, Italy, 15–17 December 1993. A longer version from which this is adapted, is available on the SHGAPE web site (Society for the History of the Gilded Age and the Progressive Era), Dec. 1997.

1. See the classic work, Richard Hofstadter's, *The Age of Reform: From Bryan to F.D.R.* (New York: Vintage Books, 1955); and the recent work by James Livingston, *Pragmatism and the Political Economy of Cultural Revolution, 1850–1940* (Chapel Hill: University of North Carolina Press, 1994). For some of my own views, see M. J. Sklar, *The Corporate Reconstruction of American Capitalism, 1890–1916: The Market, the Law, and Politics* (Cambridge, Mass.: Cambridge University Press, 1988), esp. ch. 1, and M. J. Sklar, *The United States as a Developing Country: Studies in U.S. History in the Progressive Era and the 1920s*) (Cambridge, Mass.: Cambridge University Press, 1992), esp. chs. 1, 2, and 7.
2. The best of the past few decades' business history may be characterized as the social, organizational, and economic history of the business firm—of the enterprise, relatively narrowly conceived. More recently, leading scholars have increasingly recognized the necessity of having a larger conception of enterprise and relating its evolving shape to that of society and its broader forces and trends. This work may be thought of as a marriage of the invaluable business history of such institutional scholars as A. D. H. Kaplan, Edith T. Penrose, Alfred D. Chandler, Jr., and his younger colleagues, to the venerable sociological-economic history of such scholars as John R. Commons, Thorstein Veblen, Joseph A. Schumpeter, Peter F. Drucker, Adolf A. Berle, Gardiner C. Means, Thomas Cochran, Louis Hacker, Edward Kirkland, and John K. Galbraith. Among the latter in the mid- to late twentieth century, Berle and Galbraith, and most persistently and incisively Drucker, have led in bringing together the two bodies of work, yielding rich and fruitful concepts, perspectives, and paths of research. To those of us who knew his lectures and seminar work and have read his writings with care, William A. Williams's significant and lasting contribution, resides in large part in his pioneering efforts along these matrimonial lines in the interpretation of the political-economic history of the United States.

   See Alfred D. Chandler, *The Visible Hand: The Managerial Revolution in American Business* (Cambridge, Mass.: Harvard University Press, 1977); Alfred D. Chandler, Jr., and Herman Daems, eds., *Managerial Hierarchies* (Cambridge, Mass.: Harvard University Press, 1980); Louis Galambos, "What Makes Us Think We Can Put Business History Back into History?" *Business and Economic History,* 2d ser., 21 (1992), 1–11; William Lazonick, *Business Organization and the Myth of the Market Economy* (Cambridge, Mass.: Cambridge University Press, 1991); Leslie Hannah, *The Rise of the Corporate Economy: The British Experience* (London: Methuen, 1983); Michael E. Porter, *The Competitive Advantage of Nations* (New York: Free Press, 1990); Oliver Williamson, *The Economic Institutions of Capitalism* (New York: Free Press, 1985). William A. Williams, *The Contours of American History* (Cleveland: World, 1961); W. A. Williams, *The Great Evasion* (Chicago: Quadrangle, 1968).
3. For an elaboration of these and related questions see my *United States as a Developing Country*, ch. 1.
4. Karl Marx, *Capital* (Moscow: Foreign Languages Publishing House, 1959), 3:427–32; Sklar, *United States as a Developing Country,* 30–34. See Scott R. Bowman's invaluable

work, *The Modern Corporation and American Political Thought: Law, Power, and Ideology* (University Park, Pa.: Pennsylvania State University Press, 1996), esp. ch. 4.

5. See Charles A. Conant, "Crises and Their Management," *Yale Review* 9 (February 1901): 374–98; George W. Perkins, "The Modern Corporation," in *The Currency Problem and the Present Financial Situation,* edited by E. R. A. Seligman (New York: Columbia University Press, 1908), 155–70. For the classic formulation and explication of administered markets under corporate capitalism, see Gardiner C. Means, *The Corporate Revolution in America: Economic Reality vs. Economic Theory* (New York: Collier Books Edition, 1964).
6. See Chandler, *Visible Hand*, especially 1–12 for a summary statement, and Chandler, *Scale and Scope: The Dynamics of Industrial Capitalism* (Cambridge, Mass.: Harvard University Press, 1990), esp. chs. 1 and 2, for an overview; also, Lazonic, *Business Organization and the Myth of the Market Economy.*
7. See Sklar, *United States as a Developing Country,* chs. 1, 5, 7; Livingston, *Pragmatism and the Political Economy of Cultural Revolution,* ch. 1.
8. Woodrow Wilson, *The State* (Boston: D. C. Heath, 1906), 625.
9. For cases and discussion, see Sklar, *Corporate Reconstruction*, 49–51; John R. Commons, *Legal Foundations of Capitalism* (1924; Madison: University of Wisconsin Press, 1957), 6–7, 11–46; J. Willard A. Hurst, *The Legitimacy of the Business Corporation in the Law of the United States, 1780–1970* (Charlottesville: University Press of Virginia, 1970), 65, 68–71; Morton J. Horwitz, "Santa Clara Revisited: The Development of Corporate Theory," in *Corporations and Society: Power and Responsibility* edited by Warren J. Samuels and Arthur S. Miller (New York: Greenwood Press, 1987), 13–63.
10. The leading cases were: *United States v. Trans-Missouri Freight Association,* 166 U.S. 290 (1897); *United States v. Joint Traffic Association,* 171 U.S. 505 (1898); *United States v. Addyston Pipe & Steel Co. et al.,* 175 U.S. 211 (1899).
11. T. Roosevelt, "The Trusts, the People, and the Square Deal," *Outlook* 99 (18 November 1911): 649–56; T. Roosevelt, "Where We Cannot Work with Socialists," and "Where We Can Work with Socialists," *Outlook* 91 (20 and 27 March 1909): 619–23, 662–64. For my analysis of Roosevelt's position see Sklar, *Corporate Reconstruction,* 184–203, 278–85, 334–64.
12. *Standard Oil Co. of New Jersey v. United States,* 221 U.S. 1; *American Tobacco Co. v. United States,* 221 U.S., esp. 179–180. See Sklar, *Corporate Reconstruction,* 166–75.
13. John Bates Clark, "Reform or Revolution," 27 January 1913, J. B. Clark Papers, Rare Books and Manuscript Library, Butler Library, Columbia University, New York City.
14. Wesley Clair Mitchell, "Reasons for Studying Socialism," 17 April 1916, and "Money Economy and Economic Efficiency," n.d. W. C. Mitchell Papers, Rare Books and Manuscript Library, Butler Library, Columbia University, New York City.
15. Henry Carter Adams, "Economics and Jurisprudence" (1896), in Henry C. Adams, *Two Essays,* edited by Joseph Dorfman (New York: Augustus M. Kelley, 1969), 152, 159–60.
16. Frederick Jackson Turner, "The Significance of History" (November 1891), and "Social Forces in American History" (January 1911), in *Frontier and Section: Selected Essays of Frederick Jackson Turner,* edited by Ray A. Billington (Englewood Cliffs, N.J.: Prentice-Hall, 1961), 17, 21, 161; Werner Sombart, *Why Is There No Socialism in the United States?* (1906; White Plains, N.Y.: International Arts and Sciences Press, 1976); and see James Livingston, "Why Is There Still Socialism in the United States?" *Reviews in American History* 22 (1994): 577–83.

CHAPTER 23

CENTER AND PERIPHERY IN THE HISTORY OF SCIENCE

Miriam R. Levin

1. Conceptual Centers and Peripheries

On the disciplinary map of historical practice, science now lies at the periphery. Yet the rise of science to social and economic prominence remains a powerful trope and an important thread in modern history. In fact, in the development of the professions, science has held a more influential position than history, while in the past three decades, the methods and concerns of historians have increasingly influenced the work of historians of science. In the late nineteenth century historians based their emerging profession's standards on those of science, while in the first half of the twentieth the social stature of scientists became the measure of their own aspirations. Ideals of truth seeking, fact finding, precision, empiricism, and "objectivity" of research methods, which defined academic professionalism among historians, had their source in nineteenth-century notions of science. By the turn of the century, the men who trained in science, practiced it, and taught it in universities exemplified these ideals and testified to their social viability.[1]

If anything, historians of science were more permeated by these ideals than other historians, being doubly dosed with the moral medicine of objectivity. Without questioning their subjects' expressed values, the histories they wrote carefully delineated the theories and experiments of great male scientists, showing how these interconnected to form a progressive chain of ideas. Their history of science focused on individual scientists who advanced human understanding of the laws that governed the natural world through the exercise of the scientific method.[2] This advance toward truth entailed a triumphal struggle for freedom from the tyranny of religious ideas, institutions, and leaders, first in Europe and then in mid-nineteenth-century America. Science and its professional practitioners also appeared to be the engine of national progress both material and moral, for they epitomized the virtues of intellectual freedom, democracy, and meritocracy.[3]

Since the 1960s, historians of science, like other historians, have challenged their predecessors' claims to objectivity and drawn on other disciplines for new perspectives. And, like their colleagues, they have broken apart the old synthesis and challenged the old narrative. There is a difference here, however, which distinguishes historians of science from other historians of this new generation. They not only assumed a critical stance toward their profession's unselfconscious positivism, but they questioned and critically analyzed scientists' moral and intellectual claims on objective judgment and truth seeking. As a result they helped other historians weaken the progressive narrative framework on which modern western and especially United States' history had been hung.[4]

However idealized scientists' explanations for the continuous growth in their economic influence and social status, it is difficult to deny the cultural significance science (and technology, understood commonly as its twin) assumed in Western industrializing society. Since we no longer can take the ideology of science at face value, we need to study its history to produce a more accurate narrative that takes into account recent work in the social history of science, women's history, the social studies of science and anthropology, and sets that work within the context of efforts to build a new social center of elites congenial to industrial capitalism.

Writing on the cusp of these shifts in viewpoint, the sociologist Edward Shils observed that every society has a central space within its structure. In his essay, "Center and Periphery," he described it as a power zone, which "impinges in various ways on those who live within the ecological domain in which the society exists."[5] The zone, while not necessarily at the geographic center of the social unity, represents the main values of an elite, which are carried to those on the edges through various institutions. It is to Christian men and women engaged in academic science that I want to turn now, exploring their role in forming a particular kind of zone in nineteenth- and twentieth-century America.

To be precise, I want to propose that we reexamine the history of the American scientific profession in light of the history of American Protestantism—of evangelical Protestantism during the Second Great Awakening, specifically. I want to argue that rather than being an impediment to the development of science in industrial society, evangelical religious leaders helped establish a new value system and center of power and influence in American society that gave great authority to a select group of men *and* women working in higher education. Together they formed a self-selected elite in academe who were dedicated to the scientific study of nature and able to extend their influence over geographic space and through time by founding additional institutions and producing graduates. Science faculties' escape from religion was not the source of the drama of change that ensued. Industrial capitalism was.

I want first to sketch the major shift that has occurred in the interpretation of the rise of the scientific profession as a result of the work of Thomas Kuhn and historians of women in science. A critical view of their efforts will provide a sense of what has changed and what still needs explaining in the development of a profession where the motivations behind the relationship of men and women to one another and to the emerging sciences remain obscure. I will then explore the ways in which men and women engaged in higher education and committed to academic science within the evangelical Protestant movement felt they constituted an important part of the leadership of an emerging power center. This can be done by looking at the circumstances in which a particular institution, Mount Holyoke Female Seminary, whose faculty had strong ties to the movement and to academic scientific activities, was founded and passed its first decades.[6] This is to demonstrate that whether or not these men and women agreed on explicit meanings or the distribution of power, organized religion seems to have provided them with certain common values, goals, and above all a set of loosely connected institutions from which they could launch their efforts. From their bases in colleges and seminaries they built networks and established traditions that still exist, although much altered and no longer hegemonic. Among these values were factors that countenanced the study of nature by both men and women as a means of gaining social authority.

I will sketch out how this rethinking of the relationship between religion and science helps us understand the working relationship that developed between men and women engaged in academic science. Together they came to constitute a powerful agent of cultural change as members of an elite group who helped introduce the new value system into American society and who benefited from it. I will conclude by suggesting how this revision of the history of the scientific profession might bring science back into the center of history.

2. Historiographical Changes

In the 1960s Thomas Kuhn's book *The Structure of Scientific Revolutions* was a key factor in opening up questions that brought the history of science into a postpositivist, postempiricist stage. As Arthur Danto said of Kuhn's work,

> His theory of scientific revolution . . . opened the way to discussing science as a human and historical matter . . . the natural sciences themselves became matters for the kinds of interpretation the earlier theorists had identified as the methodological prerogative of the human sciences: ways of reading the world.[7]

Kuhn's work changed the entire perspective of historians working on the history of science by proposing that science was a social activity, its premises, methods, subject matter, and lines of inquiry all socially determined by members of a self-selected group.

Historians of science saw that science might be studied as a social activity like any other. As a result of their efforts along this line, the master narrative of the rise of the scientific profession lost its idealistic luster and simple linear trajectory because historians challenged some of its assumptions, claims, and explanations for scientists' success by focusing on the internal dynamics of professional development. A whiggishness persisted in the histories of scientific professionalization which appeared in the 1970s and 1980s; but now scientific progress was the subject of inquiry rather than an unselfconsciously adumbrated theme.[8] These historians from the 1970s and 1980s argued that scientists in industrializing society were producers who specialized in certain forms of knowledge and engaged in building an enterprise whose product was in demand. Originally situated in the colleges and a few governmental posts, men of science moved their seat of power after the Civil War to the newly founded universities—and to their research laboratories within these institutions. Through associations, journals, graduate training, research, and degree granting, scientists at these secularly oriented universities gained control over scientific practice, turning it into a profession. Through articles and lectures by a variety of science popularizers and disseminators, they gained public support for, if not complete understanding of, science.[9] In the twentieth century, physicists and chemists aligned with government agencies and private industry gradually exercised more influence on a national scale than men in any other field of science.

The dynamic that fueled this successful process derived its energy in great part from male scientists' struggle to secularize science by freeing themselves from churchmen's influence in the colleges rather than from their belief in God or faith in the power of individuals to enact positive change.[10] In addition, certain changes in the public's attitude associated with changes in the American economy acted as positive incentives for men of science to struggle for intellectual and social prominence. In this industrializing society, public enthusiasm for scientific activities along with the economic support scientists won in universities, government, and industry also reinforced their aggressive efforts to expand scientific activity.[11]

In sum, these studies on the professionalization of science from this period now presented a more nuanced picture that contextualized the development of science and its relationship to the growth of industrial capitalist society. They only implicitly criticized Merton's thesis that science was compatible with liberal democratic ideals in its internal workings and intellectual foundations, and that much of the scientific community's success was due to having embraced these ideals in practice.[12]

The major challenge to this picture of science as a liberal profession open to all intellectual worthies came from women historians of science. They were quick to point out its strongly masculine bias and to discredit its meritocratic claims. They also began to identify women who had worked in the field. As they examined the record of women in science, they began to ask why women were frequently not included in the history of professional science. They also sought to explain how the few women they identified had been able to participate in science and how they had functioned. Margaret Rossiter synthesized a great deal of this research in her important and influential book *Women in American Science,* published in 1982.[13] Using the basic outlines of the new master narrative, she drew together an enormous amount of research by other scholars to support a compelling thesis, which was summed up in her book's subtitle: *Struggles and Strategies from 1830 to 1940.*

Research on the intellectual and cultural history of science identified biases in male scientists' attitudes toward women that colored men's conceptions of nature and natural law and affected the manner in which they interpreted data and even set up experimental hypotheses. Although not working on American science, Londa Schiebinger, in examining how assumptions about differences in men's and women's intellectual and physical powers were reflected in eighteenth-century anatomical depictions of human skeletons, suggested that certain carryovers existed from one country to another.[14] Anthropologist Emily Martin's research revealed the manner in which biologists' assumptions about male aggressiveness and female passivity affected the questions they asked in research on fertility.[15]

One major result of these women's efforts was to stretch the master narrative to include women. Rossiter's work and that of a number of other historians of women in science is set within the model of society as divided into separate spheres, that of men and that of women. Women wishing to enter science were understood to be breaking into a sphere of masculine culture which has mechanisms consciously devised to keep out or at least to keep down women by relegating them to lower levels of scientific work. The few who reached the highest levels were mavericks, extremely unconventional individuals, who had to undergo enormous psychological stress.

In this revised scenario, women are included only in the sense of being outsiders attempting to break into an elite circle of men. Rossiter's book and much research on the social history of women in science is informed by what Linda Kerber has called the second phase model of separate spheres,[16] the construct that women and men inhabit different social spaces and even physical spaces. Men's world is that of public life and women's that of the home and private life. Each has its own culture, ways of behaving, values, goals, duties, and even ways of thinking. According to this view, historians interpreted women's wishing to or needing to earn a living as breaking into a male world, which recognized the home as the only legitimate place for women. In Kerber's words, "Margaret W. Rossiter's *Women Scientists in America* provides, among many other things, a case study in the strategies of boundary maintenance and renegotiation."[17]

In the interpretation based on separate spheres, women who met the terms of success established by the profession were anomalies, and those who did so at the most exalted levels even more so. A number of historians of women in American science have looked at these special cases to identify how individual women, some married but most single, managed to make major contributions to research in their fields. For example, Pnina Abir-Am and Dorinda Outram published a collection of biographical essays that showed how supportive husbands, fathers, and academic mentors played important roles in helping these women negotiate the biases against women in the profession.[18] These cases were treated as exceptions that made the rule, and as a consequence took on the character of anecdotes in the history of feminism.

Evelyn Fox Keller's work on gender and science and her biography of geneticist Barbara McClintock also began from the premise of separate spheres.[19] In another book she argued that the few women who did make significant contributions and gained recognition from men for their research did so only through tremendous psychological transformations that involved crossing the personality boundaries that distinguished female from male types. Keller quoted Nancy Hopkins, a prominent woman scientist working in the 1970s, on this point:

> Obviously the intellectual processes involved in "real" science are as natural (or unnatural) to women as they are to men. But "professional science" was constructed by and for men (a certain type of man), and a woman who chooses to conquer this world at its higher echelons usually requires a major overhaul of self and world views.[20]

In light of the construct of separate spheres, women's experiences in the male world of science had analogies with the class struggle and racial segregation. Historians depicted middle-class women who sought to participate in scientific work as at first relegated to separate women's colleges. As the profession matured in the twentieth century, men limited women's access to doctoral education, steered them into repetitive tasks considered "women's work in science," and assigned them lower membership status in professional organizations. Like members of the labor movement, a number of these women founded organizations similar to mutual aid societies to represent their interests in an effort to gain some of the benefits male scientists enjoyed.[21]

These historians identified the real abuses women suffered, their profound despair and great triumphs over adversity. They also brought to light how adaptive and persistent women had been. Moreover, they established without a doubt that there were individual men in scientific organizations and institutions who effectively restricted women's participation as scientific activities became more structured, specialized, and centered in universities. Women may have shared some of the values of the emerging elites, but they were far from the center of power. In any case, it was a scenario in which women did not count as historical actors in the sense that male scientists did not see them as seriously affecting the direction of research or the organization of scientific work, or even as absolutely necessary to the profession's rise to power—there was a sense that, as with semiskilled factory labor, if some other social group had been available at lower cost, they would have been trained to perform the same work.

3. Religion and Men and Women in Science

I have tried to show that the critical revision of the history of the scientific profession had two interrelated facets. There are in fact two rather frayed features of the new narrative that are especially perspicuous. These require some reweaving if we are to understand how the scientific profession took the form it did in the United States and why it became so socially significant. First, the emphasis on the social construction of science has tended to place the old progressive ideology on the back burner, while historians examine the "real" social groups and circumstances that defined scientific activity. Thus, an idea that at one time had some historical authority is being left unattended, perhaps because it now seems a product of false consciousness. Second, we have little idea of what motivated a small but growing number of unmarried women to seek paid employment requiring or at least rewarding scientific knowledge, nor of why a number of men over several generations agreed not only to educate them but to hire them as well. Personal inclination alone is not enough to account for the numbers and the persistence over time. If science is socially constructed by men, then resorting to separate spheres does not explain why women wanted to enter scientific work, for it assumes that they had no "natural" place within it. As they now stand, these women seem acculturated.

These observations are not unconnected, for they point to the possible existence of a common value system that brought men and women into scientific work and formed part of a common culture. Moreover, they suggest that those values and that culture were infused with ideals of progress and of getting ahead in American society. It is recognized by historians of the early republic that men and (by 1848) women who fought to extend the right to vote did so for the acknowledged reason that voting gave them access to office holding as a way to exercise political and economic power. It seems logical to ask then why at about the same time did a few men and women with some scientific knowledge begin to find employment in evangelized institutions of higher education? What sort of power might holding academic posts teaching science offer them?

To formulate the questions in a more positive and historical way, was there some feature or features of antebellum American society that presented science as a highly valued and inclusive activity so far as the women in question were concerned? How might this feature constitute a context that helped shape the division of labor between men and women, as well as the ways in which they taught science and did research then and later? And how might this context have served as a bridge between men and women in science and the larger society, allowing them to extend their influence and authority?

A good direction to set out in might be that indicated by the late anthropologist M. Z. Rosaldo, who advocated finding an approach that would "help us understand how men and women both participate in and help to reproduce the institutional forms that may oppress, liberate, join or divide them."[22] In pursuit of that approach, we can gain much by heeding Joan Scott's enjoinder that those interested in the history of gender relations focus on shifting power relationships between men and women.[23] This interactive view of social processes is important for it leads us to think about these men and women committed to scientific work as part of an influential, elite group. The subject here is not the history of gender relations *per se,* but the history of why, how, and with what consequences men and women engaged in a particular and, for them, very significant activity.

To build on this notion of an emerging scientific community that included women, however, we need to have some framework within which social interactions formed and political struggles between these men and women played out. Relationships between people or groups depend on the existence of certain common understandings about what is at stake, as well as about values and goals. One person's opportunity is another's obstacle. There is also the need for a vocabulary with which to communicate. What sort of historical context is it that set men and women into these interactive relationships, gave them a common framework, modes of thinking, values, and institutions that encompassed them, providing a basis on which relationships could be defined, founded, structured, and developed?

One place to look for such a consensus is in the history of religion in antebellum America; to be exact, in the history of Protestantism and of the role played by its nineteenth-century variant, evangelical Protestantism, in the structuring and development of higher education.[24] Initially the opportunities for women to teach science came not directly from the growing market for scientific knowledge, but from evangelical Protestant churchmen in need of administrators and teachers for women's seminaries. These were the same individuals who also expanded new opportunities for men interested in science to earn their living by teaching college, thus giving members of both sexes an institutional base and the imprimatur of a sacred endeavor. Unlike the power to participate in political life by voting, science was a symbol of intellectual power over nature defined as marketable knowledge produced in institutions of higher education, to which a select number of women were privy and within which an even smaller group could earn their living. Women's engagement in science was as members of a group of intellectual and moral elites. As will be discussed below, their dependence on men for the latest scientific information made them vulnerable and also gave them leverage in this tripartite relationship.

Put this way, historically the evangelical churchmen provided a network of institutional settings where the interests of three groups could meet, find accommodation with one another, and advance their own purposes for a time in what seemed a common endeavor. They educated an elite who would lead society to new moral levels. Academic science proffered to women uninterested in direct access to political life an alternative avenue to the exercise of power. Unmarried women committed to earning their living teaching in seminaries could see science opening opportunities for social and economic influence. In the democratizing atmosphere of Jacksonian America, Susan B. Anthony may have thrown over teaching to work for voting rights because she felt men blocked women teachers from exercising social authority, but a small number of ambitious teachers found teaching science offered them opportunities to do so. And unlike those seeking the vote, these women had the benefit of belonging to the growing national network of institutions in which those with scientific knowledge came to exercise some sway.[25]

The ministers who led the evangelical movement drew their strength from unsettled populations of rural northeast communities strongly affected by the forces of industrial capitalism. The ministry itself had felt the winds of change in the form of political forces that disestablished the old theocracies in the 1820s, making way for the leadership in state and local governments of Protestants with an interest in capitalist investment in manufacturing and land development.[26] These men of the church turned their energies to saving the world from the sins of material excess, hoping to control the course of capitalist development. They did so in part through holding revivals and founding churches but also through the more formal and enduring (and entrepreneurial) means of founding and reforming educational institutions.[27]

Male colleges and single-sex seminaries were especially important to the churchmen, for they could use these institutions of higher education to form a sanctified elite of new social leaders.[28] Their foremost product was to be ministers, teachers, and wives for the ministry, but the churchmen also sought to influence the minds and morals of male students who could pursue evangelical ends through other professions becoming important in the communities: law, medicine, banking, and commerce. They supported the education of women to be their wives and the mothers of their children. In fact, they turned the market for higher education to their own advantage, seeking to give this demand a particular shape and character. They were even able to generate additional demand. While growing enthusiasm for higher education among a hard-pressed rural citizenry and an emerging middle class in the towns helped spur the passion for college and seminary founding in these years, the churchmen also found the demand for primary education in the newly settled western lands opened job opportunities for teachers, which graduates committed to evangelical goals, could fill. Missions here and abroad became another source of demand for seminary and college graduates.[29]

These churchmen supported the inclusion of science courses in the college and seminary curriculum. From their perspective, science could further religious ends. Natural law was holy law, and God was imminent in the phenomena of the physical world. The systematic study of nature was a means of gaining insight into God's grand design as well as a process of mental discipline.[30] It was a step toward salvation open to men and women alike, as all souls were equal in God's eyes.[31] Putting science in the curriculum was also partly a way of accommodating local popular interest in scientific discoveries and manufacturers' support for scientific education as a pedagogical and economic tool. In order to offer courses such as natural philosophy, natural history, chemistry, physiology, and geology, the churchmen needed college and seminary faculty with some knowledge of or interest in these subjects. In this way they provided an opportunity for a small number of men and women to develop an institutional base and some expertise. We are not, however, talking about specialists or numerous wealthy institutions with elaborate and costly facilities and equipment at this time. Nevertheless it was a beginning that endowed science teachers at a few institutions with social status and influence and an aura of sanctity second only to that possessed by teachers of theology.[32]

Men interested in science could benefit from the jobs these policies created. Their primary interest was in scholarship, however.[33] For them, nature was a source of information and science a means of systematically studying, demonstrating and reasoning about its character and organization. They came to the colleges with the primary intention of pursuing its study and educating students to do the same. It is not presently possible to say from where all the men who found posts teaching science in the antebellum colleges had come, or from where they gleaned their scientific knowledge and pedagogical methods. Several of those who would become active in the formation of the earliest scientific societies came to the colleges with a fair amount of knowledge gained from work on state and federal government surveys. Among them was Edward Hitchcock, minister, geologist, founder of the American Geological Society, professor and then president of Amherst College, and friend of Mary Lyon.

It is clear that college science faculty also desired to proselytize their own interests. Moreover, if not at once, eventually a number of them saw the benefits of supporting the higher education of women in science. As early as the teens there were some among them who, like the churchmen, supported the education of women in science to provide companionate wives for themselves and future male science faculty. Like the churchmen, they wanted helpmates who shared their outlook, understood their work, and could assist them in it.[34] By the 1830s we find a number who felt science education for women would provide them with seminary, academy, and primary school teachers committed to formally disseminating the scholarly knowledge they were gathering and organizing.

Although neither the churchmen nor the men of science were clear about whether women would or should be in charge of women's higher education, they needed personnel. A few women read this need as an opportunity for women to gain more authority, a higher status, and job security in educational work, which included science studies. Here was a chance for women from the small, hard-pressed farm families of New England: if they possessed the right abilities, ambitions, and fortitude, as well as connections in the evangelical community, they could join forces with men in a great cause. Moreover, it proffered them a foothold in institutional structures where they might have some autonomy and wield social influence of some import. They might have local women and their own networks of teachers to use as leverage in negotiating with churchmen and college men. The men certainly were aware that women comprised by far the largest number of evangelical adherents, constituted an important financial resource, and (many of them) supported higher education for their daughters.[35] Unlike some of the men who came with experience in specialized scientific work identified with economic development of natural resources, the women came with experience in teaching and an academic knowledge of science gained from study with men. In a society with limited employment opportunities for women, their links to emerging capitalist development had been indirect or very localized. They had chosen or were forced to choose work paid in cash or barter by parents and students who viewed education as an investment in an unclear future.[36]

One woman who saw that women teachers could exploit these circumstances to their own advantage was Mary Lyon, who founded Mount Holyoke Female Seminary in 1837.[37] Lyon's ability to assess the attitudes of churchmen and college men toward women and then to manage those attitudes to her advantage went a great way in making her effort a success. As she expressed it, the challenge was to make her project attractive to men without arousing their "fear [of] the effect on society of so much female influence, and what they will call female greatness."[38]

Lyon herself came from a hardscrabble farm in the hills of western Massachusetts, where she had learned early on the virtues of trading services for self-betterment and economic improvement. In fact, her life reveals in miniature that move from the culture of agricultural self-sufficiency to rural capitalism in the geographic region so well detailed by Christopher Clark.[39] As a young girl she kept house for her brother in exchange for his paying her school fees. After teaching in small-town academies, she taught in a women's seminary, where she and other teachers and students shared the housekeeping and cooking to keep down expenses. Using a small savings from her teaching, she was able to attend the influential Byfield Female Seminary in 1821, where she gained the additional education, manners, skills, and connections that would qualify her to teach a better class and level of student.

Here she studied with one of the most important men to provide women with formal scientific education in these years: Reverend Joseph Emerson, principal of the seminary. Emerson, although ordained, was a committed schoolman who prepared his women students to use their intellects by training them in philosophy, logic, disputation, and the science of physics. "It is thinking, thinking intensely, that nerves the mind, that makes the scholar," he said.[40] The aim of studying nature, for Emerson, was to produce women who could question, reason, and seek new information, not to subordinate them to religious authority. At Byfield, Lyon developed an interest in chemistry, which she would eventually teach at Mount Holyoke.

In the following years she underwent conversion to evangelical Protestantism. Thus certified in the eyes of the church and committed to a life of good works, she conceived the idea of founding a women's seminary primarily for the training of teachers. It was a way to advance her own goals by improving the status of a select group of women drawn from the large and unregulated population of women teachers. She also met Edward Hitchcock and his wife during the 1820s. They provided her with additional education in scientific subjects and ideas for teaching science, some of which she observed by attending Hitchcock's courses at Amherst College. The Hitchcocks probably helped her to pursue her project by introducing her to local influential church members. Encouraged by offers of support from the president and trustees of Amherst College and the minister and deacons of the South Hadley Congregational Church, Lyon opened Mount Holyoke Female Seminary in South Hadley in 1837.[41]

Under these favorable circumstances, Lyon worked out a division of labor between the evangelical clergy and Mount Holyoke teachers on the one hand and between male college faculty and women seminary teachers on the other. In these arrangements, she stressed the high goals they all had in common and pointed out the desirability of women teachers. But as she did so she also forged an economic rationale that argued for equal funding for equivalent work, and wrapped it in an appealing image of self-sacrifice intended to win her supporters, students, and faculty. These varied threads are skillfully woven together in the righteous language of the early missives she wrote for the seminary. In one, for example, she clearly joined her forces with those of the churchmen, describing teachers as aids, but also suggesting these women were equal if not superior to churchmen on the basis of their moral stature and economic utility. "Fill the country with ministers," she wrote, "and they could no more conquer the whole land and secure their victories, without the aid of many times their number of self-denying teachers."[42] In a prospectus in which she defined the goals of the seminary, she described it as designed to

> fit young women to be educators rather than mere teachers . . . wives and mothers . . . and also to establish the principle that the education of the daughters of the church calls as rightfully for the free gifts of the church as does that of her sons.[43]

From the beginning she made science a central attraction of the seminary's curriculum, but also a symbol of the institution and an expression of its special character. Describing the "grand features of this institution [as] an elevated standard of science, literature, and refinement, and a modest standard of expense," she also made certain to mention that here faculty would see to it that everything would be "guided and modified by the spirit of the gospel."[44] Still a bit later she enthusiastically declared Mount Holyoke a "castle of science," as she increased the number of courses and classrooms devoted to science and systematized all facets of seminary living to conform to what she called a natural system in which God's laws were manifest.[45] Her statements wrapped the radical implications of women who taught subjects at the college level within respectable religious and conventional social cloth. Among these subjects, she gave the study of nature a special place.

Lyon presented the study of science so that it appeared under the aegis of evangelical objectives, but was generally compatible with the objectives of the college men. However, as she managed it, science teaching was not entirely under the college men's control either. In practice, guided by her sense of where wise accommodation with them was necessary and useful, she arranged with them to divide the responsibilities for teaching science between visiting male faculty from colleges and technical institutes in surrounding towns and her own faculty, including herself. For the most part these men delivered the lectures, and the teachers supervised the recitation of the lectures. Just who inaugurated such policies is not known, but the men also helped Mount Holyoke faculty move up in status, serving as models for these working women to emulate. The amorphous nature of divisions in scientific labor at this time left leeway for the women faculty to attempt moving into more intellectually adventurous areas of science teaching being defined by men, while working to distance themselves from a lower class of teachers in primary schools and from less scholarly finishing school faculty. They were also anxious to make it clear they were not from the laboring classes.

This was a precarious business, which the teachers attempted to sort out within their sense of what might be socially possible and personally desireable for women in their position. Gentility was an issue. Thus, one teacher wrote that her colleague, Miss Mary C. Whitman gives "very interesting lectures. She calls it talking. She became most discouraged to day [*sic*] with the Galvanic Battery, & said she believed it was not for a lady to manage."[46] This jockeying for a place, gingerly pushing upward into male elites' company while aggressively pushing back the working classes was a process that filled some of the women faculty with mixed emotions: ambition, hope, despair, and self-deprecation, for example, mingled together.

Men could have the advantage of greater specialized knowledge gained through experience working outside academe. They certainly felt fewer social constraints than did the women teachers so far as taking the floor to lecture or to inaugurate innovative subject matter and teaching methods. It is not easy, therefore, to determine whether Mary Lyon or Edward Hitchcock was first to propose a course on human physiology specially tailored to women. It was Hitchcock, however, who delivered the lectures and demonstrated his points to the women faculty and students using a mannequin of his own devising. In his assumption of this activity, he not only took responsibility for and control over information concerning women and their bodies, but also helped establish formal conventions for its presentation and dissemination in the name of efficiency.

The result was a complex sociological and psychological readjustment of working relationships. As Miss Whitman recounted,

> To make the lectures more profitable, the school is to be divided into classes to recite the lectures. All the teachers will hear classes. The Manikin is exhibited to us. How clear an idea it does give us of the human system . . . He is so perfectly modest in all his descriptions of the human frame, that one cannot possibly *fear* he will say any thing undesirable.[47]

There was a certain thrilled anxiety women teachers experienced concerning their new working personalities and the boundaries and filters on communication they were helping establish with male college faculty to give shape and order to their working relationships. Distancing themselves from their own bodies required an objectification of themselves, of their very sexuality, even as they raised their social status as teachers. The terms they chose to describe this process reveal a strong affinity with emerging capitalist ways of viewing the world in terms of cost and profit.

This was of course a situation in flux. Outside the walls of academe in the 1840s and 1850s capitalist investment in manufacturing, communication, and transportation grew, as did private and public support for scientific information gathering, and the education and moral improvement of immigrants, Native Americans in newly acquired territories, and non-Christian inhabitants of foreign lands. Churchmen as well as male and female faculty who taught science drew strength and advantages from these changes, each in a way that clarified and hardened distinctions between churchmen and college men and between college men and seminary women. The churchmen, aware of the prospects for missionary work at home and abroad now more than ever saw the value of having teachers skilled in moral discipline, and they sought to impose this pedagogical objective on the design of all courses, including science, offered in colleges and seminaries. Mount Holyoke women felt these pressures when they hosted churchmen who denigrated "the value of mere learning" to them.[48]

Male science faculty could take the circumstances as an opportunity to separate themselves from the churchmen on the issue of moral development versus scholarship. In the process they also distinguished themselves from male scholars of other subjects and from women scholars in general, but not from evangelical religious values broadly defined. This effort at professional self-definition is well captured in a speech Hitchcock presented at Andover Theological Seminary in 1852, in which he came to grips with what it meant to be a scientist, rather than a man of the church or a teacher. He defined his role in the following way:

> He is a man who loves Nature, and with untiring industry endeavors to penetrate her mysteries. With a mind too large for narrow views, too generous and frank for distorting prejudice, and too pure to be the slave of appetite and passion, he calmly surveys the phenomena of nature, to learn from thence the great plan of the universe as it lay originally in the divine mind. . . . and we may be sure that whatever goes by the name of science, which contradicts a fair and enlightened exhibition of revealed truth, is only false philosophy.[49]

They came to designate themselves a special category of men who performed a specialized and highly exalted kind of work. Their narrow goals differed from those of churchmen, as did their means, but their interest in exploring the large framework of the universe, their long-term objectives, had equal weight and comparable moral benefits.

In fact, Mary Lyon did not choose to follow the churchmen, nor did she feel closed off from science as a scholarly endeavor. Having already made the arrangement that visiting male faculty would take charge of lectures and her own female teachers would concern themselves with the recitations and demonstrations, after 1845 Lyon hardened this division of labor and committed herself to seeing that the circumscribed work women did was done in her words "perfectly"—that is, with precision and attention to detail. In this context, Miss Whitman's misgivings concerning the lower-class connotations of handling equipment were swept aside. Its use now took on a more positive connotation, for it promised greater mastery over nature—a sign of expertise. To this end Lyon outfitted newly enlarged quarters for teaching science with the latest equipment and drove her teachers to learn to use it. She also ensured herself an expanded power base when her graduates founded sister and daughter institutions modeled on Mount Holyoke on the North American continent and abroad.[50]

The division of labor and expansion allowed her to continue to serve both clienteles for women's education and to ensure a large market for graduates that covered a growing spectrum of teaching-related employment. If it meant backing off from the effort to enter into the more intellectually challenging dimensions of science teaching that put it squarely in company with theorizing, this move did not close off access to new information or new ways of teaching science, or the possibility of adding new bits of information to the big picture through, for example, careful observation of botanical specimens. Her choice was an interesting amalgam that stopped short of making claims for herself and her teachers as scientists in Hitchcock's terms, but allowed for them to be scientists' helpmates. She also included them among this elect group of Christians, for after all those who sought truth and those who sought perfection were both moved by the highest aims of the gospel. And she could leave aside altogether the politically volatile, vexing question of what to do when biblical and scientific explanations didn't coincide. In the process Lyon also made the persona of the woman science teacher both less "ladylike" and less domestic.

This little vignette suggests that the clerical leaders of the Second Great Awakening provided the basis for and helped shape a scientific culture that included men and women. They did so by giving special authority and social status to a select group of men and women whom they had drawn to the colleges and seminaries they oversaw. There are three major ways in which these churchmen aided the formation of this culture. First, they provided the institutional settings that gave these ambitious (unmarried) men and women bases of operation that were semi-independent of one another. Within their own single-sex schools and in cooperation with other institutions, these faculty defined the nature of academic science, developed their skills, and sorted out the work. These institutions also provided them with a vehicle for extending their authority and that of science into the wider society through the students they educated. Thus, they could actually feel they were carrying out the evangelical agenda, however they may have modified it. Teaching became a specialized form of proselytizing in which they disseminated interest in science into the general population while holding fast to the belief that they worked for the common good. Second, the evangelical clergy identified the function of these institutions with a set of values that gave those who taught the scientific study of nature a moral right to claim to be leaders in building a new society. What they had not realized was that the science faculty could adjust these values to their own interests and to changing opportunities in the wider society. Third, in their concern to use these institutions to manage the course of rural capitalism, the churchmen connected the science faculty directly to market forces. Increasing public interest in science, divested of its overt associations with theology, gave science faculty increasing say over the churchmen in defining the aims and content of their courses, in budgetary expenditures and other activities related to exercising more power and influence in a group. In these three ways, churchmen opened the door to men and women to work out a set of arrangements with one another, a set of customs rooted in single-sex institutional relationships.

These male and female evangelicals each had their own view of the situation and of how their values could help them secure power and influence in this newly forming leadership. Emerging customs that defined men's and women's social roles could constrain or open opportunities for defining one's occupation. It took some risk to interpret changes in the educational market as favorable both to expansion of faculty members' authority as scholars and to the advance of the public good. These men and women may have moved from the word to the spirit of the gospels, but they remained Protestants. Nevertheless, it was the spirit of the gospels that served as their general guide and justification for the actions they took and decisions they made.

Thus, these male and female science faculties built on a foundation laid by evangelical clergy, creating a culture that was defined by Protestants, even if the language was most often divested of religious references. Expanding their influence, shifting with the market, and adapting to new institutional forms, the members of this intellectual elite remained almost exclusively Protestant in origin as late as 1940.[51] They held the posts in science in higher education. Their students held the positions in all the new institutions being opened in newly acquired territories: in secondary and primary schools; in government and industry, as well as in the other professions; in business; in local school boards; and in middle-class homes raising children. And they were jealous of these holds on society, limiting access of Jews and Catholics until the 1920s and practicing a benevolent paternalism toward a select number of African Americans.[52] If we add to their ranks the faculty in colleges and seminaries allied with evangelicalism and those in state teachers' colleges, then the scale and scope of their influence is even greater.

4. Closing the Loop

It is helpful here to return to the ideas of Edward Shils mentioned earlier in this essay. Shils had proposed we consider society in terms of a center and a periphery connected to one another. At the center is a group of elites whose values are those that dominate the rest of society. These elites can be geographically scattered, but the society usually is bounded geographically.[53] The history of the scientific profession whose American origins I have sketched out above can be considered in terms of the formation of such a new elite center in American society during the nineteenth and twentieth centuries. Protestant and middle class in character, its membership included a select number of women. Evangelical in spirit, its members accommodated well to the expansive character of first commercial and then industrial capitalism. It is not difficult to understand how, by the turn of the century, America had become a society with a population deeply committed to a vision of progress that echoed the commitment of the center to scientific truth and Protestant morality.

To say this is to recall Max Weber's study of the connections between Protestant beliefs and culture and the development of capitalism, as well as Robert Merton's study on Puritans and the scientific revolution of the seventeenth century. While these men examined the interplay between society and culture, belief and action, they accepted that men were the actors who mattered at the time. As Merton observed in the preface to the 1970 edition of his study, the question about what are the modes of interplay between society, culture, and science is germane to every historical epoch in which "men are at work in science." If we read men and women for the nineteenth and twentieth century in the United States, then we can begin to see how the socially patterned interests and motivations in the social sphere of science have been intertwined and interdependent with those in other social spheres in this later period.[54] To do so broadens the sphere of science and forces us to consider professionalization as the product of contingencies in which individuals within a religiously defined social group responded to what they perceived as opportunities in a variety of ways that meshed with one another.

It is thus possible to imagine how members of the other professions emerging in the late nineteenth century took science as their guide. Graduates of the same institutions as their scientific role models, they too partook of that education in science within this expansionistic Christian context. If they, like the scientists, sometimes went abroad for an education in German research methods, and if they rejected ministerial authority, they still carried with them a sense that their work was informed by the moral quest, evangelistic spirit, and social ambition that motivated men and women in academic science.

All of this brings me back to the beginning of this essay with its remarks about the different positions science has held in the discipline of history. Its practitioners have ceased to be models of virtue or seekers of some absolute truth whom historians emulate. The preceding reconsideration of the cultural institutions that marked the early formation of the scientific community in the United States suggests, however, that the history of science should be more central in the histories of industrializing America we research, publish, and read.[55]

Notes

I wish to thank Gunnar Broberg, Jonathan Friedman, Kaisa Ekholm-Friedman, and Elyn Frykman for their kind support and assistance.

1. Peter Novick, *That Noble Dream: The "Objectivity Question" and the American Historical Profession* (Cambridge, Mass.: Cambridge University Press, 1988), 33–34. On the history of professionalization, with special reference to the place of science as a model, see Bruce A. Kimball, *The "True Professional Ideal" in America* (Cambridge, Mass.: Blackwell, 1992); Alexandra Oleson and John Voss, eds., *The Organization of Knowledge in Modern America, 1860–1920* (Baltimore and London: Johns Hopkins University Press, 1976); Burton J. Bledstein, *The Culture of Professionalism: The Middle Class and the Development of Higher Education in America* (New York: W. W. Norton, 1976); Gerald Geison, ed., *Professions and Professional Ideologies in America* (Chapel Hill and London: University of North Carolina Press, 1983), esp. the introductory essay; Samuel Haber, *The Quest for Authority and Honor in the American Professions, 1750–1900* (Chicago: University of Chicago Press, 1991); Thomas L. Haskell, *The Emergence of Professional Social Science* (Urbana: University of Illinois Press, 1977).
2. Novick, *Noble Dream,* 296, and n. 27. Charles Coulston Gillispie, *The Edge of Objectivity: An Essay in the History of Scientific Ideas* (Princeton, N.J.: Princeton University Press 1960).
3. Robert K. Merton, "Science and Technology in a Democratic Order," *Journal of Legal and Political Sociology* 1 (1942). Also see Novick, *Noble Dream,* 296, and n. 28.
4. Novick, *Noble Dream,* 526 ff.; Georg G. Iggers, *Historiography in the Twentieth Century: From Scientific Objectivity to the Postmodern Challenge* (Hanover, N.H.: Wesleyan University Press, published by University Press of New England, 1997), 97–134 are relevant, but especially the section on the revival of narrative, 97–100; Joyce Appleby, Lynn Hunt, Margaret Jacobs, *Telling the Truth about History* (New York: Norton, 1994), 160–97.
5. Edward Shils, *Center and Periphery: Essays in Macrosociology* (Chicago and London: University of Chicago Press, 1975), 3.
6. The material for the section on Mount Holyoke is drawn from Miriam R. Levin and Pamela E. Mack, *Religion, Science and Sex at Mount Holyoke (1837–1949),* book manuscript in preparation.
7. Thomas S. Kuhn, *The Structure of Scientific Revolutions,* 2nd ed. (Chicago: University of Chicago Press, 1970). See Novick, *Noble Dream,* 526–33, for a discussion of Kuhn's ideas and influence. The quotation is from Novick, 526, and n. 2.
8. The process of shifting away from internalist history of science has engendered heated controversy between historians of science, sociologists of science, and scientists over the question of what scientists are really about. For the most recent episode involving Professor Alan Sokal and the editors of the journal *Social Text,* see the documentation on the web at http://weber.u.washington.edu/~jwalsh/sokal/articles. The literature on the history of

the scientific profession includes: Sally Gregory Kohlstedt, *The Formation of the American Scientific Community: The American Association for the Advancement of Science 1846–60* (Urbana: University of Illinois Press, 1976); Robert V. Bruce, *The Launching of Modern American Science, 1846–1876* (New York: Alfred A. Knopf, 1987), 75–93; Stanley Guralnick, *Science and the Ante-bellum American College* (Philadelphia: American Philosophical Society, 1975). George H. Daniels, *American Science in the Age of Jackson* (New York: Columbia University Press, 1968), esp. ch. 2, presents a more positive image of the antebellum college. On American higher education with references to science education see: Oleson, *Organization of Knowledge;* Roger L. Geiger, *To Advance Knowledge: The Growth of American Research Universities, 1900–1940* (New York and Oxford: Oxford University Press, 1986); Thomas Bender, Peter D. Hall, et al., "Institutionalization and Education in the Nineteenth and Twentieth Centuries," *History of Education Quarterly* 20, no. 4 (winter 1980): 449–72; and Colin B. Burke, *American Collegiate Populations: A Test of the Traditional View* (New York: New York University Press, 1982), 11–12, and 11, n. 1 for a critical overview of the literature on this subject. Studies produced in the later 1970s and 1980s have corrected both the image of the antebellum colleges as backwaters and the concept of a "university revolution" in the late nineteenth century. See Michael B. Katz, "The Role of American Colleges in the Nineteenth Century," *History of Education Quarterly* 23, (summer 1983): 211–13. Among these works are: Burke, *American Collegiate Populations*; and Peter Dobkin Hall, *The Organization of American Culture, 1700–1900: Private Institutions, Elites, and the Origins of American Nationality* (New York: New York University Press, 1982).

Other studies have concentrated on the role played by organizations and institutions in creating scientific specialists. Paul Mattingly, *The Classless Profession: American Schoolmen in the Nineteenth Century* (New York: New York University Press, 1975), argues that the history of professionalization in the colleges is best understood in terms of the professionalization of teaching in which faculty at different types of institutions defined their functions in light of the emerging bureaucratic structure of American education. Also important here is Bruno Latour and Steve Woolgar, *Laboratory Life: The Construction of Scientific Facts* (Princeton, N.J.: Princeton University Press, 1986).

On women and scientific professionalization: Margaret Rossiter's *Women Scientists in America: Struggles and Strategies to 1940* (Baltimore: Johns Hopkins University Press, 1982), esp. chs. 2, 3, 4, and 7, establishes the existence of active, professionally motivated faculty at women's colleges from the late nineteenth century on. On women and professionalization also see: Joyce Antler, *The Educated Woman and Professionalization, 1890–1920* (Ph.D. diss., SUNY Stony Brook, 1977); Sally Gregory Kohlstedt, "In from the Periphery: American Women in Science, 1830–1880," *Signs,* 4 (1978): 81–96 and 43; Mary Kinnear, *In Subordination: Professional Women, 1870–1970* (Montreal: McGill-Queen's University Press, 1995); Roberta Frankfort, *Collegiate Women: Domesticity and Career in Turn-of-the-Century America* (New York: New York University Press, 1977); Helen Lefkowitz Horowitz, *The Power and Passion of M. Carey Thomas* (New York: Knopf, 1994).

9. Daniel Goldstein, "'Yours for Science': The Smithsonian Institution's Correspondents and the Shape of Scientific Community in Nineteenth-Century America," *Isis* 85, no. 4 (December 1994): 573–99; Sally Gregory Kohlstedt, "Parlors, Primers, and Public Schooling: Education for Science in 19th Century America," *Isis* 81, no. 4 (December 1990): 425–45; Kohlstedt, "Reassessing Science in Antebellum America," *American Quarterly* 29, no. 4 (winter 1977): 444–53; Elizabeth Keeney, *The Botanizers: Amateur Scientists in Nineteenth Century America* (Chapel Hill: University of North Carolina Press, 1992), 22–27,

51–68; John C. Burnham, *How Superstition Won and Science Lost* (New Brunswick, N.J.: Rutgers University Press, 1987).

10. See Kuhn's comment in Novick, *Noble Dream,* 510. Also, see James Turner, *Without God, without Creed: The Origins of Unbelief in America* (Baltimore: Johns Hopkins University Press, 1985).
11. See Turner, 136; and Richard Whitley, "Changes in the Social and Intellectual Organization of the Sciences: Professionalization and the Arithmetic Ideal," in *The Social Production of Scientific Knowledge* edited by Everett Mendelsohn et al. (Boston: D. Reidel, 1977), 145. Daniel Kevles, *The Physicists* (New York: Random House, 1979), is a study in the rise to power of a particular group of men and how they came to epitomize their profession.
12. See discussion of Merton in Novick, *Noble Dream,* 296 and n. 28.
13. Margaret Rossiter, *Women,* 1982. Other collections include: Martha Moore Trescott, ed., *The Dynamo and the Virgin Revisited: Women and Technological Change in History: An Anthology* (Metuchen, N.J.: Scarecrow Press, 1979); Pnina G. Abir-Am and Dorinda Outram, eds., *Uneasy Careers and Intimate Lives* (New Brunswick, N.J.: Rutgers University Press, 1987); Abir-Am et al., eds., *Creative Couples in the Sciences* (New Brunswick, N.J.: Rutgers University Press, 1995).
14. Londa L. Schiebinger, *The Mind Has No Sex? Women in the Origins of Modern Science* (Cambridge, Mass.: Harvard University Press, 1989).
15. Emily Martin, *The Woman in the Body: A Cultural Analysis of Reproduction* (Boston: Beacon Press, 1988).
16. Linda Kerber, "Separate Spheres, Female Worlds, Woman's Place: The Rhetoric of Women's History," *Journal of American History* 75, no. 1 (June 1988): 9–39.
17. Kerber, "Separate Spheres," 27.
18. Abir-Am and Outram, *Uneasy Careers.*
19. Evelyn Fox Keller, *A Feeling for the Organism: The Life and Work of Barbara McClintock* ((New York: W. H. Freeman and Co., 1983).
20. Nancy Hopkins, "Women Scientists and Feminist Critics of Science," in *Learning about Women: Gender, Politics, and Power,* edited by Jill K. Conway, Susan C. Bourque, and Joan W. Scott (Ann Arbor: University of Michigan Press, 1987), 79.
21. Rossiter, *Women,* 267–312.
22. Quoted in Kerber, "Separate Spheres," 38.
23. Joan Scott, *Gender and The Politics of History* (New York: Columbia University Press, 1988), 3–5.
24. Elizabeth Fox-Genovese in her review of Linda Kerber's book suggested the importance of further exploring the connections between women's new roles in the republic and religion and industrialization. *The Journal of American History* 68, no. 1 (June 1981): 119–21. Important work on the intersection of science and religion in this period includes: Theodore Dwight Bozeman, *Protestants in an Age of Science: The Baconian Ideal and Antebellum American Religious Thought* (Chapel Hill: University of North Carolina Press, 1977); Ralph Henry Gabriel, *Religion and Learning at Yale: The Church of Christ in the College and University, 1757–1957* (New Haven: Yale University Press, 1958); Louise L. Stevenson, *Scholarly Means to Evangelical Ends: The New Haven Scholars and the Transformation of Higher Learning in America, 1830–1890* (Baltimore: Johns Hopkins University Press, 1986); Thomas Le Duc, *Piety and Intellect at Amherst College, 1865–1912* (New York: Columbia University Press, 1946); Stanley Guralnick, "Geology and Religion before Darwin: The Case of Edward Hitchcock, Theologian and Geologist (1798–1864)," *Isis* 63 (1972): 529–43; Philip J. Lawrence, "Edward Hitchcock: The Christian Geologist," *American Philosophical Society Proceedings* 116 (1972): 21–34; John Hedley Brooke, "Science and the Fortunes of Natural Theology: Some Historical Perspectives," *Zygon: Jour-*

nal of Religion and Science 24 (1989): 3–22; Turner, *Without God, without Creed;* David C. Lindberg, and Ronald L. Numbers, eds., *God and Nature: Historical Essays on the Encounter between Christianity and Science* (Berkeley: University of California Press, 1986). For background see Donald G. Mathews, "The Second Great Awakening as an Organizing Process, 1780–1830: An Hypothesis," *American Quarterly* 21, no. 1 (spring 1969): 23–44. Susan Juster, *Disorderly Women: Sexual Politics and Evangelicalism in Revolutionary New England* (Ithaca, N.Y.: Cornell University Press, 1994), esp. chs. 2, 5, and 6.

25. Among organizations that served to link colleges and seminaries by placing their graduates were the American Board of Missions and the Society for the Promotion of Collegiate and Theological Education in the West. See Arthur C. Cole, *A Hundred Years of Mount Holyoke College* (New Haven: Yale University Press, 1940); Mattingly, *Profession,* 104–12.
26. For a discussion of the complex cultural, economic, and social changes occurring in this region during these years, see Christopher Clark, *The Roots of Rural Capitalism: Western Massachusetts, 1780–1860* (Ithaca, N.Y.: Cornell University Press, 1990).
27. The exact number of colleges and theological and female seminaries founded in these years is not known; however, it is possible to gain some rough idea from the figures provided by Oscar and Mary Handlin. They estimate that between 1820 and 1870 the number of colleges rose to five hundred. The lifespans of these institutions were often quite limited as many fought losing battles with costs and competition for clientele. Oscar and Mary Handlin, *The American College and American Culture: Socialization as a Function of Higher Education* (New York: McGraw-Hill Book Co., 1970), 19 and 25–28. See also David F. Allmendinger, *Paupers and Scholars: The Transformation of Student Life in Nineteenth-Century New England* (New York: St. Martin's Press, 1975).
28. For example, Bowdoin College in one decade produced 113 lawyers, 36 state representatives, 17 state senators, 6 judges, 8 members of the U.S. House of Representatives, 6 members of the U.S. Senate, 2 secretaries of the treasury and one president of the United States: Wilmott B. Mitchell, "A Remarkable Bowdoin Decade, 1820–1830" (a paper read at a meeting of the Town and College Club, Brunswick, Maine: Bowdoin College, 1952), 22–23. Laurence R. Veysey, *The Emergence of the American University* (Chicago: University of Chicago Press, 1965); Frederick Rudolph, *The American College and University: A History* (New York: Knopf, 1962); and Frederick Rudolph, *Curriculum: A History of the American Undergraduate Course of Study Since 1636* (San Francisco: Josey-Bass Publishers, 1981). Also see Thomas Bender, et al., "Institutionalization and Education."
29. Leonard I. Sweet, *The Minister's Wife: Her Role in Nineteenth Century American Evangelism* (Philadelphia: Temple University Press, 1983), 9, 153–154. Cole, *A Hundred Years of Mount Holyoke,* 117, reports that the church, like other Calvinist institutions, cooperated with agencies such as the American Board of Commissions for Foreign Missions, holding monthly "concerts" offering prayers for the salvation of the world. Cole reports that "An important factor in arousing missionary interest was found in the visits of returned [male] missionaries and of missionary executives, who usually addressed the school." Among other places, they came from Western Reserve College, Canada, the Creek and Cherokee nations, Persia, Syria, India, China, and the Sandwich Islands. For the period after the Civil War, see Patricia R. Hill, *The World Their Household: The American Women's Foreign Mission Movement and Cultural Transformation, 1870–1920* (Ann Arbor: University of Michigan Press, 1985).
30. See Guralnick, "Geology and Religion," and Turner, *Without God, without Creed.*
31. David Noble, *A World without Women* (Oxford: Oxford University Press, 1992), 250–56.
32. Teachers' enthusiastic adoption of equipment in common school classrooms is discussed in Deborah Warner, "Commodities for the Classroom: Apparatus for Science and Educa-

tion in Antebellum America," *Annals of Science* 45 (1988): 387–97. Also see Sally Gregory Kohlstedt, "Parlors, Primers, and Public Schooling: Education for Science in 19th Century America," *Isis* 81 (1990): 425–45; Kohlstedt, "Reassessing Science in Antebellum America," *American Quarterly* 29 (1977): 444–53. Mattingly, *Classless Profession,* 38, 146, comments on the college men's initial aversion to a whole range of classroom aids because they threatened to corrupt the intellectual tone and hence weaken the scholarly basis of their claim to higher social status and authority. In the end, they embraced the new apparatus because of the way it engaged students' attention, according to Mattingly. It is possible to see that one could place different interpretations on the use of equipment, depending on whether it was viewed as a mechanical skill or a means of obtaining more precise information.

33. Lillian B. Miller, *The Lazzaroni: Science and Scientists in Mid-Nineteenth Century America* (Washington: Smithsonian Institution Press, 1972). For a particularly clear example of the Lazzaroni trying to control American science and failing, see Mary Ann James, *Elites in Conflict: The Antebellum Clash Over the Dudley Observatory* (New Brunswick, N.J.: Rutgers University Press, 1987). Russell Henry Chittenden, *History of the Sheffield Scientific School of Yale University, 1846–1922* (New Haven: Yale University Press, 1928); Louise L. Stevenson, *Scholarly Means to Evangelical Ends* (Baltimore: Johns Hopkins University Press, 1986).
34. For a classic formulation of the perfect female partner for the male college science teacher, see the dedication "To My Beloved Wife" in Edward Hitchcock, *The Religion of Geology and Its Connected Sciences* (London: Blackwood & Col, 1851), ii–iii. Sweet, *The Minister's Wife,* explores the boundaries and opportunities which this position opened to women to participate in the work of the evangelical ministry. See also Abir-Am, *Creative Couples.*
35. For a discussion of the literature with reference to women's entering the work force and women's education, see Linda Kerber, "Separate Spheres," 16–17, 24.
36. Clark, *Roots of Rural Capitalism,* 89–90, 115.
37. A new biography of Lyon is much needed. The two that exist are Edward Hitchcock, et al., *The Power of Christian Benevolence Illustrated in the Life and Labors of Mary Lyon* (Northampton, Mass.: Hopkins, Bridgeman, 1851); and Beth Bradford Gilchrist, *The Life of Mary Lyon* (New York: Houghton-Mifflin, 1910). See also Cole, *One Hundred Years.*
38. Cole, *One Hundred Years,* 19. Also see the comment in Gilchrist, *Life,* 184.
39. Clark, *Roots of Rural Capitalism.*
40. Cole, *One Hundred Years,* 6–7.
41. It is possible she worked to elicit this invitation, for, as one of her former students described her, Lyon felt there was "the greater chance of success, attained with less friction, for a scheme which appeared to originate with men." Gilchrist, *Life,* 184.
42. Letter from Mary Lyon, 1836, quoted in Kathryn Kish Sklar, "The Founding of Mount Holyoke Female Seminary: A Case Study in Educational Change," in *Women of America: A History,* edited by Carol Ruth Berkin and Mary Beth Norton (Boston: Houghton-Mifflin Co., 1979), See also 178–201 for an excellent discussion of Lyon's strategies.
43. February 1837, quoted in Sarah D. (Locke) Stow, *History of Mount Holyoke Seminary, South Hadley, Mass., during Its First Half Century, 1837–1887* (South Hadley: Mount Holyoke Seminary, 1887), 72.
44. Stow, *History,* 54.
45. Bonnie Shmurak and Bonnie S. Handler, "'Castle of Science': Mount Holyoke College and the Preparation of Women in Chemistry, 1837–1941," *History of Education Quarterly* 32, no. 3 (fall 1992), 315–41.
46. Susan Tolman, *Journal Letter,* January 27, 1847, Mount Holyoke College Archives (MHCA).

47. Lucy T. Lyon, *Journal Letter,* February 21, 1844, MHCA.
48. Rev. Rufus Anderson of the American Board of Commissioners for Foreign Missions spoke out against "the exaggerated estimate placed by parents on the value of mere learning to their daughters." He then denigrated intellectual aspirations as a threat to the social order (Cole, *One Hundred Years,* 47).
49. Quoted in Daniels, *American Science in the Age of Jackson,* 52 and n. 38. Biographical information on Edward Hitchcock includes: Daniels, *American Science in the Age of Jackson,* 213; Kohlstedt, "The Geologists' Model for National Science, 1840–1847," *Proceedings of the American Philosophical Society* 118 (1974): 179–95; Guralnick, "Geology and Religion"; Philip J. Lawrence, "Edward Hitchcock: The Christian Geologist," *American Philosophical Society Proceedings,* 116 (1972): 21–34.
50. Cole, *One Hundred Years,* 99. For other references to Lyon's almost obsessive focus on systematic organization, see Cole, 43, 105, 125. Among the sister and daughter seminaries, some of which later became colleges, were Lake Erie Female Seminary, Mills Female Seminary, and schools in Madras, India, and South Africa.
51. M. Elizabeth Tidball and Vera Kistiakowsky, "Baccalaureate Origins of American Scientists and Scholars," *Science* 193 (1976): 646–52. Kenneth Hardy, "Social Origins of American Scientists and Scholars," *Science* 185 (1974): 497, places Mount Holyoke second in the period 1920 to 1939. His article also presents information purporting to establish a causal relationship, rather than just a correlation, between religious values and the production of scientists.
52. See for example the account of the African American biologist E. E. Just's experiences in Kenneth Manning, *Black Apollo of Science: The Life of Ernest Everett Just* (New York: Oxford University Press, 1983), 41–42, 69–70, 139–46, 162–63, *passim.*
53. Shils, *Center and Periphery,* 3–5.
54. Turner, *Without God, without Creed,* 232 ff. For a discussion of the precedents for this approach, see David Landes, *The Unbound Prometheus* (Cambridge, Mass.: Cambridge University Press, 1968), 30–32, and 31 n. 2; Max Weber, *The Protestant Ethic and the Spirit of Capitalism,* translated by Talcott Parsons (London: Unwin University Books, 1968); Robert Merton, *Science Technology and Society in Seventeenth Century England* (New York: Harper & Row, 1970), ix.
55. See the review of new textbooks for the history of American technology and science in David E. Nye, "A Moment of Synthesis: Recent Textbooks in the History of Technology," *Journal of Technology and Culture* 39, no. 2 (April 1998): 292–98, esp. 98 and n. 9. Two historians of American science and technology, Daniel Kevles and Merritt Roe Smith, are collaborating with U.S. historians to write a general history of nineteenth- and twentieth-century America which integrates developments within and outside the scientific and technological communities into a reconceptualized version of that history. Two examples here are the ripple effect legal decisions concerning commerce had on early-nineteenth-century industrialization and the inauguration of the nuclear power industry in the midst of cold-war politics. (Personal communications to the author from Prof. Kevles and Prof. Smith.) It remains to be seen how the culture of progress, Protestantism, and women's place within this culture will be treated, but the general direction this project is taking promises to be a fruitful one to pursue in future.

CHAPTER 24

WORK IN THE MOCTEZUMA BREWERY

John Womack

IN THE EARLY 1900S, Moctezuma ranked among Mexico's newest breweries. Opened in 1895 in one of the country's main industrial cities, Orizaba, Veracruz, in the Sierra Madre's cool, humid foothills some seventy-five miles from the Gulf, the brewery was enlarged in 1897 and again in 1907. It was a very promising business. Work at the Moctezuma Brewery in the 1900s did not affect the federal government. It had negligible importance in the national economy. Its product was only for pleasure and conspicuous consumption, and it sold in a very competitive market. But by 1908 work at Moctezuma mattered considerably statewide and substantially in Orizaba, for the capitalists who owned the company were highly influential, made the brewery a good customer of the Mexican Railway, the local interurban railroad, and the local electric company, and paid sizable taxes to the state and the city.[1] Also the 450 men and boys who worked at the brewery formed the fourth largest contingent of workers in the city.[2]

Like work at the textile mills nearby, this work took place in a modern factory. By 1908 "an enormous establishment" of several large buildings across seven or eight acres, the brewery was in production practically year-round.[3] It included an industrial supply of water and an industrial sewer. It had industrial transportation via two spurs on the Mexican railway, which it faced just across the square south, and the interurban track on the street along its east side. Its two central towers five stories high, three boilers for 175 horsepower, two steam engines, electric power lines carrying three-phase

60-cycle alternating current at 6,600 volts, and many motors, pumps, and machines constituted industrially powerful and industrially mechanized means of production. Big windows for some rooms, solid walls for others, sawtooth roofs on some buildings, and shacked vents on the roofs of others provided industrial control of light and climate.[4] The work happened in "order and precision," in "various and multiple operations," and in an industrially certain sequence.[5] Administratively, based mainly on the buildings, the division of labor was by then in fifteen departments: *cuartos calientes,* "hot rooms," the brewhouse; *casa de maquinaria,* the new "machine house," or machinery department; *cuartos fríos,* "cold rooms," the stockhouse; *hielo,* the ice plant; *patio,* the yard; *establos,* the barns; *obras,* construction and maintenance; *secadora,* the drying plant; *envase,* packages, the new barrel- and bottle-storage sheds; *bodega,* the storehouse; *embarrilado,* barreling; *embotellado,* bottling; *tonelería,* the cooper shop; *cajonería,* the box factory; and *taller mecánico,* mechanical repairs, the machine shop. In practice there were at least three times as many subdivisions among craftsmen, workmen, and laborers. Whistles at 6 A.M. and at 6 P.M. six days a week signalled the standard industrial day and week.[6] And production as such was "phenomenal," in the aggregate and in the articles actually produced.[7] The 114,096 barrels of beer recorded in 1908, for example, were actually some 36,000 kegs and ponies and some 33,000,000 pint bottles of beer.[8]

As at other factories work happened continually out in the brewery yard on the yard boss's orders. There seven days a week, day and night at the gates and patrolling along the walls and fences, were the *porteros,* the watchmen. There also seven days a week, in the barn or out in the corral north of the buildings, were the barn foreman and two or three stable boys, who took care of horses, mules, harness, and wagons, especially the brewery's two Abresch delivery wagons.[9] There Monday through Saturday at work in construction and maintenance from 6 A.M. to 6 P.M. were several masons, carpenters, handymen, and two or three gangs of laborers, often as many as fifty or sixty men and boys. And there every working day for the same twelve hours was the yard crew, the brewery's second largest department of workers, some one hundred men and boys, working usually in various gangs unloading freight. Two or three times a week a Mexican Railway yard crew would remove an empty boxcar from the spur along the front of the brewery, and spot a car loaded with nineteen tons of good, clean, bagged pale malt in front of the brewhouse. A brewery yard crew would rig a chute from the loaded car down into the brewhouse's basement, into a belt-and-bucket elevator's boot, and every day when called go feed the elevator, for three and a half or four hours unloading, opening, and emptying forty to forty-five 93-pound bags of malt an hour down the chute. Almost every week a railroad yard crew would remove another empty boxcar from the same spur, and spot next to the car of malt a car loaded with thirty tons of bagged rough rice, and daily for one and a half or two hours a brewery gang would unload, open, and empty forty to forty-five 100-pound bags of rice an hour down the chute and into the boot. Once a week, from a refrigerator car only that day on the spur, a gang would quickly unload sixteen 175-pound bales of cold, green hops and grunt them up to cold storage on the brewhouse's second floor. Once or twice a week from a car of firewood on the spur a gang would unload its twelve to thirteen cords and stack them alongside the track under a wood shed, and daily another gang would carry two and a half or three cords back to the boiler room. Every day a railroad yard crew would remove six or seven empty boxcars from the spur west around by the bottle storage sheds, and spot there six or seven cars loaded with cases and boxes of empty bottles. Usually every day an interurban teamster would bring a car of empty packages, barrels, and boxes of empty bottles, around to the sheds too. From these cars every day a yard gang would unload the barrels, cases, and boxes, eighteen hundred to two thousand of them, 110,000–120,000 bottles a day, and carry them into the sheds.[10]

In and out of the yard and back and forth across it through the day teamsters from the brewery barn would be driving wagons, sometimes alone, sometimes with a yard gang in tow. Nearly every day a driver would take a wagon out across the square to the railroad freight dock, pick up boxes of fittings, boxes of crowns, cases of labels, drums of caustic soda, barrels of lubricating oil, cylinders of ammonia, and other packages of supplies, and deliver them back at the storehouse, on the street along the east side. Every morning two Abresch drivers would take these wagons out to the brewery's wholesale agency on the same street, pick up barrels and boxes of beer, and leave to make local deliveries, and every afternoon return to the sheds with empty barrels and boxes of empty bottles, which a yard gang would unload. At least once a day a driver would take a wagon of heavy supplies from the storehouse around to the various departments that wanted them, where a yard gang would unload them.[11] At least once a day a driver would collect a wagonload of trash and garbage and take it to the incinerator at the drying plant, out by the storage sheds, where a yard crew would unload it. Usually twelve to fifteen times a day a driver would take a wagonload of spent grains to the drying plant, and a yard gang would unload them.

Out in the sheds, eight sheet-iron halls that baked under the sun and chilled under the rain, the work was like that of the yard gangs, but static, detailed, and discriminating. In the one shed for barrels, every morning the cooper would spend a couple of hours examining yesterday's returns, usually 140 to 145 kegs and ponies. At each he would hook out the bung and any still-corked vent, take the barrel by the chime, knock it lightly on the belly with the hook, and listen for the tone, dead from the damaged ones, clear and ringing from the sound ones. The damaged his apprentice would mark and set aside for repair. The sound he would feel with a finger through the bunghole, to tell if the surface inside it was smooth or rough. The rough, he would mark and set aside for relining.[12] Once they had enough good barrels, from yesterday's returns and earlier ones by then repaired and relined, 140 to 145, the cooper would tell the yard boss, and on his orders a yard gang would load them on a wagon alongside the shed, which a driver would take to the front of the bottle house, where the same gang would unload them.

In the sheds for bottles, from 6 A.M. to 6 P.M., amid the constant racket of wood clacking on wood and glass jingling, the shed gang would be receiving and sorting bottles. The cases were shipments of new wares from the United States, dark brown *medias,* pints, factory-clean; the boxes, shipments of returned pints, dirty, often with wire around the neck, and typically with at least part of a label still stuck on them. Broken boxes and chipped, cracked, and broken bottles the gang would throw into the trash. The good bottles it would dewire, rebox, the bottles *acostados* (lying down in the box), ten across, six deep, and stack them on *armones,* two-wheeled carts waiting alongside the sheds. Carters would continually push the loaded carts to the front of the bottle house, eighteen hundred to two thousand boxes a day. There another yard gang would continually unload the carts and restack the boxes.[13]

Also as at other factories six days a week from 6 A.M. to 6 P.M. a warehouse gang worked in the storeroom. Its men would unload the supply wagon, truck or carry the packages to the proper place to store them, stack or shelve them, watch for leaks of any liquid, and continually remove and reload packages for delivery to their destination. Likewise in the agency a gang would unload the kegs, ponies, and boxes trucked there, saddle the barrels, stack the boxes, watch for leaks, load the Abresch wagons, and load the interurban cars for delivery in the mill towns up the valley.

But, being a brewery, Moctezuma was an odd sort of factory. The definitive work there, brewing and fermenting, was a combination and succession of mechanical, chemical, and biological operations. However orderly, precise, industrial, it remained the practice of an ancient art: "the mechanisms do not form a connected series," the chemical "play of delicate affinities" and the biological reactions were always "somewhat uncertain," and the operations were significantly "manual."[14] Both brewing and fermenting operations were also intrinsically occasional, differentiated into sequential tasks. Unlike operations in a textile mill, they could not happen simultaneously and continuously but only by the batch, one after another.[15] Each brew was therefore a particular event. Puffs of black smoke would rise episodically from one of the seventy-foot chimneys behind the brewhouse, a white plume of vapor would stream from the old or the new eighty-five-foot ventilator, and whiffs of cooking grains and hops would drift through the neighborhood, for two, three, or four hours at a time. In 1908 this happened one, two, or three times a day ordinarily six days a week, fifty weeks of the year, altogether some 145 brews in the 60-barrel kettle and some 425 brews in the 250-barrel kettle, each one numbered and dated.[16] And every time the brew's author, the brewmaster, was there. This was not for technical supervision. The brewmaster knew mysteries of water, heat, grains, and time that he did not think he ought to know how to explain. He had not learned them at an academy, but from his experience, his "practical education." For the eight different beers then made at the brewery he carried in his head not formulae but recipes. When he appeared, it was to keep the authoritative record, announce a peremptory order, give masterly direction, or declare a conclusive judgment. On any day Monday through Saturday he would have a brew started whenever he reckoned was best, maybe at 4 A.M., maybe at 7:30 A.M., maybe at 10 P.M. During the brews he read gauges and his watch, thermometer, and saccharometer, but made his decisions by sight, smell, taste, and feel. And on any day Monday through Saturday work ended in the brewhouse whenever he ruled that the day's work was done, maybe at 7:30 P.M., maybe at 9:30 P.M., maybe at 1:00 the next afternoon. Similarly in the stockhouse each batch in fermentation bore a number and a date, had its page in the brewmaster's records, underwent his practical tests day or night at the hours he determined, and on his word that it was beer counted as a batch done. So in the "hot rooms" and the "cold rooms" the working day and the working night were irregular, arbitrary, and indefinite. Only between tasks could workers eat or go to the toilet.[17]

It was also unusual for a factory that one of the processes of production, fermentation, required the adoption and development of a life. This life was that of the microbes in the yeast that fermented the brews into beer, *saccharomyces cerevisiae,* the type at Moctezuma named Chicago No. 1. It was of a cultivated and inhibited kind. It could not fight other microbial forms, mold, bacteria, mycoderma, wild yeast, which would ferment a brew into an acid or a solvent. Even free of them, it needed special care—"Proper nourishment, proper temperature, sufficient air, exclusion of adverse influences generally"—or it would weaken, sicken, and die. Consequently the brewmaster insisted on cleanliness, "the first consideration in every brewery," especially in the stockhouse. Consequently, he depended on the cold there, temperatures between twenty-three and fifty-two degrees Fahrenheit, low enough to chasten the undesired forms of life, but high enough to permit the privileged to reproduce. Given the natural temperatures in Orizaba, annually averaging sixty-five degrees, rising to eighty or higher most days every month, and into the nineties in May, production was possible then only through mechanical refrigeration.[18] And since the brews came one after another, and the microbes never took a night off or a Sunday or a holiday, the refrigeration had to run practically all the time. While the brewmaster kept charge of the brews in the cold, there was another master in charge of making the cold, the *maestro de maquinaria,* the master mechanic in the machinery department, who logged in at 6 A.M. and out at 6 P.M., but stood responsible at any hour for having every cold room at the right degree of cold. As sure as the brewmaster was of his art, so was the *maestro* of his several trades. From his experience as a practical stationary engineer (except for his weakness in electricity), he was a master of mechanical observation, olfaction, gustation, palpation, and auscultation, a devotee of the log, precautions, and precision, a virtuoso in fashioning woods and metals, and a wonder at erecting, running, and repairing all manner of machines. In his department and in the stockhouse, work went round the clock, two shifts a day, seven days a week, a daily and a nightly effort to preserve a vital condition.[19]

Most unusually for factory work, and most important, production took a long time, for the process of fermentation lasted from three or four to six months.[20] Compared to the volume of the brews daily started or the volume of the beer daily finished, the volume of the stocks in the process on any day was ordinarily therefore at least seventy times greater. This was why the cold rooms at Moctezuma by 1908 measured some 800,000 cubic feet.[21] As one, two, or three brews were done on brewing days in 1908, so from 27,000 to 38,000 barrels, all the brews stocked since the day before to nearly six months before, averaging the work of the past 120 days, were every day still in the course of production, all zymologically alive, all perishable. Probably 90 percent of the brews in the process wanted to be at about thirty-four degrees Fahrenheit. If the refrigeration was not right even for some hours, much less failed altogether, the brews of the previous 120 days would go bad, and 120 days of refrigeration would go for nought.

Only in finishing its product did this factory function on a classic factory system. Since the final product consisted of not only a perishable article of consumption but also a clean, durable container, not merely beer, but beer in decontaminated kegs, ponies, and pint bottles, all ready for retail, the final processes of production were barreling and bottling. And since the product was daily "a very large number of individuals," beers in scores of kegs and ponies and scores of thousands of bottles, "a great multitude of things, all of exactly the same kind," both processes required factory organization.[22] Already in 1900 the barreling and the bottling department had some notable machines. By 1904 they had some impressive series of maneuvers and mechanisms. By 1908, featuring "maximum order and the most scrupulous cleanliness," they ran on the latest line for mechanized and continuous operations.[23] In these departments the chiefs were department *cabos,* foremen. There the working day was the standard.

Moctezuma's most significant and complicated installation was its main power plant, which as the master mechanic directed the work there gave heat, force, and, most important, incessant cold.[24] At first the master had only a single train of work to supervise. The original plant had one source of power, the 60-horsepower boiler, one prime mover, the 75-horsepower engine, and one main line-shaft. The boiler's steam went on a twenty-four-hour variable load, for heat for steeping and boiling in the brewhouse, for heat for cleaning and pasteurizing in the bottle house, and for power on the engine driving by direct connection the fifteen-ton refrigerating machine and turning by belt the shaft for the plant's pumps and elevator and the brewing, barreling, and bottling machinery. There was no excess capacity for an emergency: some surplus power, but no spare engine or machine for making cold.[25] By 1901 the new equipment required the master to conduct several different operations. The plant had three sources of power, three prime movers, and two main line-shafts. One source, one of the two 100-horsepower, wood-fired, Cook boilers in the shed at the northwest corner of the brewhouse, was on a usually twelve-hour variable load entirely for heat for the brewhouse and the bottle house. The other boiler, on a twenty-four-hour variable load, powered both of the two 140-horsepower Corliss engines in the brewhouse, which together continuously cranked around two ten-foot flywheels bolted to forty-inch pulleys on a six-inch main line-shaft, which in turn transmitted (at peaks) 160 horsepower up the line for the then new one hundred-ton horizontal double-acting Vilter plant's pumps and elevator and the brewing machinery. The third source was Segura, Braniff's Iztaczoquitlán hydroelectric plant. Its power, transmitted to the transformer substation near the Mexican railway station and stepped down to 220 volts, went on a twelve-hour variable load into the bottle house to the third prime mover, the 200-horsepower Westinghouse motor, which from 6 A.M. to 6 P.M. turned a forty-inch pulley on the bottle house's six-inch main line-shaft for barreling and bottling.[26] There was by then the standard excess capacity for the most important duty. If either boiler wanted shutting down, brewing could stop, and the other boiler could keep both engines going for refrigeration. If the one hundred-ton machine wanted stopping, the engines could be reconnected to two, by then old, fifty-ton Vilter machines for the regular cold. If either of the engines broke down, the one hundred-ton machine could be disconnected and the good engine connected to its old fifty-ton machine for enough cold to get the stocks through the emergency.

By 1908 the plant's divisions were systematic, and the master mechanic on his daily morning and evening rounds walked through a new order. Of the two 100-horsepower boilers, one on a twenty-four-hour variable load steamed only for heat, in brewing, barreling, and bottling; the other was a spare. From Iztaczoquitlán, where by then the plant was Orizaba Electric Light and Power's, high-tension lines brought the current at 6,600 volts also on a variable twenty-four-hour load into the brewery's new substation, behind the brewhouse, in the west wing of the new machine house. There in the high-tension room on the second floor, through three conductors, closed disconnecting switches, and a closed oil circuit-breaker behind the first panel of a two-panel, marble switchboard, the current flowed onto the main bus-bar behind the switchboard.[27] Thence branched two 6,600-volt circuits. On one the current flowed through three conductors to the bus-bar behind a marble-paneled switchboard on the machine house's first floor, in the engine room, and from this bar through a closed oil circuit-breaker it went in six phases through six conductors into the armature winding on the stator of the new, 500-horsepower Westinghouse synchronous motor. Beside the marble board on the first floor, from behind a slate switchboard, direct current from the motor's 15-horsepower exciter flowed back into the motor's field. The motor delivered the power in mechanical motion. On its bedplate, bearings, and shaft, the shiny, black electromagnetic machine stood about nine feet high, measured about eight feet wide and eight and a half feet long at its base, and weighed some ten tons. Its squirrel-cage-wound, salient-field-pole rotor, constantly revolving at 225 revolutions per minute, driving the exciter by direct connection, drove at the same speed a fifty-six-inch, twenty-grooved flywheel, which drove by the American rope system across about twenty feet, a fourteen-foot, twenty-grooved wheel, which in turn drove at a constant 75 revolutions per minute the old and the new one hundred-ton Vilter compressors. The other 6,600-volt circuit was the source of two low-voltage circuits. From behind the second panel of the second-floor switchboard, through a closed oil circuit-breaker, three conductors carried single-phase currents down to the substation's first floor into three, single-phase, 75-kilowatt transformers in parallel. From them, through three conductors back up to the second floor and through a closed, low-tension, air circuit-breaker on the first panel of a three-panel, slate switchboard, three single-phase currents at 220 volts flowed onto the main low-tension bus-bar behind all three panels of the board. Through air circuit-breakers on the second and third panels two wires from the second carried single-phase current for light, and three wires from the third panel carried three-phase current for power, to the cut-out cabinets in all the brewery's departments, to the various light and motor switches, and into the lights and motors that were on. Of these ordinarily the largest was the old 200-horsepower motor, removed to the new repair shop to turn its line-shaft.[28] So the power available sufficed for any foreseeable emergency. If Iztaczoquitlán went down, if the 500-horsepower motor failed, or either of the one hundred-ton machines, the spare boiler would drive the otherwise idle steam engines and thereby the two old fifty-ton compressors, to keep the stocks cold enough for many hours.

Finally, between the central buildings and the bottle-storage sheds, stood a small, simple power station for destruction and by-production at the drying plant. On the brewery's rule of cleanliness, daily destruction of trash and garbage, including usually 500 to 550 pounds of wet, spent hops, was a sanitary necessity. And by-production turned a daily mess into a useful substance. On an average working day eleven or twelve tons of dry malt and rice went into the brewery, and thirteen or fourteen tons of wet, spent grains came out. Left wet for more than twenty-four hours, they would ferment and rot. Dried, they would make two and a half to three tons of sweet meal, "an unsurpassable food for cattle" in the dairies round the city and upcountry.[29] The plant comprised the incinerator, to burn the waste; a ninety-foot chimney, to give good draft on wet refuse and throw gases, smoke, and fumes high and far away; and inside an adjacent frame building the old 75-horsepower boiler, a little motor, and the motor-driven dryer, a horizontal, sheet-iron drum about twenty-two feet long, five feet in diameter.[30]

The continuous work for power and refrigeration happened then on the master mechanic's orders in the boiler room and in the new machine house. At the boilers, water-tube, upright, quick steamers, a day-shift and a night-shift fireman by turns watched the gauge of the one lit, tended its feed heater and pump, and threw cord wood into its furnace.[31] On a rare, easy night, nothing brewing, the hardest duty was staying awake. Taking the shift at 6 P.M., the fireman would test the safety valve, climb the ladder up to the boardwalk by the water-gauge glass, blow down the column, test the glass's water level by the gauge cocks, climb down, blow off the mud drum, and examine and oil the pump. He would have no more to do until 5 A.M. but keep an eye on the gauges, about every hour toss a chunk of wood into the furnace, and sooner or later clean the fire and the ash pit. Only on the last hour of his shift would he fire fast, every six or seven minutes, to raise the day's steam for the bottle house. On the rare day without a brew the fireman would fire the furnaces only about every ten minutes, to maintain the heat for cleaning and pasteurizing; any time after noon he would clean the fire and the pit. On brewing days, however, the brewmaster would usually have the master mechanic calling for thousands of pounds of steam an hour at least three times a day. For a 250-barrel brew from 10 P.M. to 1 A.M., a 60-barrel brew from 6 to 9 A.M., and another 250-barrel brew from 2 to 5 P.M., plus the regular needs for bottling, the night fireman would fire every two or three minutes during the first brew, clean the fire and haul ashes between 1 and 5 A.M., and fire again every two or three minutes from 5 to 6 A.M., and his fellow on the day shift would work twice as hard, firing every two or three minutes from 6 to 8 A.M., not quite so fast the next hour, more slowly the next two, and only every ten minutes the next three hours, when he would clean the fire and haul ashes, but practically nonstop, a chunk every minute or two, from 2 to 5 P.M.

Notes

1. J. R. Southworth, *El estado de Veracruz-Llave* (n.p., 1900), 124; Morcom to Minister of Communications, October 8, 1907, Archivo Histórico de la Secretaría de Comunicaciones y Obras Públicas, C 1/315; A. Rodríguez Sariol, "Datos de la Empresa de luz eléctrica," August 24, 1907, and Eduardo Vignon, "Relación de las Industrias establecidas en este Municipio correspondiente al año de 1906," September 18, 1907, Archivo Municipal de Orizaba (henceforth AMO), 257/6; "Datos Ministrados al Museo Comercial de Filadelfia," November 6, 1906, AMO, 244/9; "Padrón de causantes del derecho de patente," October 31, 1906, and "Fábricas y Molinos," November 1, 1906, AMO, 259/1; *Periódico Oficial de Veracruz,* July 3, 1906, June 22, 1907, July 11, 1908. Steven H. Haber, *Industry and Underdevelopment: The Industrialization of Mexico,* 1890–1940 (Stanford: Stanford University Press, 1989) 85–86, 113–20.
2. Percy F. Martin, *Mexico of the 20th Century,* 2 vols. (New York: Dodd, Mead & Co., 1907), 2:23b.
3. Ibid. *El Reproductor,* January 18, 1906. "Escritura," July 13, 1906, in "Testimonios de la escritura constitutiva de 'Cerveceria Moctezuma,' S.A.," July 15, 1960, Archivo de Manuel Gómez Morín, 144.
4. *El Reproductor,* July 27, 1895, February 22, March 8, and March 15, 1900; Southworth, *Veracruz,* 124, 131; "Mexican Brewery and Ice Plant," *The Western Brewer,* January 15, 1901, 21–26, 29; "Cervecería Moctezuma, S.A.," September 1904, 391–92; Julio Zárate, *Album del estado de Veracruz* (n.p., n.d.), 44–45; Auguste Génin, *Notes sur le Méxique* (Mexico City: Imprenta Lacaud, 1908–10), 5; Eugenio Espino Barros, ed., *México en el centenario de su independencia* (Mexico City: Müller Hnos, n.d. [1910?]), 173; Miguel Alemán Velasco, ed., *Documentos gráficos para la historia de México: Veracruz, 1858–1914* (Mexico City: Editora del Sureste, 1988), 145; José M. Naredo, *Estudio geográfico, histórico y estadístico del cantón y de la ciudad de Orizaba,* 2 vols. (Orizaba: Imprenta del Hospicio, 1989), 2:260, 264–67; *McGraw Central Station Directory and Data Book, 1921–1922* (New York: McGraw Hill, 1922), 805; "Vista de la ciudad de Orizaba," in *Orizaba: Monumento en honor de los hijos del estado de Veracruz, defensores de la patria en los años de 1847 y 1848* (Xalapa: Tip. del Gobierno del Estado Orizaba, 1903), frontispiece; "Panorama del Cerro de Borrego desde la Cervecería Moctezuma-Noroeste," *Panorama Moctezuma,* Papers of Manuel Escobar; Bernardo García Díaz and Laura Zevallos Ortiz, *Orizaba* (Mexico City: Archivo del Estado de Veracruz, 1989), 50–51.
5. R. G. Eslava, "Orizaba," *El Reproductor,* January 12, 1905.
6. Roberto Saviñón, "Primera parte del informe . . . de la visita que practicó a la Cervecería Moctezuma, S.A.," March 13, 1922, and "Continuación del informe correspondiente a la Cervecería Moctezuma, S.A.," March 31, 1922, Archivo General de la Nación, Departamento de Trabajo (henceforth AGN-DT), 17/1/6/6 (old style); J. Martínez Garza, "Datos

sobre algunas industrias manufactureras establecidas en Orizaba," *Boletín de la Secretaría de Fomento,* ep. 2a., vol. 3 (1903–4), 189–92; "Mexican Brewery," 24–26; J. A. Celis O. and R. M. de la Mora "Plano General de la Cervecería," November 25, 1940 (for a copy of which I thank Christian Reiterhardt of Cervecería Cuauhtémoc); interview with Manuel Zorrilla Rivera, April 28, 1975; interview with Gabriel Camaleño, July 27, 1977; interviews with Jorge Fleischmann, August 15, September 7, 1977. *cf* Testimony by Samuel Gompers, in U.S. Industrial Commission, *Report of the Industrial Commission,* 19 vols. (Washington, D.C.: Government Printing Office, 1900–1902) 17:410–12; and Ludwig Andorfer, *Die Rationalisierun in der Brauindustrie unter Berücksichtigung ihrer Einwirkung auf die Arbeiterschaft* (Nürnberg: F. Carl, 1929), 44–49.

7. Adolfo Dollero, *México al día* (Mexico City: Libería de la V[da] de C. Bouret, 1911), 732.
8. "Producción de la 'Cervecería Moctezuma,' S.A., desde su fundación hasta la fecha," December 31, 1939, and Jorge Fleischmann to Verlag Hans Carl, March 17, 1953, Archivo de la Cervecería Moctezuma; interview with Gabriel Camaleño, July 26, 1977; interviews with Jorge Fleischmann, August 31, September 7, 1977; "Mexican Brewing and Breweries," *One Hundred Years of Brewing* (Chicago: H. S. Rich and Co., 1903), 636; E. Struve, *Die Bierbrauerei und die Bierbesteurung in den haupt-Kulturländern* (Berlin: Paul Parey, 1909), 462.

   On measurements of beer, see Robert Wahl and Max Henius, *American Handy-Book of the Brewing, Malting and Auxiliary Trades* (Chicago: Wahl-Henius Institute, 1901), 80, 96, 102, 915. On kegs and ponies, see Edward H. Vogel, Jr., et al., *The Practical Brewer* (St. Louis: Master Brewers Association of America, 1946), 141. On variations then in the contents of pint bottles, see Allen R. Smart, "Twentieth-Century Brewery Accounting," *The Western Brewer,* November 1912, 238, and "Bottled Beer," ibid., May 1914, 213.
9. Zorrilla Rivera, April 28, 1975; Camaleño, July 26, 1977. On the Abresch wagons, *The Brewer's Journal,* March 1, 1905, 215; "Chas. Abresch Co.," *The Western Brewer,* January 1908, advertisement on page 14.
10. Zorilla Rivera, April 28, 1975; Camalaño, July 26, 1977; Fleischmann, August 31, September 7, 1977; Saviñón, March 13, 1922, AGN-DT, 17/1/6/6; A. Mantel, "The Brewing Industry in Mexico," *The Western Brewer,* November 15, 1901, 446; Eslava, "Orizaba":l; Martínez Garza, "Datos," 191; Southworth, *Veracruz,* 124; Espino Barros, *México,* 173; Alemán Velasco, *Documentos,* 145; "Ayer 1896" and "Chalet de botellas de vidrio, 1907," Escobar papers; Albert de Baer, "Mexico," *United States Consular Reports* 324 (September 1907), 145–46; Gonzalo Arzamendi, Jr., "La influencia del medio en la seguridad e higiene industrial, aplicada a la industria cervecera," September 1964, 3–4, in Biblioteca Henry O. Sturm, Jr., Asociación Nacional de Fabricantes de Cerveza. Cf. "Allsopp's Bottling Plant," *The Western Brewer,* February 15, 1901, 65.
11. On the storehouse and agency, "Mexican Brewery," 26. On the incinerator and drying plant, Eslava, "Orizaba":l; Espino Barros, *México,* 173; Alemán Velasco, *Documentos,* 145; Fleischmann, September 7, 1977.
12. Interview with Luis E. Sánchez, August 10, 1977; G. J. Siebel, "Handling and Pitching of Packages," *The Western Brewer,* June 15, 1897, 1047, 1049; F. P. Hankerson, *The Cooperage Handbook* (Brooklyn, N.Y.: Chemical Publishing Co., 1947), 138; Kenneth Kilby, *The Cooper and His Trade* (Fresno, Calif.: Linden Publishing Co., 1989), 19, 41. Cf. George Ehret, *Twenty-Five Years of Brewing* (New York: Gast Lithograph and Engraving Co., 1891), 96–102.
13. Camaleño, July 26, 1977; interview with Daniel Sierra Rivera, September 5, 1977; Mantel, "Brewing Industry," 446; de Baer, "Mexico," 146; Charles H. Sulz, *A Treatise on Beverages* (New York, 1888), 388–92; Philip Dreesback, *Beer Bottlers' Handy Book* (Chicago: Wahl-Henius Institute, 1906), 100; Raoul M. Vázquez to Luis E. Sánchez, May 31, 1977 (for a

copy of which I thank Luis E. Sánchez); "Esteban González Rojas" and "Andrés Durán Alvarado," Escobar papers.

14. Andrew Ure, *The Philosophy of Manufactures* (London: Charles Knight, 1835), 2, 13. A good summary of contemporaneous practice in the industry in the United States followed also by large breweries in Mexico, is Robert Wahl, "Brewing and Malting," in *Industrial Chemistry: A Manual for Student and Manufacturer,* edited by Allen Rogers and Alfred B. Aubert (New York: D. Van Nostrand Co., 1913), 688–704.
15. Carl Rach, "Brew House Arrangement and Mashing Methods," *The Western Brewer,* October 15, 1901, 406–7; R. Norris Shreve, *The Chemical Process Industries,* 2nd ed. (New York: McGraw Hill Book Co., 1956), 1, 9–22.
16. "Producción," December 31, 1949, Archivo de la Cervecería Moctezuma; Fleischmann, September 7, 1977; Fred Ophuls and A. B. Stickney, *The Thermal Engineer in the Brewery* (New York, 1933), 16. Cf. Carl Rach, "Four Months of Strenuous Work in the Two Largest Breweries of Indiana," *The Brewers' Journal,* May 1, 1904, 287–89, and June 1, 1904, 335–36. On the kettles, "Mexican Brewery," 21; "Cervecería Moctezuma," 392; Saviñón, March 31, 1922, AGN-DT, 17/1/6/6.
17. Sánchez, August 10, 1977; Fleischmann, August 15 and September 7, 1977. Cf. Leonardo M. Mayer, "¿De manera hijo que quieres ser maestro cervecero?" November 1961, Biblioteca Sturm; Charles Russert, "Mission of America's Brewing Academies," *The Western Brewer,* October 15, 1901, 403–5; Frank Keeling, "Status of the Modern Brewer," *The Brewers' Journal,* May 1, 1902, 291–94; Testimony by Gompers, *Industrial Commission,* vol. 7, 625, 650; Charles Booth, *Life and Labour of the People of London,* 17 vols. (London: MacMillan & Co., 1902), 2nd ser., 3:122; Emil Wolff, *Lohnsystem und Löhne in der Brauindustrie* (Berlin: Carl Heymanns Verlag, 1912), 86–94, 148–59.
18. On the yeast, Fleischmann, September 7, 1977. On the special care it required, Wahl and Henius, *American Handy-Book,* 516–618, 520–22, 542–43, 742; J. E. Siebel, "Pure Yeast and Beer Taste," in *Original Communications of the Zymotechnic Institute* (Chicago: Zymotech Institute, 1891), 32–34; "The Production of Pure Beer," *The Western Brewer,* January 1904, 11. On temperatures in Orizaba, Naredo, *Estudio,* 2:6; Moisés T. de la Peña, *Veracruz económico,* 2 vols. (Mexico City: Gobierno del Estado de Veracruz, 1946), 1:31.
19. Fleischmann, August 31, September 7, 1977. Cf. "Brewmasters and Engineers," *The Western Brewer,* November 1905, 526; G. J. Patitz, "Engineering Problems in the Brewery Power Plant," ibid., April 1912, 171.
20. Sánchez, August 10, 1977; Fleischmann, September 7, 1977; Martínez Garza, "Datos," 190. Cf. Wahl and Henius, *American Handy-Book,* 758–59; J. G. Friedhoff, "Cellar Treatment," *The Western Brewer,* March 15, 1901, 93; Lorenz Herzinger, "Fermentation and Cellar Work," ibid., May 15, 1901, 182; Francis Wyatt, "Notes on Bottle Beer Brewing," ibid., January 1907, 30; Ophuls and Stickney, *Thermal Engineer,* 4.
21. "Mexican Brewery," 21, 22, 29; *The Western Brewer,* April 1907, 188; *The Brewers Journal,* May 1, 1907, 314; *Modern Mexico,* October 1907, 30.
22. Charles Babbage, *On the Economy of Machinery and Manufactures,* 4th ed. (London: John Murray, 1835), 120, 268.
23. Eslava, "Orizaba"; "Mexican Brewery," 22–26, 28; "Cervecería Moctezuma," 392.
24. Lorenzo Campano, *Manual del cervecero y del fabricante de bebidas gaseosas y fermentadas,* new ed. (Mexico City: Libería de la V*da* de C. Bouret, 1927), 1; "Brewing in Milwaukee," *The Western Brewer,* January 15, 1895, 85–89, 99; G. E. Lob, "The Power Question in the Brewery," ibid., March 1912, 133–35; Max Delbrück, *Illustriertes Brauerei-Lexikon* (Berlin 1910), 544–46; Ophuls and Stickney, *Thermal Engineer,* 16–18.
25. *El Reproductor,* July 27, 1895; Zárate, *Album,* 45.
26. *El Reproductor,* June 18, 1896; ibid., July 30, 1906; *The Western Brewer,* September 15, 1896, 1699; ibid., October 15, 1896, 1922; "Mexican Brewery," 21–26, 29; Zárate, *Album,* 44;

Southworth, *Veracruz,* 124–25; Martínez Garza, "Datos," 191–92; Rodríguez Gaviol, August 24, 1907, and Vignon, September 18, 1907, AMO, 257/6. For the boilers, the steam engines, and the fifty-ton and the one hundred-ton compressors, see The Vilter Manufacturing Co., *Refrigerating and Ice Making Machinery, Catalogue A* (Milwaukee, Wis.: Vilter Manufacturing Co., 1909), 29, 33–35; and "Calderas verticales del año 1906," "Motores 'Corliss' para casos de emergencia, 1922" "Compresoras de amoniaco, para casos de emergencia, 1922," and "Compresoras de amoniaco, enero 1922," photographs, in *Album de la Cervecería Moctezuma, Orizaba, Ver.* (Mexico City, 1922). Cf. William Nottberg, "Electric Power for Breweries," *The Western Brewer,* January 15, 1906, 25–27; *Electric World,* February 3, 1906, 293; C. F. Hettinger, "How to Generate and Utilize Power in Breweries," *The Western Brewer,* May 15, 1906, 226–28; Otto Luhr, "Economy and Simplicty in Brewery Power Plants," ibid., December 15, 27, 1909, 628–29.

27. Fleischmann, September 7, 1977. On Orizaba Electric Light and Power, *POV,* January 4, 1908; *Electric Review,* January 4, 1908, 32; *McGraw Central Station Directory,* 805; Roberto Saviñón, "Informe . . . correspondiente a la visita que practicó en la Planta Eléctrica de Iztaczoquitlán," February 26, 1922, AGN-DT, 17/1/6/6; Westinghouse Electric and Manufacturing Co., Detail and Supply Department, *Circular No. 1504: Alternating Current Switchboards,* May, 1909, 1–16. Cf. Frank Koester, *Hydro-electric Developments and Engineering* (New York: D. Van Nostrand Co., 1909), 280–308; Warren H. Miller, "Alternating-Current Industrial Power Plants," *Electrical World,* June 3, 1909, 1376–79; William Koedding, "The Application of Electrical Power in the Brewery," *The Western Brewer,* March 15, 1912, 111–12; H. W. Peck, "Modern Practice in Switchboard Design," *The Electric Club Journal,* December 4, 1904, 634, May 1905, 311–15, June 1905, 380–83, August 1905, 508–11, and October 1905, 634–40; "Fulton Ice Company's Plant," *Refrigerating World,* January 1924, 13–15.

28. Fleischmann, August 15, September 7, 1977. For the motor's switchboard, see "Freezing plant, brewery at Orizaba," photograph in The Epicure, "How to See Mexico," *Overland Monthly,* July 1910, 39. For the motor, ibid., 39; "Compresoras de amoniaco, enero 1922," *Album de la Cervecería;* Dollero, *México,* 782; Westinghouse Electric and Manufacturing Co., *Circular No. 1133: Westinghouse Revolving Field Alternators,* June 1906, 3–11; "Westinghouse, Doing It Electrically," *Refrigerating World,* February 1917, 5; Educational Department, Westinghouse Electric and Manufacturing Co., *Synchronous Motors: Westinghouse Extension Course Number 14* (E. Pittsburgh, 1931), 8–9, 42, 78, 86–100. For the compressors in 1908, "Freezing plant," in The Epicure, "How to See Mexico," 39; "Compresoras de amoniaco, enero 1922," *Album de la Cervecería; The Western Brewer,* July 15, 1907, 402; *Ice and Refrigeration,* July 1907, 33; *Modern Mexico,* October 1907, 31. (The authors of the last three articles mistook Moctezuma's new total refrigerating capacity for its newly acquired refrigerating capacity.) On the wiring for lights and motors, "Departamento de botellería en 1908," "Departamento de embotellado en 1920," "Departamento de embotellado, 1921," "Lavadoras de botellas, 1920," "Lavadoras de botellas, vista del subsuelo en 1922," and "Máquina de hacer clavos, 1922," *Album de la Cervecería;* R. G. Hudson, "Wiring of Buildings for Light and Power," in *American Handbook for Electrical Engineers,* edited by Harold Pender (New York: John Wiley and Sons, 1914), 1938–40, 1949–50, 1952, 1963. For the old motor in its new place, "Máquina de hacer clavos, 1922," *Album de Cervecería.*

29. Saviñón, March 31, 1922, AGN-DT, 17/1/6/6.

30. Fleischmann, September 7, 1977. Eslava, "Orizaba"; Espino Barros, *México,* 173; Aleman Velasco, *Documentos,* 145. Cf. Wahl and Henius, *American Handy-Book,* 871–73; Felix Mendelsohn and Maurice E. Stern, *Brewers and Bottlers Universal Encyclopedia* (Chicago: Brewers Publishing Co. of America, 1910), 165, 237; W. Goslich and K. Fehrmann, *Brauerei-Maschinenkunde,* 2 vols. (Berlin: Paul Parey, 1914–1920), 2:318–20.

31. "Calderas verticales del año 1906," *Album de la Cervecería;* "Mexican Brewery," 21; Cecil H. Peabody and Edward F. Miller, *Steam Boilers* (New York: John Wiley and Sons, 1905), 27–29.
32. Camaleño, July 26, 1977; N. Hawkins, *Maxims and Instructions for the Boiler Room* (New York: Theo Audel and Co., 1901), 14, 18, 24–27, 37–47, 196–201, 218–21; Robert H. Thurston, *A Manual of Steam-Boilers* (Babcock and Wilcox), 28, 110–11; *Steam,* 298–300; *Coal Miners' Pocketbook,* 11th edition (New York: 1916), 426, 434–35; Arthur D. Pratt, "Steam Boilers," in *Mechanical Engineers' Handbook,* 936–37; Otto Luhr, *Mechanical and Refrigerating Engineers' Handbook* (Chicago: 1913), 306.

CHAPTER 25

FAULKNER'S SOUTH: IS THERE TRUTH IN FICTION?

Louis Ferleger and Richard H. Steckel

"Both Faulkner and Warren, though they did not claim to be historians, actually knew their Southern history very well.... So Faulkner, like any other great literary artist, provides us with scenes set against the backdrop of history. Because of it those scenes gain in energy and power over our minds and affections.... What Faulkner has done [in *Absalom, Absalom!*], therefore, is to force the reader to find the proper measure of history for himself. Everything in the book is drama. The reader is allowed to watch the various characters try to piece together the few bits of fact that they possess, try to imagine why the character did and said this or that, and to take part himself in the process of constructing what actually happened and why. But the reader in doing this will necessarily become involved in a second process: that of assessing the degree to which one can ever find the truth in history."[1]

William Faulkner concluded his 1950 Nobel address with this observation: "When the last ding-dong of doom has clanged and faded from the last worthless rock hanging tideless in the last red and dying

Reprinted with permission of *The Journal of Mississippi History.* The longer original article appeared in volume LX, Summer 1998, no. 2: 105–121.

evening, that even then there will still be one more sound: that of his puny inexhaustible voice, still talking."[2]

Faulkner's reference to "his puny inexhaustible voice" is not a historical accident. His characters are "puny," "gaunt," "weak," or "small." Despite the hundreds of thousands of pages of comment and criticism written about his work, readers have missed his distortion of Southern health. Faulkner's novels inaccurately describe the physical attributes of Southerners and this has created false and misleading historical images.

For many, Faulkner's South is the South they know and love. A novel's descriptions of a region, society, or culture often strikingly illuminate a historical period and create stark images that may leave readers with a deeply ingrained sense of people and places. Whether these images are useful as factual descriptions of the period is another matter. In a review of the work of Dickens and other novelists of England's Industrial Revolution, historian William Aydelotte concludes that the novels are suspect as a factual source. He argues instead that novels may be useful for understanding the history of opinions since they "show not the facts of the age, but the mind of the novelist, not social conditions, but attitudes toward social conditions."[3] The economic historian Alexander Gerschenkron maintained, instead, that novels, plays, and other literary materials were valuable factual sources for understanding Russian economic history in an environment where little information was available by other means.[4] While fictional characters may accurately portray certain dimensions of history, they can also misrepresent historical reality—in Faulkner's case, by making Southerners look weak and unfit.

Readers of history, science, economics, and literature must come to terms with their images of the past, which often are shaped and molded elsewhere. As Edmund White recently observed, "A book exists only when a living mind recreates it."[5] And perceptions of the South are recreated by literature or movies based upon literature. Far too many readers of Southern novels attribute factual content to fictional characters and situations; for them the South is Faulkner's South. As the distinguished Faulkner scholar Cleanth Brooks once put it: "Most of us identify Faulkner with the South, and it is natural that we should do so, for his fiction is filled with references to its history, its geography, its customs; and his prose often employs its special idiom."[6]

Faulkner's rich descriptions of race relations, merchant-landlord interactions, and the Civil War display a keen sensitivity to historical nuance and detail that remains forceful today. Few novelists have Faulkner's power to describe complicated social and historical relationships without reducing them to mere love affairs or sordid endings. Yet Faulkner's powerful narrative descriptions of Southern life and health leave a lasting, but distorted, impression of an impoverished population that yearned for better times and a healthier life.

The greatness of Faulkner's novels hardly depends upon their description of the health conditions of Southerners, but throughout his work, he does painstakingly create images of their physical traits, eating habits, and stature. Generally, his characters have extraordinarily complex social and emotional lives but are not healthy or robust. This is true for men and women, black or white, almost irrespective of age or social class. Faulkner describes his characters as physically vulnerable weaklings, who consume great quantities of alcohol and smoke prodigious amounts of tobacco. After reading Faulkner's novels, it may be shocking to learn that the South was not a distinctly unhealthy region.

Faulkner's inexorable tendency to diminish the stature and health of his characters begins in his early novels. In *Pylon,* J. A. Prufrock looks "like a cadaver out of a medical school vat" and his "stick like arm, the brittle light and apparently senseless hand like a bundle of dried twigs too."[7] Faulkner describes one man as

> something which had apparently crept from a doctor's cupboard and, in the snatched garments of an etherised patient in a charity ward, escaped into the living world. He saw a creature which, erect, would be better than six feet tall and which would weigh about ninety-five pounds, in a suit of no age or color . . . which ballooned light and impedimentless about a skeleton frame as though suit and wearer both hung from a flapping clothesline; a creature with the leashed, eager loosejointed air of a halfgrown highbred setter puppy.[8]

The picture of physical debility endured as Faulkner moved on to his greatest novels. *Absalom, Absalom!* displays an array of characters with unattractive, stunted features: "A man with a big frame but gaunt now almost to emaciation"; "the small slight child whose feet, even when she would be grown would never quite reach the floor . . . as against Ellen who, though small-boned also, was what is known as fullbodied . . . Not fat: just rounded and complete"; "Ellen was in her late thirties, plump"; "He had filled out physically. . . . The fat, the stomach, came later."[9]

Throughout the novel, many of the characters physically deteriorate or become sick. Faulkner's descriptions of both children and adults reveal his obsession with the deterioration and permanent alteration of fleshly characteristics: "But there she was, with the eleven year old boy who looked more like eight . . . the magnolia-faced woman a little plumper now, . . . followed by a gigantic negress carrying a silk cushion and leading by the hand the little boy . . . a thin delicate child"; "he would never be other than light in the bone and almost delicate—the boy with his light bones and womanish hands"; "I remember how I remained one afternoon when school was out and waited for the teacher, waylaid him; he was a smallish man"; "So they hauled him out of his cave under the river bank: a little man"; "the small furious grim implacable woman not much larger than a child"; "the tiny gnomelike creature in headrag and voluminous skirts."[10]

In *Light in August* and *The Sound and the Fury,* Southerners are repeatedly portrayed as physically unappealing. In *The Sound and the Fury* Faulkner describes some Southerners "fat as you is"; he writes "Only Doc Peabody is fat. Three hundred pounds."[11] But these descriptions pale compared with those in *Light in August.* Here Faulkner's characters are "that small man"; "puny"; "a tall man, and he was thin once. But he is not thin now. His skin is the color of flour sacking and his upper body in shape is like a loosely filled sack falling from his gaunt shoulders of its own weight, upon his lap"; one has a face "at once gaunt and flabby. . . . That part of his torso visible above the desk is shapeless, almost monstrous, with a soft and sedentary obesity"; another is "dumpy, obese, gray in color, with a face like that of a drowned corpse"; and another is "a tub of a man, with the complete and rocklike inertia of a tub."[12]

Faulkner was unrelenting in his negative images of Southern physical attributes. In *Mosquitoes* he writes that Fairchild "looked more like a walrus than ever."[13] In *Go Down, Moses,* he refers to the sheriff as "a tremendous man, fat," and to Molly as "the thin, almost fleshless arm beneath the layers of sleeve, dry and light and brittle and frail as a rotted stick," and to Major de Spain as "the short plumpish grey-haired man."[14]

As I Lay Dying includes dozens of physical descriptions of weak, old, and sick Southerners. When characters *are* tall, Faulkner usually makes them also gaunt or obese.[15] In *The Town,* Faulkner describes one character as "a tall gaunt man," and another as "tall, with his big belly," thereby diminishing the characters' physical advantages. For the most part, however, the characters in *The Town* are, as in Faulkner's other novels, "fat," "big bull," "a little dried-up feller," and possessed of a "big gut."[16]

Flags in the Dust, Faulkner's third novel, originally appeared in 1929 in a greatly edited version as *Sartoris.* The physical descriptions are familiar: "fat," "thin," "plump," "mountainous," and so on.[17] The characters in *Requiem for a Nun* fared no better: "a frail irascible little man weighing less than a hundred pounds—would the fifteen pounds of lock even then fail to bring his weight up to that of a normal adult male"; another has a "fat shapeless body"; and a third is "a frail anemic girl with narrow workless hands lacking even the strength to milk a cow."[18]

If we credit Faulkner's physical descriptions, Southerners were indeed sorry specimens—frail, weak, and puny or fat and unhealthy—none of whom could be expected to enjoy the average life span that Northerners commonly attained during the twentieth century. Faulkner's physical descriptions create the impression of a feeble, exhausted, and unfit population.

One would never suspect that Southerners have a history of height advantages over Northerners. Yet they have just that. A well-nourished population fares better than poorly nourished ones. Faulkner's novels contain richly detailed descriptions of the food and fluids consumed. His characters eat meat and flour products, many starches, and garden vegetables and fruits; these descriptions suggest that Southerners had sufficient nutrients available to be healthy, robust, and industrious.

Typically, a male character in a Faulkner novel is drunk at some point, and many remain inebriated for long periods of time. While Faulkner describes his characters as drinking various liquids, alcohol is always among them. Tobacco is also ubiquitous. In conversation after conversation, Faulkner portrays Southerners as heavy drinkers, smokers, and chewers of tobacco. As we now know, smoking and habitual consumption of alcohol can seriously undermine health and longevity.[19] Among the hundreds of examples, Faulkner writes in *Absalom, Absalom!*: "And Grandfather (he was young then too) brought some champagne and some others brought whiskey . . . sat around the fire with the champagne and the whiskey . . . filling the room with alcohol snoring . . . holding out the bottle of whiskey already uncorked."[20]

Faulkner, of course, drank heavily himself and may well have projected his own habits onto others. He was also very conscious of his small stature.[21] Yet we should err in simply assuming that he represented his characters as looking and behaving as he did. The force and vigor of Faulkner's literary accomplishment preclude any such mechanical reading. Yet when all appropriate respects to his talent have been paid, one is still left with the haunting suspicion that Faulkner perceived the South through the prism of his feelings about himself. And it is even possible that his complex feelings about his own place in his world led him to put other Southerners down to size.

How much truth is there in Faulkner's fiction? Not much when it comes to longevity and heights. The South of the early twentieth century did as well as the North in a crucial measure of a population's well-being: life expectancy at birth. In the 1930s, the earliest period for which life expectancy statistics are available for the entire country, the average length of life in the South was almost identical to that of the United States as a whole: about sixty-three years for white males and sixty-seven years for white females. In Faulkner's home state of Mississippi life expectancy at birth was over sixty-two years for white males and sixty-seven years for white females.[22]

Southerners have a history of height advantage over residents of the North that appeared as early as the mid-eighteenth century. Among native-born troops who fought in the French and Indian War, those from the South and the Middle Atlantic states were nearly identical: sixty-eight inches, only an inch below modern height standards.[23] The regional similarity persisted in the American Revolution, but by the Civil War native-born Southern troops had a height advantage over their Northern counterparts of approximately one inch.[24] Evidence from the world wars shows that Southerners were also relatively tall in the twentieth century. Average heights among World War I troops were 67 inches for Northeasterners and sixty-eight for Southeasterners and soldiers from the South Central. Similarly in World War II the South held its one-inch height advantage over the North.[25]

Southerners were actually taller than Northerners. What does a one-inch height advantage mean? It means that Southerners had a better history of net nutrition than Northerners. The height of an individual reflects the interaction of genetic and environmental influences during the period of physical growth. Although genes are important determinants of individual height, studies of genetically similar and dissimilar populations under various environmental conditions suggest that differences in average height across most populations are largely attributable to environmental factors, especially diet and disease. Studies of populations in Europe, New Guinea, and Mexico show that differences in average height between populations are almost entirely the product of the environment. Data from well-nourished populations in several developed and developing countries show that children from Europe or of European descent, from Africa or of African descent, and from India or the Middle East have similar growth profiles. Europeans and people of European descent and Africans and people of African descent who grew up under good nutritional circumstances have nearly identical stature.[26]

The evidence on living standards in Faulkner's South is unambiguous. Incomes were low but growing rapidly and health—life expectancy and heights—were approximately as good or better than the national average.[27] Reasonably good health in the face of poverty is not a puzzle and may be observed in societies that are low in population density on arable land and remote from commercial centers. Ireland before the famine of the 1840s provides a good example.[28] The abundant arable land supported a good diet by providing garden produce, game, fish, and inexpensive foodstuffs. Perhaps more important, the low population density and lack of commercial activity limited the spread of communicable diseases. The example of cholera, which spread along trade and migration routes, illustrates this point. The South of the early twentieth century did have isolated health problems, such as hookworm and pellagra.[29] But in the most important dimensions of living standards, especially height and life expectancy, the South performed respectably and much better than generally recognized.

Literature influences peoples' perceptions of the past and the present, as much inaccurately as accurately. Many Southern novelists have undoubtedly contributed to the view that Southerners are physical weaklings. But Faulkner has been especially influential through his powerful literary accomplishments. And Faulkner's physically pathetic characters, with their yearning for better health, belie the reality that health and nutrition in the South was as good or better than the national average. Thus his novels, which are widely taken to capture the psychocultural "truth" of the region, present a skewed picture of its material reality.

The ideas of novelists are more powerful than commonly thought. Practical people, who believe themselves to be exempt from literary influences, are usually the slaves of some "great literary artist." Madmen in authority, who hear voices in the air, are distilling their frenzy from some literary scribbler of a few years back.[30] On the question of Southerners' health, Northerners—and Southerners too—have been slaves of Faulkner's imagination.

Notes

1. Cleanth Brooks, *On the Prejudices, Predilections, and Firm Beliefs of William Faulkner* (Baton Rouge: Louisiana State University Press, 1987), 15, 60, 158.
2. *New York Times,* December 8, 1993.
3. William O. Aydelotte, "The England of Marx and Mill as Reflected in Fiction," *Journal of Economic History,* Suppl. 8 (1948): 42–58.
4. Alexander Gerschenkron, "A Neglected Source of Economic Information on Soviet Russia," in *Economic Backwardness in Historical Perspective: A Book of Essays,* edited by Alexander Gerschenkron (Cambridge, Mass.: The Belknap Press of Harvard University Press, 1962), 296–317; ibid., "Reflections of Soviet Novels," 318–40.
5. *New York Times,* December 21, 1993.
6. Cleanth Brooks, *William Faulkner, First Encounters* (New Haven: Yale University Press, 1983), 1.
7. William Faulkner, *Pylon* (New York: Random House, 1935), 20–21, 24, 56, 64, 135, 179.
8. William Faulkner, *Absalom, Absalom!* (New York: Random House, Modern Library Collection, 1936), 32, 65, 68, 73, 80, 85, 126. See also *The Hamlet* (New York: Random House, 1964, 3rd edition), 5–10, 47, 51, 63, 323.
9. *Absalom, Absalom!* 193–200, 214, 225, 242, 256, 324, 352, 368, 375.
10. William Faulkner, *The Sound and the Fury* (New York: Random House, The Modern Library Edition, 1992), 23, 128.
11. William Faulkner, *The Sound and the Fury,* 23, 128.
12. William Faulkner, *Light in August* (New York: Random House, 1959), 42, 70, 72, 82, 275, 330; see also 106, 111, 247, 249, 271, 282, 322–23, 325, 326, 328, 342, 348, 352, 382.
13. William Faulkner, *Mosquitoes* (New York: Liveright Publishing Corporation, 1955), 80.

14. William Faulkner, *Go Down, Moses* (New York: Random House, Modern Library Edition, 1955), 63, 119, 126, 137, 166, 238, 311, 317, 373, 379.
15. William Faulkner, *As I Lay Dying* (New York: Random House, International Collector Library, 1957), 26–28, 30–31, 33–34, 63, 84, 85, 105.
16. William Faulkner, *The Town* (New York: Random House, 1955), 11, 20, 38, 90, 147, 160, 197, 206, 363.
17. William Faulkner, *Flags in the Dust* (New York: Random House, 1973), 15, 23, 25, 71, 87, 218.
18. William Faulkner, *Requiem for a Nun* (New York: Random House, 1966), 17, 37, 217, 221, 229, 236, 258.
19. Phyllis B. Eveleth and James M. Tanner, *Worldwide Variation in Human Growth* (Cambridge, Mass.: Cambridge University Press, 1990), 205; Terry C. Blum, Paul Roman, and Jack K. Martin, "Alcohol Consumption and Work Performance," *Journal of Studies on Alcohol* 54, (1993): 61–70; Andrew J. Treno, Robert Nash Parker, and Harold D. Holder, "Understanding U.S. Alcohol Consumption with Social and Economic Factors: A Multivariate Time Series Analysis, 1950–1986," *Journal of Studies on Alcohol* 54 (1993): 146–56; Dale M. Heien and David J. Pittman, "The External Costs of Alcohol Abuse," *Journal of Studies on Alcohol* 54 (1993): 302–7.
20. *Absalom, Absalom!,* 219, 237, 257. For other examples of alcohol and tobacco consumption see *Pylon,* 83, 98, 119, 126, 128, 184, 240; *Absalom, Absalom!,* 17, 20, 26, 40, 51, 63, 108, 139, 186, 209, 217, 221, 226, 229–31, 239, 247, 256–58, 265, 282, 301, 315–16, 322; *Mosquitoes,* 72, 97, 193, 208, 237, 261, 266, 285, 289, 317, 336, 341; *Go Down, Moses,* 147, 192, 344; *The Town,* 52, 68, 83, 108, 155, 159, 225, 357; *As I Lay Dying,* 6, 32, 123, 125–26; *Requiem for a Nun,* 4, 5, 15, 21, 70, 81, 85, 92, 103, 122, 127, 129, 130, 135, 135–36, 142, 157, 175, 198, 223, 243; *Flags in the Dust,* 33, 42, 110–11, 121, 124, 130, 177, 281, 336; *The Hamlet,* 9, 39, 54, 89, 206, 293; William Faulkner, *Soldiers' Pay* (New York: Liveright Publishing Corporation, 1954), 10, 23, 27,40, 67.
21. We are indebted to Cleanth Brooks for this point, personal communication, August 8, 1993. According to Stephen B. Oates, Faulkner "idolized his grandfather, who stood six feet tall . . ." In addition, Oates states that Faulkner, "acutely conscious of his small stature, . . . longed all his life to be tall like his father, his grandfather, and especially his great-grandfather. Fully grown at five feet, five and a half inches in height, he had his mother's small, shapely feet, thin mouth, and delicate chin." See *William Faulkner: The Man and the Artist* (New York: Harper and Row, 1987), 9, 14. This point is reinforced in Joel Williamson, *William Faulkner in Southern History* (New York: Oxford University Press, 1993), 166.
22. National Office of Vital Statistics, *State and Regional Life Tables, 1939–41* (Washington: U.S. Government Printing Office, 1948).
23. Kenneth L. Sokoloff and Georgia C. Villaflor, "The Early Achievement of Modern Stature in America," *Social Science History* 6 (1982): 453–81.
24. Benjamin Apthorp Gould, *Investigations in the Military and Anthropological Statistics of American Soldiers* (New York: Hurd and Houghton, 1869), 123.
25. Bernard D. Karpinos, "Height and Weight of Selective Service Registrants Processed for Military Service during World War II," *Human Biology* 30 (1958): 292–321.
26. Reynaldo Martorell and Jean-Pierre Mabicht, "Growth in Early Childhood in Developing Countries," in *Human Growth: A Comprehensive Treatise,* Volume 3, edited by Frank Faulkner and James M. Tanner (New York: Plenum Press, 1986), 241–62.
27. The South was poor relative to other regions of the United States, yet the economy was growing relatively rapidly in Faulkner's era. The most comprehensive study of regional income patterns was conducted by Richard A. Easterlin in 1961. Since the national

accounts were not established until the 1930s, he used census data on productive activity and market prices to approximate income by region in earlier years. He reports that per capita income in the South was 51 percent of the national average in 1880 and 1900. Yet, in 1920 the South's position had risen to 62 percent and by 1950 it was 73 percent of the national average. Despite low incomes in the South of Faulkner's formative years (he was born in 1897), the region prospered in that income grew faster than in the North or the West. The South's economic performance can be put into perspective by noting that average per capita income for the entire country in the first half of the twentieth century was growing at approximately 1.68 percent per year, or doubling every forty-one years. In moving from 51 percent of the average in 1900 to 62 percent of the average in 1920, the South grew at 2.65 percent per year, which amounts to a doubling every twenty-six years. Few nations with populations as large as the South's attained this level of economic growth over a period as long as twenty years until the post–World War II Asian economic miracles (Japan, South Korea, Taiwan, etc.) appeared on the scene. Little is changed in this analysis if the time period is extended from 1900 to 1950. In the first half of the century, Southern per capita income grew at an annual rate of 2.4 percent and doubled every twenty-nine years. Though poor by national standards, the Southern economy had a vibrancy and a zest for growth exceeding that in other regions. These data suggest that Southerners were industrious and hard working. See "Regional Income Trends, 1840–1950," in *American Economic History,* edited by Seymour Harris (New York: McGraw-Hill, 1961), 525–47.

28. Stephen Nicholas and Richard H. Steckel, "Tall But Poor: Nutrition, Health, and Living Standards in Pre-Famine Ireland," *Journal of European Economic History,* 26 (1977); 105–34.
29. Elizabeth W. Etheridge, *The Butterfly Caste: A Social History of Pellagra in the South,* (Westport: Greenwood Publishing Company, 1972).
30. With apologies to John Maynard Keynes, *The General Theory of Employment, Interest and Money* (New York: Harcourt, Brace and World, 1936), 383.

CONTRIBUTORS

EDWARD BERKOWITZ, professor of history at George Washington University, writes on social welfare policy including, most recently, a history of the Institute of Medicine and a biography of Wilbur Cohen.

JOHN PATRICK DIGGINS is distinguished professor of history at the Graduate Center of the City University of New York. His most recent books include *The Promise of Pragmatism* and *Max Weber: Politics and the Spirit of Tragedy.*

LOUIS FERLEGER is national director of the Historical Society and professor of history at Boston University. He is editor of *Agriculture and National Development: Views on the Nineteenth Century* and coeditor of *Slavery, Secession, and Southern History.*

ELIZABETH FOX-GENOVESE teaches history at Emory University. Her books include *Within the Plantation Household: Black and White Women of the Old South* and *Feminism Without Illusions: A Critique of Individualism.*

EUGENE D. GENOVESE is president of The Historical Society. He has recently published *A Consuming Fire: The Fall of the Confederacy in the Mind of the White Christian South.*

ROCHELLE GURSTEIN teaches history at the Bard Graduate Center. She has published *The Repeal of Reticence: America's Cultural and Legal Struggles Over Free Speech, Obscenity, Sexual Liberation and Modern Art.*

VICTOR DAVIS HANSON is professor of Greek and classics at California State University, Fresno. Most recently, he is the author of *The Wars of the Ancient Greeks* and *The Soul of Battle.*

GERTRUDE HIMMELFARB is professor emeritus of history at the City University of New York. Her most recent books are *The De-Moralization of Society: From Victorian Virtues to Modern Values* and *The Two Cultures: A Moral Divide.*

RUSSELL JACOBY teaches history at the University of California, Los Angeles. The author of *Social Amnesia, Dialectic of Defeat,* and *The Last Intellectuals,* he will publish *The End of Utopia* this year.

DONALD KAGAN is Hillhouse professor of history and classics at Yale University. His most recent book is *On the Origins of War and the Preservation of Peace.*

ALAN CHARLES KORS, professor of history at the University of Pennsylvania, is the author of several books on the French Enlightenment and currently is editor-in-chief of the *Oxford Encyclopedia of the Enlightenment.*

BRUCE KUKLICK is Nichols professor of American History at the University of Pennsylvania. He is at work on a book entitled *Intellectuals and War, 1945–1973.*

ELISABETH LASCH-QUINN, associate professor of American history and director of American studies at Syracuse University, is the author of *Black Neighbors,* editor of *Women and The Common Life,* and author of forthcoming books on interracial etiquette since the 1960s and the social origins of contemporary debates about the family.

MIRIAM R. LEVIN is associate professor of history, and a member of the graduate program in History of Science, Technology, Medicine, and the Environment at Case Western Reserve University. Her books and articles on industrial culture and science education in the United States include *Cultures of Control,* which is forthcoming.

DANIEL C. LITTLEFIELD is professor of history and Afro-American studies at the University of South Carolina and author of *Rice and Slaves: Ethnicity and the Slave Trade in Colonial South Carolina.*

WALTER A. MCDOUGALL is the Alloy-Ansin professor of international relations and history at the University of Pennsylvania. He edits *Orbis, A Journal of World Affairs,* and is most recently the author of *Promised Land, Crusader State: The American Encounter with the World Since 1776.*

PAUL A. RAHE is Jay P. Walker professor of history at the University of Tulsa. His book, *Republics Ancient and Modern: Classical Republicanism and the American Revolution* has been issued in a three-volume paperback edition.

DIANE RAVITCH is research professor of education at New York University and senior fellow at the Brookings Institution. Her latest book was *National Standards in American Education.*

LEO P. RIBUFFO, George Washington Distinguished Professor of History at George Washington University, is author of *The Old Christian Right: The Protestant Far Right from the Great Depression to the Cold War* and *Right Center Left: Essays in American History.*

PHILLIP M. RICHARDS is an associate professor in the department of English at Colgate University. He has published literary criticism in *Early American Literature, American Quarterly,* and *Cultural Studies,* and literary journalism in *Commentary, Dissent,* and *Harper's.*

MARTIN J. SKLAR is professor of history at Bucknell University. He has published *The Corporate Reconstruction of American Capitalism, 1890–1916* and *The United States as a Developing Country.*

RICHARD H. STECKEL is professor of economics and anthropology at Ohio State University and a research associate at the National Bureau of Economic Research. His most recent book, edited with Roderick Floud, is *Health and Welfare During Industrialization.*

DEBORAH A. SYMONDS is associate professor in and chair of the history department at Drake University. Her most recent publication is *Weep Not for Me: Women, Ballads, and Infanticide in Early Modern Scotland.*

MARC TRACHTENBERG is professor of history at the University of Pennsylvania. He has most recently published a book on the Cold War, *A Constructed Peace: The Making of the European Settlement, 1945–1963.*

SEAN WILENTZ is the Dayton-Stockton professor of history and director of the Program in American Studies at Princeton University. His most recent book, with Paul Johnson, is *The Kingdom of Matthias.*

JOHN WOMACK is the Robert Woods Bliss professor of Latin American history and economics at Harvard University. His books include *Zapata and the Mexican Revolution* and *Rebellion in Chiapas.*

PERMISSIONS

For essays in this volume that have been previously published, the editors wish to thank:

Eugene D. Genovese, "A New Departure" originally was published as "Restoring Dignity to the Historical Profession" in the *Los Angeles Times,* May 31, 1998. Reprinted by permission of the author.

Marc Trachtenberg, "The Past under Siege," *Wall Street Journal,* July 17, 1998. Reprinted by permission of the author.

Alan Charles Kors, "The Future of History in an Increasingly Unified World" originally was presented in a slightly different form at the Presidential Plenary Session of the American Historical Association, December 1992. Reprinted by permission of the author.

Daniel C. Littlefield, "Politics and Multiculturalism" originally was published in slightly different form in the *OAH Council of Chairs Newsletter,* October/December 1991. Reprinted by permission of the author.

Rochelle Gurstein, "On the Obsolescence of 'Puritanism' as an Epithet" appeared in a slightly different form as "'Puritanism' as an Epithet: Common Standards and the Fate of Reticence" in *Salmagundi,* No. 101–102, Winter–Spring 1994. Reprinted by permission of *Salmagundi* and the author.

Gertrude Himmelfarb, "Postmodernist History" previously was published in *On Looking into the Abyss: Untimely Thoughts on Culture and Society* (Knopf, 1994). Reprinted by permission of the author.

Russell Jacoby, "A New Intellectual History?" appeared in the *American Historical Review,* April 1992. Reprinted by permission of the American Historical Association.

Leo P. Ribuffo, "Confessions of an Accidental (or Perhaps Overdetermined) Historian" appears by permission of the author.

Deborah A. Symonds, "Living in the Scottish Records Office" appears by permission of the author.

Bruce Kuklick, "Writing the History of Practice: The Humanities and Baseball, with a Nod to Wrestling" appears by permission of the author.

Victor David Hanson, "The Dilemmas of the Contemporary Military Historian" appears by permission of the author.

Paul A. Rahe, "Aristotle and the Study of History: A Manifesto" appears by permission of the author.

Donald Kagan, "What Is a Liberal Education?" appears by permission of the author.

Edward Berkowitz, "The Death of Jane Addams," appeared in an earlier form in *The Word & I,* January 1997. Reprinted by permission of the author and *The World I,* a publication of the Washington Times Corporation.

Diane Ravitch, "The Controversy Over National History Standards" was presented before the American Academy of Arts and Sciences on April 9, 1997. Reprinted by permission of the author.

John Patrick Diggins, "The National History Standards" was previously published in *The American Scholar,* Autumn 1996, 65:4. Reprinted by permission of the author.

Sean Wilentz, "Clio Banished?: Battles over History in the Schools" appears by permission of the author.

Walter A. McDougall, "Whose History? Whose Standards" was previously published in *Commentary* 99:5 (May 1995) 36–43.

Martin J. Sklar, "Capitalism and Socialism in the Emergence of Modern America: The Formative Era, 1890–1916" originally was presented at the Fifth International Week on the History of the Enterprise, December 1993, and has been significantly revised in this version. Copyright © 1999 by Martin Sklar. Reprinted by permission of the author.

Miriam R. Levin, "Center and Periphery in the History of Science," appears by permission of the author.

John Womack, "Work in the Moctezuma Brewery" appears by permission of the author.

Louis Ferleger and Richard H. Steckel, "Faulkner's South: Is There Truth in Fiction?" was previously published in *The Journal of Mississippi History,* Vol.

LX, Summer 1998, no. 2:105–121. It appears by permission of the authors and *The Journal of Mississippi History*.